Theory into Practice

An Introduction to Literary Criticism

Ann B. Dobie

Australia Canada Mexico Singapore Spain United Kingdom United States

Theory into Practice
An Introduction to Literary Criticism
Ann B. Dobie

English Editor: *Bill Hoffman*
Development Editor: *Camille Adkins*
Project Manager, Editorial Production: *Barrett Lackey*
Permissions Editor: *Beverly Wyatt*
Production Service: *G&S Typesetters, Inc.*
Copy Editor: *Rosemary Wetherold*
Cover Design: *Beverly Baker*
Cover Printer: *Malloy Lithography*
Compositor: *G&S Typesetters, Inc.*
Printer: *Malloy Lithography*
Cover Image: *Rene Magritte* **Les Promenades d'Euclide (Euclidean Walks). 1955**
Oil on canvas, 64 1/8" X 51 1/8" (163 X 130 cm). The Minneapolis Institute of Arts, Minneapolis, Minnesota

Printed in the United States of America
4 5 6 7 8 9 06 05 04 03
For more information contact Heinle, 25 Thomson Place, Boston, MA 02210 USA,
or you can visit our Internet site at http://www.heinle.com

ISBN: 0-1550-6858-X

Library of Congress Catalog Card Number: 2001095957

Contents

ACKNOWLEDGMENTS

I am grateful for having had help from many quarters in writing this book. First I must thank my students, for whom and from whom I have learned more than I can measure. They have always been some of my most effective teachers. I am also appreciative of the honest and helpful responses of my colleagues to what and how I wrote. In particular, I thank Suzanne Moore for sharing her computer expertise by helping me identify useful Web sites and Judy Gentry, Duane Blumberg, Maurice DeQuesnay, Patricia Rickels, and Mary Ann Wilson for reading parts of the text and advising me on matters about which they know far more than I. There were anonymous reviewers, too, whose comments helped to shape much of what appears here. I am grateful for their constructive suggestions for revision. To my friends who have listened patiently to accounts of the progress of my writing I owe hours of reciprocal listening. And to my husband I give thanks for his unflagging encouragement and support.

To the Student: An Introduction to *Theory into Practice*

If you are a person who reads on your own for pleasure or for information, you probably are in the habit of talking with other readers about what you find interesting. You share the questions a book raised for you, compare it with other works by the same writer, and reminisce about what it made you recall from your own experience. The discussion is probably informal, spontaneous, and momentary. You may not even remember it a couple of days later.

Theory into Practice: An Introduction to Literary Criticism invites you to join a similar conversation, the main difference being that it will be more thoughtful, prepared, and memorable than the casual one just described. If those seem like intimidating terms, a look at the table of contents will reassure you that it begins with critical approaches that are not far removed from the friendly conversation mentioned earlier. They will ask you to engage in forms of literary talk that you are probably already comfortable with. As your critical skills improve, you will be introduced to newer, and probably less familiar, schools of criticism.

The new approaches have appeared as part of a dramatic shift that has taken place in literary criticism over the past several decades. In a college literature class not too long ago you would probably have been expected to read from a biographical, historical, or formalist approach, the critical perspectives covered in the opening chapters of *Theory into Practice,* but the situation is dramatically different today. The forms of criticism available to (and expected of) a good reader have grown more complex and sometimes a bit troubling. They have certainly grown more numerous. Some fundamental assumptions and practices regarding the reader's role have changed with them, making your job as student and critic less easily defined and prescribed than it once was. Consider how the following changes have redefined your responsibilities.

The literary canon, once accepted as a cultural heritage to be passed down from one generation to another, is no longer a stable body of texts that all readers agree upon. Instead, it is now a conflicted, disputed set of materials that stay in flux. The "master works" have been challenged by others drawn from popular culture, and serious attention is paid to materials that once were not deemed worthy of study in higher education. Your task, now that the "masterpieces" are no longer accepted as such, is to decide what a masterful text is after all and to which ones you would award that label.

Teachers, too, have changed, at least some of them. Once regarded as dispensers of knowledge and wisdom through the medium of the class lecture, they relieved the student of having to do much more than take down what was said, remember it, and demonstrate on occasion an understanding of it. The premise was that the teacher had the answer, and the student would learn it. Many effective classrooms operated under that system, for decades producing well-educated people who were good critical readers. Some still do, but today most teachers acknowledge that with the multiplicity of readings provided by the numerous new critical approaches, no single interpretation will suffice. Competing systems of inquiry create differing and sometimes conflicting understandings of any given work, and those disagreements, as Gerald Graff argues in *Beyond the Culture Wars,* can provide healthy debate that makes us better readers and critics. In short, in many of today's classrooms you are not expected to be the passive receptor of information or experience. Instead, you are required to assume the role of coparticipant in the making of a text. As a good reader, you cannot remain a silent partner in the conversation about a text, because what you have to say about it helps create it.

Another influence on current literary criticism is the sheer volume of information that is readily available on any subject. The amount of data that can be found on the Internet alone is almost overwhelming. Its effects on literary study are apparent in critics' frequent use of material that is drawn from nonliterary sources. In many of the newer approaches it is not enough to identify metaphors or rhyme schemes in a poem. Now you may be expected to use ideas from anthropology, sociology, or economics to explain what it means. The cross-disciplinary demands of today's critical approaches ask you to use everything you know—and more.

Perhaps the most demanding aspect of the reader's new role, but also probably the most important, is that you are put in the position of questioning basic assumptions about everything, not just literature. You may find that task to be a disquieting one, given that reading to affirm what we already know and accept is certainly a more comfortable position to be in. However, much of the vitality of the new approaches comes from the fact that they closely connect literature with our lives. They do so by making us look hard at what we often take for granted to see if it is valid, justifiable, and true. They make us examine values and practices that are so much a part of our lives that they exist, most of the time, beyond our questioning and evaluation.

Such practices are not universally accepted or approved. Some powerful voices have been raised in opposition. Allan Bloom in *The Closing of the American Mind,* for example, argues strongly against changes in the traditional curriculum, objecting to the inclusion of studies of popular culture and its products, which he sees as a less rigorous and significant body of subject matter than that which has been the staple of college curricula for several decades. Other detractors have objected to the political edge that many of the current critical perspectives have developed. Those who make such protests deny the validity of treating poetry or fiction as political documents that reveal the shortcomings of a society, promote the agendas of reformists, or serve to publicize an ignored minority. Whatever happened to literature as art, aesthetics, timeless beauty? they ask. Doesn't looking at a text from a political point of view demean its existence? Doesn't literature transcend the transience of political concerns?

Two counterarguments are commonly used to justify the political aspect of today's literary criticism. Those critics who espouse the first agree with George Orwell's assertion: "No book is genuinely free from political bias. The opinion that art should have nothing to do with politics is itself a political attitude." Simply put, there is no escaping politics. It is present in every assumption made about the social order, even when nothing explicitly labeled as political is being addressed.

The second justification points out that our culture is not a homogeneous one and that numerous minorities are no longer willing to pretend that it is. Previously silent voices are now calling for new definitions of cultural identity, celebrating their uniqueness and refusing to deny their own backgrounds and blend in with the rest. Their efforts are as influential in literature as in life; in both arenas they have ramifications that are political in nature. In the case of literature, their stand has led to new readings of both contemporary and traditional works and to recognition of previously overlooked writers.

Clearly the conversation about literature to which this book invites you is not a simple one. It is fraught with conflicts and disagreement. It questions traditional assumptions and practices. It requires you to evaluate what is and to reflect on what you think should be. You will not agree with everything that is said in the discussions; you will not agree on all points with fellow students or even your instructor. The resulting dissonance is expected and justifiable because intellectual engagement, not consensus, is the purpose. Your responsibility is to try out the techniques presented here so that you can make your own informed judgments about literature, literary criticism, and the world beyond them.

To play a competent part in any conversation requires being able to use the language in which it occurs with skill and effectiveness. To talk about literature means knowing the language of criticism. *Theory into Practice* is designed to help you understand that language, or languages, for each critical perspective has its own manner of speaking and writing. This text is, then, more than simply an invitation. It is a guide that will help you move from familiar conversations to others that may challenge your traditional ways of thinking. For each approach it will give you historical background, explanations of basic principles, extensive examples, suggestions for writing your analysis, a model student essay, a glossary of terms, recommended Web sites, and lists for further reading. At the end, in "Information at a Glance," you will find brief statements about purposes, assumptions, strategies, strengths, and weaknesses of each approach.

As you make your way through the schools of criticism discussed here, you will be dealing with complex ways of reading, analyzing, and interpreting literature that ask you to think long and deeply. If you approach them with a willingness to master their basic principles, to apply their strategies, and to make informed choices about their validity and effectiveness, they will help you discover the inexhaustible richness of reading critically. You are urged to make use of all the help that *Theory into Practice* offers as you join the critical conversation.

Works Analyzed in the Text

Poems

John Donne, *Elegy 19, On His Mistress Going to Bed,* Chapter 9
Robert Frost, *Nothing Gold Can Stay,* Chapter 1
Robert Frost, *Stopping by Woods on a Snowy Evening,* Chapter 8
Edwin A. Robinson, *Richard Cory,* Chapter 3
Alfred, Lord Tennyson, *Ulysses,* Chapter 4

Short Stories

Sherwood Anderson, "The Egg," Chapter 4
Angela Carter, "The Tiger's Bride," Chapter 10
Kate Chopin, "Désirée's Baby," Chapter 2
William Faulkner, "Barn Burning," Chapter 2
Ernest J. Gaines, "The Sky Is Gray," Chapter 9
Nathaniel Hawthorne, "Young Goodman Brown," Chapter 4
James Joyce, "Araby," Chapter 3
Bobbie Ann Mason, "Shiloh," Chapter 8
Guy de Maupassant, "The Diamond Necklace," Chapter 5
Frank Norris, "A Deal in Wheat," Chapter 5
Edgar Allan Poe, "The Masque of the Red Death," Chapter 7
Eudora Welty, "Death of a Traveling Salesman," Chapter 7
Edith Wharton, "The Other Two," Chapter 6

Letters

Letters of Abigail and John Adams, Chapter 6

Autobiography

Jill Ker Conway, excerpt from *The Road from Coorain,* Chapter 10

Remembrance

Zora Neale Hurston, excerpt from *The Eatonville Anthology,* Chapter 10

Play

James Baldwin, *Blues for Mister Charlie,* Chapter 10

I

THE RELATIONSHIP OF READING AND WRITING

Reading is to the mind what exercise is to the body.
JOSEPH ADDISON, English essayist

How can I know what I think till I see what I say?
E. M. FORSTER, English novelist and essayist

READING AND WRITING IN COLLEGE

Reading and writing seem to be inseparable acts, rather like two sides of the same coin. Sometimes we even say the three words as if they were only one: reading-and-writing. Their connections are echoed in the advice every successful writer gives fledgling ones to "read, read, read." So, too, we know that good readers grow more perceptive and insightful if they "write, write, write."

It all sounds so easy and natural. When we encounter a book that touches our emotions or disturbs our assumptions, for example, we want to share our reactions with someone else. We may call a friend to talk about it, or if there is nobody to listen, we may turn to writing to explain what we are thinking and feeling about what we have read. It is then we all too often discover that putting what we think about a novel or a poem down on paper in a form that someone else will find interesting (and intelligible) is not so simple. In school, where reading and writing are assigned, the problem can be more serious. Students sometimes struggle not only with expressing their opinions but also with finding them. Reading works that someone else has chosen for them, students may have trouble identifying something to write about. In the worst-case scenario, they may not even understand what they've read very well.

Academic survival depends on developing skills that will allow you to explore the meaning, aesthetics, or craft of a text and then write about the insights you've discovered. They are the skills of a literary critic, a person who examines how a piece of writing works, what it has to say about the culture or author that produced it or about human nature in general, why it was written, in what ways it is similar to other works, and how it ranks in comparison with them. In short, to be a successful critic you need to be a resourceful reader, one who can utilize the principles of more than a single school of literary analysis and write with insight and understanding, as well as clarity and grace.

The writing you are asked to do in literature classes can take many forms, from marginal notes to quick journal entries and freewriting sessions, perhaps eventually going through many drafts to become a full-blown piece of academic discourse. But, of course, it may also take final form as a letter to a friend, a poem for your eyes only, or the answer to an essay question on an examination. The purpose and audience for your writing will determine how your critical pieces take shape and what that shape is. What does not change is that the reading-writing connection can be a valuable one for you, because by writing responses to what you read, you are likely to understand it better, remember it longer, relate it to other experiences more often (both those you have and those you read about), and use it more effectively.

We read and respond, then talk and write. The text we ultimately publish, whether as rough notes, a reading log, a creative effort, examination questions, or a research report, is literary criticism, an effort to share our experiences with someone else.

ENGAGING THE TEXT

Regardless of the assignment you are given, practicing literary criticism requires more than a single effort or skill. Even answering a question in class requires that you think about your response before speaking. Written criticism takes even more care. Whether you are dealing with a long research paper or an essay question on an exam that has a time limit, the job calls on you to carry out several complex tasks, and the process can be overwhelming if you try to think about them all at once. As a result, getting started is the hard part for many people. Where to begin isn't always obvious. To gain some control over the process, you can use some fairly simple techniques to help make your initial approach. They take little time but can pay big dividends later.

The techniques suggested as starting points here involve connecting reading and writing so that you can discover what you have to say. They include making marginal notations, keeping a reading log, and using prewriting strategies. It is likely that some of them will work better for you than others. For example, some readers find that making entries in a log disrupts their enjoyment of a text, but others make it a regular part of their reading process. You will have to be the judge of which strategies are most effective for you and which you find to be unproductive. The important step is to incorporate those that help into your own reading-writing process. Here are some that you may want to make a routine part of your approach to engaging a text.

ADDING MARGINAL NOTATIONS

One of the reasons that reading and writing seem to be two parts of a whole is that they sometimes take place at the same time. During the first reading of a work, for example, you may find yourself underlining sentences, putting question marks or checks in the margins, highlighting passages, or circling words that you don't understand. In fact, you may not think of such cryptic markings as writing at all, but they are representations of what you are thinking and feeling as you go through a text. And because nobody takes in a work completely the first time through, they can serve as starting points for the next reading. They will help you find those passages and ideas that you wanted to think about some more or perhaps didn't understand at all. You will be glad when you return to a work that when you were there the first time, you left some footprints to follow when you came back. Look at how a first-time reader responded to Robert Frost's poem "Nothing Gold Can Stay."

NOTHING GOLD CAN STAY

Nature's first green is gold, → How can green be gold?
Her hardest hue to hold.
Her early leaf's a flower; Lots of rhyme in this poem!
Something "subsides" to itself? But only so an hour.
Then leaf subsides to leaf.
So Eden sank to grief,
What does Eden have to do w/ nature? So dawn goes down to day. Opening sounds get repeated, too.
Nothing gold can stay.

The advantage of marginal notations is that they don't interrupt your reading very much. They are, however, usually too terse and superficial to serve as the basis of a full-scale analysis. Several other techniques that will connect your reading with your writing in more substantive ways include keeping a reading log and using prewriting strategies.

KEEPING A READING LOG

You will have the rough beginnings of a reading log if you have made marginal and textual notes while you were reading. A log simply amplifies the process and thus requires a separate notebook for your comments. You may even want to skip the marginal markings and use the notebook from the beginning.

Several different kinds of information, depending partly on how familiar you are with a work, will be appropriate for your reading log. When you read something for the first time, you are likely to make notes about relatively basic information. If you are reading a narrative, for example, you may want to answer such questions as the following:

- Where is the action happening?
- What are the relationships of the characters?
- Which character(s) do I find to be the most interesting?
- Which one(s) do I care for most?
- Which one(s) do I dislike the most?

You might even want to pause in the middle to speculate about the following:

- What do I want to happen?
- What am I afraid will happen?
- What do I think will happen?
- What have I read that prompted the answers to these questions?

If you are reading a poem, you may want to record answers to questions like these:

- Who is the speaker of the poem?
- What do I know about him or her?
- What is the occasion for saying it?
- Where is it taking place?
- Who is listening?
- Which lines seem to be the most important ones?
- Do they give me insight into the poem as a whole?

Another way of beginning to think about a work is to jot down questions, memories it has called up, arguments with the ideas, or speculations about how the author came to write it. These considerations will help connect you with what you have read, not simply focus your attention on the text itself. They will make it more meaningful to you as an individual. It is often in personal interaction with a work that you begin to make meaning as a writer-critic.

When you are more familiar with the work, you will want to address more complex issues in your reading log or journal. You have several different models to follow, including the following:

- A learning log (sometimes called a double-entry log or a dialectical log) in which you divide a page into vertical halves, noting page numbers, phrases, or words from the text on one side and your own response on the other. On your side of the page you may express confusion, record definitions of words you don't know, question connotations, argue with the text, note the recurrence of an image—whatever you think you need to return to later.
- A dialogue journal that uses the same format but devotes one side of the page to your comments and leaves the other half for comments from another reader (student, friend, teacher, etc.).
- A "what if" journal that asks for a response to hypothetical questions, such as these: If you could talk to the author (or one of the characters or the narrator), what questions would you ask? What objections would you raise?
- A vocabulary journal that records all the words you are unfamiliar with.
- A personal writing journal that can include informal freewrites on a passage or a scene; a descriptive paragraph, poem, or short narrative about an experience the text brings to mind; or an imagined conversation between two characters.

At the end of a reading, a summary paragraph about your reactions as recorded on your half of the double-entry log will help you pull together what you think about the work. A word of caution: don't let too much time pass between the reading a work and writing your summary paragraph. Responses fade quickly, and the longer you wait to set down your feelings and ideas, the less pointed and vibrant they will be.

USING HEURISTICS

Sometimes the notes made in your reading log are an end to the process. Perhaps you do not need or want to do anything more with the work in question, and so you leave it to go on to other texts. However, if you have been assigned a class paper dealing with a particular poem or have an upcoming examination over a given novel, you will want to continue your study.

The point now is to stimulate your own thinking, to find out more about your responses to the reading than the immediate, brief notes in your reading log can tell you. One of the ways to probe further is to use prewriting strategies, the same discovery processes you have used in other writing situations. You are in a good position to do so, as comments from the reading log can serve as starting places. There are many ways of beginning, and you should use the ones that are helpful and productive for you. Some of the most popular techniques include brainstorming, listing, freewriting, making analogies, and clustering. If you want to know more about how they work, you can find explanations in most writing handbooks and rhetoric texts.

SHAPING A RESPONSE

Up to this point, you have mostly been gathering your responses and ideas, thinking through the work and your involvement in it. As you learn about all of the different critical perspectives to follow, you will begin to read more deeply and with more understanding. Although these perspectives are presented here as discrete approaches to analysis and criticism, in actual practice they rarely stand alone. You will find that they often complement and supplement each other. The strategies just discussed can be used to explore them, helping you to achieve greater understanding and pleasure from what you read.

At some point—and you will have to be the judge of when that happens—you will want to share your ideas with someone else. Whether you simply talk about a work with a friend, make an oral class presentation, or prepare a fully developed written text, you will need to make some decisions about how to present your opinions and ideas. To do so, you will want to be aware of the context of your presentation: its purpose, audience, and voice.

DETERMINING A PURPOSE

As noted earlier, marginal notations and log entries are often made without any purpose beyond recording them. However, independent presentations usually have another reason for being, one that determines how you proceed. Relatively short analytical essays (such as those based on comparison and contrast or on cause and effect), and even personal essays, are commonly assigned in college literature classes, but on occasion you may be asked to produce a longer paper. For example, you may be required to examine the issues treated in the work, the controversies and ideas it presents. You can examine characters in a narrative or describe and analyze the structure of a work. More closely focused still are papers about imagery, symbolism, prosody, or point of view. There is, obviously, no shortage of possible topics. Two of the most troublesome (and critical) forms in which you are likely to be asked to write are those of examinations and research papers. The rest of the chapters in this book will discuss making literary analyses and composing extended papers that report them from a wide variety of perspectives, but here are some suggestions for how to proceed when your purpose is to answer essay test questions or compose a research paper.

ANSWERING ESSAY QUESTIONS

Assuming that you have carefully prepared for an exam, you have several strategies that can help you write effective answers to the essay questions you find on it. First, recognize the intent behind the questions. Some are designed simply to assess whether you have read assignments or whether you have ingested specific information. On the other hand, sometimes an instructor expects you to demonstrate that you have done more than memorize material—that you can draw inferences from it, relate it to other information, evaluate it, agree or disagree with it. In short, you may be asked to show that you can think critically about a subject. Finally, on some rare occasions you may be expected to be creative. A question such as, If you could invite any three authors whose work you have studied to a party with each other, whom would you invite and what do you think they would talk about? asks for more than data or even inferences. It expects you to be inventive and imaginative.

A second consideration involves how extensive the answer should be. If the directions ask for "brief identifications," you should be highly specific and to the point, reserving valuable time for the rest of the examination. If, on the other hand, you are directed to "discuss thoroughly," you will need to begin with a broad statement of fact or opinion and then move into its explanation by citing causes, comparisons, examples, or other more specific proof and logic.

Finally, an important point to keep in mind while composing any answer is that you must address the question that is asked. Probably the biggest cause of low scores on essay examinations is that students do not keep to the topic or follow directions. All too often they stray off into discussing a related topic—for example, giving a plot summary instead of making a comparison of two characters. One way to stay on task is to begin a discursive answer by partially restating the question. For example, if your test question reads, "How does the imagery found in the poems of Robert Frost reflect his own life?" you should begin your answer in the same way, saying something like, "Robert Frost's life is reflected in his poems in images such as birch trees, stone walls, and snowy evenings, which are typical of New England, where he lived."

WRITING RESEARCH PAPERS

A research paper differs from other papers that deal with literary topics in two ways. First, it involves the use of secondary sources, publications about the work you are discussing. The pieces of writing discussed earlier usually require using only the literary work itself. Second, because it will be presented as academic discourse, the style will be more formal than that of some of the other work you have done.

Many of the conventions that you follow will depend on your instructor. Although some general guidelines almost always apply, you should be sure that you understand and use the guidelines that are given for your particular assignment. They may vary somewhat from the suggestions that follow.

- You will enjoy the project more if you choose a topic that interests you. Because you will be spending many hours working with it, you will not want to suffer through dealing with a subject you find boring or irrelevant.
- Keep a reputable handbook for writers at your side. Many helpful books can guide you step-by-step through the process of finding the materials you need in the library, taking relevant notes, and documenting sources. If your instructor has suggested or required a particular one, be sure to get it and use it.
- Start early. Good research cannot be done quickly. You will need time not only to write the paper but, even before composing a draft, to consider the various data and opinions that you read in order to come up with your own ideas.
- With all the work that goes into a research paper, it should be more than a scrapbook of other people's ideas. It should reflect your own. If you begin to feel that you have nothing to contribute to the rich critical dialogue that has preceded your study, you can use several strategies to find your own opinions. First, remember that you can argue with other critics. If you disagree with the conclusions drawn by one of your secondary sources, you have the basis for critical argument. Another way of finding your own point of view is to look at a work from a perspective that has not been traditionally used. For example, feminist critics are providing some surprising new readings of well-known texts by looking at them (for the first time) through women's eyes. Finally, you can interact with the work on a personal level by asking yourself early on how you respond to it and why. Some brainstorming on that topic may lead you to ideas that you can go on to investigate and test by examining the ideas of other critics.
- Your paper will probably run between five and fifteen pages, although length is one of those matters that instructors often stipulate. Regardless of how long it is, in its final form it should have an introduction, a well-developed discussion section, a conclusion, and a list of sources cited. Not only should the introduction announce the topic to be discussed, and perhaps your particular focus, but it should also provide an attractive, inviting beginning. The discussion section, as the heart of your explanation or argument, should follow a clear plan of development, using examples from the work itself and references to secondary sources to strengthen your case. The conclusion need not be long if you have been clear in

the preceding sections. It should simply provide a satisfying sense of completion to the paper.

KNOWING YOUR AUDIENCE

Just as your purpose will affect what you write and how you write it, the audience (your reader) too will influence both the information you include and the form and style you use to communicate it. Imagine, for example, that as a result of driving too fast on a rain-slick street, you were responsible for sliding into the back of another car. How would you write an account of the accident for the police report? To your parents? In a letter to a friend who habitually drives too fast? In each case the basic facts would be the same, but the details would vary. The language would change, because different readers provide different obligations and opportunities. The same situation is true for writing literary criticism.

When you are making notes in a reading log, the primary audience is yourself. Consequently, you are not likely to worry about writing in complete sentences or editing for correctness. You may have even developed a personal shorthand to save time. When you use those notes as the basis of a commentary to be shared with a writing group, however, you will need to revise them so that they are more easily understood by others. That is, you will move to standard forms of expression.

The research paper is likely to be the most formal assignment you are asked to carry out. It is written in academic prose, a relatively impersonal, formal, tightly organized type of discussion that is addressed to a well-informed and intelligent audience whom you may not know personally. Traditionally this situation has meant that the writer avoids all colloquialisms, slang, abbreviations, or references to the self, probably includes some technical terms and headings for the different sections, and always documents references to other scholars' work. Some of this impersonal formality seems to be receding currently, with more acceptance of the use of the first-person personal pronoun *I*. However, readers of research reports retain a strong preference for formal academic prose, which you will probably want to honor.

CHOOSING A VOICE

Your writer's "voice" changes just as your audible one does in different situations. As the audience grows more distant and unknown, your writing continues to become more formal and impersonal. When, for example, you write an answer to an essay question on an examination, you are hoping to assure an instructor, who may or may not know you well, that you have mastered a body of material or a set of skills or that you have the ability to think critically. The expression will, of necessity, differ significantly from the short notes you made for yourself in your log.

One reason that the audience affects the form and language of your writing, your voice, is that you change roles as you deal with different people. Remember the car accident you hypothetically had on the slick street? When writing to the police and to your parents, you were dealing with authority figures, people you were expected to treat with deference and respect. When you composed the accident report, you were acting as a responsible citizen trying to get the facts down as clearly as possible. With your parents, you were probably acting as a defendant trying to explain that it wasn't entirely your fault. In the letter to your friend, on the other hand, you were writing as an equal, making remarks that were half-informative and half-entertaining. Your personality changed with the audience, thereby causing your written "voice," the representation of who you were in that piece, to change as well.

When you are writing literary criticism, your voice will differ, depending not only on the audience but also on the purpose of your piece. Short, personal questions and reminders are basically starting points for more serious thinking later. Reading logs are ruminative in nature; they explore ideas, possibilities for dialogues with others. You take examinations to exhibit what you know and can do. The purpose of the research report is to explore a topic in depth, possibly turning up new and interesting perspectives on it in the process. Basically you are moving through several roles, from novice to questioner, authority figure, and researcher and critical thinker. As your persona changes in each case, your voice will change, adjusting to the role you have assumed.

HELPING THE PROCESS

In writing classes, you have probably already been introduced to the process by which a piece moves from a rough draft (based on exploratory beginnings discussed earlier) to a final, polished one that is ready to be shared with readers. Remember that the process is not a lockstep affair. Instead of a sequence of separate stages, each one completed before the next is begun, it is a fairly jumbled procedure in which you move forward and then go back to change what you have already done, thereby necessitating changes in what follows. The main point to remember is that effective writing is usually the result of numerous false starts, multiple versions, a substantial number of small changes, and maybe even some big ones.

The chapters that follow will give you ample suggestions for prewriting, drafting a text, and revising it. They will also provide lists of printed sources and Web sites that can help you find information about the approach you are using to analyze a poem or a piece of fiction. You can also set up some collaborative efforts of your own, as well as refer to additional mechanical and printed aids that can help you with just about everything from comma splices to the composing process in general. Here are some suggestions for both collaboration and more impersonal assistance.

COLLABORATION

One of the myths about writing is that it is a solitary activity. We have all seen cartoons of the lonely poet waiting for inspiration by the light of a flickering candle. Real writers, however, know that they are not alone at all. They are heavily dependent on an audience that responds to what they've written. Only by getting reactions from other readers can a writer know if the work has succeeded or where it has missed the mark. A beginning writer also profits from working with supportive peers who can sense strengths and weaknesses that she is unaware of. In the end, the story or poem belongs to the person who wrote it, but a little help from one's friends along the way can be invaluable.

Collaboration can begin by a simple sharing of initial reactions to a work. A brief reading of the comments and questions recorded in a reading log, for example, can form the basis for discussion of any aspect of a story or poem. If everyone agrees, then everyone can feel validated; if opinions vary widely, which is the more likely event, there is much to be examined and discussed.

Although the instructor has the responsibility for arranging shared sessions in class, you can do much on your own. It may mean making arrangements to meet outside of class, but the rewards can be worth the trouble. If you want to have the support and suggestions of your friends and colleagues, you can do much of what a teacher would ask you to do in a workshop situation. Consider trying the following suggestions.

If you are ready for more extended sharing than has been described so far, a brief freewriting of five to ten minutes, or perhaps some clustering or listing, can provide material for discussion. If you do not feel comfortable working with a group, you may find it more productive at this stage to be paired with another person. The two of you can simply read each other's informal responses and react to them, or you can be more organized about the process by consciously finding one thing to agree with or to compliment. Later, when you feel ready, your pair can be combined with another to form a group of four to continue your discussions and sharing. If you have more than one such group, you can hold a larger session in which each quartet selects its strongest piece to share with everyone.

Sometimes you will want or need to share something longer than the short pieces of freewriting or journal entries. One way to generate a more extended discourse is to try what Richard Adler calls "answering the unanswered question." That is, ask yourself what you do not understand or where you wish you had more information. Another possibility is to use David Bleich's technique of first asking yourself what you think is the most important word in the work, then the most important passage, and, finally, the most important feature. For each answer, specify why you find it to be the most important. Your answers will reflect you as an individual with a unique perspective on the text. Your experiences and opinions will lead you to shape a response that is different from those of your colleagues. You will have a unique response to share with them.

When you share a more fully developed piece of writing, you will probably need to follow a more formal process. Several models of collaborative revising are helpful. The element common to all of them is their positive nature. Collaboration is most productive when it takes place in an atmosphere of support and affirmation, not one steeped in negative criticism. The point is to help each other achieve more effective writing by making helpful comments.

One popular model of a writing group involves having the writer read her piece to the entire group, not stopping until she reaches the end, then pausing briefly for the group to write brief responses to it. Another uses a series of questions that the group is asked to answer about each writer's paper. They can be formulated to suit the needs of the occasion, but they usually involve questions such as the following:

- What is the main idea of this paper?
- Did the opening sentence make you want to hear the rest? Why or why not?
- Were there enough examples to make the major points clear?
- Were the examples interesting, appropriate, and vivid?
- Did you have a satisfying sense of closure at the end?

Whatever approach your group chooses, remember that, as the writer, you have the final say in what happens in your paper. You are free to implement or reject the suggestions you receive. Most of the time, however, it is a good idea to pay attention to what your audience says.

On some occasions you may find it impossible to assemble a writing group to help you shape or polish a piece of writing, but there are a few strategies you can use when working alone. They can help you distance yourself from your work so that you are more likely to see and hear it as another reader might. You can, for example, read the piece aloud. Your ear will pick up problem areas (wrong words, missing punctuation, even underdeveloped points) that your eye has missed. Listen as a stranger to the language, and ask yourself what is missing, what is unclear. It is easier to remove yourself from the author's seat if you allow yourself time to forget what you have written. That is, if you can put a piece away for several days without reading it or even thinking much about it, then when you take it out again, it will sound as if someone else has composed it. You may be surprised at the awkward passages you discover when you come back to a text with fresh eyes (and ears).

REFERENCE MATERIALS

In addition to the assistance that critical friends can provide, you will also find it helpful to keep a good reference book or two by your side while you are writing. Remember that handbooks, dictionaries, and rhetoric texts are all helpful in composing, revising, and editing your manuscript.

Today the solitary writer can also benefit from technological assistance. The computer is no substitute for a human reader (yet), but it does an excellent job of finding misspelled words and is (sometimes) helpful in identifying ungrammatical constructions. Even highly skilled writers use such devices to create final copy that is as close to being error-free as possible. Also, the opportunities computers provide for producing visually attractive copy have made it mandatory that the papers you produce have a professional look to them. No excuses will justify a sloppy presentation. Any reader expects a clean, well-designed format that invites attention.

Technology can also help you find material that will enrich your reading. The information available on the Internet is increasing at an astonishing rate that shows no signs of slowing down. Information from the Internet has many advantages for the user, not the least of which is its easy accessibility. However, anyone who uses it should be aware of some of its shortcomings. Simply put, it is not always reliable. First of all, because of the easy access, anyone can create a Web site or post comments to various groups. The result is that not all information on the Internet can be trusted. You must always question the source of material that you find there. Even addresses that end in *.edu,* which some people tend to assume are reputable ones because they are located at universities, can pose problems. As students come and go and courses change, these sites are very likely to move or disappear without warning. As a result, even some of those listed in this book may no longer be active.

SUMMING UP

As you have seen in this chapter, the relationship of reading and writing is not a simple one. Making analyses and writing papers that explain them are made manageable, however, by adopting a method that does not require you to work on all of its aspects at once, a method that instead allows you to concentrate on one or two tasks at a time. Engaging a text, shaping a response, and finally sharing it with other readers is demanding but satisfying, because it not only leads us to new insights about ourselves and our world but also puts us in touch with a community of thinking people.

RECOMMENDED WEB SITES

New Web sites devoted to various literary interests are coming online in ever-increasing numbers. Some of them are general sites that deal with a wide variety of critical approaches; some are more specialized. Lists of the latter will appear in the discussion of each school of criticism.

GENERAL INFORMATION SITES

A few Web sites that provide general information and criticism about individual figures, movements, and areas of study include the following:

http://muse.jhu.edu/

A site that allows you to subscribe online to several educational journals in the arts and humanities.

http://www.iath.virginia.edu/elab/elab.html

A guide to using hypertext technology. Known as the Electronic Labyrinth, it evaluates hypertext and its potential for writers.

http://www.academic.marist.edu/1/hsite.htm
A list of hypertext sites and critical essays.

http://www.georgetown.edu/crossroads/asw/lit.html#hypertext
An American Studies site that provides links to an extensive set of resources.

http://www.cwrl.utexas.edu/~daniel/
A list of links to sites featuring student writing and projects on a variety of literary topics.

http://vos.ucsb.edu/
Information on any arts or literature topic. The site is named Voice of the Shuttle.

http://lists.village.virginia.edu/~spoons/
A clearinghouse for email discussion lists on literary topics, including criticism. Known as the Spoon Collective, it has information on how to subscribe to various email discussion lists and general information about the subject matter of specific ones.

Literary Criticism Sites

On the Internet you can also find Web sites that address literary theory in general. They present primary sources, definitions of terms, bibliographies, and other information that can be helpful supplements to your study. Some good sites are listed below.

http://www.cumber.edu/litcritweb/
Called the LitCrit Web, this site tells you about or links you to information about a variety of critical theories and critical practice.

http://www.home.earthlink.net/mandal/Michele/projects/hyper/hypercritical.html
A student site that defines and explores the theories behind several schools of criticism.

http://www.runet.edu/~jmking/amlit/crit2.html
A page posted by a student that gives an essay on different types of literary criticism.

http://fyl.unizar.es/FILOLOGIA_INGLESA/BIBLIOGRAPHY.HTML
A bibliography of literary studies and criticism listing over 100,000 entries, specially focused on English-speaking authors and on criticism or literary theory written in English. It can be searched in Spanish.

http://130.179.92.25/Arnason_DE/Backmaterials.html
An extensive glossary of critical terms. It also has notes on formalist and structuralist material, with a list of links to discussions of theoretical background.

http://www.press.jhu.edu/books/hopkins_guide_to_literary_theory/
General information on literary theory.

http://www.newi.ac.uk/rdover/popfic/critical.htm
Very brief summaries of various theories.

http://omni.cc.purdue.edu/~felluga/theory.html
An undergraduate introduction to critical theory.

http://www.brocku.ca/english/courses/4F70/index.html
A list of links to information on several types of literary criticism.

SUGGESTED READING

Abrams, M. H. *A Glossary of Literary Terms.* 7th ed. Fort Worth, Tex.: Harcourt, 1999.

Adams, Hazard. *Critical Theory since 1965.* Tallahassee: Florida State Univ. Press, 1986.

———. *Critical Theory since Plato.* Revised ed. Fort Worth, Tex.: Harcourt, 1992.

Bressler, Charles. *Literary Criticism: An Introduction to Theory and Practice.* 2d ed. Upper Saddle River, N.J.: Prentice Hall, 1999.

Carpenter, Scott. *Reading Lessons: An Introduction to Theory.* Upper Saddle River, N.J.: Prentice Hall, 2000.

Eagleton, Terry. *Literary Theory.* Minneapolis: University of Minnesota Press, 1996.

Groden, Michael. *The Johns Hopkins Guide to Literary Theory and Criticism.* Baltimore: Johns Hopkins Univ. Press, 1994.

Harkin, Patricia. *Acts of Reading.* Upper Saddle River, N.J.: Prentice Hall, 1999.

Harmon, William, and C. Hugh Holman. *Handbook to Literature.* 8th ed. Upper Saddle River, N.J.: Prentice Hall, 2000.

Heilker, Paul, and Peter Vandenberg. *Keywords in Composition Studies.* Portsmouth, N.H.: Heinemann, 1996.

Kaplan, Charles, and William Anderson, ed. *Criticism: Major Statements.* 4th ed. Boston: Bedford/St. Martin's Press, 2000.

Keesey, Donald. *Contexts for Criticism.* 3d ed. Mountain View, Calif.: Mayfield, 1998.

Lentricchia, Frank. *Critical Terms for Literary Study.* 2d ed. Chicago: Univ. of Chicago Press, 1995.

Rivkin, Julie. *Literary Theory: An Anthology.* Malden, Mass.: Blackwell, 1998.

Selden, Raman. *A Reader's Guide to Contemporary Literary Theory.* 3d ed. Lexington: Univ. Press of Kentucky, 1993.

Staton, Shirley F., ed. *Literary Theories in Praxis.* Philadelphia: Univ. of Pennsylvania Press, 1987.

Storey, John. *An Introductory Guide to Cultural Theory and Popular Culture.* Athens: Univ. of Georgia Press, 1993.

Tyson, Lois. *Critical Theory Today: A User-Friendly Guide.* New York: Garland, 1999.

2

Familiar Approaches

Almost every literary work is attended by a host of outside circumstances which, once we expose and explore them, suffuse it with additional meaning.

RICHARD D. ALTICK, *The Art of Literary Research*

Reviewers are usually people who would have been poets, historians, biographers, if they could: they have tried their talents at one or the other, and have failed; therefore they turn critics.

SAMUEL TAYLOR COLERIDGE, *Lectures: Shakespeare and Milton*

CONVENTIONAL WAYS OF READING LITERATURE

Taking a course in literary criticism is an exercise in discovering how many different ways you can read a single text. Some of the approaches will be familiar ones, so familiar that they may seem to be not so much special strategies for dealing with a work but simply the natural way to read. Others may seem more bizarre and complex, at least at first. The perspectives discussed in this chapter are those you are likely to recognize, because they have probably served as the organizing bases for courses you have taken or assignments you have been given. They include approaching a text from a social viewpoint, which involves history and biography; seeing it as representative of a particular genre; fitting it into the whole body of a writer's work; or applying particular ways of thinking to it, such as comparison and contrast or cause and effect. They are "tried and true" methods that continue to be helpful to understanding literature.

A Social Perspective

To understand the discussion that follows, you should read the short story "Barn Burning," by William Faulkner, which begins on page 217.

Nobody lives a completely isolated existence. Each of us is a product of more biological, intellectual, emotional, and spiritual influences than we can recognize—much less name. The reverse is true as well: to some degree each human being affects the world she lives in, some in monumental ways, some in quiet, unnoticed ones; some leave the world better for their having lived in it; some seem bent on destruction. All of us affect the world in some way.

When we apply this assertion to works of literature, we can say that they are products of a time, a place, and an individual and that they have the capacity to affect, and perhaps even change, the world into which they are introduced. Hippolyte Taine (1828–1893) was one of the earliest theorists to explore this idea. Hoping to establish a scientific basis for literary criticism, he tried to make interpretations by applying the methods of biological science to literature. He looked at the historically verifiable causes of a text. He wanted the facts. Three major factors, he announced, determine a work of art's unique character: *"race, milieu et moment."* By the term *race,* Taine referred to national characteristics that are typically found in works of art produced by the creative artists of a given country. His meaning is close to what is today called cultural. Consider the music of Duke Ellington or George Gershwin. Could a listener ever think it was by a Russian composer? What is it that makes *Rhapsody in Blue* peculiarly American? It is, Taine would say, its "racial" characteristics. When Taine spoke of *milieu,* he was referring to the environment of the artist, the sum total of her experience. It includes family background, education, travel, marriages and love affairs, income—all those forces that combine to create the individual as a unique human being. *Moment* is a reference to the less personal influences in a writer's life, to those that govern not the individual but the age. It points to the major intellectual currents of a period, its governing ideas and assumptions. His idea is reflected in the categories into which literature is sorted: classical, romantic, absurdist, and so on. Such labels are a way of referring to a group of identifiable characteristics that held sway at a particular literary period.

A more modern statement of the social approach comes from Austin Warren. In his *Theory of Literature,* he names three areas that are of interest to the social critic. First he notes the importance of the heredity and environment of the writer, which help explain social attitudes and opinions that appear in his work. In the short story "Barn Burning," for example, we find evidence of William Faulkner's own family background. Born in 1897 near Oxford, Mississippi, into a society that still had vivid memories of the Civil War, Faulkner grew up in a family whose roots were buried deep in the history of the state. His great-grandfather had been a colonel in that war, as well as a prominent figure in the postwar South as it struggled to rebuild its society. In that era he played numerous roles—including those of a lawyer, politician, financier, politician, railroad builder, and general public figure. His end was a violent one, at the hands of a business rival. Faulkner's grandfather continued the family businesses, and his maternal grandmother lived with Faulkner's family for a number of years until her death in 1907. His father, a man who preferred hunting and fishing to "polite society," worked at one time for the railroad but later became business manager of the University of Mississippi. His mother provided an early literary influence on the writer-to-be. Although Faulkner left Oxford before completing high school, he returned in 1919 after having served as a member of the British Royal Flying Corps during World War I. Back in his native state, he continued to read and write but expressed no particular professional ambition. After publishing a volume of poetry, *The Marble Faun* (1924), he moved on to New Orleans, where he met Sherwood Anderson and other writers who encouraged him to write about his native region. In 1929 he returned again to Oxford, where he married his high school sweetheart and where he lived until his death in 1962. The family lore, the identification with place, the knowledge of people and events of the Civil War, and the war's lasting effects on the defeated South are all evident in "Barn Burning." The characters, drawn from more than a single social class, are typical of those he would have known or heard about. The conflicts among the tenant family, the town merchants, and the landed gentry were drawn from firsthand experience or local legend. The effect is a sense of depth of awareness and understanding that cannot come from simply reading about a place and its people or even from observing it as an outsider, for that matter.

Warren goes on to call attention to the world that is presented in the work itself. What culture and society are being depicted? How does the fictive (or poetic) world reflect its outer world? Faulkner's created place, Yoknapatawpha County, Mississippi, which Malcolm Cowley called "Faulkner's mythical kingdom," has become almost synonymous with the one in which he lived. It has a physical presence with dimensions (2,400 square miles lying between the hills of north Mississippi and the black bottomlands), population (15,611 people of all classes and types), and a history (beginning with the story of the nephew of a Chickasaw chief and moving forward to narratives in which the old order meets the modern world). Faulkner's works can be described as sociological studies of all classes of people, from the aristocratic old families and county-seat lawyers to the tenant farmers and bootleggers. All are defined by speech, attitudes, food, and houses that are true to their status and background. In "Barn Burning," for example, Major de Spain's world, briefly glimpsed by Sarty through the opened front door as "a suave turn of carpeted stair and a pendant glitter of chandeliers and a mute gleam of gold frames" is a far cry from that of the unlettered, uncultured Abner Snopes, but both are a part of the time and place that Faulkner knew at first hand. Malcolm Cowley sees Yoknapatawpha finally as the story of the South in general, a region settled by aristocrats and ambitious people who took the land from the Indians with the idea of founding an enduring and civil society. Their efforts were corrupted, however, by slavery, interrupted by the Civil War, and ultimately defeated by people like the Snopeses, who were unprincipled and exploitative.

Finally, Warren turns his focus on the world that the work entered—that is, the audience for which it was intended. What kind of impact did it have on its readers? How was it critically received? This last area of interest has more recently been the concern of a group of critics known as the receptionists, about whom you will learn more later. They are interested in how the reading public responded to a given work in different periods. In Faulkner's case, the news was not always good. In the early 1930s he had a hard time making a living. His fiction did not have a ready audience, because it was difficult and experimental. Neither *The Sound and the Fury* nor *As I Lay Dying,* complex because of their multiple narrators and interior monologues, was a popular success. Faulkner tried to support himself by selling short stories to national magazines, but his earnings did not meet his needs. After publishing *Sanctuary,* a sensational (sometimes called sordid) work to produce income, he found a more durable means of earning money by writing for the movies while he continued to produce his novels. His last major novelistic effort was a series about the rise of the Snopeses and the decline of the old-line families. Using some of the characters introduced in "Barn Burning," he extended their stories through *The Hamlet* (1940), *The Town* (1957), and *The Mansion* (1959). His acceptance as a major fiction writer of this century was signaled by his being awarded the Nobel Prize in 1950.

Several schools of criticism that have recently adapted and applied a social perspective in ways that go beyond traditional approaches have grown powerful enough to warrant separate study. The receptionists, for example, are discussed in in chapter 7 (Reader-Response Criticism). Even more distinctive are the Marxists, treated in chapter 5. Their approach was widely practiced in the 1930s by such luminaries as Granville Hicks, Cecil Day-Lewis, Archibald MacLeish, and others. More recently, critics using the principles and techniques of the new historicism, covered in chapter 9, have challenged basic premises and goals of traditional historical literary study. They reject, for example, the assumption that one can know with any certainty what actually happened in any particular event, or that a period can be understood by determining its defining spirit, or that history unfolds in a sequence of causes and effects that is positive and progressive. To make their case, they do not limit their focus to literature, but in their effort to understand a period in all its dimensions, they turn also to nonliterary documents and information more often left to sociologists and anthropologists.

For several reasons the social approach, as it has been traditionally practiced, has waned in importance over the past few years. Certainly the influence of the new critics diminished its role (see chapter 3). The reluctance of readers to judge the worth of a work by its social relevance, their desire to value it for its aesthetic qualities, and their aversion to studying society rather than literature caused people to turn away from this perspective to others that serve them in different ways. Nevertheless, history and biography, once the principal means of approaching a literary text, are still in widespread use, although contemporary critics seldom make them their entire or even their central focus. Although some readers find such approaches to offer less opportunity for creative reading, and others object that connecting a work to an author's life or his times provides little opportunity for considering how or how well a poem or piece of fiction works, and still others protest that the reader's attention is directed to nonliterary and even nonaesthetic matters that are of only peripheral concern to the work itself, many people still find history and biography to be helpful means of extending the understanding of a story, a poem, or a play.

One of the most important reasons that history and biography are helpful is that knowledge of the past gives readers a way to understand the language, ideas, and purposes of literature more deeply and clearly. (The reverse is also true: as artifacts produced in a certain period, works of literature give historians a way to see the past.) For example, such knowledge can make a reader aware of social trends and conventions that would have influenced a writer's attitudes and tastes. It can clarify allusions to local and historical events and explain special uses of individual words and expressions. On a less general level, it can explain the origins of a specific work, clarify the source of the author's convictions, and reveal her deep concerns and conflicts. In short, it can show us why certain artists wrote as they did. It can even identify differences between contemporaries. Of course, matters can get complex when the biographical information (or what we know about an author's values) is contradictory to what a story implies, and such conflicts need to be resolved. Sometimes it is simply a matter of recognizing that the content of a work and the author's life are never the same, but on other occasions sorting out fact from fiction involves the skills and resources of the trained researcher. For most readers (and students), historical and biographical information won't make a bad story good or a good story better, but it can draw attention to literary qualities that might be missed by a reader from another period.

In the classroom, history and biography are certainly alive and well, often serving as the basis of lectures and writing assignments—even providing the organizing principle of many survey courses. Part of their appeal for teachers and students is that they furnish background against which a text can be more readily understood. By providing the reader with a sense of the world in which a writer lived and worked, they can enhance and clarify the meaning of a text. Such knowledge can also aid interpretation by preventing gross misreadings. In short, even if you do not choose to make history and biography your only analytical strategies, they can be used to supplement, complement, and support other, more complex ones.

Several characteristics distinguish historical and biographical studies. For one, they are primarily descriptive, not analytical or evaluative in nature. Also, they tend to be lengthy, because the background to a work has to be described, and the work has to be shown to fit the description. Some critics think history and biography are more appropriate for fiction (especially the novel) than for lyric poetry, but others have applied them effectively to poems. Obviously, a historical novel that recounts real events of great consequence lends itself easily and naturally to an examination of the real world outside the fictive one; a novel written as social protest or calling for reform can easily be studied for its impact on the situation it depicts. Poetry, too, however, can be studied from this perspective. Marxist critics, for example, have repeatedly managed to demonstrate that poems reflect class struggle or the writer's own background, and F. W. Bateson, in *English Poetry: A Critical Introduction,* goes so far as to organize literary history into six chronological schools, assign a social order to each, then show how individual poems reflect the writer's response to his social world.

Today most readers who use biographical and historical information to complement other methods of analysis turn to more than a simple recitation of the facts of an author's life or of the publication of the text. They search out the social and intellectual concerns of both the writer and of his society. They look for other works of the same period with which they can draw comparisons regarding themes, style, and genre. Sometimes they make comparisons between a specific work and others by the same author.

Whether you are using a historical-biographical approach as your sole perspective or using it to complement another means of analysis, you will find the following questions to be helpful aids to thinking and organizing your ideas.

- Where does this work fit into the chronology of the author's published works?
- Are the events of the plot based on the author's own experiences?
- How old was the author when the text was written?
- Is the setting (time and place) one in which the author lived? If not, how did he become knowledgeable about them: travel? reading? research?
- Are any of the characters based on people the author knew?
- Is one of the characters based on the author herself?
- How do the issues addressed (or conflicts depicted) reflect controversies, questions, and problems of the author's day?
- How does this work exemplify the definition of the intellectual or literary period in which it was produced—for example, classicism or romanticism?
- What are the attitudes of the author, either implied or explicit, about the central concerns of the text? Why does he have them?
- Does the language include words with archaic meanings? If so, what did they mean when the author used them?
- What writers and texts can be said to have influenced the writing of the work under consideration?

THE EFFECTS OF GENRE

To understand the discussion that follows, you should read the short story "Barn Burning," by William Faulkner, which begins on page 230.

Another traditional approach, the study of genre, represents some of the earliest literary criticism we have, going all the way back to Aristotle's classification of forms in his *Poetics* (fourth century B.C.). Viewing poetic art as an imitation or representation of reality, he grouped literary works according to the means, objects, and manner of the imitations. The term *means* refers to the medium of the work—for example, music, prose, or verse; *objects* refers to the nature of the situation or characters being imitated; and *manner* is the point of view, which can be the voice of a character, the author's own voice, or the voice of an actor. Recall, for example, that Aristotle defined tragedy as dealing with noble actions of great magnitude (objects), in artistically enhanced language (means) and presented in a dramatic, not narrative form (manner).

Throughout much of literary history, readers have found it helpful to be able to approach a new work with certain preconceived notions about what would be found there and what would be expected of the person who chose to read it. By knowing the elements commonly found in a story or poem or what shape it is likely to take, a reader can come to it with certain expectations and, hence, ways of understanding it. Conversely, to mistake the category into which a work fits can result in serious misreading. For example, to expect a lyric poem to have the sweep and grandeur of an epic would stand in the way of enjoying the lyric poem's personal and musical qualities.

Genre criticism was somewhat less powerful in the nineteenth century, but it had a small renaissance in the 1940s when a group known as the Chicago School (because many of the early members were at the University of Chicago) called for an approach to criticism that was less narrowly focused than that of the new critics (see chapter 3). They found in Aristotle the foundations of a system that could be extended in ways that would provide a broader and more comprehensive approach to literature. R. S. Crane, for example, argued in *Critics and Criticism* (1952) for the need to determine the kind of artistic object an author intended to produce before considering other elements of the work: "to what extent, and with what degree of artistic compulsion any of the particular things the writer has done at the various levels of his writing, down to the details of his imagery and language, can be seen to follow from the special requirements or opportunities which the kind of whole he is making presents to him."

Another way of approaching the study of genre was advanced by Northrup Frye in his *Anatomy of Criticism* (1957). He reserved the term *genre* for distinctions based on what he called the "radical of presentation," the relationship between an artist and the audience in the presentation of the work. He saw four such relationships and thus four major genres: *epos,* in which the poet speaks or recites to an audience; *drama,* in which the artist's words are enacted by characters before an audience; *lyric,* in which the audience seems to be overhearing a poetic speaker who does not direct the work to them; and *fiction,* in which the artist writes to a reading audience.

Genre studies take a number of different forms, but they usually have several basic aspects in common. Initially they attempt to determine what the genre of any given work is. The issue is more important than it might seem, for sometimes readers of the same text disagree about what kind of work they are reading, causing them to approach it with different expectations and afterward to judge it by different criteria. When we pick up a new novel, for example, our experience with other novels causes us to look for similar elements and strategies of development and to evaluate the new one by how well those elements and strategies are used. Our assumptions about fiction mean that we expect to meet interesting characters, listen to a narrator who may or may not be someone in the story, and find descriptive passages—perhaps even some philosophical commentary. We hope to enjoy a compelling plot, complete with conflict and resolution; a setting that logically contains the characters and maybe even extends our understanding of them; and symbols that become meaningful because they properly belong in the world of the story. With poetry, on the other hand, we expect to hear music in its sounds and rhythms, see images, recognize patterns, and savor ambiguity and figurative language. Similarly, we approach drama knowing that it will work out its narrative through dialogue, monologue, soliloquy, and action, because it does not have the luxury of authorial description or commentary.

Subcategories have additional distinctions. For example, lyric poetry is vastly different from epic poetry, and we do not expect of the latter the brevity and subjectivity of the former. The popular forms of certain periods of literary history set up their own special presumptions. A Wordsworthian sonnet will not read like Whitman's blank verse, but both are poetry. Certainly we read (or see) *Oedipus Rex* with a mind-set that is different from the one we bring to *The Sunshine Boys,* but both belong to the genre known as drama. If for some reason we mistake the genre of a text, we are likely to be disappointed and confused. To take Jonathan Swift's "A Modest Proposal" as a straightforward suggestion for curing the social ills of eighteenth-century Ireland by selling the children for food, instead of the ironic satire that it really is, would lead the reader to assume that the author was a sadistic monster. In short, whether dealing with major or minor categories of genres, our expectations partly shape how we receive the text. A question that sometimes affects genre is, What is the authentic text? That, too, is a more complicated matter than it seems because writers sometimes publish different versions of the same work. Charles Dickens wrote an unhappy ending to his novel *Great Expectations,* but when the reading public objected, he published a more pleasing one. Which is the authentic one? Further complicating the situation is that printing errors are likely to be repeated and finally accepted as the correct text. James Joyce's *Ulysses,* written in English that is characterized by original and daring wordplay and first typeset by French printers, still leaves readers wondering what was intentional and what was accidental. To make such determinations, scholars usually need access to manuscripts and other hard-to-find documents. Such study also requires knowledge of linguistics, literary history, and other even more specialized fields. As a result, textual criticism is a field of study in itself that is difficult for anyone but trained researchers to pursue. Nevertheless, all readers should at least be sure they are dealing with a standard edition and be aware of any disputed words or passages. To identify a genre with any certainty, a reader must have a stable text.

Once the text has been identified and the genre determined, a genre study examines how a text complies with, varies, or deviates from other works of its kind. We can ask, then, what makes "Barn Burning" a story? The answer is that it acts like one. It has what we expect a story to have—a narrator, in this case a third-person omniscient one; characters who outwardly engage in dialogue and action but whose inner souls we grow to know as well; a plot that begins with exposition, quickly moves to develop a conflict that rises to a climax, and at the end comes to a close with a denouement. The narrator describes the country store that serves as a makeshift courthouse so that we know its smells and its hard nail kegs that serve as seats. He tells us about the grandeur of Major de Spain's home and, by contrast, the harsh life of Sarty's family. On some level we begin to notice the recurrence of images of fire—candles burning, the small fire of the Snopeses' camp, the large one that consumes Major de Spain's barn. Point of view, developed characters, an ordered plot, description, and motifs and symbols make "Barn Burning" a story.

Certainly we recognize its moves as typical of short fiction, but if "Barn Burning" were totally consonant with expectations, we might easily grow bored. When the characters are stereotypes, the causality of the plot is forced, or the dialogue is mundane, a text is likely to become too predictable and thereby lose our interest. That makes a second question necessary: How does "Barn Burning" employ the conventions of the short story so that it holds our interest? Certainly it is grounded in characters who sound real and true. They speak in ways that define them as people of a particular place and time, of certain economic and educational levels. We believe they exist. Their problems are also of interest to us. We ache for Sarty's desperate need to respect his father as it conflicts with his innate understanding of the mean and destructive nature of his father's acts. The increasing viciousness of Abner is balanced against Sarty's hope, carrying us forward to his ultimate decision to betray his father to Major de Spain. We are more likely to stay focused on a story that not only uses the techniques of fiction in highly competent, even artistic ways but also surprises us by deviating from them from time to time. That leads to a third question: How does "Barn Burning" break the rules to create its own presentation? In the case of "Barn Burning," one element that makes it distinctive is Faulkner's prose style. It is easily recognized because it has certain characteristics that are not common in the style of other fiction writers. (At least they were not highly evident in writers who preceded Faulkner, though he has often been imitated and even parodied since his work went into publication.) He makes sentences, for instance, that we do not expect. We hear something new and interesting, for example, in his account of Sarty's running away from Major de Spain's house toward his unknown future. Listen to the complexity—and the music—of this one sentence:

> He could not hear either: the galloping mare was almost upon him before he heard her, and even then he held his course, as if the very urgency of his wild grief and need must in a moment more find him wings, waiting until the ultimate instant to hurl himself aside and into the weed-choked roadside ditch as the horse thundered past and on, for an instant in furious silhouette against the stars, the tranquil early summer night sky which, even before the shape of the horse and rider vanished, stained abruptly and violently upward: a long, swirling roar incredible and soundless, blotting the stars, and he springing up and into the road again, running again, knowing it was too late yet still running even after he heard the shot and, an instant later, two shots, pausing now without knowing he had ceased to run, crying "Pap! Pap!", running again before he knew he had begun to run, stumbling, tripping over something and scrabbling up again without ceasing to run, looking backward over his shoulder at the glare as he got up, running on among the invisible trees, panting, sobbing, "Father! Father!"

As readers, we are caught up in the power of this very long sentence that quickens its pace and increases its intensity as it goes on. The story rushes forward on its back. Such complexity could easily spin out of control, and it is interesting to ask how Faulkner manages to keep it going. A close look reveals that it is actually several utterances in one. That is, the sentence breaks down into units—some long, some short—that are set off from those next to it by commas and colons. For example, the unit that reads "knowing it was too late yet still running even after he heard the shot and, an instant later," fifteen words, is followed by the staccato two-word unit that reads "two shots," then by the nine-word unit "pausing now without knowing he had ceased to run." The pauses between units of unequal length, not always coming where the reader would expect them, provide a rhythm that both controls the speed of the sentence and calls attention to important narrative elements, such as the firing of the shots. The images, too, are rich and exotic, filled with the sound of the galloping horse, the sight of the early night sky that silhouettes the action, and the kinesthetic appeal of the boy's running and falling and running again. Though Faulkner's sentences, such as this one, may not be thought of as a deviation from traditional storytelling, their daring complexity gives his fiction its own personality. They make it anything but predictable or boring.

CONVENTIONAL WAYS OF WRITING ABOUT LITERATURE

Sometimes you will receive an assignment that is based less on specific subject matter than on a way of thinking about a text. It might be an approach that could be applied to many texts, not just the one assigned for study. For example, instead of asking you to use historical background to explain the role Abner Snopes played in the Civil War, your instructor might assign an essay that analyzes the motives of Snopes or that compares and contrasts Sarty with the character of another boy depicted in a story about coming of age in difficult circumstances. Such assignments ask you to use a specific thinking technique, which has its own rules of governance, instead of looking for a body of information that may be ordered in numerous ways. Some of the more common assignments that take this form include making an explication, doing an analysis, comparing and contrasting, and studying the works of a single author. Each of them requires that you formulate a response, your own argument about the topic. The statement of that position is commonly referred to as your thesis statement.

EXPLICATION

An explication, sometimes called by its French name, *explication de texte,* usually examines a fairly brief work, or sometimes a single passage from a larger one. In it you are expected to present an interpretation of the work, explain its meaning, or show how the writer achieves a particular effect. To do so you will make a close reading, noting all the nuances of the language and style, assessing how they fit together to create the whole.

It is important to remember that an explication is not a summary. That is, it is not a brief recitation of plot, which can result from following the chronological sequence of events, or a paraphrase of a poem, which comes from examining it line by line or stanza by stanza. You will do better to think about the work or passage in terms of significant literary elements, such as symbols, motifs, or figurative language, and then point out the meanings and effects they have.

ANALYSIS

An analysis of anything involves dividing it into its parts, then noting how they relate to or create the whole. It is a traditional assignment popular with teachers of literature, because it can be applied to the study of characters, plot structure, and imagery—a wide variety of literary elements. For example, if you were asked to analyze the character of Sarty in "Barn Burning," you would think about various aspects of his being, such as his family background, societal pressures, education, and experiences. How do they work together so that in the end he runs away from his childhood into adulthood?

Sometimes an analysis traces the stages of development of an event. In the case of Sarty's final act, for example, you would look for signs of his evolving decision, for formative events that change the way he sees his life—and that of his father. It is a process, not a single unchanging entity. In an analysis you will not be able to discuss every aspect of a work, nor do you need to. You will restrict your concern to those issues that are pertinent to the character or literary element that you are analyzing.

COMPARISON AND CONTRAST

Essay questions on examinations often take the form of comparison and contrast because the form allows an instructor to assess your knowledge about more than one topic in a single question. It also makes evident your ability to think critically, as it asks you to assess the similarities and differences of two persons or things, usually with a view to evaluating their worth relative to each other.

When you meet such an assignment, you will do well to begin with a simple list of how your two topics are similar and different in significant ways. If you are comparing two works, they should have some meaningful point of commonality—for example, the subject, author, or setting. The word *significant* is important here, because you cannot draw meaningful inferences from your study if you are dealing with trivial instances of comparison, and in the end you will want to draw conclusions about which is better, stronger, more important, longer-lasting, or more desirable. Without such a central idea, an organizing focus, your information will remain disconnected bits of data that mean nothing.

There are several different ways to present your conclusions, but two basic organizational patterns are always available. Say you are comparing "Barn Burning" with "Spotted Horses," another short story by Faulkner. Using the first pattern, you can present your discussion of "Barn Burning" in the first half of your paper, then turn your attention to "Spotted Horses," noting where the two stories share meaningful similarities but also diverge in other important ways. The second pattern presents one piece of information at a time about each story. For example, you might discuss the setting of each story, then the symbolism, followed by the theme. (Of course, there should be strong connections among the elements you choose to examine.) Both models call for a conclusion in which you make inferences and generalizations about the essential sameness, difference, or relative worth of the two texts.

STUDY OF A SINGLE AUTHOR'S WORKS

An analysis of several works by the same author takes the basic techniques of comparison and contrast one step further, for it continues to search for characteristics that recur from one work to another, albeit sometimes with variations and changes. You are trying to find the creative fingerprints of the artist—what makes her unique and, thereby, recognizable.

Regardless of how many works by a single author that you choose to consider in your analysis, you should prepare yourself by reading as many as possible. The more you have read of a single writer's work, the easier it will be for you to identify typical attitudes, concerns, and strategies. You will know that you are ready to discuss significant characteristics when you can recognize a poem or story as probably having been written by a particular person, although the authorship was not disclosed.

Topics that grow out of such studies are numerous. For example, you can focus your attention on a given theme or issue, the recurring treatment of certain social values, repeated stylistic characteristics, or reflections of the author's own experiences. In all cases you will want to trace the appearance of whatever you are examining through several works of the same author.

SUMMING UP

The approaches to reading texts and writing literary analyses that are explained in this chapter are probably not new ones for you, given that they have been standard classroom methods of teaching for many years. That they have been popular with teachers for decades is evidence of their usefulness. They will provide a good starting place for you to begin your literary explorations, and later they can be valid means of extending other approaches.

RECOMMENDED WEB SITES

When you are interested in doing historical-biographical research, you will find information quickly by doing an Internet search on the literary time period and/or the author's name. In addition, the following Web sites are particularly helpful for this kind of study.

http://www.ipl.org/ref/litcrit/
The Internet Public Library online literary criticism site. An excellent source for all types of criticism, but especially for the historical-biographical study.

http://www.ipl.org/ref/litcrit/guide.html
Another part of the Internet Public Library site.

MODEL STUDENT ANALYSES

A Look at the Background of Kate Chopin's "Désirée's Baby": A Biographical Study

Jahleh Kazemi-Richard

Kate O'Flaherty Chopin was born into an elite French Creole family in St. Louis, Missouri, on February 8, 1851. In her book entitled *Kate Chopin: A Critical Biography,* Per

Seyersted emphasizes that through her mother, Eliza O'Flaherty, the family had strong roots in this growing city, roots that reached as far back as the 1700s, when French settlers had made their way to America.

Chopin's ancestry also included Irish forebears through her father, Thomas O'Flaherty, who emigrated from his native Ireland to St. Louis in 1825. In his adopted city he became a successful merchant, and his family grew to hold a prominent place in society there. He married Eliza in 1844, four years after his first wife died giving birth to a son named George. Her Creole family welcomed him warmly, and her mother, Mme. Charleville, moved in with the couple after she became a widow. In 1848 Thomas and Eliza had a boy, Thomas O'Flaherty, Jr., followed by Kate two years later. Another daughter was born after Kate, but she lived for only a few years.

Unfortunately, this was not the only loss the family experienced while Kate was growing up. On November 1, 1855, Thomas O'Flaherty, who was one of the founders of the Pacific Railroad, died tragically when a bridge collapsed under the inaugural train he was riding on. His death greatly affected his daughter, who had not yet reached five years of age. Seyersted comments, "What had been a gay and joyous home, in which the Captain's wit and humor had been much in evidence, now was a place of sorrow. There was no one to carry on his activities, and the household became more reclusive."

During Kate O'Flaherty's childhood, St. Louis was a booming economic center for trade. It was also a Southern stronghold of aristocratic French and American antiabolitionists. Describing the city's pre–Civil War political climate, Seyersted writes, "In the 1850's, cosmopolitan St. Louis was the scene of bitter fights among its national groups. . . . Earlier, Elijah P. Lovejoy, a St. Louis publisher, had been forced out of town and later killed in nearby Alton, Illinois, by an angry mob who resented his abolitionist campaign." The O'Flaherty family definitely held strong Southern sympathies during the Civil War. In fact, George, Kate's half-brother, who joined the Confederate army and was captured in 1862, died from typhoid fever as he was being exchanged back to his regiment a month after Mme. Charleville passed away.

These new losses plunged the then twelve-year-old Kate into despair, and she secluded herself from school and her peers for almost three years. She was raised by the women of the household and after a time took up her studies at a Roman Catholic convent, where she became fluent in French and acquired a good basic knowledge of the French and British classics. When she graduated from the Academy of the Sacred Heart in 1868, she was ready to take a graceful dip into the fashionable society life of a southern belle. From what is known of her during that time, however, it appears that she did not care for all the dances she attended and preferred reading and studying novels of all kinds. She seemed especially interested in novels depicting strong-willed female protagonists. According to Seyersted, "Kate O'Flaherty seems also to have been greatly interested in Mme. De Stael's two novels *Delphine* and *Corinne,* the one dealing with a woman who finds her passion for her lover more important than what the world says of it, and the other with an English poetess who settles in Italy in order to live and work unhampered by the narrow English moral laws."

Such a background fails to suggest the life Kate Chopin was to lead. Instead of accepting the sheltered, privileged existence her well-to-do Catholic girlhood foreshadowed, she chose to ignore convention by smoking, going about the city unaccompanied, and later by writing scandalous books—or so they were judged to be at that time. How did she grow to be so independent? And where did the storytelling impulse come from?

Victoria Richelet Verdon, her great-grandmother, seems to have been an important early influence on both her social practices and her writing. A strong-willed woman who had at one time owned keelboats that traveled between St. Louis and New Orleans, Victoria Verdon encouraged Kate to face life boldly. Then, too, she was also a practiced storyteller. In Father Daniel S. Rankin's *Kate Chopin and Her Creole Stories,* we learn that her grandmother, Mme. Charleville, also entertained Kate with stories, specifically historical tales about Louisiana. She would reward her granddaughter's musical endeavors, for example, by recounting how St. Louis was settled by French colonists from New Orleans while it was still part of the Louisiana Purchase. Many of these stories centered around intimate relationships between men and women, relationships that were sometimes of a questionable nature. They are significant since complex relationships between men and women form the crux of many of Chopin's own stories.

At twenty-five Kate O'Flaherty met Oscar Chopin, a young Creole originally from northwestern Louisiana who was working at a St. Louis bank. Married in 1870, they settled in New Orleans after a short honeymoon trip to Europe. When his business there failed, he became the manager of a family cotton plantation and a village store in central Louisiana. The couple moved to Cloutierville, near Natchitoches, where they lived with their six children until Oscar's death from swamp fever in 1883. Inconsolable, she returned to St. Louis a year later, only to face the loss of her mother as well, leaving her alone with her children and her writing. It was then that she attempted for the first time to get her work published and recognized. Her career would last only a little over ten years, but in that time she would complete two novels, as well as over 150 stories, poems, and reviews.

"Désirée's Baby" appeared in *Vogue* in 1893. It was one of a series of tales about people with Cajun and Creole backgrounds entitled *Bayou Folk* (1894). The stories, which appeared in various periodicals, established her as an important local-color fiction writer of the day. Earlier, in 1890, she had published a first novel, *At Fault* (printed at her own expense), but it was *Bayou Folk* and a second collection of stories, *A Night in Acadie,* that made her reputation.

"Désirée's Baby" is the story of a young girl who is adopted by a wealthy Creole family, the Valmondes. Madame Valmonde, not having been able to conceive children herself, dotes on Désirée with the love and tenderness of a true mother. She believes that Désirée has been "sent to her by a beneficent Providence." The neighbor's son, Armand Aubigny, is a cruel plantation and slave owner who falls madly in love with her when he sees her leaning against the fence that separates their two properties one day. He impetuously decides to marry her despite her "unknown origins."

At first, Armand seems happy with his wife, and his newfound marital bliss even affects his behavior toward his slaves. Désirée clearly tells Mme. Valmonde about her husband's change after the arrival of her newborn son saying, ". . . he hasn't punished one of them,—not one of them—since baby is born. Even Négrillon, who pretended to have burnt his leg that he might rest from work—he only laughed, and said Négrillon was a great scamp." In a short while, however, conflict arises out of the presence of the baby boy. Mme. Valmonde is the first character to hint that something is amiss. On seeing him one morning, she is surprised by his appearance: "'This is not the baby!' she exclaimed, in startled tones." Mme. Valmonde has noticed that the color of the baby is not "white," but she is unable to share this knowledge with her unknowing daughter.

Three months later, Armand starts to avoid his wife and returns to his old brutal behaviors. Désirée is distressed and doesn't understand this new turn in their relationship until she compares the skin of a mulatto boy who is fanning the baby with her son's skin and realizes that they both have a yellowish tint to them. Seized with dread, she asks her husband what this could mean. His answer is painfully short. "'It means,' he answered lightly, 'that the child is not white; it means that you are not white.'" A panicked Désirée then writes to her adopted mother in a final effort to prove her "white" racial identity, but Mme. Valmonde simply urges her to come back home to her (where she won't be judged by her origins). Désirée, completely rejected by her husband, takes her baby out into the swamps and is never heard from again.

Chopin leaves the reader with an unexpected twist of events at the end of this sad story. While burning all of his wife's possessions, including love letters she wrote to him while they were courting, Armand accidentally runs across a letter his mother had written to his father that contains a "dark" family secret. "'But, above all,' she wrote, 'night and day I thank the good God for having so arranged our lives that our dear Armand will never know that his mother, who adores him, belongs to the race that is cursed with the brand of slavery.'"

Like most of Chopin's works, "Désirée's Baby" deals with a marital relationship, but it is unique in the sense that it is her only story that deals with racial segregation in such a clear and direct manner. At a time when racial tensions were high, Chopin managed artfully to blur the lines between "black" and "white." Through "Désirée's Baby," she boldly questions the morality of a society that would cruelly and superficially rank human beings by their appearance, their "color." It can be argued that Armand is the real victim of this story because he is duped by the establishment into being cruel to his own people and losing his precious wife and child. Chopin teaches us that true love knows no color and no artificial boundaries. In the end, Mme. Valmonde is a heroine because she accepts Désirée as her child and gives her unconditional love without even wanting to know her true origins or her race.

In many ways "Désirée's Baby" is typical of much of Kate Chopin's work. Its use of an exotic Louisiana setting, its exploration of complex male and female relationships, the creation of sensuous Creole characters, and the inclusion of French expressions are found throughout her subsequent stories and novels. For example, her last novel, *The Awakening* (1899), has many of the elements found in "Désirée's Baby." Because the novel's rediscovery was largely reponsible for the author's current critical acceptance, stories such as this one become even more interesting as early depictions of the themes for which Kate Chopin was to be known.

Good versus Evil in Kate Chopin's "Désirée's Baby": A Comparative Study

Andrea E. Segura

Kate Chopin explores the theme of good versus evil in her short story "Désirée's Baby," using the differences between Désirée and her husband, Armand Aubigny, to shed light on the racial tensions of the South in the nineteenth century. Using the contrasts of good and evil, light and darkness, white and black, and male and female, Chopin creates a rich text that depicts the futility of racial prejudice.

"Désirée's Baby" is the story of a young southern girl, of unknown heritage, who is adopted by the Valmonde family. The story traces Désirée from the time of her arrival at the Valmonde plantation to her marriage to Armand Aubigny. Chopin's short story ends with the birth of their child and the banishment of Désirée and her son because of the realization that the child is biracial.

In the text, Désirée is characterized as good and Armand as evil. Thinking of the child her husband found, Madame Valmonde speculates about the child's arrival: "In time Madame Valmonde abandoned every speculation but the one that Désirée had been sent to her by a beneficent Providence to be the child of her affection, seeing that she was without a child of the flesh." In contrast, Armand is compared to Satan when he realizes that his child is biracial. "And the very spirit of Satan seemed suddenly to take hold of him in his dealing with the slave."

By virtue of her kind and gentle nature, Désirée finds that her happiness depends on the mood of her husband. "When he frowned she trembled, but loved him. When he smiled, she asked no greater blessing of God." As a result of her goodness, Désirée is abused by her husband for most of the story.

Armand shows the true nature of his character when faced with the realization that his child is biracial. The so-called love he felt for Désirée is replaced with hatred and disdain.

"'It means,' he answered lightly, 'that the child is not white; it means that you are not white.'" He feels nothing but apathy at her decision to leave. To Armand, Désirée is now an embarrassment that he no longer wants to face. He banishes her and their child to the woods to die.

Chopin also uses images of light versus darkness in "Désirée's Baby" to distinguish between the nature of Désirée and Armand. Désirée, who is consistently dressed in white, is portrayed as the epitome of virtue and grace. "The young mother was recovering slowly, and lay full length, in her soft white muslins and laces upon a couch." Her light countenance is in stark contrast to the dark-skinned Armand and his plantation, L'Abri. "Big solemn oaks grew close to it, and their thick-leaved, far-reaching branches shadowed it like a pall." Whereas Armand is dark and menacing, Désirée is glowing and kind. "Désirée's face became suffused with a glow that was happiness itself."

In the patriarchal system of the nineteenth-century South, being male was privileged over being female. Armand rules the home with an iron fist. He appears to become a kinder and gentler man at the onset of his marriage. "Marriage and later the birth of his son had softened Armand Aubigny's imperious and exacting nature greatly." Unfortunately this change is short-lived.

Désirée, in the role of the cowering female, is forced to beg unsuccessfully to stay in her home after the true race of her son is revealed. "'Shall I go, Armand?' she asked in tones sharp with agonized suspense." The "good" woman is forced to leave her home at the whim of her "evil" husband. In contrast to Armand, who wields power over the entire plantation, including its people, Désirée is not even in control of her own destiny or the destiny of her child.

The theme of white versus black is one of the strongest elements in "Désirée's Baby." The slaves at L'Abri are cruelly treated by their master. "Young Aubigny's rule was a strict one, too, and under it his negroes had forgotten how to be gay." Désirée and her child are banished from their home because of the suspicion that she is black. Armand also withdraws his love because of this "crime." "Moreover, he no longer loved her, because of the unconscious injury that she had brought upon his home and name."

To be black is equated with being unworthy of love, kindness, and basic human rights. In an ironic twist in the plot, Kate Chopin shows the fallacy of racial prejudice in the ending of "Désirée's Baby." There is a sense of poetic justice when Armand learns that it is he, not Désirée, who "belongs to the race that is cursed with the brand of slavery."

Kate Chopin's short story "Désirée's Baby" is a complex tale that ultimately focuses on good versus evil. Chopin explores racial prejudice by focusing on the differences between Désirée and Armand Aubigny. She uses imagery and dialogue to breathe life into this cautionary tale. Chopin does not insult the reader with pat answers and a strained happy ending. She creates a complicated text that reveals the evil and futility of racial prejudice.

3

Formalism

Poetry does not inhere in any particular element but depends upon the set of relationships, the structure, which we call the poem.

Robert Penn Warren, "Pure and Impure Poetry"

Formalism probably has the distinction of having more names than any other recently developed school of criticism. The model, as defined by American and English critics, has been called the New Criticism (long after it was no longer new), as well as aesthetic or textual (because of its primary concerns), or ontological (because of its philosophical grounding). Then, too, there is **Russian formalism,** which shares some fundamental characteristics with its western cousin, but it is the former (by whatever name you choose to call it and referred to here as formalist criticism) that in the 1930s revolutionized the work of scholars, critics, and teachers in this country. For decades people learned to read, analyze, and appreciate literature using this approach, making it one of the most influential methods of literary analysis that twentieth-century readers have encountered.

Its sustained popularity among readers comes primarily from its providing a way to understand and enjoy a work for its own inherent value as a piece of literary art. Emphasizing close reading of the work itself, formalism puts the focus on the text as literature. It does not treat it as an expression of social, religious, or political ideas; neither does it reduce it to being a promotional effort for some cause or belief. As a result, it makes those who apply its principles and follow its processes better, more discerning readers.

HISTORICAL BACKGROUND

Any new school of criticism is both an offspring of those that have preceded it and a reaction against them. The New Criticism, with its emphasis on unity and form, is the direct descendant of the aesthetic theories of the romantic poets (and philosopher-critics before them). Samuel Taylor Coleridge, for example, believed that the spirit of poetry must "embody in order to reveal itself; but a living body is of necessity an organized one—and what is organization but the connection of parts to a whole, so that each part is at once end and means!" Form to him was not simply the visible, external shape of literature. It was something "organic," "innate." He explained that "it shapes as it develops itself from within, and the fulness of its development is one and the same with the perfection of its outward form. Such is the life, such the form."

The New Criticism was more directly born as a reaction against the attention that scholars and teachers in the early part of this century paid to the biographical and historical context of a work, thereby diminishing the attention given to the work itself. Instead of dealing directly with a poem, for example, they were likely to treat it as a sociological or historical record. It could be an excuse to indulge one's fascination with the lives of writers and their friends. And when the critics and scholars did directly address the text, they tended to describe their own impressions of it. Clearly, something more scientific was called for, some better way of understanding and evaluating a poem or play.

Enter the New Criticism, a theory of literature that would have a reader understand and value a work for its own inherent worth, not for its service to metaliterary matters. The movement began informally in the 1920s at Vanderbilt University in discussions among John Crowe Ransom, Robert Penn Warren, Allen Tate, Cleanth Brooks, and others who were interested in getting together to talk about literature. For three years they even published a literary magazine called *The Fugitive.* Not only influenced by each other but also bolstered by the work of theorists from abroad, such as T. S. Eliot, I. A. Richards, and William Empson, they began to develop their ideas of how to read a text. Important to their thinking, for example, was Eliot's announcement of the high place of art as art rather than as expression of social, religious, or political ideas. They were influenced, too, by his explanation of how emotion is expressed in art. He called it the objective correlative, "a set of objects, a situation, a chain of events which shall be the formula of that *particular emotion;* such that when the external facts, which must terminate in sensory experience, are given, the emotion is immediately evoked." From Richards, who was concerned with the investigation of meaning, they adopted the practice of working toward the scrupulous explication of poems. Later the Fugitives would become well known for their own poems and stories, but they are also remembered for beginning to formulate principles of literary analysis that would shape the habits of serious readers for several decades to come.

The New Criticism went on to develop a sense of the importance of form (leading at some point to its being called formalism), their practice of the close reading of texts, and an appreciation of order. It asserted that understanding a work comes from looking at it as a self-sufficient object with formal elements, laws of its own that could be studied. To know *how* a work means became the quest. In time, formalist principles were set firmly in place with their acceptance by prestigious literary journals such as the *Kenyon Review* and *Sewanee Review* and by college adoptions of Brooks and Warren's texts *An Approach to Literature* (with John Purser in 1936),

Understanding Poetry (1939), *Understanding Fiction* (1943), and *Understanding Drama* (by Brooks and Robert Heilman in 1948). It was also supported by the publication of anthologies such as *The House of Fiction,* by Caroline Gordon and Allen Tate (1950). The wide dissemination of formalist principles led, finally, to their dominance of American, and to some extent English, literary studies for the decades of the 1940s and 1950s and into the 1960s.

READING AS A FORMALIST

To understand the following discussion, you should read the short story "Araby," by James Joyce, which begins on page 230.

The critic who wants to write about literature from a formalist perspective must first be a close and careful reader who examines all of the elements of a text individually and questions how they come together to create a work of art. Such a reader, who respects the autonomy of a work, achieves an understanding of it by looking inside it, not outside it or beyond it. Instead of examining historical periods, authorial biographies, or literary styles, for example, she will approach a text with the assumption that it is a self-contained entity and that she is looking for the governing principles that allow it to reveal itself. The correspondences between the characters in James Joyce's short story "Araby" and people he knew personally may be interesting, for example, but for the formalist they are less pertinent to understanding how the story creates meaning than are other kinds of information that it contains within itself.

Because formalism calls for a close reading of the text, the first time through you cannot expect to notice all the subtleties and details that will ultimately figure in your analysis. It is on subsequent readings that the formalist perspective begins to take shape. The second time around, you may begin to notice repetition of words and images, patterns of sound, multiple meanings, and ambiguous dialogue. You will ultimately investigate every detail of a work for its contribution to and connection with the whole. Such observations made by the scrupulous reader are the key to discovering how all the formal elements of the text work together. Some of the main elements that call for attention are form, diction, and unity—and the various literary devices they subsume.

FORM

Coleridge's concept of the organic, inherent nature of form in a literary work (noted earlier) is reflected in the formalists' assumption that although the external, easily noted ordering of a poem or story (its rhyme scheme or sequence of events leading to a climax, for example) may be significant in an analysis, form is actually the whole that is produced by various structural elements working together. It grows out of the work's recurrences, repetitions, relationships, motifs—all the organizational devices that create the total effect. Together they are the statement of the work. Form and content are inseparable.

What a poem or prose work means depends on how it is said, so to understand it, the formalist reader-writer pays attention to how all parts of the work affect each other and how they fit together. In early readings, then, you may find it helpful to make marginal notations where words and phrases recur. If the wording is not repeated exactly as it was before, there may be synonyms that echo important ones. Images, too, can gain significance by appearing more than once. They may be random or may form a regular pattern, but either way they deserve to be noted because they begin to create form and unity.

In a narrative, the point of view from which a story is told is a significant shaping force. Because the reader is given only the information that the narrator knows, as he or she understands it and chooses to share it, the storyteller controls the reader's perception of the fictive world and thereby determines how the reader grasps the integral and meaningful relationship of all its parts. Of course, the omniscient narrator, who speaks with a third-person voice, is assumed to see all, but if a major or minor character in the narrative recounts the narrative, the reader must question how that teller's part in the story affects his or her understanding and presentation of it. Is the narrator reliable? Biased? Does the narrator have a reason to leave out events or reshape them? What is the ethical stance of the teller?

Your reading log can also be used to address a number of issues regarding the formal qualities of a text. Some relevant questions such as these can help you start to think about them.

- Does this work follow a traditional form, such as the Petrachan sonnet form, or does it chart is own development?
- How are the events of the plot recounted—for example, in sequential fashion or as a flashback?
- How does the work's organization affect its meaning?
- Does the denouement in a plot surprise or satisfy you?
- Does it provide closure to the narrative or leave it open?
- What is the effect of using a particular meter—say, anapestic tetrameter?
- What is the effect of telling a story from this point of view?
- What sounds are especially important in developing this piece? Where do they recur? (In poems, be sure to look for more than end rhyme.)
- What rhythms are in the words? (This question is applicable to prose as well as poetry.)
- Where do images foreshadow later events?
- How does the narrator's point of view shape the meaning?
- What visual patterns do you find in this text?
- What progressions of nature are used to suggest meaning—for example, sunrise/sunset, spring/winter?
- If you were to make a chart of the progress of this plot or poem, what would it look like?

Sometimes, particularly in works written in the last few decades, form is hard to determine. Conventions that serve as guideposts for the reader may be few. Theater of the absurd, for instance, delights in a lack of traditional elements that an audience looks to for help. No form is also form, however. Notice how the seeming absence of form suggests a chaotic world in which there is no meaning.

As a formalist, then, you will look for meaning in all the organizational elements at hand, even those that seem distorted or "absurd." But simply listing them is not enough. You must then determine how their interaction creates meaning. What is the effect of the whole? How do the parts of the poem that give it order come together to assume a unique shape that presents readers with a unique experience? How does structure become meaning?

Looking at "Araby," for example, the reader easily recognizes that the narrative unfolds chronologically, but she also perceives that more is taking place here than a simple sequence of events involving a romantic desire to go to a bazaar. On the surface of the story little seems to happen, but beneath it more subtle conflicts and changes are transpiring. With that recognition it is possible to see "Araby" as an initiation story in which the protagonist begins with childish dreams, moves through a test of will and commitment, and arrives at a new, adult sense of the world. The boy's maturation could be described as a downward emotional spiral as he moves from a sense of the holiness of the world to frustration with its obstacles and then rage at its emptiness. The bottom of the spiral is marked by his recognition of the futility of his efforts to make it otherwise. Though the process begins as he listens to the sounds of innocent child's play, it ends with a recognition of man's aloneness in a darkened world.

The form of "Araby" can be described in other ways as well. You can, for example, compare it to other stories of quest, in which the protagonist searches for a holy relic, traveling from place to place (in this case making the train journey, which he must take alone) and enduring ordeals in the service of his mission. You can also describe it as circular, for it begins with physical death (a priest had died in the back room, where the air is still musty, and the garden is yellowed and "straggling") and ends with the death of innocence and belief that those images foreshadow. You could even say that it is a mythic pattern, as it recounts a single episode from childhood to suggest the larger pattern of human experience in which innocence is succeeded by knowledge, dreams by reality, childhood by adulthood.

DICTION

Words hold the keys to meaning. A formalist will look at them closely, questioning all of their **denotations** (explicit dictionary meanings) and **connotations** (implied but not directly indicated meanings). As Cleanth Brooks posits, the reader must consider how a word or phrase creates meaning that no other word or phrase could. **Etymology** (the history of a word) becomes significant, and **allusions** to other works may import surprising meanings. Tracing allusions is a sticky point for formalists because it means going outside the text to find meaning. Nevertheless, if the reader is to explore all facets of the text, it is important to discover everything that a given reference suggests.

The locution that has more than a single possibility for interpretation is valued for the richness it brings to the whole. Unlike the scientist, who strives for directness and singularity of meaning, the poet, who speaks of experience, uses **ambiguity** to reach for meaning through language that is suggestive, compressed, and multileveled. The poet may, for example, choose words that can bear the load of several, sometimes divergent meanings, as Gerard Manley Hopkins does in "The Windhover." In that poem he uses the word *buckle,* which can mean "crumple" but also suggests "join" or "bend" and perhaps other possibilities.

When an incident, object, or person is used both literally (as itself) and figuratively (as something else), it becomes a **symbol.** In other words, a symbol refers simultaneously to itself and to something beyond the self as well, to expand the meaning of the text and provide additional possibilities for the discovery of meaning. A flag is a flag, for instance, but it also makes a viewer think of freedom and country. Symbols are often recognizable because they grow out of images or phrases that recur with more than normal frequency or that receive an inordinate amount of attention by the narrator. Such is the case with the train trip the boy in "Araby" must take to reach the fair. As he travels alone through the dark night, the journey becomes more than a physical one; he is also moving psychologically from innocence to knowledge, from childhood to adulthood. Because it is meaningful in the context of the images, plot structure, and other elements of the story, the symbol contributes to the unity of the story.

In your reading log, you will find it helpful to take note of the quality of language in a selection. You can

- Record any words you do not know.
- Find words that appear more than once. Do their meanings change with subsequent use? Or do they grow more powerful?
- Look for words that suggest meanings that they do not explicitly state.
- Identify terms (titles of books, quotations, paraphrases) that point to other works that would add meaning to the one you are reading.
- Look up the history of words that appear at important points of a story or poem. Do other, older meanings suggest anything about their use here?
- Where did you find ambiguity? How does it suggest additional meanings?
- What are the important symbols, and how do they create unity?

When applied to "Araby," these approaches reveal that its language is particularly rich and subtle, with connotations radiating out of words that initially seem to be merely literal or factual. The opening paragraph alone—with its use of "blind" (twice), its reference to the school as a prison (at the end of the day setting the boys "free"), and its description of the uninhabited, detached house in a neighborhood of "brown imperturbable faces"—suggests a society in which something important has been lost, a world in which dreams will not survive. It stands in contrast to the language used to describe the boy's private, inner world where he worships Mangan's sister, whom he thinks of as a holy figure surrounded by an aura of light. Describing his devotion, he stresses its sacred nature by using Christian language. He says, "I imagined that I bore my chalice safely through a throng of foes. Her name sprang to my lips at moments in strange prayers and praises which I myself did not understand."

The ambiguity in "Araby," its use of words that suggest more than a single meaning, creates a sense of mystery that is part of both the boy's devotion to holy mysteries and the mystery of human life. For instance, the descriptions of Mangan's sister, who does little and says only a few words, imply that she is both human and holy. When the boy recounts his vision of her, he says, "The light from the lamp opposite our door caught the white curve of her neck, lit up the hair that rested there and, falling, lit up the hand upon the railing. It fell over one side of her dress and caught the white border of a petticoat, just visible as she stood at ease." In his words she is both a sexual and a sacred being. He is attracted by her sensuality but also sees her as a holy icon surrounded by light.

Obviously the diction of "Araby" suggests more than a first reading might indicate. The formalist critic will push on its language to reveal meanings that are not readily noticed, in an effort to find suggested meanings rather than explicit ones. The result is an enriched understanding of the experience of the boy, his world, and his understanding of it.

UNITY

If a work has unity, all of its aspects fit together in significant ways that create a whole. Each element, through its relationship to the others, contributes to the totality of the work, its meaning. Patterns that inform and give its parts relevance to the rest often appear as verbal motifs, images, symbols, figurative language, meter, rhyme, sound. The narrator's point of view can also be an important unifying element. Unity is not easily achieved, however, for the formal elements that are eventually reconciled by the reader will resist, contradict, and contrast each other and threaten the orderliness of the work. Their opposition, which must be overcome if the work is to achieve wholeness, gives it the complexity one finds in life itself.

Unity is created, for example, when a single **image** or **figure of speech** is extended throughout a work or when several images or figures form a pattern. The appearance may be a relatively simple repeated reference to a color or a sound, or the more complicated use of figurative language, an intentional departure from normal word meaning such as a metaphor. For example, when a word or phrase is used to refer to a person or object to which it is not logically applicable, as in Emily Dickinson's assertion that "hope is the thing with feathers," the metaphorical statement is an imaginative way of identifying one thing with another. Stretched and elaborated, images and figures grow rich and complex, as is easily noticed in the poems of the metaphysical poets, whose works the New Critics celebrated. To see how the protracted, embellished use of an image or figure can enhance and complicate meaning, you can read John Donne's "A Valediction: Forbidding Mourning" or shorter poems such as "The Silken Tent," by Robert Frost, or Emily Dickinson's "I Like to See It Lap the Miles."

In the most powerful works the elements do not come together easily or comfortably. In fact, the formalist critic looks for them to resist each other, creating what Allen Tate called **tension,** the push of conflicting elements resisting each other. Tension often appears in the form of **irony** (the use of a word or a statement that is the opposite of what is intended), **paradox** (a contradiction that is actually true), and ambiguity (a word, statement, or situation that has more than one possible meaning.) For example, the point of view of a piece of fiction becomes more complicated, and more interesting to a formalist, if the narrator is not aware of the whole story but must tell it from limited knowledge or understanding. The possibilities for paradox, irony, and ambiguity grow when the storyteller operates without fully comprehending the dimensions of the events and characters of the narrative.

In your reading journal you may want to ask some questions about the unity of the selection you are studying. You can ask

- What images are extended or elaborated?
- Where do several images work together to create meaning?
- What is paradoxical in the work? How is it both contradictory and true?
- What is ironic in the work?
- Do all of the elements cohere in ways that generate meaning?
- Are the verbal motifs, images, figures of speech, symbols, meter, rhyme, and sound consistent? If not, what did you have to reconcile?

"Araby" is rich in paradox, ambiguity, and irony, but it is the last one that most clearly creates tension in this story. For example, the hall, when the boy finally arrives at the bazaar, is in darkness and silence "like that which pervades a church after a service." He recognizes that despite his devotion, his fidelity, and his desire to serve his dream, he has come too late. What he has expected, indeed what the reader feels he has deserved, has not come to pass. His situation is an ironic one in which he finds the opposite of what he made his journey to reach. Araby, the place of romance and enchantment, is as mundane as his own neighborhood. His holy quest has led to darkness.

Paradox often occurs along with irony, and many elements in Joyce's story are paradoxical. The boys' school, for example, is called the Christian Brothers' School, but it is described as a prison. In fact, the references to Christian objects and symbols that abound in the story are mostly paradoxes. The boy's garden, for example, has a central (dying) apple tree, he prays in the back room (where the priest died), and at the end of the story a voice calls out, in an inversion to God's command "Let there be light," that the light has gone out. There is paradox, too, in the boy's devotion, in that it is simultaneously sad (because it is doomed) and laughable (because it is childish). And Mangan's sister, both holy and profane, is perhaps not simply ambiguous but paradoxical.

Along with the irony and ambiguity, such paradoxes require the reader to reconcile them in order to resolve the tension they create so that the text becomes a unified whole. As Robert Penn Warren points out in "Pure and Impure Poetry," the poet "wins by utilizing the resistance of his opponent—the ambiguity, irony, and paradox, which, since everything in the work has to be accounted for, the reader must resolve to discover meaning."

WHAT DOESN'T APPEAR IN FORMALIST CRITICISM

If the formalist critic is to approach a work with a heightened awareness of form, diction, and unity (including finding and examining the significance of ambiguity, paradox, and irony), some other analytical techniques are strenuously to be avoided. They include the heresy of paraphrase, the intentional fallacy, biographical examination, and the affective fallacy. Because they lead the reader away from the poem instead of *into* it, they are not considered to be valid critical tools.

Paraphrase

If a reader accepts the principles of formalism, any change to a text—whether it be in form, diction, or unifying devices—makes the work no longer itself. To restate a poem or summarize a story is to lose it. Its uniqueness disappears. Any alteration of wording or structure or point of view changes the meaning of the original and cannot, therefore, be valid.

Intention

What an author intended to do is not important, argue the formalists. What the author actually did is the concern of the reader. In *The Verbal Icon,* William Wimsatt and Monroe Beardsley question whether an author's intentions can ever be known, as they often lie below the conscious level. Even if they are overtly stated, they may not have been carried out. Authors, they observe, are not necessarily reliable witnesses of such matters. One can add that neither are they necessarily good critics of their own work. Sometimes they don't even recognize how good it actually is.

Biography

Studying the details of an author's life, and by extension the social and historical conditions in which a work was produced, may be interesting, but it does little to reveal how a poem means. The work is not the writer, nor the writer the work. To confuse the two is to be led away from what happens in the work.

Affect

If readers digress by paying attention to the writer's biography, they also go astray by paying attention to their own reactions to the work. By asking about its effect on an audience, particularly the emotional effect, the critic shifts attention to results rather than means, from the work to the responses of someone outside the text. Such an approach will lead to no single meaning. It can impose no standards. It results, say the formalists, in pure subjectivism.

Obviously, the formalist approach is not without its weaknesses and, needless to say, those who would point them out. Chief among the complaints is that the formalists have elevated the study of technique to the exclusion of the human dimension, that they have turned reading into the solving of clever puzzles and have lost the connections literature has with people and their lives.

Other objections come from those who find formalism too restrictive. David Daiches, for example, argues against such a narrow focus on a piece of literature as a work of art. It is, he asserts, many things at once: a social document, a record of a writer's thoughts and experiences, a commentary on life. To narrow the range of its possibilities is to diminish it.

Finally, critics have charged that formalism works less well with some works, perhaps even certain genres, than others. It has proved to be especially helpful with lyric poetry but less effective in understanding the essay or long, philosophical poems. (Obviously, it is easier to deal with the formal elements of short texts than those of long ones.) That it has not worked particularly well for analysis of contemporary poetry suggests that, for the time being, it is more likely to be found as part of other critical approaches than in essays that are purely formalist in their techniques. Certainly it is alive and well in classrooms, where it still teaches students to read closely and analytically and to support their interpretations with examples drawn from the text under consideration.

WRITING A FORMALIST ANALYSIS

Prewriting

When you approach the actual writing of your analysis, you may find that your reading log is mostly filled with definitions of words or lists of images. It is now time to see how they are woven together, even those that do not naturally fit. You may want to revisit the text, looking for patterns (recurrences that appear with such regularity that they are eventually anticipated), visual motifs, and repeated words and phrases; for significant connotations, multiple denotations, allusions, and etymological ramifications to meaning; for unity, as expressed by the meaningful coherence of all elements of the work; and for the tension produced by paradox and irony.

Another approach to prewriting is to spend some time freewriting about what you have read. You can begin with a symbol or a strong image and see where it takes you. If the text has the unity a formalist looks for, any single observation is likely to lead you to an understanding of the other aspects of the text to which it is connected.

Drafting and Revising

The Introduction

A common way of beginning a formalist analysis is to present a summary statement about how the various elements of the work come together to make meaning. Such an opening announces the core of the analysis that the rest of your paper will explain in more detail. Of course, if this is the approach you want to use, you will need to write at least a draft of your discussion before working on the introduction, because you have to know what you are going to say before you can summarize it.

An introduction that follows this pattern will undoubtedly clarify your topic and intentions for your readers, but it may not be the most attractive or interesting way of addressing them. A more colorful alternative is to begin by making direct reference to the text itself. For example, if you are working with a short story, you can recount a particularly meaningful incident from it, or if you are writing about a poem, you can quote a few lines from it, followed by an explanatory comment of why the excerpt is important to understanding the work as a whole.

The Body

The main part of your paper will be devoted to showing how the various elements of the text work together to create the meaning. You will want to touch on the form, diction, and unity, citing examples of how they operate together and reinforce each other to develop a theme, a meaning that has some universal human significance. Your job is to describe what you find in the work, then to assess its effect on the whole. Where you find conflicts, aspects of the work that do not seem to lead to the same ends, you must work to resolve the tension they create.

If a repeated image is dominant in a story, or a repeated phrase particularly insistent, you may want to give it first place in your discussion. That is, you can choose to begin with the most significant element in the work, letting it subsume the other aspects that formalists consider important. On the other hand, you may decide to treat form, diction, and unity as equally significant, giving roughly the same amount of consideration to each.

You will want to give a good bit of attention to any instances of paradox and irony in the selection, explaining how their presence creates tension and how their resolution provides satisfaction. This is a good opportunity to draw examples from the text or to quote significant passages. As in all critical essays, references to the work that illustrate your discussion will both strengthen and clarify what you are saying.

It is important to remember that you will find it more effective to organize your discussion around the literary elements you have examined rather than follow the sequence of events in a narrative or the stanzaic progression of a poem. For the writer who tries to move sequentially through the text as the author has constructed it, making analytical comments along the way, the temptation to forsake analysis and simply summarize the work is hard to resist.

The Conclusion

The end of your paper is an appropriate place to state (or reiterate) the connection between form and content. Up to this point, you have been describing how the text operates in particular ways and explaining the meaning that emerges from them. Now you have the opportunity to make some generalizations about the overall relationship of form and content. Now you can decide whether you have explored a text that has its own laws of being and operates successfully within them, one in which the formal elements, not easily reconciled, eventually are harmonized to make meaning.

GLOSSARY OF TERMS USEFUL IN FORMALIST CRITICISM

Affective fallacy Concern for the effect a work has on the reader. According to the formalists, to use affect as a criterion of judgment is a mistake because the work is judged by what it *does* instead of what it *is*.

Allusion A brief reference to a character, person, event, or situation outside the work in which it is made.

Ambiguity Wording that suggests more than one meaning or interpretation.

Connotation Meaning associated with a word in addition to its denotative, or dictionary, meaning.

Denotation The core or specific meaning of a word without any associated or suggested meanings.

Etymology The study of the origins of words or of a specific word.

Figure of speech Words used in more than their literal sense. They may appear as similes, metaphors, synecdoches, metonymies, and other forms.

Image A mental picture created by references to the senses. As a descriptive strategy, it can represent or enhance the understanding of a person, event, or object.

Intentional fallacy Concern for the author's purpose in writing the work. To the formalist, this way of determining the meaning and effectiveness of a work is erroneous because it is based on information outside the text.

Irony A statement or situation in which the meaning is the opposite of what is said, done, or expected.

Motif A recurring phrase, image, or scene in a work.

Paradox A statement that seems to contradict itself but is actually true.

Paraphrase A reworded version of a passage or work usually made by someone other than the original writer. To a formalist, it cannot substitute for what it restates.

Point of view The perspective from which a narrative is told—for example, first-person or omniscient.

Russian formalism A school of criticism active in Russia and Czechoslovakia in the early part of the twentieth century that worked to establish a scientific basis to explain how literary devices produce aesthetic effects. In the 1940s and 1950s it influenced the development of the New Criticism. Its leaders included Viktor Shklovsky and Mikhail Bakhtin.

Structure The statement made by a work; the essential, basic meaning.

Symbol Someone or something that is a literal presence but also represents something beyond the self. The physical object or person usually refers to something abstract.

Tension The energy created by conflicting elements in a work, usually appearing in the form of ambiguity, irony, and paradox.

Unity The coherence of the elements of a work that creates a sense of an organic whole.

RECOMMENDED WEB SITES

http://www.cnr.edu/home/bmcmanus/tools.html
A starting point for readers just beginning to work with formalist criticism.

http://www.members.aol.com/arkmast/narr03.html
A treatise on narratology.

http://sun3.lib.uci.edu/~scctr/Wellek/wellek/1976.html
A New Critical bibliography.

http://www.sun3.lib.uci.edu/indiv/scctr/Wellek/wellek/index.html
A bibliography of Rene Wellek's work, with links to other relevant sites.

http://www.northshore.net/homepages/hope/KJnarrative.html
Another site on narratology.

http://130.179.92.25/Arnason_DE/Backmaterials.html
A formalist-structuralist link.

SUGGESTED READING

Brooks, Cleanth. *The Well Wrought Urn: Studies in the Structure of Poetry.* Rev. ed. London: Dobson, 1968.

Brooks, Cleanth, and Robert B. Heilman, eds. *Understanding Drama: Twelve Plays.* New York: Holt, 1948.

Brooks, Cleanth, and Robert Penn Warren, eds. *Understanding Fiction.* 3d ed. Englewood Cliffs, N.J.: Prentice Hall, 1979.

———. *Understanding Poetry.* 4th ed. New York: Holt, Rinehart, and Winston, 1976.

Brooks, Cleanth, John T. Purser, and Robert Penn Warren, eds. *An Approach to Literature.* 5th ed. Englewood Cliffs, N.J.: Prentice Hall, 1975.

Cowan, Louise. *The Fugitive Group: A Literary History.* Baton Rouge: Louisiana State Univ. Press, 1959.

Daiches, David. The New Criticism: Some Qualifications. *College English* 39 (February 1950): 64–72.

Eliot, T. S. *The Sacred Wood: Essays on Poetry and Criticism.* London: Methuen, 1964.

Empson, William. *Seven Types of Ambiguity.* New York: Noonday Press, 1955.

Krieger, Murray. *The New Apologists for Poetry.* Westport, Conn.: Greenwood Press, 1977.

Ransom, John Crowe. *The New Criticism.* Westport, Conn.: Greenwood Press, 1979.

Richards, I. A. *Practical Criticism: A Study of Literary Judgment.* New York: Routledge, 2001.

Tate, Allen. *Collected Essays.* Denver, Colo.: Alan Swallow, 1959.

Wimsatt, W. K., Jr. *The Verbal Icon: Studies in the Meaning of Poetry.* Lexington: Univ. Press of Kentucky, 1954.

MODEL STUDENT ANALYSIS

Robinson's "Richard Cory": A Formalistic Interpretation

Frank Perez

For readers who are inclined to extract didactic moral lessons from poetry, the central theme of Edwin Arlington Robinson's short poem "Richard Cory" may appear to be that wealth, charm, and popularity, at least for the people in the poem, do not necessarily equate to personal happiness and fulfillment. However, a close reading of the poem suggests that the real theme of the poem is that appearances can sometimes be misleading. In the poem, the townspeople admire Richard Cory and "wish that we were in his place." But this adulation is misguided, for in the last line we learn that Richard Cory commits suicide. That this climactic bit of information comes at the end of the poem is important because it contributes to the thematic and structural potency of the poem and resolves the ironic tension that it also creates.

The poem consists of four heroic (or elegiac) quatrains and is written in iambic pentameter. In the first stanza the townspeople describe Richard Cory and state they "looked at him" when he went downtown. The description continues in the second stanza but takes on an air of admiration: "But still he fluttered pulses when he said, / 'Good-morning,' and he glittered when he walked." This admiration is directly stated in the third stanza: "In fine, we thought that he was everything / To make us wish that we were in his place." The positive descriptions of Richard Cory and the emulation suddenly stop in the fourth stanza and shift instead to a description of the daily misery of the townspeople. The last two lines of the poem deal with Richard Cory's suicide. The abrupt ending of the poem (indeed, the brevity of the poem itself) serves to effectively convey the sense of shock and "unfinished business" that normally accompanies news of a suicide or sudden death.

The chief irony of the poem is that the speaker(s)—in this case the ambiguously plural "We people on the pavement"—are quite taken with a man who is miserable to the point of suicide. This situation is paradoxical and can be explained only in terms of the tension that the last line of the poem creates. This tension is twofold. First, there is the tension between the outward description of Richard Cory as given by the townspeople and the inner description of Richard Cory as indicated by the fact that he kills himself. Second, there is a conditional tension between Richard Cory and the state of the townspeople. Not only does the startling revelation of Richard Cory's suicide in the last line create this tension, but it also simultaneously forces an interpretation of the poem that resolves the tension.

The first of the aforementioned tensions is most clearly illustrated in the poem's diction, particularly in the title and in the words used to describe Richard Cory in the first ten lines. His name may suggest "rich man" or may even be an allusion to Richard the Lionhearted (Richard Coeur de Lion). The townspeople's description of Richard Cory is filled with words laced with regal connotations: "He was a gentleman from sole to crown," "imperially slim," "he was rich—yes, richer than a king." In addition, Richard Cory is described as charming: "He was a gentleman," "he fluttered pulses when he said, / 'Good-morning,' and he glittered when he walked," he was "admirably schooled in every grace." Such sycophantic adoration reaches a zenith in lines 11–12: "In fine, we thought that he was everything / To make us wish that we were in his place." Yet, despite his popularity, Richard Cory is in reality a suffering figure who takes his own life. But this dark side of Richard Cory is lost on the townspeople, who appear to be enraptured with the outward trappings of wealth and success. This dichotomy between the outward appearance of success and the reality of inner turmoil is not fully realized until we learn of Richard Cory's death in the last line of the poem.

The fact that the townspeople do not realize this dichotomous tension between Richard Cory's outward and inner states is evidenced in the second tension of the poem—the tension between Richard Cory and the state of the townspeople. In stark contrast to the description of Richard Cory's apparent life of ease, the townspeople are depicted as miserable, hardworking sorts: "So on we worked, and waited for the light, / And went without the meat, and cursed the bread; . . ." The word "so" comes immediately after the line "To make us wish that we were in his place" and thereby suggests that these people were driven by material urges to emulate Richard Cory.

There is no indication in the poem that the townspeople realize the error of their positive assumptions about Richard Cory. In addition, there is no internal evidence within the poem to indicate that the people cease their material striving after Richard Cory's death; the most any close reader can say on this matter is that he or she simply does not know what the townspeople's reaction is to Richard Cory's death. To infer anything else would be to read into the poem something that is not there—a critical no-no in the interpretive analysis of poetry. Also, the poem gives absolutely no evidence whatsoever for the cause of Richard Cory's suicide. Hence, it would be a mistake to interpret the poem as a moral lesson warning against the dangers of materialism. Rather, the safest interpretation is that appearances can sometimes be misleading.

4

Psychological Criticism

Novelists who go to psychiatrists are paying for what they should be paid for.

Unknown Source

Human beings are fascinating creatures, and we can be said to take a psychological approach when we try to understand them. The questions we ask about characters are the same ones we are likely to ask about our friends. "Why'd he want to do something dumb like that?" we say. Or we shake our heads and comment, "I knew that wasn't going to work. I don't see why she had to try it." We never seem to run out of speculation about other people's motives, relationships, and conversations or, for that matter, our own. There are our dreams, too, puzzling as to their source, bizarre in their form, and ambiguous as to their meaning but powerful enough to frighten, please, and intrigue us.

HISTORICAL BACKGROUND

Aristotle knew that human beings are endlessly interesting. As far back as the fourth century B.C. he commented on the effects of tragedy on an audience, saying that, through pity and fear, tragedy created a catharsis of those emotions. He was only the earliest of many writers and critics down through the centuries to question why we are drawn to write stories and poems and why we like to read them. Does literature make us a better person? Matthew Arnold believed it could. Poetry, he said, could "inspirit and rejoice the reader." Where does the impulse to write come from? Wordsworth said it springs from "emotion recollected in tranquillity." What is creativity? Coleridge thought that there were two types: the primary imagination, described as "the living power and prime agent of all human perception," and the secondary one, "identical with the primary in the *kind* of its agency, and differing only in *degree* and in the *mode* of its operation." Even Friedrich Nietzsche spoke of personalities as being Apollonian, by which he meant that they were guided by the use of critical reasoning, or Dionysian, referring to personalities ruled by creative-intuitive power.

All such questions and theories are psychological ones. They are efforts to explain the growth, development, and structure of the human personality. Until the latter part of the nineteenth century, however, such speculation lacked the broad theoretical basis that would give validity to those early attempts at devising theory. It was then that Sigmund Freud (1856–1939) advanced his startling theories about the workings of the human psyche, its formation, its organization, and its maladies. His students and followers, such as Alfred Adler, Otto Rank, and Carl Jung, would build on his ideas to probe the workings of the human psyche in order to understand why people act as they do. Of particular interest to literary critics is Jung, who provided the concepts of the collective unconscious, myths, and archetypes that have helped readers see literature as an expression of the experience of the entire human species. Later, in the 1950s, Northrup Frye developed Jung's ideas in ways that were more directly applicable to literature. More recently Jacques Lacan has received serious interest for his efforts to build on Freud's work, turning to new linguistic theories to assert that language shapes our unconscious and our conscious minds, thereby giving us our identity.

Preceding the significant contributions to come from Jung, Lacan, and others, Freud began the quest for understanding by providing new ways of looking at ourselves. The power of his theories is evident in the number and variety of fields they have affected, fields as disparate as philosophy, medicine, sociology, and literary criticism. Although they do not provide an aesthetic theory of literature, which would explain how it is beautiful or why it is meaningful in and of itself, their value lies in giving readers a way to deepen their understanding of themes that have always been present in Western literature, themes of family, authority, guilt. Too, they provide a framework for making more perceptive character analyses. With Freudian theory, it is possible to discover what is not said directly, perhaps what even the author did not realize he was saying, to "read between (or perhaps beneath) the lines."

The absence of an aesthetic theory makes psychoanalytic criticism both more and less useful to a reader. On the one hand, because it does not contradict other schools of criticism, it can be used as a complement to them. That is, instead of ruling out other perspectives on a text, it can exist alongside them, even enrich and extend them. The French feminist critics, a case in point, have made good use of the ideas of Jacques Lacan in the formation of their own critical approaches. On the other hand, the lack of an aesthetic theory means that psychoanalytic criticism can never account for the beauty of a poem or the artistry that has created it. The reader must turn to other types of analysis to explore those other dimensions of literature.

PRACTICING PSYCHOLOGICAL CRITICISM

To understand the discussion that follows, you should read the short story "Young Goodman Brown," by Nathaniel Hawthorne, which begins on page 234.

Today the psychological literary critic can base her inferences on the work of numerous important theorists, but it is Freud's ideas that have provided the basis for this approach, and it is his ideas that are still fundamental to it. To work as a psychological critic, whether you are directly applying Freudian theory or working with the ideas of his followers, it is necessary to understand some of his concepts about the human psyche.

FREUDIAN PRINCIPLES

As a neurologist practicing in Vienna in the late nineteenth century, Sigmund Freud was troubled that he could not account for the complaints of many of his patients by citing any physical cause. Diagnosing them as hysterics, he entered upon analyses of them (and himself) that led him to infer that their distress was caused by factors of which perhaps even they were unaware. He became convinced that fantasies and desires too bizarre and unacceptable to admit had been suppressed, buried so deeply in the unconscious part of their being that, although the desires did not have to be confronted directly, they led to neuroses that caused his patients' illnesses. He concluded that the unconscious plays a major role in what we do, feel, and say, although we are not aware of its presence or operations.

He did not come by these ideas easily or quickly. As early as 1895 he published, with Joseph Breuer, *Studies in Hysteria,* an important work asserting that symptoms of hysteria are the result of unresolved but forgotten traumas from childhood. Five years later he brought out *The Interpretation of Dreams,* in which he addressed the fundamental concepts of psychoanalysis, a treatment in which a patient talks to an analyst about dreams, childhood, and relationships with parents and authority figures. (Freud was not alone in asserting the close relationship between dreams and art. In 1923 Wilhelm Stekel published a book on dreams, saying that no essential difference exists between them and poetry, and around that same time F. C. Prescott, in *Poetry and Dreams,* argued for a definite correspondence between the two in both form and content.) Using free association, slips of language, and dreams, Freud found ways for an analyst to help the patient uncover the painful or threatening events that have been repressed in the unconscious to make them inaccessible to the conscious mind. When such ideas are applied to literature, the process is called psychoanalytic criticism, and the same topics and techniques form the basis for analyzing literary texts.

Just after the turn of the century, Freud himself began to apply his theories to the interpretation of religion, mythology, art, and literature. His first piece of psychoanalytic criticism was "Delusions and Dreams" in Jensen's *Gradiva* (1907). In it he psychoanalyzed the central character, noting the oedipal effects behind the plot. The concern with literature soon turned to the writers themselves and to artists in general as he questioned why art exists and why people create it. In that search he wrote monographs on Dostoyevsky, Shakespeare, Leonardo da Vinci, Goethe, and others. His sense of the artist, finally, was that he is an unstable personality who writes out of his own neuroses, with the result that his work provides therapeutic insights into the nature of life not only for himself but also for those who read. As Freud commented in *Lectures on Psycho-Analysis,* "The artist has also an introverted disposition and has not far to go to become a neurotic."

In 1910 the depth that Freud's approach could add to literary analysis was made apparent in a (now classic) essay on *Hamlet* by Ernest Jones, in which he argues that Hamlet's delay in taking revenge on Claudius is a result of the protagonist's own "disordered mind." More specifically, Jones sees Hamlet as the victim of an oedipal complex that manifests itself in manic-depressive feelings, misogynistic attitudes, and a disgust for things sexual. According to Jones, Hamlet delays his revenge because he unconsciously wants to kill the man who married his mother, but if he punishes Claudius for doing what he himself wished to do, that would in a sense mean that he was killing himself. Also derived from his oedipal neurosis, his repressed desire for Gertrude, who is overtly affectionate toward him, causes him to treat Ophelia with cruelty far out of proportion to anything she has done. When he orders her to a nunnery, the slang meaning of "brothel" makes it clear that he sees all women, even a guiltless one, as repugnant. And throughout the play his disgust toward sexual matters is apparent in the anger evoked in him by the marriage of Claudius and Gertrude as well as in his repulsion of Ophelia.

Since Freud's era, and since Jones's landmark essay appeared, psychoanalytic criticism has continued to grow and develop, generating, for example, the related genre of **psychobiography.** Today it shows few signs of slowing down. Nevertheless, it is still Freud's work that provides the foundation of this approach. Not all of his explanations of how the mind operates are applicable to literary criticism, but the six that follow have had enormous impact on the way we understand what we read. They have even affected the way writers construct their works.

The Unconscious

Probably the most significant aspect of Freudian theory is the primacy of the unconscious. Hidden from the conscious mind, which he compares to that small portion of an iceberg that is visible above the surface of the water, the unconscious is like the powerful unseen mass below it. Because the conscious mind is not aware of its submerged counterpart, it may mistake the real causes of behavior. An individual may be unable to tell the difference between what is happening and what she thinks is happening. In short, our actions are the result of forces that we do not recognize and therefore cannot control.

In Nathaniel Hawthorne's short story "Young Goodman Brown," for example, Brown finds himself in just such a dilemma. Even well past the events of his night in the forest, he is not sure of what was real and what was a dream. His journey is a psychological, as well as physical, one, for he moves from the security of consciousness to the unknown territory of the unconscious, a powerful force that directs him in ways he neither expects nor understands. He leaves the village of Salem, where social as well as spiritual order prevails, to go into the forest, where the daylight, and the clarity of vision and understanding it seems to confer, gives way to darkness and frightful confusion of perceptions. In the end, he can no longer tell reality from dreams, good from evil.

The Tripartite Psyche

In an effort to describe the conscious and the unconscious mind, Freud divided the human psyche into three parts: the id, the superego, and the ego. They are, for the most part, unconscious. The id, for example, is completely unconscious, and only small parts of the ego and the superego are conscious. Each operates according to different, even contrasting, principles.

The **id,** which is the repository of the **libido,** the source of our psychic energy and our psychosexual desires, gives us our vitality. Because it is always trying to satisfy its hunger for pleasure, it operates without any thought of consequences, anxiety, ethics, logic, precaution, or morality. Demanding swift satisfaction and fulfillment of biological desires, it is lawless, asocial, amoral. As Freud describes it, it is "only a striving to bring about the satisfaction of the instinctual needs subject to the observance of the pleasure principle."

Obviously the id can be a socially destructive force. Unrestrained, it will aggressively seek to gratify its desires without any concern for law, customs, or values. It can even be self-destructive in its drive to have what it wants. In many ways it resembles the devil figure that appears in some theological and literary texts, because it offers strong temptation to take what we want without heeding normal restraints, taboos, or consequences. Certainly it appears in that form in "Young Goodman Brown." The id is personified in the person of Brown's fellow traveler, who appears to Brown immediately after he thinks to himself, "What if the devil himself should be at my very elbow!" The narrator suggests the embodiment of Brown's id in the figure by describing him as "bearing a considerable resemblance" to the young man. Even before the older man's appearance, from the very outset of the journey, Brown recognizes that he is challenging acceptable behavior by leaving the highly regulated life of Salem, and the pull of the id to disregard the usual restrictions and participate in acts normally forbidden in the village intensifies as he walks deeper into the forest. As Hawthorne points out, Brown becomes "himself the chief horror of the scene."

To prevent the chaos that would result if the id went untamed, other parts of the psyche must balance its passions. The **ego,** which operates according to the reality principle, is one such regulating agency. Its function is to make the id's energies nondestructive by postponing them or diverting them into socially acceptable actions, sometimes by finding an appropriate time for gratifying them. Although it is for the most part unconscious, the ego is the closest of the three parts of the psyche to what we think of as consciousness, for it mediates between our inner selves and the outer world. Nevertheless, it is not directly approachable. We come closest to knowing it when it is relaxed by hypnosis, sleep, or unintentional slips of the tongue. Dreams, then, become an important means of our knowing what is hidden about ourselves from ourselves.

The third part of the psyche, the **superego,** provides additional balance to the id, for it furnishes a sense of guilt for behavior that breaks the rules given by parents to the young child. Similar to what is commonly known as one's conscience, it operates according to the morality principle, for it provides the sense of moral and ethical wrongdoing. Although parents, who enforce their values through punishments and rewards, are the chief source of the superego, it is expanded by institutions and other influences later in life. Consequently, it works against the drive of the id and represses socially unacceptable desires back into the unconscious. Balance between the license of the id and the restrictions of the superego produces the healthy personality, but when unconscious guilt becomes overwhelming, the individual can be said to be suffering from a guilt complex. When the superego is too strong, it can lead to unhappiness and dissatisfaction with the self.

For Goodman Brown, the descent into the unconscious (the night in the forest) presents a conflict between the superego (the highly regulated life he has known in Salem) and the id (the wild, unrestrained passions of the people in the forest). Lacking a viable ego of his own, he turns to Faith, his wife, for help. Unfortunately, she wears pink ribbons, a mixture of white (purity) and red (passion), which indicates the ambiguity of goodness and Brown's clouded belief in the possibility of goodness throughout the remainder of his life.

The Significance of Sexuality

Prior to Freud, children were thought to be asexual beings, innocent of the biological drives that would beset them later. Freud, however, recognized that it is during childhood that the id is formed, shaping the behavior of the adult to come. In fact, Freud believed that infancy and childhood were periods of intense sexual experience during which it is necessary to go through three phases of development that serve specific physical needs, then provide pleasure if we are to become healthy, functioning adults. The first phase is called the oral phase, because it is characterized by sucking, first to be fed from our mother's breast, then to enjoy our thumbs or, later, even kissing. The second is the anal stage, a period that not only recognizes the need for elimination but the presence of another erogenous zone, a part of the body that provides sexual pleasure. In the final phase, the phallic stage, the child discovers the pleasure of genital stimulation, connected, of course, to reproduction. If these three overlapping stages are successfully negotiated, the adult personality emerges sound and intact. If, however, these childhood needs are not met, the adult is likely to suffer arrested development. The mature person may become fixated on a behavior that serves to fulfill what was not satisfied at an early age. The early years, therefore, encompass critical stages of development because repressions formed at that time may surface as problems later.

Around the time the child reaches the genital stage, about the age of five, he or she is ready to develop a sense of maleness or femaleness. To explain the process by which the child makes that step, Freud turned to literature. Referring to the plot of Sophocles' *Oedipus Rex,* he points out that the experience of Oedipus is that of all male children. That is, just as Oedipus unknowingly kills his father and marries his mother, a young boy forms an erotic attachment to his mother and unconsciously grows to desire her. He consequently resents his father because of his relationship with the mother. Fearing castration by the father, the male child represses his sexual desires, identifies with his father, and anticipates his own sexual union. Such a step is a necessary one in his growth toward manhood. The boy who fails to make that step will suffer from an oedipal complex, with ongoing fear of castration evident in his hostility to authority in general.

In the case of girls, the passage from childhood to womanhood requires successful negotiation of the Electra complex. In Freudian theory the girl child, too, has a strong attraction for her mother and sees her father as a rival, but because she realizes that she has already been castrated, she develops an attraction for her father, who has the penis she desires. When she fails to garner his attentions, she identifies with her mother and awaits her own male partner who will provide what her female physiognomy lacks.

In "Young Goodman Brown," Hawthorne clearly implies that Brown's troubling impulses are sexual ones, and they are not his alone. The sermon of the devil figure promises Brown and Faith that they will henceforth know the secret sins of the people of Salem: "how hoary-bearded elders of the church have whispered wanton words to the young maids of their households; . . . how fair damsels—blush not, sweet ones—have dug little graves in the garden, and bidden me, the sole guest, to an infant's funeral." The catalogue leaves no doubt that sexual passion is part of the human condition, and left unrestrained, it leads to grave offenses. Freud explains that as both boys and girls make the transition to normal adulthood, they become aware of their place in a moral system of behavior. They move from operating according to the pleasure principle, which dictates that they want immediate gratification of all desires, to an acceptance of the reality principle, in which the ego and superego recognize rules, restraint, and responsibility. Goodman Brown, unable to discern reality or define moral behavior, remains outside the adult world.

The Importance of Dreams

The vast unconscious that exists beneath the surface of our awareness seems closest to revelation when we sleep. Our dreams, according to Freud, are the language of the unconscious, full of unfulfilled desires that the conscious mind has buried there. Their content is rarely clear, however, for even in sleep the ego censors unacceptable wishes. Through the use of symbols that make repressed material more acceptable, if not readily understandable to us, the ego veils their meaning from direct apprehension that would produce painful recognition. As in literature, the process may take place through **condensation.** For example, two desires of the psyche may be articulated by a single word or image in a dream, just as they are in a poem. Condensation can also take place through **displacement,** moving one's feeling for a particular person to an object related to him, much as metonymy uses the name of one object to replace another with which it is closely related or of which it is a part. When dreams become too direct and their meanings too apparent, we awaken or, unconsciously, change the symbology. Interestingly, Young Goodman Brown is never certain whether he has dreamed his experience or not. Indeed, the ambiguity and uncertainty about the other villagers and their part in the satanic communion haunt him for the rest of his life. He returns to the village and the light of day, but what is real and what is fantasy eludes him. The meanings of the symbols remain unrevealed to him.

As a window into the unconscious, dreams become valuable tools for psychoanalysts in determining unresolved conflicts in the psyche, conflicts that a person may suspect only because of physical ailments, such as headaches, or psychological discomfort, such as claustrophobia. When a reader meets them in literature, they offer rich insights into characters that their outer actions, or even their spoken words, might never suggest. Because they are meaningful symbolic presentations that take the reader beyond the external narrative, they are valuable tools of the critic using a psychoanalytic approach.

Symbols

Freud's recognition of the often subtle and always complex workings of sexuality in human beings and in literature led to a new awareness of what symbols mean, in literature as well as in life. If dreams are a symbolic expression of repressed desires, most of them sexual in nature, the images through which they operate are themselves going to be sexual ones. Their sexuality is initially indicated by shape. That is, physical objects that are concave in shape, such as lakes, tunnels, and cups are assumed to be female **(yonic)** symbols, and those that are convex, those whose length exceeds their diameter, such as trees, towers, and spires, are assumed to be male **(phallic).** Although Freud himself objected to a general interpretation of dream symbols, insisting that they are personal and individual in nature, such readings are not uncommon. Sometimes this approach to understanding symbols has been pushed to ridiculous extremes, but it undeniably has the capacity to enrich our reading and understanding in ways that we would not otherwise discover.

The symbols in "Young Goodman Brown" are replete with sexual suggestion that is rarely made explicit in the story. Many of those that play a part in Brown's initiation, such as the devil's staff, which is described as "a great black snake, a living serpent," are male images, suggesting the nature of Brown's temptation. The satanic communion is depicted as lighted by blazing fires, with the implication of intense emotion, especially sexual passion. The burning pine trees surrounding the altar, again masculine references, underscore that the repressions of nature exercised in the village give way to obsessions in the forest. There are female symbols, too. For example, entering the forest suggests returning to the dark, womblike unknown. And what if Young Goodman Brown has not actually undergone the experience and has only dreamed it? The event is still significant, because dreams can function as symbolic forms of wish fulfillment.

Brown's nighttime journey, the nature of which is powerfully deepened by the symbolic imagery, leaves its mark on him. He is thereafter a dark and brooding man, leading Richard Adams ("Hawthorne's Provincial Tales") to argue that Brown fails to mature because he fails to learn to know, control, and use his sexual feelings. That is, he cannot love or hate; he can only fear moral maturity. He never manages to emerge from his uncertainty and consequent despair. He has been required to acknowledge evil in himself and others, including his wife, so that he can recognize goodness, but having failed the test, he is left in a state of moral uncertainty. The result is moral and social isolation.

Creativity

The connection between creative expression and the stuff of dreams was not lost on Freud. His curiosity about its sources and nature is reflected in the monographs he wrote on creative artists from various times and cultures, pieces on Leonardo da Vinci, Shakespeare, and Michelangelo, for example. He recognized that the artist consciously expresses fantasy, illusion, and wishes through symbols, just as dreams from the unconscious do. To write a story or a poem, then, is to reveal the unconscious, to give a neurosis socially acceptable expression. Such a view makes the writer a conflicted individual working out his problems. Freud explained the idea this way in *Lectures on Psycho-Analysis:*

> The artist has also an introverted disposition and has not far to go to become a neurotic. He is one who is urged on by instinctual needs which are too clamorous. He longs to attain to honor, power, riches, fame, and the love of women; but he lacks the means of achieving these gratifications. So, like any other with an unsatisfied longing, he turns away from reality and transfers all his interest, and all his libido too, to the creation of his wishes in the life of fantasy, from which the way might readily lead to neurosis.

In the process of engaging in his own therapy, says Freud, the artist achieves insights and understanding that can be represented to others who are less likely to have found them.

Such views have led some critics to focus their attention not on a text but on the writer behind it. They see a work as an expression of his unconscious mind, an artifact that can be used to psychoanalyze the writer, producing psychobiography. (A good example of this genre is Edmund Wilson's *The Wound and the Bow.*) Of course, to do such a study, one needs to have access to verifiable biographical information as well as expertise in making a psychological analysis. Most literary critics, while they may be able to find the former, usually lack the latter. And, indeed, one might ask whether such an undertaking is literary criticism at all.

Summing Up

In the end, when you make a Freudian (psychoanalytical) reading of a text, you will probably limit yourself to the consideration of the work itself, looking at its conflicts, characters, dream sequences, and symbols. You will use the language Freud provided to discuss what before him did not have names, and you will have an awareness that outward behavior may not be consonant with inner drives. You will avoid oversimplification of your analysis, exaggerated interpretations of symbolism, and excessive use of psychological jargon. If you do, you will have the means to explore not only what is apparent on the surface but what is below it as well. As Lionel Trilling pointed out in *The Liberal Imagination,* Freud has provided us with "the perception of the hidden element of human nature and of the opposition between the hidden and the visible."

CARL JUNG AND MYTHOLOGICAL CRITICISM

Once a favored pupil of Freud, Carl Jung (1875–1961), a Swiss physician, psychiatrist, and philosopher, eventually broke from his mentor, then built on his teacher's ideas in ways that made Jung, too, an important figure in the new field of psychoanalysis. His insights have had significant bearings on literature as well.

Like his teacher, Jung believed that our unconscious mind powerfully directs much of our behavior. However, where Freud conceived of each individual unconscious as separate and distinct from that of others, Jung asserted that some of it is shared with all other members of the human species. He describes the human psyche as having three parts: a **personal conscious,** a state of awareness of the present moment that, once it is past, becomes part of the individual's unique **personal unconscious.** Beneath both of these is the **collective unconscious,** a storehouse of knowledge, experiences, and images of the human race. It is a racial memory, shared and primeval, often expressed outwardly in myth and ritual. Young Goodman Brown's presence at the forest gathering, for example, can be described as participation in a ritual binding past and present. As Jung explains it, "This psychic life is the mind of our ancient ancestors, the way in which they thought and felt, the way in which they conceived of life and the world, of gods and human beings." Its contents, because they have never been in consciousness, are not individually acquired. They are inherited.

The relevance of these ideas to literature lies in the correspondences in plots and characters that literary scholars began to find in works by writers in disparate circumstances who could not have been known to each other. Gilbert Murray, for example, was so struck by the similarities he found between Orestes and Hamlet that he concluded they were the result of memories we carry deep within us, "the memory of the race, stamped . . . upon our physical organism." That is why such criticism is sometimes called a mythological, archetypal, totemic, or ritualistic approach, each name pointing to the universality of literary patterns and images that recur throughout diverse cultures and periods. Because they elicit perennially powerful responses from readers the world over, they suggest a shared commonality, even a world order. As a result, archetypal criticism often requires knowledge and use of nonliterary fields, such as anthropology and folklore, which provide information and insights about cultural histories and practice.

Although the collective unconscious is not directly approachable, it can be found in **archetypes,** which Jung defined as "universal images that have existed since the remotest times." More specifically, he described an archetype as "a figure . . . that repeats itself in the course of history wherever creative fantasy is fully manifested." It is recognizable by the appearance of nearly identical images and patterns (found in rituals, characters, or entire narratives) that predispose individuals from wholly different cultures and backgrounds to respond in a particular way, regardless of when or where they live.

Archetypes may have originated in the unchanging situations of human beings, such as the rotating seasons or the mysteries of death, but they are not intentionally created or culturally acquired. Instead, they come to us instinctually as impulses and knowledge hidden somewhere in our biological, psychological, and social natures. As John Sanford explains it, archetypes "form the basis for instinctive unlearned behavior patterns common to all mankind and assert themselves in certain typical ways." In literature we recognize them and respond to them again and again in new characters or situations that have the same essential forms we have met before and have always known. For example, when we meet Huckleberry Finn or the Ancient Mariner (as Maud Bodkin pointed out in *Archetypal Patterns in Poetry*), we are connecting with archetypes, re-creations of basic patterns or types that are already in our unconscious, making us respond just as someone halfway around the world from us might.

Archetypes appear in our dreams and religious rituals, as well as in our art and literature. They are media for the telling of our myths, which, according to Jung, are the "natural and indispensable intermediate stage between unconscious and conscious cognition." By becoming conscious of what is generally unconscious, we integrate our lives and formulate answers for things that are unknowable, such as why we exist, why we suffer, and how we are to live. By uniting the conscious and unconscious, they make us whole and complete.

Living fully, Jung believed, means living harmoniously with the fundamental elements of human nature. In particular, we must deal with three powerful archetypes that compose the self. They are the shadow, the anima, and the persona. All three are represented in literature.

The **shadow** is our darker side, the part of ourselves we would prefer not to confront, those aspects that we dislike. It is seen in films as the villain, in medieval mystery plays as the devil, and in powerful literary figures like Satan in *Paradise Lost*. Young Goodman Brown clearly confronts (and rejects) his shadow in the figure of his nocturnal traveling companion. The **anima,** according to Jung, is the "soul-image," the life force that causes one to act. It is given a feminine designation in men (like Brown's Faith), and a masculine one (animus) in women, indicating that the psyche has both male and female characteristics, though we may be made aware of them only in our dreams or when we recognize them in someone else (a process Jung refers to as **projection**). The **persona** is the image that we show to others. It is the mask that we put on for the external world, which may not be at all what we think ourselves to be inside. The persona and anima can be thought of as two contrasting parts of the ego, our conscious personality. The former mediates between the ego and the outside world, the latter between the ego and the inner one.

To become a psychologically healthy, well-balanced adult—or, as Jung says, for **individuation** to occur—we must discover and accept the different sides of our selves, even those we dislike and resist. If we reject some part of the self, we are likely to project that element onto others, that is, transfer it to something or someone else, thereby making us incapable of seeing ourselves as wrong or guilty. Instead, we see another person or institution to be at fault. In these terms, Young Goodman Brown's despondency can be seen as the result of his failure to achieve individuation. He projects his shadow on the forest companion and later on the entire community. He fails to nurture his anima, leaving Faith behind and in the end suspecting her of the faithlessness he has committed. And, finally, his persona, the face that he shows to the world, is a false one. He is not the "good man," the pious Puritan he claims to be. The healthy individual develops a persona that exists comfortably and easily with the rest of his personality. Young Goodman Brown, unable to integrate all parts of his personality, dies an unhappy neurotic, or as Hawthorne puts it: "they carved no hopeful verse upon his tombstone, for his dying hour was gloom."

There are, of course, many different archetypes, but some are more commonly met than others. Some of the characters, situations, and symbols that frequently elicit similar psychological responses from diverse groups of people can be found in the lists that follow. Whenever you meet them, there is the possibility that they carry with them more power to evoke a response than their literal meanings would suggest.

Characters

- **The hero.** Heroes, according to Lord Raglan in *The Hero: A Study in Tradition, Myth, and Drama,* are distinguished by several uncommon events, including a birth that has unusual circumstances (such as a virgin mother), an early escape from attempts to murder him, a return to his homeland where, after a victory over some antagonist, he marries a princess, assumes the throne, and only later falls victim to a fate that may include being banished from the kingdom only to die a mysterious death and have an ambiguous burial. The archetype is exemplified by such characters as Oedipus, Jason, and Jesus Christ. Sometimes the story may involve only a journey during which the hero must answer complex riddles, retrieve a sacred or powerful artifact, or do battle with superhuman creatures for the purpose of saving someone else, perhaps a whole people. The quests of some of the knights in Tennyson's *Idylls of the King,* such as those made by Gawain and Galahad, are examples.
- **The scapegoat.** Sometimes the hero himself becomes the sacrificial victim who is put to death by the community in order to remove the guilt of the people and restore their welfare and health. On occasion, an animal suffices as the scapegoat, but in literature the scapegoat is more likely to be a human being. Again, Jesus Christ is an example, but a more recent retelling of the story is found in Shirley Jackson's "The Lottery."
- **The outcast.** The outcast is a character who is thrown out of the community as punishment for a crime against it. The fate of the outcast, as can be seen in *The Ancient Mariner,* is to wander throughout eternity. Hawthorne's Young Goodman Brown also finds himself separated from his community following his refusal to join in the forest communion. He cannot listen to the hymns of the assembled congregation on the Sabbath, kneel with his family at prayer, or trust in the virtue of Faith, his wife. He is lonely and alone.
- **The Devil.** The figure of the Devil personifies the principle of evil that intrudes in the life of a character to tempt and destroy him, often by promising wealth, fame, or knowledge in exchange for his soul. Mephistopheles in the legend of Faust is such a figure, and certainly the old man whom Young Goodman Brown

meets in the forest is one too. He carries a snakelike staff and purports to have been present at ancient evil deeds. Brown even refers to him as "the devil."

- **Female figures.** Women are depicted in several well-known archetypes. The Good Mother, such as Ma Joad in *The Grapes of Wrath,* is associated with fertility, abundance, and nurturance of those around her. The Temptress, on the other hand, destroys the men who are attracted to her sensuality and beauty. Like Delilah, who robs Samson of his strength, she causes their downfall. The female who inspires the mind and soul of men is a spiritual (or Platonic) ideal. She has no physical attractions but, like Dante's Beatrice, guides and directs and fulfills her male counterpart. Finally, women are also seen as the Unfaithful Wife. As she appears in Flaubert's *Madame Bovary,* the Unfaithful Wife, married to a dull, insensitive husband, turns to a more desirable man as a lover, with unhappy consequences.
- **The Trickster.** A figure often appearing in African-American and American Indian narratives, the Trickster is mischievous, disorderly, and amoral. He disrupts the rigidity of rule-bound cultures, bringing them reminders of their less strict beginnings. For example, in the tales of Till Eulenspiegel, which date back to the sixteenth century, Till, a shrewd rural peasant, outwits the arrogant townspeople and satirizes their social practices.

Images

- **Colors** have a variety of archetypal dimensions. Red, because of its association with blood, easily suggests passion, sacrifice, or violence. Green, on the other hand, makes one think of fertility and the fullness of life, even hope. Blue is often associated with holiness or sanctity, as in the depiction of the Virgin Mary. Light and darkness call up opposed responses: hope, inspiration, enlightenment, and rebirth in contrast with ignorance, hopelessness, and death.
- **Numbers,** too, are invested with different meanings. The number three points to things spiritual, as in the Holy Trinity; four is associated with the four seasons (and by extension with the cycle of life) and the four elements (earth, air, fire, and water). When three and four are combined to make seven, the union produces a powerful product that is perfect and whole and complete.
- **Water,** another common image, is often used as a creation, birth, or rebirth symbol, as in Christian baptism. Flowing water can refer to the passage of time. In contrast, the desert or lack of water suggests a spiritually barren state, as it does in T. S. Eliot's *The Waste Land.*
- **Gardens,** and other images of natural abundance, often indicate a paradise, a state of innocence. The best-known, of course, is the Garden of Eden.
- **Circles** can be presented simply or in complex relationships with other geometric figures. By their lack of beginnings and endings, they commonly suggest a state of wholeness and union.
- The **sun,** like the seasons, makes one think of the passage of time. At its rising it calls to mind the beginning of a phase of life or of life itself; at its setting it points

to death and other endings. At full presence it may suggest enlightenment or radiant knowledge.

Situations

- The **quest** pursued by the hero, mentioned earlier, usually involves a difficult search for a magical or holy item that will return fertility and abundance to a desolate state. Certainly the boy in James Joyce's "Araby" goes to the bazaar in search of a fitting offering for Mangan's sister, whom he has sanctified with his young love. It is both a holy quest and a romantic one. A related pattern is that of the need to perform a nearly impossible task so that all will be well. Arthur, for example, must pull the sword from the stone if he is to become king. Often found as part of both these situations is the journey, suggesting a psychological as well as physical movement from one place, or state of being, to another. The journey, like the travels of Ulysses, may involve a descent into hell.
- **Death and rebirth,** already mentioned in connection with the cycle of the seasons, is one of the most common of all archetypes in literature. Rebirth may take the form of natural regeneration, that is, of submission to the cycles of nature, or of escape from this troubled life to an endless paradise like that enjoyed before the fall into the sufferings that are part of mortality. Coleridge, for example, in "Kubla Khan" presents a landscape that is both savage and holy, a landscape of heaven and hell, ending with a vision of a transcendent experience in which the speaker/holy man has "drunk the milk of Paradise."
- **Initiation** stories deal with the progression from one stage of life to another, usually that of an adolescent moving from childhood to maturity, from innocence to understanding. The experience is rarely without problems, although it may involve comedy. In its classic form it requires that the protagonist go through the initiation alone, experiencing tests and ordeals that change him so that he can return to the family or larger group as an adult member.

NORTHRUP FRYE AND MYTHOLOGICAL CRITICISM

In 1957, Northrup Frye advanced the study of archetypes, at least as they apply to literature, with the publication of *Anatomy of Criticism,* in which he presents a highly structured model of how myths are at the basis of all texts. Although he did not accept Jung's theories in their entirety, he used many of them as the basis of his efforts to understand the functions of archetypes in literature. He spoke of a "theory of myths," by which he really referred to a theory of genres as a way of understanding narrative structures. All texts, he concluded, are part of "a central unifying myth" exemplified in four types of literature, or four **mythoi,** that are analogous to the seasons of the year. Together they compose the entire body of literature, which he calls the **monomyth.** Specific works of each type contain archetypes and patterns that are like those found in ritual or myth.

The mythos of summer, for example, is the romance. It is analogous to the birth and adventures of innocent youth. It is a happy myth that indulges what we want to happen—that is, the triumph of good over evil, problems resolved in satisfying ways. Autumn, in contrast, is tragic. In the autumn myth the hero does not triumph but instead meets death or defeat. Classic tragic figures, like Antigone or Oedipus, are stripped of power and set apart from their world to suffer alone. In the winter myth, what is normal and what is hoped for are inverted. The depicted world is hopeless, fearful, frustrated, even dead. There is no hero to bring salvation, no happy endings to innocent adventures. Spring, however, brings comedy: rebirth and renewal, hope and success, freedom and happiness. The forces that would defeat the hero are thwarted, and the world regains its order. And, according to Frye, every work of literature has its place in this schema.

Currently the mythic or archetypal approach is less frequently used than it was in earlier decades. Some readers complain that it overlooks the qualities of individual works by its focus on how any given text fits a general pattern. When a novel is seen as but one of many instances of death and rebirth, for example, its uniqueness is ignored and its value diminished. However, the process of relating a single work to literature in general, and finally to human experience as a whole, gives it stature and importance in the eyes of other readers. It relates literature to other areas of intellectual activity in a reasoned, significant manner. Certainly it is worth knowing and sometimes using, for it yields insights about both literature and human nature that other approaches fail to provide. It considers a work in terms of its psychological, aesthetic, and cultural aspects, making such an analysis a powerful union of three perspectives.

JACQUES LACAN: AN UPDATE ON FREUD

Since the 1960s the Freudian approach, which had waned in popularity, has experienced a renascence due to the ideas of a French psychoanalyst named Jacques Lacan. His work has been described as a reinterpretation of Freud in light of the ideas of structuralist and poststructuralist theories, particularly those of Ferdinand de Saussure (see chapter 8). Whereas Freud's concept of the unconscious as a force that determines our actions and beliefs shook the long-held ideal that we are beings who can control our own destinies, Lacan has further weakened the humanist concept of a stable self that is governed by attributes of consciousness (such as rationality and self-reflection) by denying the possibility of bringing the contents of the unconscious into consciousness, as his predecessor had hoped to do. Freud wanted to make hidden drives and desires conscious so that they could be managed, but according to Lacan, the ego can never replace the unconscious or possess its contents, for the simple reason that the ego, the "I" self, is only an illusion produced by the unconscious. How we develop this illusion is of particular interest to the Lacanian critic.

Like Freud, Lacan acknowledges the importance of the unconscious in our conscious behavior. He differs from his predecessor, however, by asserting that the unconscious is structured like a language. Even Freud, who conceived of it as a disordered, even chaotic collection of wishes and desires, alluded to the condensation and displacement of dreams, processes that are similar to metaphor and metonymy. Even his analysis of unconscious symbolism was often based on verbal techniques—puns, word associations, and slips of language. Lacan expands such ideas by turning to Saussure, with a few modifications. Unlike Saussure, who saw a **signifier** and a **signified** as two parts of a **sign,** Lacan sees in the unconscious only signifiers that refer to others signifiers. Each has meaning only because it differs from some other signifier. It does not ultimately refer to anything outside itself, and the absence of any signified robs the entire system of stability. In these terms the unconscious is a constantly moving chain of signifiers with nothing to stop its shifting and sliding. The signified that seems to be "the real thing" is actually beyond our grasp, for, according to Lacan, all we can have is a conceptualized reality. We cannot go outside language. Nevertheless, we spend our lives trying to stabilize this system so that meaning and self become possible.

Our movement toward adulthood means developing several parts of our personality in search of a unified and psychologically complete self, which, although it can never be achieved, can be approached by stabilizing the sliding of signifiers. Consequently, we move through three parts of our personality, or Orders, as Lacan calls them: the Real, the Imaginary, and the Symbolic, corresponding to the experience of need, demand, and desire. Underlying the process, so the assumption goes, is language as the shaper of our unconscious, our conscious minds, and our sense of self.

The new infant exists in a state of nature, a psychological place characterized by wholeness and fullness. Unaware of its separateness from the mother or any other object that serves its needs, the infant does not recognize a distinction between itself and anything else. Some Lacanians recognize this as the Real Order, though others see it as part of the Imaginary Order, reserving the Real for the final stage of development. (This disagreement will be explained more fully below.)

Somewhere between six and eighteen months of age, the baby begins to perceive the distinctions between itself and the surrounding world, an experience that certainly identifies the **Imaginary Order.** It is a preverbal stage in which the baby becomes aware of its body only in bits and pieces, whatever is visible at any given moment, but it does not yet conceive of itself as whole, although other people can be recognized as whole. Lacan explains that at some time during the Imaginary Order the baby will see itself in a mirror, giving it a sense of its possible wholeness because it looks like other objects, like beings with discrete boundaries. When the awareness of being separate comes, as it must if the individual is to move from nature to culture, the sense of unity with others and other objects is lost and, along with it, the sense of security that it provided. With the baby desiring a return to that earlier period of oneness with the mother, its needs at this point turn into demands, specifically demands for attention and love from another that will erase the separation that the baby now knows, but such a reunion is not possible. One can never return.

Identification of the mirror image as the "self" is misleading, however, because the image is not the actual "self." The infant only thinks it is and uses it to create the ego, the sense of "I." Thus the "self" is always manufactured, an acceptance of an external image instead of an internal identity. It is known as an "ideal ego," because it is whole, nonfragmented, having no lack or absence. In other words, the individual makes up for the union that has been lost by misconceiving of the self as whole and sufficient, but such an assumption is illusory.

When the infant realizes it is not connected to that which serves its needs, it experiences irretrievable loss, making it necessary for language to take the place of what is lacking. The **Symbolic Order,** which overlaps with the Imaginary, introduces language, which a person must enter to become a speaker and thereby designate the self as "I." By stopping the play and movement of signifiers so that they can have some stable meaning, it masters the individual and shapes one's identity as a separate being. Because in the Symbolic Order everything is separate, to negotiate it successfully, a person must master the concept of difference, difference that makes language possible (that is, we know a word such as *light* because it is not the word *fight*) and difference that makes genders recognizable.

According to Lacan, there are biological sexual differences, but gender is culturally created. Whereas the Imaginary Order is centered in the mother, The Symbolic Order is ruled by what he calls the "Law of the Father," because it is the father who enforces cultural norms and laws. Because the power of the word and being male are associated, the boy child must identify with the father as rule giver, and the girl must acknowledge that, as such, the father is her superior. Both male and female experience a symbolic castration, a loss of wholeness that comes with the acceptance of society's rules. The ultimate symbol of power Lacan calls the **phallus,** referring not to a biological organ but to a privileged signifier, the symbol of power that gives meaning to other objects. Neither males nor females can possess it totally, though males have a stronger claim to it. Instead, we human beings go through life longing for a return to the state of wholeness when we were one with our mother, manifested in our desire for pleasure and things. But wholeness will always elude us.

Some disagreement exists about the nature of the **Real Order,** partly because it is a difficult concept to grasp, and partly because Lacan himself changed his mind about it. Some scholars see it as the condition of the infant: prelinguistic, unified, full, and complete. Language is not needed, because there is no lack or absence, and when language appears, the Real is lost. Others argue that because the Real symbolizes what is external to an individual, all that she is not, the Real cannot exist until the subject and the Symbolic are formed because nothing can be outside the Symbolic until it exists. That would make the Real the final phase of psychic development. The important thing to understand about the Real Order is that it is beyond language, either preceding it or exceeding it. In fact, it is beyond language, the individual, or representation because in it there is no loss, lack, or absence.

For the literary critic, Lacan's ideas are interesting because they provide more ways of understanding and analyzing characters. A reader can look for symbolic representations of the Real, the Imaginary, and the Symbolic Orders to demonstrate how the text depicts the human being as a fragmented, incomplete being. In "Young Goodman Brown," for example, evidence of the three orders points to lack and absence that make wholeness impossible. The protagonist longs for the wholeness provided by the Real, but it eludes him. He does not know and can never know the true "self," and he resists the acceptance of society's rules, the power of the group. Clearly suffering from a loss that he can never recover, he exemplifies the fragmented being who is unable to achieve the completeness he desires.

Lacan's ideas are also germane to the work of the critic because he acknowledges that literature offers access to the Imaginary Order and a chance to reexperience the joy, *jouissance,* of being whole, as we once were with our mother.

WRITING PSYCHOLOGICAL CRITICISM

PREWRITING

Once you are accustomed to taking a Freudian, mythological, or Lacanian approach, you will begin to notice meaningful symbols and pay close attention to dream sequences just as a matter of course. If you are not used to reading from these perspectives, however, during prewriting you may want to be intentional about noting aspects of a work that could be significant with them.

If you are interested in using Freudian theory, you can begin by making notes about a selected character, then write a paragraph of description about her.

- What do you see as the main traits of the character?
- How are those traits revealed?
- What does the narrator reveal about the character?
- In the course of the narrative, does he change? If so, how and why?
- Does the character come to understand something not understood at the outset?
- How does the character view himself or herself?
- How is he viewed by the other characters?
- Do the two views agree?
- What images are associated with the character?
- What are the main symbols?
- Which symbols are connected with the character or forces that affect the character?
- Does the character have any interior monologues or dreams? If so, what do you learn about the character that is not revealed by outward behavior or conversation?
- Are there conflicts between what is observable and what is going on inside the character? Are there any revealing symbols in them?
- Where do the characters act in ways that are inconsistent with the way they are described by the narrator or perceived by the other characters?
- How can you explain a character's irrational behavior? What causes do you find? What motivation?

An archetypal approach can start with these questions:

- What similarities do you find among the characters, situations, and settings of the text under consideration and other works that you have read?

- What commonly encountered archetypes do you recognize?
- Is the narrative like any classic myths you know?
- Where do you find evidence of the protagonist's persona? anima/animus? shadow?
- Does the protagonist at any point reject some part of her personality and project it onto someone or something else?
- Would you describe the protagonist as individuated—that is, as having a realistic and accurate sense of self?

You can begin a Lacanian approach by considering the following questions:

- Where do you recognize the appearance of the Real, Imaginary, and Symbolic Orders?
- Is the character aware of the lack or absence of something significant in the self?
- Are there objects that symbolize what is missing or lacking?

DRAFTING AND REVISING

The Introduction

When you are writing an analysis of a work of literature from any of these three forms of psychological criticism—Freudian, mythological, or Lacanian—your reader will find it helpful if you announce at the outset what the primary focus will be. Because such studies can look at a single character, the relationships among characters, meaningful symbolism, narrative patterns, or even the life of the author, an indication of the direction your paper will take makes it easier for others to follow the development of your discussion.

Another approach is to comment on similarities and differences between the work you are dealing with and other works by the same author. If you have determined that the elements of the poem or story you are analyzing are typical of a given writer, that is, for example, that the conflicts faced by a particular character are similar to those that have been developed in some of her other works, noting those correspondences in the introduction can help convince the reader that what you say is valid. On the other hand, if the work under analysis is atypical of what one anticipates from a given writer, then revealing at the beginning that it is a departure from the expected can garner attention.

If you have discovered parallels between the text you are writing about and others that you have read, you may want to mention the similarities you have discovered. If the situations or relationships among the characters have reminded you of those found in classic myths, fairy tales, Greek drama, or even more modern works, mentioning those correspondences will turn your discussion to a mythic perspective.

The Body

Because of the number and diversity of topics you have to choose from when doing psychoanalytic (and related) criticism, there is no formula for the organization of the body of the paper. There are only suggestions that may help you structure the way in which you report your ideas.

As always, you cannot expect your audience to accept your analysis simply as stated. You will have to prove your case by using tenets of psychological or critical theory to explain, for example, that a certain character cannot keep a job because he is resistant to authority as a result of having unresolved issues with his father, or that another is projecting an undesirable part of her personality when she blames a good friend for provoking a quarrel that she herself began. You do not have to refer to all of the principles explained in this chapter, but you should incorporate all the points that help to support your position.

If you have chosen to take a character as the principal topic of a Freudian analysis, you may have already discovered what you want to reveal about him when you were prewriting. If not, it may be necessary to return to those notes in order to expand and deepen them so that you eventually arrive at an understanding of some struggle the character is living through, an epiphany he or she experiences, or the motivation behind some particular behavior. It will be that understanding that you address in the body of your discussion. You may find the following strategies to be helpful.

- Reveal what is happening in the character's unconscious as it has been suggested by images, symbols, or interior monologues.
- Identify the nature of the character's conflicts, looking for indications of whether he or she has the attitudes of a healthy adult male or female. If not, then the neurosis needs to be identified and its source examined.
- Because any changes in the outlook or behavior of a character signal that some struggle has been resolved, for good or ill, assess their meaning.
- Examine whether a character operates according to the pleasure principle, the morality principle, or the reality principle.
- Explain a character's typical behavior by determining whether the personality is a "balanced" one or whether it is dominated by the id or the superego.
- Look carefully at any dreams that are recounted or alluded to. What repressed material are they putting into symbolic form? What are they really about?
- Probe the meanings of symbols by thinking about them in terms of their maleness and femaleness.
- Find some particular behavior that a character is fixated on, then trace it to some need or issue from childhood that went unsatisfied or unresolved.
- Note any conflicts or events in the author's life that are reflected in the text.

Using a mythological approach, you can explore one or several of the following topics.

- Show how characters follow (or vary from) well-established patterns of behavior or re-create well-known figures from literary history—for example, from Greek mythology.
- Look at similarities and contrasts in the personal conscious and personal unconscious to determine whether they reflect the same desires and impulses or if they are in conflict.

- Locate any instances in which the collective unconscious of a character is revealed, perhaps through a dream or vision.
- Identify archetypal images and situations and explain how they work together to create meaning.
- Examine instances in which the persona, anima/animus, and shadow of a character are revealed, including instances of rejection and projection.

To use Lacan's ideas as the basis of your discussion, you can consider the following points.

- Identify the Real, Imaginary, and Symbolic Orders in the narrative and explain the position of a character in relation to them.
- Locate those occasions on which a character recognizes that she is a fragmented being yearning for wholeness and explain their causes.
- Explain how certain objects symbolize that which is lacking in a character's life.

The Conclusion

The psychological analysis is one of the occasions on which a summary conclusion may be welcomed by the reader. Because the discussion is likely to have covered some unusual ground and used some unusual terminology (for literary criticism), a brief reiteration of the major points followed by a general conclusion may be in order. You should take care not simply to say everything again but to assume a more global view, looking at the analysis as a whole. If you discussed multiple points, for example, you will probably need to rename them and tie them all together, showing how they extend and reinforce each other. If you focused on only one topic, such as character or imagery, then a simple reiteration of the themes that grew out of what you found should suffice.

Glossary of Terms Useful in Psychological Criticism

Anima/animus The life force within an individual. It is both life itself and the creator of life. It is made up of contragender elements of the self and belongs to the personal and collective unconscious.

Archetypes Inherited ideas or ways of thinking generated by the experiences of the human race that exist in the unconscious of an individual. They are universal and recurring images, patterns, or motifs representing typical human experience that often appear in literature, art, fairy tales, myths, dreams, and rituals. They unite the conscious and the unconscious, helping to make an individual whole.

Collective Unconscious The inherited collective experience of the human race.

Condensation The use of a single word or image in a dream to articulate two references.

Displacement Moving one's feelings for a particular person to an object related to him.

Ego In Freudian terms, the part of the psyche that mediates between the inner self and the external world. As such, it helps regulate the id by postponing its urges or by diverting them into socially acceptable actions.

Id An unconscious part of the psyche that is the source of psychic energy and desires. It operates for the sole purpose of finding pleasure through gratification of its instinctual needs.

Imaginary Order A term used by Jacques Lacan to refer to the psychic stage during which the infant begins to recognize its separateness from other objects and to develop a sense of self.

Individuation Successful discovery, acceptance, and integration of one's own shadow, anima/animus, and persona. It is a psychological maturation.

Libido The instinctual energies and desires that are derived from the id.

Monomyth Northrup Frye's term for literature, composed of four mythoi.

Mythoi Four narrative patterns that, according to Northrup Frye, exhibit the structural principles of the various genres. He associates each with a season of the year.

Persona Jung's term for the social part of an individual's personality. It is the being that other people know as one's self.

Personal conscious A state of awareness of the present moment.

Personal unconscious A storehouse of past personal experience no longer extant in the personal conscious.

Phallic symbol A masculine symbol. It is recognizable because its length exceeds its diameter.

Psychobiography The use of a psychoanalytic approach to understand a writer.

Real Order A term used by Jacques Lacan to refer to the physical world beyond the individual, language, or representation because in it there is no loss, lack, or absence. Some readers understand it to exist during early infancy (before language) and others understand it to exist as the final phase of psychic development (after the Symbolic).

Shadow Jung's term for the dark, unattractive aspects of the self. An individual's impulse is to reject the shadow and project it on someone or something else.

Sign The combination of a signifier and a signified.

Signified The concept or meaning indicated by a signifier

Signifier A conventional sound, utterance, or written mark.

Superego The part of the psyche that provides discipline and restraint by forcing unacceptable desires back into the unconscious. It is formed early on by parents and later by social institutions and other models.

Symbolic Order A term used by Jacques Lacan to refer to the psychic stage in which an individual learns language and it shapes his identity.

Yonic symbol A feminine symbol. It is recognizable because it is concave—for example, a bowl or a cave.

RECOMMENDED WEB SITES

Web sites devoted to some of the topics covered in this chapter should be used with caution. Although the ones listed below are deemed helpful, many sites that are connected to philosophical, psychological, and religious slants, both traditional and nontraditional ones, are not. Some take extreme positions of belief. In particular, the Web surfer looking for information on Jung, archetypes, and myths needs to be aware that a search can lead to so many different topics that the initial quest can get lost. For these reasons, more than the usual thoughtfulness needs to be exerted when searching this topic on the Web.

http://www.brocku.ca/english/courses/4F70/psychlit.html
A discussion of what psychoanalysis and literature have in common and what psychoanalysis can contribute to literature.

http://www.clas.ufl.edu/users/nnh/mindbook.htm
An essay on psychoanalytic literary criticism by Norman Holland.

http://members.home.com/mikencarrie/crit15.htm
A brief discussion of Freud and art.

http://www.dragonfire.net/~brysons/academic/frye.html
Brief notes about Northrup Frye's *Anatomy of Criticism.*

http://www.cgjungpage.org
Extensive information about Jung and Jungian psychology.

http://www.daimon.ch/
An online bookstore devoted to publications on Jungian themes. It includes books, journals, and audiotapes.

http://www.mcli.dist.maricopa.edu/smc/journey/
An interactive site that takes the user on the journey of the hero archetype.

http://www.mythweb.com/
Biographies of Greek mythical characters. The graphics are colorful and entertaining.

http://www.acs.appstate.edu/~davisct/nt/jung.html
Definitions and discussions of major archetypes, including special attention to the shadow, anima/animus, and several others.

http://www.colorado.edu/English/ENGL2012Klages/lacan.html
Lengthy but readable explanation of Lacanian theory.

http://members.home.com/mikencarrie/crit25.htm
Brief overview of central ideas of Lacan.

http://www.brocku.ca/english/courses/4F70/terms.html
Explanations of key terms and concepts of Freud and Lacan.

SUGGESTED READING

Benvenuto, Bice, and Roger Kennedy. *The Works of Jacques Lacan: An Introduction.* New York: St. Martin's Press, 1986.

Bergler, Edmund. *The Writer and Psychoanalysis.* Madison, Conn.: International Universities Press, 1991.

Bodkin, Maud. *Archetypal Patterns in Poetry.* New York: AMS Press, 1978.

Campbell, Joseph. *The Hero with a Thousand Faces.* New York: MJF Books, 1996.

Felman, Shoshana. *Jacques Lacan and the Adventure of Insight: Psychoanalysis in Contemporary Culture.* Cambridge: Harvard University Press, 1987.

Fiedler, Leslie. *Love and Death in the American Novel.* Normal, Ill.: Dalkey Archive Press, 1997.
Frazer, Sir James. *The Golden Bough.* New York: Penguin Books, 1996.
Freud, Sigmund. *Introductory Lectures on Psycho-Analysis.* Trans. Joan Riviere. London: Heron Books, 1970.
———. *The Interpretation of Dreams.* Trans. Joyce Crick. New York: Oxford Univ. Press, 1999.
Frye, Northrup. *Anatomy of Criticism.* Princeton, N.J.: Princeton Univ. Press, 1957.
Hoffman, Frederick J. *Freudianism and the Literary Mind.* Westport, Conn.: Greenwood Press, 1977.
Holland, Norman. *The Dynamics of Literary Response.* New York: Columbia Univ. Press, 1989.
Jung, Carl. *The Integration of the Personality.* Trans. Stanley Dell. New York: Farrar and Rinehart, 1939.
———. Psychology and Literature. In *Modern Man in Search of a Soul,* trans. W. S. Dell and Cary F. Baynes, pp. 175–199. Fort Worth, Tex.: Harcourt, 1950.
———. *The Archetypes and the Collective Unconscious.* Trans. R. F. C. Hull. Princeton, N.J.: Princeton Univ. Press, 1980.
Lesser, Simon O. *Fiction and the Unconscious.* Boston: Beacon Press, 1957.
Murray, Gilbert. *The Classical Tradition in Poetry.* New York: Russell and Russell, 1968.
Phillips, William, ed. *Art and Psychoanalysis.* New York: World, 1963.
Trilling, Lionel. *Freud and the Crisis of Our Culture.* Boston: Beacon Press, 1955.
Wheelwright, Philip. *Metaphor and Reality.* Bloomington: Indiana Univ. Press, 1962.
Winnicott, D. W. *Playing and Reality.* New York: Tavistock, 1980.
Wright, Elizabeth. *Psychoanalytic Criticism: Theory in Practice.* New York: Methuen, 1984.

MODEL STUDENT ANALYSES

Psychological Complexity in Sherwood Anderson's "The Egg": A Freudian Analysis

Mark Wekander

Sherwood Anderson's story "The Egg" functions with a slim plot. A man leaves his happy life as a bachelor to assume the economic responsibilities of marriage and parenthood. The first step in this attempted transformation is a chicken farm that he and his wife buy. When this endeavor fails, the couple start a small restaurant near a railroad station that they run around the clock by dividing the schedule. The father attempts to attract new customers by a positive attitude and an attempt to cater to the young. The climax comes when he performs his pathetic tricks for the young Joe Kane, who is waiting for a train that is running late. He first attempts to make an egg stand on end by rolling it in his hands, then shows the young man chickens that were born freaks of nature that he has preserved in alcohol, and then boils an egg in vinegar and tries to force it down the neck of a bottle. The father's egg tricks finally scare off the customer, and the father goes in defeat to his wife.

The story, however, could be summed up as a man's marriage leads to higher goals and so to ridiculous failure, or in another way, that entering the reproductive cycle leads to defeat.

In his typical fashion, Anderson defuses the tension of plot with the first sentence: "My Father was, I am sure, intended by nature to be a cheerful, kindly man." The word *intended* already insinuates the discrepancy between nature and society. The first paragraph ends by pointing to the father's original natural state and his attempt to integrate into the world: "He had at that time no notion of trying to rise in the world."

Anderson's simple story leaves the reader with complex feelings about the ridiculous father, whose dilemma appears to be tragic, and about the son, who narrates the story and seems to replace the father and become him. Behind them both stands the mother who pushes each of them out into the world and in mysterious ways controls and checks the father.

In this slight plot with no suspense, the action is contained and does not form a strong causal chain but instead gives one the sense of viewing a series of chronological tableaux that explain the psychological relationship of the characters. The relationship among the father, mother, and son exists on two levels. On one level the son is the usurper, the oedipal child who usurps his father's position with his mother and his power. On the second level, each member of the family represents an aspect of the tripartite personality. The narrator-son is the ego; the father, who existed as a rural Pan before marriage, is the libido residing in the id; and the mother, who socializes the father and the son, functions as the superego.

The son, who has usurped his father's place with his mother and stands as a barrier to his father's sexual gratification, tells the story. He himself fears assuming his father's role as the displaced lover and is ambivalent about sexual gratification and procreation, which will lead him to the same position of exile as his father. The son as the voice of the story controls and silences the father, so the ego has suppressed the sexual desire (libido) in the id and come under the influence of the superego. Likewise, the son has usurped the father's place in bed, and the mother's affection and her aspirations for success are now placed on the son.

The egg in its dual symbolic role stands for the son-ego and for a fertility and potency that is always beyond the reach of the father. His failures with eggs begin after the narrator, the son who is the egg fertilized by his father, has been born and the father's life changes: "I came wriggling and crying into the world. Something happened to the two people. They became ambitious." The birth of the narrator reins in the father, who before marriage would "make his horse comfortable for the night," a reference to the father's easy sexuality in his idyllic unwed state. From the start the father's place in bed and the mother's affection, at least in the eye of the narrator-son, has been forfeited to the son. It is now the narrator who "lay beside her," and her dreams are that her son "would some day rule men and cities." In an oedipal revolution, the son has taken both the bed and the affection of the mother away from the father.

The father's subsequent sterility and alienation are immediately emphasized: ". . . she induced father to give up his place as a farmhand, sell his horse and embark on an independent venture of his own." The father sells his horse, a traditional symbol of male sexuality, and symbolically gives up his sexual prowess. The chicken farm and all that has to do with eggs becomes "an independent venture of his own." While the venture actually is not just the father's, the narrator-son sees the father as removed from the world occupied by him and his mother.

The story includes many incidents where the father's separateness from the mother, son, and community are emphasized. At the narrator's birth, he and the mother share the bed, and the father is exiled from sexual intercourse. The move to the restaurant signifies a more public and less sexual life. Their 24-hour-a-day restaurant means the father works while the wife is in bed and she works while he is in bed. In the final episode of the story the father comes to throw himself on his knees at the bed of his wife after the scenes of his humiliation in the restaurant. The restaurant's location also develops the theme of isolation and failure, since the house in which they establish the restaurant is not in the town of Bidwell but a mile away at the railroad station in Pickleville. The father's ride on the wagon is emblematic of his separateness. He rode alone while the mother watched "to be sure that nothing fell from the wagon," and the narrator walked "to see the wonders of the world."

The mother-superego is behind the father's socialization. She has the idea for the chicken farm, which removes the father from his idyllic life as a farmhand and makes him ambitious. Later the narrator tells us that the father has been silenced "from long association with mother and the chickens." The mother's roles are those of the superego, the mother-wife-lover in the oedipal love triangle, and instigator of plans for upward mobility or integration into society.

The move from the chicken farm to the restaurant represents a further sublimation of the libido. The father rides alone in the wagon with objects that emphasize his infertility while his wife watches to make sure that he remains there. The road figures as a symbol for sexual intercourse and viability. The son is beginning to understand "the wonders of the world," while the mother has become the restrictive eye that ensures that nothing falls into the road from the wagon, such as the father's sperm. He is left with his treasures; the deformed chickens in bottles of alcohol—in a sense eggs gone awry—and the baby carriage with its broken wheels. No other contents of the wagon are mentioned. Like the freaks in alcohol, the baby carriage represents both sexual inability and infertility. It is a reminder that there will be no more offspring, since the libido has been thoroughly controlled. The broken wheels emphasize the impotency of the father and the sublimation of libido. The only viable wheels are those on the wagon that "had been borrowed for the day from Mr. Albert Griggs, a neighbor."

The story equates sexual impotence with financial and worldly failure. The ambition of the father, a desire that the narrator-son claims is inspired by the mother, repeatedly meets with failure. The eggs of the father's chicken farm are doomed to short freakish existence or to eventual failure and fatality. The road to success, or the road of sexual intercourse, is always up. Success is "rising in the world," "getting up in the world," "rose from poverty to fame and greatness," and "upward journey through life." The male erection and the sperm rising in the uterus to fertilize the egg are also embodied in this language. But after the birth of the narrator, sexual success seems to be impossible.

The son's own conception is described both in his birth, when he came "wriggling . . . into the world," and in a dream that he has. The dream is triggered when he looks at his father's bald head, "and the bald path that led over the top of his head was, I fancied, something like a broad road . . . into the wonders of an unknown world." The father's bald head, as a male phallic symbol, inspires and frightens the child and finally becomes the metonym for his father's sexual and financial failure. When the father reaches his final humiliation, the son remembers "my own grief and fright and the shiny path over father's head glowing in the lamp light as he knelt by the bed." The child's dream of sexuality, inspired by his father's bald (impotent) head (male sexuality), incorporates the wonder of sexuality with the fear of procreation. "I was a tiny thing going along the road into a far beautiful place where there were no chicken farms and where life was a happy eggless affair." In his dream he is both the sperm moving up the uterus and the child who will have no usurper from other siblings or from children of his own. In the dream the wish fulfillment of the libido is achieved by avoiding the inevitable loss of sexual satisfaction that comes through fatherhood. The dream concerns conception but also equates happiness with "eggless" existence.

When the family leaves the chicken farm and its sterile "poor stony land," they move to Pickleville. Formerly, "there had been cider mill and a pickle factory at the station." The phallic pickle and the feminine symbol of the apple are now inoperative. They have both been closed by failure, and again Anderson associates sexual failure with financial failure.

In Pickleville, the restaurant depends on the railroad for business. An iron horse has replaced the father's horse, or sexuality. He no longer travels but waits on those who do. The father tries to subdue the usurping generation, the young people of the town of Bidwell, with his great personality and good humor. His desire for sexual success is masked as an attempt at business success. "Father became a little feverish in his desire to please." Through displacement, the father's competition with the son becomes an attempt to conquer the youth of Bidwell. Besides being the oedipal threat, the son and Joe Kane are representatives of the ego-conscious public self. The father represents the libido, which has been exiled through sublimation to the silenced subconscious.

On the second level the son as ego associates himself with his father, who is libido, while being his antagonist in the battle for his mother's affection. The episode with the eponymously phallic Joe Kane, when the father tries to impress his new customer with his egg tricks, is remembered by the son not as something he has heard but as something he himself had experienced: "For some inexplicable reason I know the story as well as though I had been witness to my father's discomfiture. One in time gets to know many inexplicable things." As ego through states of dream or reverie, he is able to access the knowledge of the libido, which has been banished to the id.

Since the son-ego is influenced by both the mother-superego and the father-libido, he must speak for the father-libido and silence him. The ego is aware of the control of the superego. As they head out in the wagon for their move to the restaurant, the narrator-son tells us that his father "from a long association with mother and the chickens . . . had become habitually silent and discouraged." Later it is the son who shapes and permits his father's speech: "That was as far as he got. My own imagination has filled in the blanks." The ego speaks for the person and with its incomplete knowledge it creates the self.

The son tells his father's story and, in doing so, his own, for as he points out, "If correctly told it [the story] will center on the egg." As ego, he is not an objective speaker but represses and ridicules sexuality. When he sees the girls skipping and singing on their way home from school, he at first imitates them and then represses himself: "I was afraid of being seen in my gay mood. It must have seemed to me that I was doing a thing that should not be done by one who, like myself, had been raised on a chicken farm where death was a daily visitor." His experience on the chicken farm, the world of sexual and financial failure, has determined his perception of the world: "They [the chickens] are so much like people they mix one up in one's judgment of life." The chicken farm with endless eggs and tragedies—adverse sexual experience—causes him to suppress sexuality. His father caged in the wagon on his way from the chicken farm to the restaurant is the symbol of this suppression.

In the incident with Joe Kane in the restaurant, the father attempts to regain his sexual prowess and reverse his fortunes. The father-libido has already become absurd as he has attempted to find a voice. "He painted a sign on which he put his name in large red letters. Below his name was the sharp command—'EAT HERE'—that was seldom obeyed." When Joe Kane enters the restaurant, the mother-supergo and son-ego are asleep upstairs. The father is confronted with the younger generation, the young man from Bidwell waiting for the train. He does not speak. "For a long time father, whom Joe Kane had never seen before, remained silently gazing at his visitor. He was no doubt suffering from an attack of stage fright." When he breaks the silence, his words mimic the sound of a barnyard rooster, "How-de-do."

His first attempt at dominating this surrogate for the younger generation, or ego, is to get an egg to stand on end. The veiled allusions to male erections continue through this episode. But as he attempts this trick, "rolling the egg between the palms of his hands," he talks. His silence is broken as he attempts to prove his sexual potency. But his talk is ridiculous because it lacks the control of the superego and the ego. The association between expression and sexuality is pointed out in the father's criticism of Columbus, a worldly success who "was a cheat," he declared emphatically. "He talked of making an egg stand on end. He talked, he did, and then he went and broke the end of the egg." The father's references to Columbus's talking are followed by his outrage at the discoverer's Gordian-knot solution to the problem.

The father's own attempts to make the egg "stand" are frustrated. His scientific explanation of how he will make the egg stand—"He explained that the warmth of his hands and the gentle rolling movement he gave the egg created a new center of gravity"—though perhaps sexually charged in connotation, are not as illogical and sexual as his earlier "mumbled" explanation of "the effect to be produced on an egg by the electricity that comes out of the human body." Unlike Columbus who breaks the egg and lets the fluid out, his own attempts are dry and his success ultimately unseen by Joe Kane. The ego has turned away from the display of the libido at the crucial moment.

In his next attempt to prove his sexual viability, he shows Joe Kane one of the freak chicks in alcohol that he has preserved from his years on the farm but only elicits the young man's disgust: "His visitor was made a little ill by the sight of the body of the terribly deformed bird floating in the alcohol in the bottle and got up to go." The father offers him a free cigar and a cup of coffee to make him stay. Though Freud himself said that "sometimes a cigar is just a cigar," here the cigar and the cup function respectively as phallic and yonic counters, a replacement for the sexuality the father cannot himself enjoy.

Finally the father becomes more explicit when he boils an egg in vinegar and attempts to force "the egg to go though the neck" of a bottle. Joe Kane, however, leaves during his attempt, and the father in his desperation throws an egg at Joe and misses him. His failed attempt to put the egg in the bottle is figured as failed coition when the speaker states, "When he thought that at last the trick was about to be consummated the delayed train came in at the station and Joe Kane started to go." The train, the iron horse, prevents the father from consummation by its own arrival and has won Joe Kane away from him. The contrast between the father's horse of the older generation and the iron horse of Joe Kane's generation is implicit. Completely defeated, he runs up to his wife and son. "He laid the egg gently on the table and dropped on his knees by the bed." The father has come up from the restaurant where he had been humiliated. His prostration next to her bed provides a visual representation of the libido ruled by the superego.

At the end of the story there is a type of temporary reconciliation. The father and mother lie in bed together. The restaurant, which is the public arena that controls and humiliates the father, is closed. The son lies in the same room, can see the egg, and listens to the "muttered conversation" of his parents. The superego (mother) and the libido (father) have reached a conciliation in the sleepy presence of the ego (the son). The fact that this happens when the lights are out and all parties are sleeping points to a truce on the level of the unconscious and a wish fulfillment for the libido that is only vaguely sensed by the narrator (ego).

But this stasis can only be temporary. The restaurant must again open at night because that is when most of its business occurs. The father will return to his suppressed state, his silence broken only occasionally.

The next morning the narrator ponders the egg on the table, but his consideration of the egg and the hen leaves no place for the rooster. "I wondered why eggs had to be and why from the egg came the hen who again laid the egg." The mystery of this cycle, which includes and excludes the father and the son, distances them from and connects them to each other: "The question got into my blood. It has stayed there, I imagine, because I am the son of my father." The son on one level is ignorant concerning sexuality, but on another level as the ego he senses the jockeying for power between the superego and the libido and realizes that it must be a problem that "remains unsolved in my mind."

The powerful inexplicable nature of "The Egg" has struck readers from the beginning. Virginia Woolf in 1925 wrote that with this story "Mr. Anderson has bored into that deeper and warmer layer of human nature." The psychological framework gives names for the story's dynamics that disturb the reader but does not reduce them to corralled categories. Its mixture of the pathetic and the absurd, the close and the distant, the specific and the undefinable, says something profound about humanity.

Water, Sun, Moon, Stars, Heroic Spirit, in Tennyson's "Ulysses": A Mythological Analysis

Tiffany N. Speer

In the poem "Ulysses," Alfred, Lord Tennyson turned to one of the classic heroes of literature to explore the nature of the heroic spirit as it approaches death. Throughout the poem, the aging king remembers all that he has achieved. He realizes that he is no longer physically capable of performing such great acts, but that his heroic virtue remains. Though age has conquered his body, he insists that his triumphant spirit will not rest. The poem is paradoxical because the hero continually compares the deterioration of his physical capabilities with the rekindling of his heroic heart and his will to survive. There are several instances in which the descriptions of life and death are allusions to universal symbols and archetypes.

In the first few lines of the poem, Ulysses introduces the topic of debate: acceptance of age and retirement without settling for submission. He signals his refusal to stop living when he says, "I will drain / Life to the lees." This statement, the intense rejection of death, the image of drinking the full cup of tea, or drinking life "down to the last drop" is a recurring idea in this poem. Perhaps Ulysses' most significant instance of acceptance in the poem comes when he pauses and states, "I am become a name." He realizes that his name alone will live on in glory because of the reputation that he made from years of leading others.

It is in this first proclamation of identity that Jungian archetypes of self are introduced. He is shadow, anima, and persona combined to make a trinity of personalities that hover around acceptance of what is to come. Through this poem, Ulysses shows all three parts of his personality, the weak, the realistic, and the strong. In fact, the poem itself becomes a trilogy of archetypes combined to suggest Ulysses' image of himself.

The idea of becoming an "idle king" weary from a life of glorious reign is unacceptable to Ulysses. He refuses to accept that because he is aging, he will no longer roam the world as he did as a young hero. He says, "How dull it is to pause, to make an end, / To rust unburnished, not to shine in use!" Words such as "dull," "end," "rust," "barren," "aged," and "dim" indicate a sense of death and decay. It is in these words that Ulysses uncovers the "shadow" that he is trying to conquer. He is aware that it exists, but because he prefers not to live it out in full, he attempts to continue on with life as he did before.

Second, Ulysses' "anima," his sense of inevitable death, controls all that he does. After stating that he will always be a valiant warrior and that "every hour is saved / From that eternal silence," Ulysses begins to reflect on the possibility of passing down his reign to his son. He contradicts himself slowly as he comments on Telemachus's abilities as a leader and begins to face the fact that he, Ulysses, will soon die. At this transition, death is personified as a "vessel," a feminine object that holds his fate. She is his anima. He seems to whisper, "There lies the port; the vessel puffs her sail; / There gloom the dark, broad seas." Because Ulysses can see that he will soon die, he is revived in the final portion of the poem. Ironically, the vision of death is the "life force" that causes him to remember that he does not have to die in spirit.

Once again, Ulysses realizes that death does not have to take hold of his heart as it does his body. He says optimistically, "Old age hath yet his honour and his toil." His persona, or the mask that he wears for the sake of others, is the attitude that he shows at the end of the poem. He admits that death is drawing near, but he also says that it is never too late to live life to the fullest. He says, "for my purpose holds / To sail beyond the sunset, and the baths / Of all the western stars, until I die." His public stance is a positive one that encourages his people to believe that no matter what happens to their bodies, their spirits and souls will never age.

Not only does this poem contain the Jungian trinity of archetypes of the self, but it also contains other physical symbols that support its structure. There is a repetition of water images, of sailing away "beyond the sunset," and "on shore, and when / Thro' scudding drifts the rainy Hyades / Vext the dim sea." These references to water indicate the passing of time, as they wash away what was old while the new things come to surface. It is always the water or ship that takes Ulysses away when he speaks of death; therefore, water indicates his eternal fate. In the beginning of the poem, he speaks of being an idle king "among these barren crags," suggesting that his life now is without water, dying, desolate, or useless. Without water he cannot live, just as without duty and adventure he refuses to live. But it is the water that continually sails him off to death. The duty, or the water of his life, is the very thing that gives him life.

Ulysses also makes many references to the elements of the sky. He mentions rain, sun, stars, moon, and sunsets, all of which are in reference to light in some kind of darkness. First, he says, "and vile it were / For some three suns to store and hoard myself, / And this gray spirit yearning in desire / To follow knowledge like a sinking star." Hiding behind the sun and not following his dreams and pursuing further knowledge are repugnant to him. Just as stars fall, his knowledge will also fall from his memory. He also uses the image "The long day wanes; the slow moon climbs" to indicate the approach of death. Each of the references to elements of the sky is a description of Ulysses' inevitable end, his final adventure.

Alfred, Lord Tennyson used many elements in his approach to the topic of death in his poem "Ulysses." Not only does the voice of Ulysses echo the three parts of the Jungian shadow, anima, and persona, but it also uses references to death as water and sky to speak of death. Ulysses argues with himself that despite age and fate, the truly heroic spirit never dies. It is through these universal symbols that Tennyson is able to completely capture the undying soul of a dying hero. The memory of him will always be present, just like the water, sun, moon, and stars.

5

MARXIST CRITICISM

The Marxist analysis has got nothing to do with what happened in Stalin's Russia: it's like blaming Jesus Christ for the Inquisition in Spain.

TONY BENN, British Labor politician

A comment that has made the rounds of many English departments over the past few years is that since the fall of the Berlin Wall and the subsequent opening of Russia to the West, Marxism has died a quiet death—except in English departments, where it is still alive and well. Even if it weren't for China and some other places in the world where Marxist theory is securely in place, the remark would be inaccurate, but it does point to the lasting viability of Marxist literary criticism, which continues to appeal to many readers and critics. It is interesting to note, however, that the principles of Marxism were not designed to serve as a theory about how to interpret texts. Instead, they were meant to be a set of social, economic, and political ideas that would, according to their followers, change the world. They are the basis of a system of thought that sees inequitable economic relationships as the source of class conflict. That conflict is the mechanism by which Western society developed from feudalism to capitalism, which, according to Marxism, will eventually give way to socialism, the system that will characterize world economic relationships. Since its inception, Marxist theory has provided a revolutionary way of understanding history.

HISTORICAL BACKGROUND

Marxism has a long and complicated history. Although it is often thought of as a twentieth-century phenomenon, partly because it was the basis of the social-governmental system of the Soviet Union, it actually reaches back to the thinking of Karl Heinrich Marx, a nineteenth-century (1818–1883) German philosopher and economist. The first announcement of his nontraditional way of seeing things appeared in *The German Ideology* in 1845. In it he introduced the concept of **dialectical**

materialism, argued that the means of production controls a society's institutions and beliefs, and contended that history is progressing toward the eventual triumph of communism. When Marx met the political economist Friedrich Engels (1820–1895) in Paris in 1844, and they discovered that they had arrived at similar views independent of each other, they decided to collaborate to explain the principles of communism (later called Marxism) and to organize an international movement. These ideas were expounded in the *Communist Manifesto* (1848), in which they identified class struggle as the driving force behind history and anticipated that it would lead to a revolution in which the workers would overturn the capitalists, take control of economic production, and abolish private property by turning it over to the government to distribute fairly. With these events, class distinctions would disappear. In the three-volume work *Das Kapital* (1867), Marx argued that history is determined by economic conditions and urged an end to private ownership of public utilities, transportation, and the means of production. Despite the variations and additions that have occurred in the century that followed, on the whole, Marx's writings still provide the theory of economics, sociology, history, politics, and religious belief called Marxism.

Although Marxism was not designed as a method of literary analysis, its principles were applied to literature early on. Even in Russia, where literature was sometimes accepted as a means of productive critical dialogue and at other times viewed as a threat if it did not promote party **ideology,** literature was linked to the philosophical principles set down by Marx and Engels. Although its place was uncertain and shifting—culminating finally in the Soviet Writer's Union, founded (and headed) by Joseph Stalin to make certain that literature promoted socialism, Soviet actions, and its heroes—it was apparent that Marxism provided a new way of reading and understanding literature.

The first major Marxist critic, however, appeared outside of Russia. He was Georg Lukács (1885–1971), a Hungarian critic who was responsible for what has become known as **reflectionism.** Named for the assumption that a text will reflect the society that has produced it, the theory is based on the kind of close reading advocated by formalists but now practiced for the purpose of discovering how characters and their relationships typify and reveal class conflict, the socioeconomic system, or the politics of the time and place. Such examination, goes the assumption, will in the end lead to an understanding of that system and the worldview, the **weltanschauung,** of the author. Also known as **vulgar Marxism,** reflection theory should not be equated with the traditional historical approach to literary analysis, for the former seeks not just to find surface appearances provided by factual details but to determine the nature of a given society, to find "a truer, more concrete insight into reality" and look for "the full process of life." In the end, the reflectionists attribute the fragmentation and alienation that they discover to the ills of capitalism.

Another important figure in the evolution of Marxism is the Algerian-born French philosopher Louis Althusser (1918–1990), whose views were not entirely consonant with those of Lukács. Whereas Lukács saw literature as a reflection of a society's consciousness, Althusser asserted that the process can go the other way. In short, literature and art can affect society, even lead it to revolution. Building on Antonio Gramsci's idea that the dominant class controls the views of the people by many means, one of which is the arts, Althusser agreed that the working class is manipulated to accept the ideology of the dominant one, a process he called **interpellation.** One way that capitalism maintains its control over the working classes is by reinforcing its ideology through its arts. Althusser went on to point out, however, that the arts of the privileged are not all the arts that exist. There remains the possibility that the working class will develop its own culture, which can lead to revolution and the establishment of a new hegemony, or power base. Althusser's ideas are referred to as **production theory.**

Marxism established itself as part of the American literary scene with the economic depression of the 1930s. Writers and critics alike began to use Marxist interpretations and evaluations of society in their work. As new journals dedicated to pursuing this new kind of social and literary analysis sprang up, it became increasingly important to ask how a given text contributed to the solution of social problems based on Marxist principles. Eventually the movement grew strong enough to bring pressures to bear on writers to conform to the vision, resulting in a backlash of objection to such absolutism from such critics as Edmund Wilson in "Marxism and Literature" in 1938.

Currently two of the best-known Marxist critics are Fredric Jameson and Terry Eagleton. Jameson is known for the use of Freudian ideas in his practice of Marxist criticism. Whereas Freud discussed the notion of the repressed unconscious of the individual, Jameson talks about the political unconscious, the exploitation and oppression buried in a work. The critic, according to Jameson, seeks to uncover those buried forces and bring them to light. Eagleton, a British critic, is difficult to pin down, as he continues to develop his thinking. Of special interest to critics is his examination of the interrelations between ideology and literary form. The constant in his criticism is that he sets himself against the dominance of the privileged class. Both Jameson and Eagleton have responded to the influence of poststructuralism, and in the case of the latter, it resulted in a radical shift of direction in the late 1970s. (For definitions and a discussion of poststructuralism, see chapter 8.)

In some ways Jameson and Eagleton are typical of the mixture of schools in literary criticism today. For instance, it is not uncommon to find psychoanalytic ideas in the writing of a feminist critic, or postcolonial (see chapter 10) notions influencing a Marxist. As groups that share an active concern for finding new ways of understanding what we read and the lives we live, their interaction is not surprising. The borrowing back and forth may make it difficult to define discrete schools of literary analysis, but in practice it makes the possibilities for literary analysis all the richer.

READING FROM A MARXIST PERSPECTIVE

To understand the discussion that follows, you will need to read the short story "The Diamond Necklace," by Guy de Maupassant, which begins on page 243.

Many of the principles of Marxism and the approach to literary criticism that it spawned have already been mentioned in the brief historical survey you just read.

Now it will be helpful to examine them in more detail and to see how they can be applied to literary texts.

ECONOMIC POWER

According to Marx, the moving force behind human history is its economic systems, for people's lives are determined by their economic circumstances. A society, he says, is shaped by its "forces of production," the methods it uses to produce the material elements of life. The economic conditions underlying the society are called **material circumstances,** and the ideological atmosphere they generate is known as the **historical situation.** This means that to explain any social or political context, any event or product, it is first necessary to understand the material and historical circumstances in which they occur.

In Guy de Maupassant's short story "The Diamond Necklace," we are given a clear picture of a society that has unequally distributed its goods or even the means to achieve them. Madame Loisel has no commodity or skills to sell, only her youth and beauty to be used to attract a husband. Without access to those circles where she can find a man with wealth and charm, she is doomed to stay in a powerless situation with no way to approach the elegant lifestyle that she desires. The material circumstances of her society have relegated her to a dreary existence from which she can find no exit. Her husband is so conditioned to accept the situation that he does not understand her hunger to be a part of a more glamorous and elegant world. He is content with potpie for his supper because he has been socially constructed to want nothing else.

The way in which society provides food, clothing, shelter, and other such necessities creates among groups of people social relations that become the foundation of the culture. In other words, the means of production structures the society. Capitalism, for example, divides people into those who own property, and thereby control the means of production, the **bourgeoisie,** and those who are controlled by them, the **proletariat,** the workers whose labor produces their wealth. (Although in American society today we have come to use the term *bourgeoisie* to mean "middle class," it originally designated the owners and the self-employed as opposed to wage earners.) Because those who control production have a power base, they have many ways to ensure that they will maintain their position. They can manipulate politics, government, education, the arts and entertainment, news media—all aspects of the culture—to that end.

The division of the bourgeoisie and proletariat in the society depicted in "The Diamond Necklace" is firmly established and maintained. Mme. Loisel's husband is a "lowly clerk," and although she has a wealthy friend from her convent days, she has none of the accoutrements that would fit her to attend a reception to which her husband has (with some manipulation) managed to be invited. The haves are separated from the have-nots in this story by what they own and what they lack and by their ample or limited opportunity to acquire wealth and power. The division grows more apparent and unbridgeable as the couple works at increasingly demeaning jobs to acquire the money to pay off their loans. Because of the debts owed to the bourgeoisie, incurred because of the loss of the necklace owned by Mme. Loisel's well-to-do friend, they sink lower and lower in the social scale, losing what little hold they once had on social position or physical comfort. In the end, Mme. Loisel has become old and unkempt, unrecognizable to her friend. And in the most unjust irony of all, she learns after ten years that her efforts have been in vain. The bourgeoisie has tricked her once again by lending her a necklace not of diamonds but of cut glass.

Marx saw history as progressive and inevitable. Private ownership, he said, began with slavery, then evolved into feudalism, which was largely replaced by capitalism by the late eighteenth century. Evident in small ways as early as the sixteenth century, capitalism became a fully developed system with the growing power of the bourgeoisie in the mid-nineteenth century. At every stage it had negative consequences because it was a flawed system that involved maintaining the power of a few by the repression of many. The result was ongoing class struggle, such as the one depicted the "The Diamond Necklace" between the bourgeoisie and the proletariat. The Marxist, then, works to reveal the internal contradictions of capitalism so that the proletariat will recognize their subjugation and rise up to seize what is rightfully theirs. As he states in a famous passage from *The Communist Manifesto,* "Let the ruling classes tremble at a Communistic revolution. The proletarians have nothing to lose but their chains. They have a world to win. Working men of all countries, unite!" Although Mme. Loisel makes no move to create a revolution, she is keenly aware of the source of her sufferings. As she tells her affluent friend, who is "astonished to be so familiarly addressed by this common personage," "I have had some hard days since I saw you; and some miserable ones—and all because of you—". The fall of the bourgeoisie and the victory of the proletariat Marx deemed to be "equally inevitable," and the new system born of such a revolution would be a classless society in which everyone had equal access to its goods and services, such as food, education, and medical care.

Some of the damage caused by the economics of capitalism, according to Marxists, is psychological. In its need to sell more goods, capitalism preys on the insecurities of consumers, who are urged to compete with others in the number and quality of their possessions: a newer car, a bigger diamond engagement ring, a second house. The result is **commodification,** an attitude of valuing things not for their utility **(use value)** but for their power to impress others **(sign value)** or for their resale possibilities **(exchange value).** Both Mme. Loisel and her wealthy friend are victims of their society's emphasis on sign value. The former is so dazzled by the glitter of jewels and gowns and fashionable people that she can find little happiness in the humble attentions of her husband-clerk, and her friend's interest in the necklace apparently extends no further than the fact that it is impressive evidence of her wealth, for she substitutes glass for the real thing. When the acquisition of things that possess sign value and/or exchange value becomes extreme, an individual can be said to practicing **conspicuous consumption.**

Because the economic system shapes the society, the methods of production are known as the **base.** The social, political, and ideological systems and institutions it generates—the values, art, legal processes—are known as the **superstructure.** Because the dominant class controls the superstructure, they are by extension able to control the members of the working classes. There is not complete agreement among Marxists as to whether the superstructure simply reflects the base or whether it can also affect the base. The group known as **reflectionists,** who subscribe to what is called **vulgar Marxism,** see the superstructure as formed by the base, making literature (and other such products) a mirror of the society's consciousness. In a capitalist society it would exhibit the alienation and fragmentation that, according to the Marxists, the economic system produces. Controlled by the bourgeoisie, texts may, at least superficially, glamorize the status quo in order to maintain a stable division of power and means. Readers may not be aware of manipulation, especially when it appears in the form of entertainment, but it is no less effective for its subtle presentation.

Other Marxists, who assume that the superstructure is capable of shaping the base, recognize that literature (and art, entertainment, and such) can be a means for the working class to change the system. By promoting their own culture, they can create a new superstructure and eventually a different base. Even Marx and Engels admitted that some aspects of the superstructure, such as philosophy and art, are "relatively autonomous," making it possible to use them to alter ideologies.

The economic base in "The Diamond Necklace" is significant to all that is depicted in the story. Mme. Loisel's husband is a clerk whose employers have power over his professional life and their social relationships with him also reflect that power. They lead very different kinds of lives. The bourgeoisie give elegant parties while the clerk and his wife eat potpie. He is not expected to fraternize with his betters except by the rare invitation (so eagerly sought after by him) that comes his way. And on such occasions it is with difficulty that Mme. Loisel can achieve the appropriate appearance—dress, jewels, wrap. As they take on less attractive jobs to pay back what is owed, they are even less acceptable in the corridors of wealth and power. In the end, Mme. Loisel's friend does not even recognize her.

MATERIALISM VERSUS SPIRITUALITY

According to Marx, reality is material, not spiritual. Our culture, he says, is not based on some divine essence or the Platonic forms or on contemplation of timeless abstractions. It is not our philosophical or religious beliefs that make us who we are, for we are not spiritual beings but socially constructed ones. We are not products of divine design but creations of our own cultural and social circumstances.

To understand ourselves, we must look to the concrete, observable world we live in day by day. The material world will show us reality. It will show us, for example, that people live in social groups, making all of our actions interrelated. By examining the relationships among socioeconomic classes and by analyzing the superstructure, we can achieve insight into ourselves and our society. For example, the critic who looks at instances of class conflict or at the institutions, entertainment, news media, legal, and other systems of a society discovers how the distribution of economic power undergirds the society. Such analyses uncover the base, the economic system, and the social classes it has produced. Since the base and the superstructure are under the control of the dominant class, the worldview of the people is likely to be a false one, and the obligation of the critic is to expose the oppression and consequent alienation that has been covered over. The Marxist is rarely content simply to expose the failings of capitalism but also desires to argue for the fair redistribution of goods by the government.

It is the material world that has created Mme. Loisel, for example, and it is the material world that destroys her. Her desire for expensive objects and the circles where they are found, generated by the capitalistic system she lives in rather than by any character flaw, lead her to make a foolish request of a friend. When she loses the "diamond" necklace, she too is lost. Her relationship with her friend, as well as any hope for a return to the glittering world of the reception, is shattered. She is destroyed not by spiritual failure but by an economic system that has created a superstructure that will not allow her a better life. She is trapped by material circumstances, and the final revelation about the false jewels deepens her sense of alienation and powerlessness.

CLASS CONFLICT

One of the basic assumptions of Marxism is that the "forces of production," the way goods and services are produced, will, in a capitalist society, inevitably generate conflict between social classes, which are created by the way economic resources are used and who profits from them. More specifically, the struggle will take place between the bourgeoisie, who control the means of production by owning the natural and human resources, and the proletariat, who supply the labor that allows the owners to make a profit. The conflict is sometimes realized as a clash of management and labor, sometimes simply as friction between socioeconomic classes. They are two parts of a whole that struggle against each other, not just physically but also ideologically. Marx referred to this confrontation as **dialectical materialism.** Actually the term includes more than class conflict, for it refers to the view that all change is the product of the struggle between opposites generated by contradictions inherent in all events, ideas, and movements. A thesis collides with its antitheses, finally reaching synthesis, which generates its own antithesis, and so on, thereby producing change.

The Marxist is aware that the working class does not always recognize the system in which it has been caught. The dominant class, using its power to make the prevailing system seem to be the logical, natural one, entraps the proletariat into holding the sense of identity and worth that the bourgeoisie wants them to hold, one that will allow the powerful to remain in control. Monsieur Loisel, for instance, is content with his lot. He aspires to no more than he has and has difficulty understanding his wife's dreams. As for Mme. Loisel, she longs for things that "most other women in her situation would not have noticed." She believes herself born for luxuries—that is, a misplaced member of the middle class. They both experience the consequent debilitation and alienation described by Marx. Before the loss of the necklace, M. Loisel is given little credit for what he does. As a "minor clerk" he has little personal connection to his labor and is given no credit for what he produces. After the loss, the situation is intensified, for the couple are finally shut out of all social contact with bourgeois society. In the end Mme. Loisel moves to carry out what Marx calls upon the proletariat to do. She realizes that her life has been controlled by others. Freed of the debt she has owed her wealthy friend, she determines to free herself of the social enslavement to her by speaking openly and honestly at last. In doing so, she becomes painfully aware of the unsuspected depth of the control the latter has had over her. The necklace is false. She has been stripped of her dreams and forced to suffer for nothing. Finally, by speaking clearly she engages in revolution by refusing to want any longer what the bourgeoisie values.

ART, LITERATURE, AND IDEOLOGIES

Ideology is a term that turns up frequently in Marxist discussions. It refers to a belief system produced, according to Marxists, by the relations between the different classes in a society, classes that have come about because of the modes of production in the society. An ideology can be positive, leading to a better world for the people, or it can be negative, serving the interests of a repressive system. The latter rarely presents itself as an ideology, however. Instead, it appears to be a reasonable, natural worldview, because it is in the self-interest of those in power to convince people that it is so. Even a flawed system must appear to be a success. An ideology, dictated by the dominant class, functions to secure its power. When such cultural conditioning leads the people to accept a system that is unfavorable for them without protest or questioning, that is, to accept it as the logical way for things to be, they have developed a **false consciousness.** Marxism works to rid society of such deceptions by exposing the ideological failings that have been concealed. It takes responsibility for making people aware of how they have unconsciously accepted the subservient, powerless roles in their society that have been prescribed for them by others.

Marx himself was a well-educated, widely read German intellectual who could discourse on the poetry, fiction, and drama of more than a single culture. He enjoyed the theater and frequently made references to literature of all kinds. He was aware, however, that art and literature are an attractive and effective means of convincing the proletariat that their oppression is just and right. Literature is a particularly powerful tool for maintaining the social status quo because it operates under the guise of being entertainment, making it possible to influence an audience even when its members are unaware of being swayed. Because it does not seem to be didactic, it can lead people to accept an unfavorable socioeconomic system and to affirm their place in it as the proper one. By doing so, it serves the economic interests of those who are in power. Marx points out that controlling what is produced is not difficult, because those who create art must flatter (or not offend) their clients who pay for it—the bourgeoisie.

Although Marxist views about literature coexist comfortably with the principles of some other schools of criticism, they stand in direct opposition to the concerns of the Formalists, for Marxist critics see a literary work not as an aesthetic object to be experienced for its own intrinsic worth but as a product of the socioeconomic aspects of a particular culture. Marxists generally accept, then, that critics must do more than explain how a work conforms to certain literary conventions or examine its aesthetic qualities. Marxist critics must be concerned with identifying the ideology of a work and pointing out its worth or its deficiencies. The good Marxist critic is careful to avoid the kind of approach that concerns itself with form and craft at the expense of examining social realities.

Instead, she will search out the depiction of inequities in social classes, an imbalance of goods and power among people, or manipulation of the worker by the bourgeoisie, and she will point out the injustice of that society. If a text presents a society in which class conflict has been resolved, all people share equally in power and wealth, and the proletariat has risen to its rightful place, then the critic can point to a text in which social justice has taken place, citing it as a model of social action. In the former instance, the Marxist critic operates a warning system that alerts readers to social wrongs; in the latter, he is a mentor to the proletariat, pointing out how they can free themselves from the powerless position in which they have been placed. The intent of both approaches is highly political, aimed as they are at replacing existing systems with socialist ones. The function of literature is to make the populace aware of social ills and sympathetic to action that will wipe those ills away.

The ideology that a text inevitably carries can be found in either its content or its form. That is, a text has both subject matter and a manner of presentation that can either promote or criticize the historical circumstance in which it is set. To many Marxists, it is content that is the more significant of the two. The "what" is more revealing than the "how."

The "what" is important because it overtly expresses an ideology, a particular view of the social relations of its time and place. It may support the prevailing ideology of the culture, or it can actively seek to show the ideology's shortcomings and failings. It can strengthen a reader's values or reveal their flaws through characters and events and editorial comment.

If the subject matter is presented sympathetically, it depicts the social relationships—laws, customs, and values—that are approved by that society, in a way that legitimizes them and, by extension, the underlying economic system that has produced them. If, on the other hand, it criticizes the prevailing ideology, it can be equally powerful and persuasive. By depicting the negative aspects of a socioeconomic system—injustice, oppression, and alienation—literature can awaken those who are unfavorably treated by it. It can make them aware that they are not free, that they (the working class) are controlled by the oppressive bourgeoisie, a self-appointed elite. It can be a means of changing the superstructure and the base because it can arouse people to resist their treatment and overthrow unfair systems. At the very least, it can make social inequities and imbalances of power public knowledge.

What is the ideology expressed by the content of "The Diamond Necklace"? It is doubtful that de Maupassant wrote the story to foment revolution among his countrymen, but in it the destructive power of the cool lack of concern of the bourgeoisie for the proletariat is unmistakably depicted. The minor clerk and his wife are almost beneath notice to those who employ them, and the lower the couple falls in their ability to live well, or comfortably, or to survive at all, the less visible or recognizable they become. The denial of beautiful clothes and jewels to Mme. Loisel (while they are available to others no more deserving than she), and the suffering that such inequities cause her, carry with them a clear social commentary. Such a society is uncaring and unjust. It exists on assumptions that allow the powerful to keep their comfortable positions only if the powerless remain oppressed and convinced that it is right that they are oppressed.

The manner of presentation (the "how") can also be instrumental in revealing the ideology of a text, especially when it brings the reader close to the people and events being depicted. For that reason, realistic presentations that clearly depict the time and place in which they are set are preferable to many Marxist readers because they make it easier to identify with an ideology or to object to it. However, others find in modern and postmodern forms evidence of the fragmentation of contemporary society and the alienation of the individual in it. The narrative that is presented in an unrealistic manner—that is, through stream of consciousness or surrealism, may make a less overt identification with the socioeconomic ills of capitalism or with socialist principles, but it can nevertheless criticize contradictions and inequities found in the world that capitalism has created. The effect of forms on the development of social commentary in a text can be understood by imagining how "The Diamond Necklace" would be changed if instead of being a realistic depiction given by an omniscient narrator, the story were presented as an internal monologue taking place in the mind of Mme. Loisel or that of her husband or even that of her convent friend. In the latter form, the ideology would shift with each one's perception of what the social system is and should be, as well as what each has to lose or gain by changing it.

Believing that all products of a culture, including literature, are the results of socioeconomic and ideological conditions, the Marxist critic must have not only an understanding of the subject matter and the form of a work but also some grasp of the historical context in which it was written. He must also be aware of the worldview of its author, who wrote not as an individual but as one who reflects the views of a group of people. Such grounding helps the reader identify the ideology that inevitably exists in a text, so that she can then analyze how that ideology supports or subverts the power structure it addresses.

To make a Marxist analysis, then, you can begin by asking questions such as the following:

- Who are the powerful people in the society depicted in the text? Who are the powerless people? Are they depicted with equal attention?
- Why do the powerful have that power? Why is it denied to others?
- Do you find evidence of class conflict and struggle?
- Do you find repression and manipulation of workers by owners?
- Is there evidence of alienation and fragmentation?
- Does the bourgeoisie in the text, either consciously or unconsciously, routinely repress and manipulate less powerful groups? If so, what are the tools they use? News? Media? Religion? Literature?

- What does the setting tell you about the distribution of power and wealth?
- Is there evidence of conspicuous consumption?
- Does the society that is depicted value things for their usefulness, for their potential for resale or trade, or for their power to convey social status?
- Do you find in the text itself evidence that it is a product of the culture in which it originated?
- What ideology is revealed by the answers to the preceding questions? Does it support the values of capitalism or any other "ism" that institutionalizes the domination of one group of people over another—for example, racism, sexism, or imperialism? Or does it condemn such systems?
- Is the work consistent in its ideology? Or does it have inner conflicts?
- Do you find concepts from other schools of literary criticism—for example, cultural studies, feminism, postmodernism—overlapping with this one?
- Does this text make you aware of your own acceptance of any social, economic, or political practices that involve control or oppression of others?

Your answers should lead you to an understanding of the ideology expressed in the text and perhaps to insight into your own. Does the work accept socialism as historically inevitable as well as desirable? Does it criticize the repressive systems? Or does it reject socialism and approve of another system that exists by promoting one group of people at the expense of another—e.g., a particular ethnic or minority group. Where do you see similar situations in your own world? How that ideology is expressed through the form of the work, the characters, the setting, imagery, and all of its other literary elements is the content of the analysis.

WRITING A MARXIST ANALYSIS

There is no prescribed form for writing a Marxist analysis. Doing so is simply a matter of applying Marxist principles in a clearly ordered manner. As a result, one such written critique may look quite different from another but be equally Marxist in its content.

PREWRITING

If you have thoughtfully answered the questions listed above, you will have material to begin your prewriting. If you take those items that yielded the most information or generated your strongest opinions and use them as the basis of a freewrite, your thinking will begin to develop along some identifiable lines. It may be that you need only see where the responses you made to some of the questions are evident in the text. Those passages should provide you with examples of your generalizations.

Some questions that will require you to go outside the text for answers, but that can be rewarding to pursue, are those that deal with the historical circumstances of the writer and his text. You may want to take the time to do some library work to examine the following topics:

- What are the values of the author's time and place? Where are they reflected in the text?
- What biographical elements of the author's life can account for his ideology? For example, to what social class did he and his family belong? Where is that evident in the text?
- What are the socioeconomic conditions of the writer's culture? Where are they reflected in the text?
- Who read the work when it was first published? How was it initially received? Was it widely read? Banned? Favorably or unfavorably reviewed?
- What were the circumstances of its publication? Was it quickly accepted, widely distributed, highly promoted? Or was it difficult to find a publisher? Was it given limited distribution?

Regardless of which topics you ultimately decide to develop, the four most important goals of your prewriting are (1) to clarify your understanding of the ideology of work; (2) to identify the elements of the text that present the ideology; (3) to determine how they promote it—that is, convince the reader to accept it; and (4) to assess how sympathetic or opposed it is to Marxist principles. It is important to remember that a text does not have to be Marxist in its orientation to yield itself to an interesting reading from this perspective. Even one that is capitalist or sexist in its outlook can be fruitfully examined to determine how it attracts the reader into accepting its ideology.

It is also reassuring to recognize that Marxist critics do not always agree with each other's reading of a given text. If your interpretation differs from others, it is not necessarily wrong, because no single Marxist reading of a work results even when the same principles are applied. In the same manner, Marxism lends itself to combination with other schools of criticism, giving it even more possibilities for variation.

DRAFTING AND REVISING

The Introduction

In a Marxist analysis it can be effective to announce the ideology of the text and its relationship to Marxist views at the outset. Because the rest of your essay will be concerned with where and how the ideology is worked out, it is important that your reader share your understanding of the stance taken by the text. If you find this approach to be too dry, boring, and didactic, you might begin with a summary of an incident in the work that illustrates the social relationships of the characters or some other socioeconomic aspect of the society as preparation for your statement of its overall worldview.

The Body

The central part of your essay will demonstrate the presence or rejection of Marxist principles in the text you are analyzing. It is in this part that the organizational principles will be of your own design. That is, you may choose to discuss each of the major characters, assess the nature of the social institutions depicted, or point out the struggles between groups of people. The approach you take will in large part be dictated by the work itself. For example, an analysis of "The Diamond Necklace" could be built around the decline of the power and place of M. and Mme. Loisel as they are forced to repay the cost of the necklace, could illustrate the unjust treatment they receive from those in the powerful, controlling classes of society, or could compare and contrast the differences between their lives and those of the rich and powerful. Of course, these are overlapping issues, and it is difficult to focus on one without the other. Once you have addressed any such topic, you will quickly find yourself with comments to make about others that are related to it.

Because there is not a particular form to follow in writing a Marxist analysis, you may fall back on some of the techniques discussed in chapter 2 (Familiar Approaches). It might be helpful to think about the usefulness of explication, comparison and contrast, and analysis. In any case, during revision you will want to be sure that each of your points is equally developed and that all are linked together in a logical sequence. Making an outline (*after* drafting) to check on whether you have managed to provide adequate coverage and coherence is helpful because it can give you an overview of what you have done. If the parts are not balanced in length, depth, or content, you will need to make adjustments.

The Conclusion

The conclusion of a Marxist analysis often takes the form of an endorsement of classless societies in which everyone has equal access to power and goods or criticism of repressive societies in which that is not the case. It may once again make a case for social reform, pointing out where the literary work under consideration has either supported or rejected social change. In either case, to write the conclusion you will need to consider how the ideology in the text affirms or conflicts with your own.

That assessment may lead to a second possibility for your conclusion. That is, you may find it interesting to reflect on what the work has revealed to you about your own ideology. Perhaps you discovered that you have uncritically accepted the principles of socioeconomic-political movements that are in themselves controlling and oppressive. Perhaps your analysis has made you aware that principles that you took as "given" or "natural" or "just the way things are" are actually socially constructed and can be changed in ways that make society more just and balanced. If so, explaining your realization can provide a powerful ending to your analysis.

Glossary of Terms Useful in Marxist Criticism

Base The methods of production in a given society.

Bourgeoisie The name given by Marx to the owners of the means of production in a society.

Commodification The attitude of valuing things not for their utility but for their power to impress others or for their resale possibilities.

Conspicuous consumption The obvious acquisition of things only for their sign value and/or exchange value.

Dialectical materialism The theory that history develops neither in a random fashion nor in a linear one but instead as struggle between contradictions that ultimately find resolution in a synthesis of the two sides. For example, class conflicts lead to new social systems.

Exchange value An assessment of the worth of something based on what it can be traded or sold for.

False consciousness People's acceptance of an unfavorable social system without protest or questioning, that is, as the logical way for things to be.

Historical situation The ideological atmosphere generated by material circumstances. To understand social events, one must have a grasp of the material circumstances and the historical situation in which they occur.

Ideology A belief system.

Interpellation A term used by Louis Althusser to refer to the process by which the working class is manipulated to accept the ideology of the dominant one.

Material circumstances The economic conditions underlying the society. To understand social events, one must have a grasp of the material circumstances and the historical situation in which they occur.

Production theory The name given to Louis Althusser's ideas about the ability of literature and art to change the base of a society. By creating and celebrating its own cultural artifacts, the proletariat can produce a revolution that replaces the hegemony of the dominant class with its own.

Proletariat The name given by Marx to the workers in a society.

Reflectionism A theory that the superstructure of a society mirrors its economic base and, by extension, that a text reflects the society that produced it.

Sign value An assessment of something based on how impressive it makes a person look.

Superstructure The social, political, and ideological systems and institutions—for example, the values, art, and legal processes of a society—that are generated by the base. Some disagreement exists among Marxists about the manner and degree of influence the base and superstructure have on each other.

Use value An appraisal of something based on what it can do.

Vulgar Marxism Another name for *reflectionism.* Those who practice it try to determine the true and complete nature of a given society.

Weltanschauung The worldview of the author.

RECOMMENDED WEB SITES

http://home.mira.net/~deller/melt/

A site for primary works of Marx, Engels, Lenin, and Trotsky, with information on Hegel, Stalin, Lenin, Trotsky, and Engels and the philosophies of each.

http://csf.colorado.edu/psn/marx/

Marxists Internet Archive is an extensive database of Marxism.

http://www.trincoll.edu/depts/phil/philo/phils/marx.html
Provides links to other Marxist sites.

http://lists.village.virginia.edu/~spoons/marxism_html/index.html
A list of nineteen email discussion lists dedicated to Marxism.

http://vos.ucsb.edu/shuttle/cultural.html#marxist
A clearinghouse site with links to several Marxist theory, ideology, and criticism sites. It also includes listings for journals devoted to Marxism.

SUGGESTED READING

Ahearn, Edward J. *Marx and Modern Fiction.* New Haven, Conn.: Yale Univ. Press, 1989.
Arvon, Henri. *Marxist Aesthetics.* Trans. H. Lane. Ithaca, N.Y.: Cornell Univ. Press, 1973.
Eagleton, Terry. *Marxism and Literary Criticism.* Berkeley and Los Angeles: Univ. of California Press, 1976.
———. *Criticism and Ideology: A Study in Marxist Literary Theory.* New York: Schocken, 1978.
Hicks, Granville. *The Great Tradition.* New York: Biblo and Tannen, 1967.
Jameson, Fredric. *Marxism and Form: Twentieth-Century Dialectical Theories of Literature.* Princeton, N.J.: Princeton Univ. Press, 1971.
———. *The Political Unconscious: Narrative as a Socially Symbolic Act.* Ithaca, N.Y.: Cornell Univ. Press, 1981.
Laing, Dave. *The Marxist Theory of Art: An Introductory Survey.* Boulder, Colo.: Westview Press, 1986.
Mulhern, Francis, ed. *Contemporary Marxist Literary Criticism.* New York: Longman, 1992.
Slaughter, Cliff. *Marxism, Ideology, and Literature.* London: Macmillan, 1980.
Williams, Raymond. *Marxism and Literature.* Oxford: Oxford Univ. Press, 1977.

MODEL STUDENT ANALYSIS

Marxist Criticism of Frank Norris's "A Deal in Wheat"

Vickie Lloyd

Frank Norris's short story "A Deal in Wheat" presents the reader with a circularity that shows the intimate economic relationship between the base (a capitalist economic system) and the superstructure (represented by a commodity trading system that favors greedy market speculators over producers). This story comprises a plain lesson to us of the impact on our lives of the lack of morality and common decency of the affluent classes who are allowed to run our economic system. Norris also exposes the false consciousness of the proletariat who are subjugated by this ruthless system.

The story begins with Lewiston, a man on the verge of losing the family farm because a wealthy speculator has driven the price of wheat down so low that he cannot break even on his crop. Lewiston leaves his panicky wife and travels to town to make one more attempt to sell his grain for a price that will cover the cost of raising and storing the grain. The grain dealer, Bridges, tells Lewiston that he can pay no more than 62 cents a bushel and that it is the fault of the wealthy men who run the market. Bridges, who is upset, claims that the situation negatively affects them both, but it is obvious that Bridges is well off and does not stand to lose his very livelihood.

Lewiston forfeits his farm to creditors, and while his wife is sent to stay with relatives, he goes to Chicago to work. Lewiston's life spirals downward, and it is only near the end of the story that he is able to recover, but only through unskilled slavelike labor. As his fortunes dissolve, the wealthy wheat dealers who caused his decline seek to destroy one another with market speculations driven by fraud. These machinations are nothing more than fun and games for the rich men but represent life-and-death struggles for the proletariat, which is negatively affected by the speculations.

When Lewiston arrives in Chicago, he has a job in a hat factory, but even that is taken away from him when an import duty on felt is repealed and the home market is flooded by cheap imports. Here we see the adverse results to the workers when government refuses to protect the jobs of its own citizens against incursions by foreign markets. Although Norris says no more about this situation, the reader is reminded that the government of a free-market economy will always be run by the wealthy and for the good of the wealthy. In such a government, the proletariat is powerless and has no say in the decisions that affect day-to-day living.

Tragically, Lewiston finds himself homeless and living a hand-to-mouth existence. His lack of success at keeping a job, coupled with the breakup of his family, lends a heartbreaking poignancy to his situation, which is repeated in any society where the ruling class is not answerable to the working class.

Juxtaposed to the poor worker, Norris shows us the moneyed capitalists who are responsible for the farmer's plight. The capitalists, Truslow and Hornung, are out to do as much damage to one another as possible, and in their war of greed, the worker is ruthlessly victimized. In the course of the story, Hornung attempts to corner the market on wheat in order to drive up the price. He sells a load of wheat to Truslow but has second thoughts: although he is set to make a fortune, he wonders if he should drive the price of wheat so high that Truslow is forced into bankruptcy. He longs to destroy his great enemy, and in this desire, Norris plainly shows us one of the more immoral facets of capitalism, that of the need for the wealthy to climb to success by oppressing others, even of the same class. The selfish destructiveness of ruthless and powerful men affects all levels of a society.

Hornung's plan backfires because Truslow perpetrates a scam on Hornung. When Hornung discovers the scam, he laughs it off, thus revealing that to both these men, their avaricious machinations are nothing more than sport. Although the two have managed to wreck the lives of untold numbers of families, they blithely go on playing their games. Unfortunately, their sport has caused the price of wheat to be driven up even further, and their game has consequences that are devastating. Many others like Lewiston are unable to make a go of the family farm, and thus another American tradition is destroyed by big business.

In a pivotal scene, Lewiston finds himself late at night in a long line waiting to receive free bread from a local bakery. Many other men who also suffer the same plight are in the line, and Norris portrays this scene in imagery that calls to mind the deathlike stillness of a cemetery. Norris describes the setting as being "very dark and absolutely deserted," with Lewiston standing in the "enfolding drizzle, sodden, stupefied with fatigue." The weary men merely stand without talking so that even their basic social need to communicate with each other has been destroyed by capitalist greed. This powerful and heartrending scene stands out because it bluntly reflects the way materialism strips away the humanity of the working class. The author's use of the dank, depressing graveyard imagery constitutes a metaphor for the death of working class people at the hands of the society that should nurture it.

One evening, as the men are standing in line, a sign is posted on the bakery door saying that the price of wheat has risen so high the bakery can no longer give away bread. Here, we see that even this small perquisite is taken away from the desperate men. Symbolically, Norris is showing us that the rapacious greed of the ruling class is stealing the very bread from the mouths of the workers.

Bread is the most basic of human food, and Norris's symbolic use of wheat speculation and the starving men awaiting handouts of free bread cuts to the very core of the economic dilemma of the worker and exposes its rotten marrow. This battle for the fundamental symbol of life is emblematic of the class struggle of the proletariat for a fair share of society's goods and services.

Also symbolically, Norris uses exchange market terminology to label Truslow as the Great Bear and Hornung as the bull. In market jargon, a bear speculator profits from a falling market, and a bull profits from a rising market. Whether the market is rising or falling, the bourgeoisie will control the purse strings of the nation, and the bottom line for both men is profit, but only for themselves. In the story, the two men display the worst characteristics of the animals they represent, recklessly attempting to destroy each other in a territorial fight with animalistic shortsightedness. The bull lords it over his herd, driving away weaker males and thus making the social decisions. The ones driven away become isolated, and, deprived of the life-giving society of the herd, they starve to death. The bear is a large predator that destroys other animals in order to survive. The bull and the bear control the power base in their territories, ensuring the maintenance of their positions by the "wealth" of their strength and size. They also manipulate their respective societies by enforcing a class structure in which the weaker males are not allowed to breed, thus even establishing control over the genetic makeup of their societies. Hornung and Truslow, in their unchecked cupidity, are like the animals because both make social decisions for the weaker proletariat and both men are unbound by moral strictures. The "weaker males" of Hornung and Truslow's society are as marginalized and alienated as the animals at the bottom of the beastly hierarchy.

Eventually, Lewiston is able to overcome his predicament by finding a job and working his way up to a steady salary. Even this small victory is downwardly quantified by the fact that it involves street cleaning. In our society's unchecked rush toward ownership of all we survey, we harshly judge and look down upon those whose slavelike work for others is seen as less than noble. Although our society could not function without the so-called blue-collar jobs such as mechanic and farmer and the unskilled labor of street cleaners and garbage collectors, these necessary occupations are severely undervalued. The spurious shame associated with these trades has been fostered by the bourgeoisie and swallowed wholesale by all, including the very workers who, like Lewiston, are forced into them by lack of better opportunity. This false consciousness further serves to alienate the workers and fragment our society.

Eventually, Lewiston is reunited with his wife, but he never forgets what it felt like to be caught in what the author describes as "the cogs and wheels of a great and terrible engine." This engine is the American capitalist economy, constructed and operated by the iron-hard and dispassionate ruling classes who feel no loyalty to the workers who oil and fuel the great engine, nor to those who are crushed by it. Lewiston and others like him are unable even to comprehend the great forces that shape their lives.

As to Truslow and Hornung, at the end of the story Norris reminds us that the two "never saw the wheat they traded in, bought and sold the world's food, gambled in the nourishment of entire nations, practiced their . . . oblique shifty 'deals,'" and went on about their destructive business "contented, enthroned, and unassailable." The author's use of the word *enthroned* calls to mind royalty and the divine right of kings. Certainly in this story, Truslow and Hornung conduct themselves with no thought to the peasants beneath them. Because of their accumulation of earthly treasures, they falsely view themselves as having passed into the realm of divinity, which gives them the right to destroy, starve, and maim with impunity the blighted workers whose fate lies in the hands of the ruling class.

"A Deal in Wheat" is a sharp lesson to materialistic societies of the rank evils of social systems that base their economy on an undervalued working class. By taking the reader from the wealthy who run the system to the poor who are most affected by the system, Norris is giving the reader a broad picture of the methods used by an unchecked bourgeoisie to destroy families and rob individuals of their humanity.

6

Feminist Criticism

Throughout history people have knocked their heads against the riddle of the nature of femininity. . . . Nor will you have escaped worrying over this problem—those of you who are men; to those of you who are women this will not apply—you are yourselves the problem.

Sigmund Freud, Lecture 33,
New Introductory Lectures on Psychoanalysis and Other Works

If a woman has her Ph.D. in physics, has mastered quantum theory, plays flawless Chopin, was once a cheerleader, and is now married to a man who plays baseball, she will forever be "former cheerleader married to star athlete."

Maryanne Ellison Simmons,
wife of Milwaukee Brewers' catcher Ted Simmons

When a school of literary criticism is still evolving, trying to make a definitive explanation of it can be a perilous undertaking. Feminist criticism, for example, is difficult to define because it has not yet been codified into a single critical perspective. Instead, its several shapes and directions vary from one country to another, even from one critic to another. The premise that unites those who call themselves feminist critics is the assumption that Western culture is fundamentally **patriarchal,** creating an imbalance of power that marginalizes women and their work. That social structure, they agree, is reflected in religion, philosophy, economics, education—all aspects of the culture, including literature. The feminist critic works to expose such ideology and, in the end, to change it so that the creativity of women can be fully realized and appreciated.

HISTORICAL BACKGROUND

Although the feminist movement stretches back into the nineteenth century, the modern attempt to look at literature through a feminist lens began to develop in the early

1960s. It was a long time coming. For centuries Western culture had operated on the assumption that women were inferior creatures. Leading thinkers from Aristotle to Darwin reiterated that women were lesser beings, and one does not have to look hard to find comments from writers, theologians, and other public figures that disparage and degrade women. The Greek ecclesiast John Chrysostom (345–407 A.D.) called women "a foe to friendship, an inescapable punishment, a necessary evil," and Ecclesiasticus (a book of the Apocrypha) states, "All wickedness is but little to the wickedness of a woman." The Roman theologian Tertullian (c. 160–230 A.D.) lectured women: "The judgment of God upon your sex endures even today; and with it inevitably endures your position of criminal at the bar of justice. You are the gateway to the devil." Even the Book of Genesis blames Eve for the loss of paradise. Revered writers of later ages have been equally ungenerous in their descriptions of the nature of women. Alexander Pope (1688–1744) asserted, "Most women have no character at all," and John Keats (1795–1821) explained, "The opinion I have of the generality of women—who appear to me as children to whom I would rather give a sugar plum than my time, forms a barrier against matrimony which I rejoice in."

It is not surprising, given widespread acknowledgment of the inferiority of the female, that women too accepted their lesser status. Even the French writer Madame de Staël is said to have commented, "I am glad that I am not a man, as I should be obliged to marry a woman." When women did recognize their talents, they sometimes worked to conceal them. Jane Austen, for example, advised, "A woman, especially, if she have the misfortune of knowing anything, should conceal it as well as she can." Or as Mae West put it, "Brains are an asset, if you hide them." Women are the staple of jokes, too. James Thurber, an often quoted misogynist, once commented, for example, "Woman's place is in the wrong."

In the late eighteenth century, however, Mary Wollstonecraft took issue with the assumptions that have allowed people to make jokes and caused women to hide their creativity. In 1792 she published *A Vindication of the Rights of Woman,* in which she depicted women as an oppressed class regardless of social hierarchy. Having experienced as a child the imbalance of power between her own mother and father, and having observed as an adult the indignities suffered by women of all classes, she recognized that they are born into powerless roles. As a result, they are forced to use manipulative methods to get what they want. She argued for women to be "duly prepared by education to be the companions of men" and called for the members of her sex to take charge of their lives by recognizing that their abilities were equal to those of men, to define their identities for themselves, and to carve out their own roles in society. She wrote,

> I earnestly wish to point out in what true dignity and human happiness consists—I wish to persuade women to endeavour to acquire strength, both of mind and body, and to convince them that the soft phrases, susceptibility of heart, delicacy of sentiment, and refinement of taste, are almost synonymous with epithets of weakness, and that those beings who are only the objects of pity and that kind of love, which has been termed its sister, will soon become objects of contempt. . . . I wish to shew that elegance is inferior to virtue, that the first object of laudable ambition is to obtain a character as a human being, regardless of the distinction of sex.

Her stand was not welcomed by all. Horace Walpole, for example, called her a in petticoats," but the words were out, and they were impossible to ignore evei

In 1929 another eloquent analysis of the position of women was published by Virginia Woolf, best known as a writer of lyrical and somewhat experimental novels. Called *A Room of One's Own,* it questioned why women appear so seldom in history. Woolf pointed out that poems and stories are full of their depictions, but in real life they hardly seem to have existed. They are absent. In the chapter entitled "Shakespeare's Sister," she pondered what would have happened to a gifted female writer in the Renaissance. Without an adequate education or a room of her own, "whatever she had written," Woolf concluded, "would have been twisted and deformed, issuing from a strained and morbid imagination." Woolf went on to argue that "if we [women] have the habit of freedom and the courage to write exactly what we think; if we escape a little from the common sitting room and see human beings not always in their relation to each other but in relation to reality; and the sky too, . . . when she [Shakespeare's sister] is born again she shall find it possible to live and write her poetry."

Individuals like Wollstonecraft and Woolf stand out as eloquent spokespersons for women. Along with them are many others whose names are less well known but whose efforts have been important to the development of women's history, both social and literary. Some of that history has been traced by Elaine Showalter, who divided it into three phases, which she called the feminine phase (1840–1880), the feminist phase (1880–1920), and the female phase (1920–present). In the first, female writers imitated the literary tradition established by men, taking additional care to avoid offensive language or subject matter. Novelists such as Charlotte Brontë and Mary Ann Evans wrote in the forms and styles of recognized writers, all of whom were male. Sometimes female writers even used men's names (Currer Bell and George Eliot, for example) to hide their female authorship. In the second phase, according to Showalter, women protested their lack of rights and worked to secure them. In the political realm, Susan B. Anthony, Elizabeth Cady Stanton, and others pushed to secure equality under the law, and some of the more radical feminists envisioned separate female utopias. In the literary world they decried the unjust depictions of women by male writers. The third phase, at its beginnings, concentrated on exploring the female experience in art and literature. For female writers this meant turning to their own lives for subjects. It also meant that the delicacy of expression that had typified women's writing began to crumble as a new frankness regarding sexuality emerged. For feminist critics it meant looking at the depiction of women in male texts in an effort to reveal the **misogyny** (negative attitudes toward women) lurking there. More recently they have turned their attention to an examination of works by female writers. These latest efforts Showalter refers to as **gynocriticism,** a movement that examines the distinctive characteristics of the female experience, in contrast to earlier methods that explained the female by using male models.

During the third period, a host of important spokespersons have raised public awareness of issues surrounding women's rights. Simone de Beauvoir in *The Second Sex* (1949) argued that French culture, and Western societies in general, are patriarchal. In them it is the males who define what it means to be human. Lacking her own history, the female is always secondary or nonexistent. Beauvoir believed that women are not born inferior but made to be so. She called for women to break out of being the "other" and realize their possibilities. Betty Friedan shocked some and cheered others with her attack on the image of the happy American suburban housewife and mother in *The Feminine Mystique* (1963). By the next decade feminists were taking their models from other social protests, such as the civil rights movement. Kate Millett, in *Sexual Politics* (1970), objected to the repressive stereotyping of women by probing the differences between biological (sexual) and cultural (gender) identities. Millet also pointed out that power in civil as well as domestic life is held by males, and literature is a record of the collective consciousness of patriarchy. That is, much literature is the record of a man speaking to other men, not directly to women. At about the same time, Germaine Greer documented images of women in popular culture and literature in *The Female Eunuch* (1970), in an attempt to free women from their mental dependence on the images presented by these sources.

Showalter acknowledges that today there is no single strand of feminism or feminist criticism, no single feminist approach to the study of literature, but there do seem to be some similarities among feminists in particular countries. American feminism, which has its stronghold in academia, has worked to add texts by female writers to the canon. Sandra Gilbert and Susan Gubar, authors of *The Madwoman in the Attic* (1979), have been influential in American feminist criticism, calling for a recognition that male writers have too long stereotyped women as either "the angel in the house" (the woman who lives to care for her husband) and "the madwoman in the attic," the woman who chooses not to be the angel. They call for writing by women, even a woman's sentence, that will more accurately capture the complexity of women's lives and nature.

Showalter points out that French feminists are primarily psychoanalytic. For their theoretical basis they have turned to their fellow countryman Jacques Lacan. They are, consequently, concerned with language, particularly with how women in the **Symbolic Order** (a phase of development) are socialized into accepting the language (and law) of the father and thereby made inferior. Hélène Cixous goes so far as to assert that there is a particular kind of writing by women that she calls ***l'écriture feminine.*** It has as its source the wholeness of Jacques Lacan's **Imaginary Order,** the prelinguistic domain of the female that is characterized by freedom from laws and a sense of "other" (see chapter 4).

The British feminists, according to Showalter, generally take a Marxist position. Protesting the exploitation of women in life and literature, which they view as connected by virtue of being parts of the material world, the British feminist critics work to change the economic and social status of women. They analyze relationships between gender and class, showing how power structures, which are male dominated, influence society and oppress women. Like Marxists in general, they see literature as a tool by which society itself can be reformed.

All three groups are gynocentric, trying to find ways to define the female experience, expose patriarchy, and save women from being the other. Those involved with literature—critics and writers—try to expand the canon to include female writers and to correct inaccurate depictions of them in the works of male writers. Interest in such topics has led to increased notice of works written by females who have been ignored or forgotten but whose texts deserve examination. *The Awakening,* by Kate Chopin, is a case in point. It was rediscovered in the 1960s, becoming a popular and critical success more than sixty years after its initial publication. The growing strength of the women's movement has also led to the establishment of women's studies programs, further fueling the interest in gender studies, which question the qualities of femininity and masculinity, and in feminist literary criticism. Such programs ask questions about the nature of the female imagination and female literary history. What, after all, is a female aesthetic? Do women use language in ways that are different from those of men? Do women have a different pattern of reasoning? Do they see the world in a different way?

Several significant studies have tried to answer such questions. They do not all agree, but in general they have challenged assumptions about how males and females use language, view reality, solve problems, and make judgments. They suggest that women and men have different conceptions of self and different modes of interaction with others. Some of the findings call for a recognition of the differences, because ignoring them inevitably leads to a suppression of women's ways of understanding and acting.

Nancy Chodorow, for example, argues in *The Reproduction of Mothering* that girls and boys develop a different concept of self because of different relationships with the mother, the primary parent in the home. Girls maintain an ongoing gender role identification with the mother from the beginning, but boys, in addition to dealing with an **oedipal attachment,** give up their primary identification with her. The result is that men tend to deny relationships, whereas women remain relational.

In another study, Carol Gilligan focuses on differences in the ways in which males and females talk about moral problems. Men, she points out, are more likely to see morality as a matter of rights and rules to be dealt with by formal reasoning. Women, on the other hand, are more likely to deal with moral issues contextually. That is, instead of applying "blind justice" provided by abstract laws and universal principles, they recognize that moral choice must be determined from the particular experiences of the participants. Conflicting responsibilities are to be resolved in a narrative, consensual manner. Gilligan's *In a Different Voice* uses the metaphors of a web, with its suggestion of connections (and entrapment as well), and a ladder, with its implications of upward movement, achievement, and hierarchies. By doing so, she counters the argument of Lawrence Kohlberg (based on a study using only male subjects) that moral development is derived from an understanding of human rights. More recently she has worked with Nora Lyons to examine the implications of self-definition, finding that many more women than men define themselves in terms of their relationships and connections to others.

Another feminist writer, Robin Lakoff, argues that women's language is inferior to that of men. She points out its patterns of weakness, uncertainty, and triviality. She goes on to assert that women should adopt the stronger male utterance if they wish to achieve equality.

A fourth study of significance comes from Mary Field Belenky, Blythe McVicker Clinchy, Nancy Rule Goldberger, and Jill Mattuck Tarule. Entitled *Women's Ways of Knowing,* it is concerned with the intellectual development of women. Recognizing that male experience has served as the model in defining the processes of intellectual maturation, they argue that the ways of knowing that women value "have been neglected and denigrated by the dominant intellectual ethos of our time." That is, "thinking" has traditionally been defined as the mental processes attributed primarily to men, processes such as abstract reasoning, the scientific method, and impersonal judgments. Belenky et al. argue that this kind of thinking does not come naturally to many women who instead are more comfortable with personal and interpersonal ways of knowing. They are more likely to value "connection over separation, understanding and acceptance over assessment, and collaboration over debate." Based on interviews with 135 women from a variety of backgrounds and ages, the study found that women develop intellectually as they find their voice, as they move from silence (in which they take their identification from external authorities) to subjective knowledge (when they turn away from others but still lack a public voice) and then to constructed knowledge (when they integrate their own intuitive knowledge with what they have learned from others).

Despite (or perhaps because of) such studies, today members of the feminist movement and the critics, male and female, who make its principles and methods the basis of their critical approach to literature are not yet in complete agreement about what those principles and methods are. In fact, there are currently many different forms of feminism and many different kinds of feminist critics, partly because of their tendency to borrow from other social and literary movements, a practice that has both enriched and complicated their work. As a result, they now find themselves the inheritors of several decades of evolution that have led to significant differences, and even some disagreements, among them.

Minority feminists—women of color and lesbians, for example—do not always align themselves with what they see as a primarily white, middle-class movement that has historically marginalized them. Their exclusion is ironic, given that their victimization has been greater than that of their white counterparts. Not only has history taken less notice of them than it has of white women, but literature too has generally overlooked them, at least until recently. Compounding their grievances is the fact that they have more than a single battle to fight. The African-American feminist critic, for example, finds herself pressured by two forces of oppression: racism and sexism. They are bound together in her experience, but she does not find that circumstance represented by mainstream feminism, which is focused only on sexism. The same situation is true for the poor, the aged, and other women who find themselves without access to power, leaving them outside the movement as it has developed with leadership vested in educated, relatively affluent white women. The response of minority feminist critics is therefore likely to be more political than that of white critics. And when one makes reference to feminism as a worldwide movement, the situation becomes even more complex, because the roles and power of women in different countries vary widely. A feminist living and working in Los Angeles is likely to have a very different life from that of a mother of five in Iraq, so how can there be "sisterhood"?

The political edge found among minority feminist critics, the Marxist feminists, and others has not been welcomed by everyone. Some complain that radical positions regarding social policy ultimately cause a reader to ignore the literary text. They object that a radical position diverts the critic from the main task at hand—to pay attention to the aesthetics of literature, not to impose a political stance on it. Such comments are formalist in nature, for they urge the reader to see the work as an autonomous entity with its own rules of being. It is an approach that lies at a great distance from the methods of those who would use literature as a tool of social protest and reform.

The definition of feminist criticism was also destabilized by the introduction of deconstruction, which since the middle 1970s has been a disruptive and transformative way of thinking about what it means to be male or female (see chapter 8). When the definition plays with the reversal of those categories, it also overturns all the other binary oppositions that are related to them: rational/emotional, active/passive, objective/subjective. The result is that it complicates what we mean when we refer to sexual identity. What do we mean when we describe someone as masculine or feminine?

Practitioners of queer theory (lesbians, gay men, bisexuals, and indeed anyone who by self-definition is not "straight") make interesting use of deconstruction's blurring and reversals of categories. Interested in questions regarding sexual identity, they view individuals not simply as male or female but as a collection of many possible sexualities that may include heterosexuality, homosexuality, or bisexuality. In other words, sexuality is neither stable nor static. It is dynamic and changing, affected by the experience of race and class and subject to shifting desire. It is a force of its own that is not just biologically conferred. Thus, heterosexuality cannot be viewed as the norm against which other sexual identities are measured.

Applied to literary criticism, queer theory raises questions about how a text represents sexual categories. Does it depict human sexuality as more complex than the essentialist terms *male* and *female* suggest? Does it show how sexual identities are indeterminate, overlapping, changing? Does it complicate what it means to be homosexual or heterosexual? Such approaches can be found in the work of gay and lesbian critics, who, although they do not necessarily share the same goals or methods, come together under the more inclusive term of *queer criticism.*

READING AS A FEMINIST

To understand the discussion that follows, you should read the letters of Abigail Adams written on March 31 and April 5, 1776, and the one from her husband, John, written on April 14, 1776, which begin on page 249.

Although feminist criticism has many strands, most critics hold some general approaches in common. More specifically, they look at literary history to rediscover forgotten texts by women, to reevaluate other texts, and to examine the cultural contexts in which works were produced. They analyze the male/female power structure that makes women the other (the inferior), and they reject it. They work to abolish limiting stereotypes of women. They seek to expose patriarchal premises and the prejudices they create. In short, by changing the literature that people read and the ways that they read it, feminist critics hope to change the world so that everyone is valued as a creative, rational being. That makes them, as a group, highly ideological, even visionary.

Despite the sprawling nature of feminist studies, it is possible to group some of the different perspectives into several overlapping approaches. Three major groups of feminist critics are those who study difference, those who study power relationships, and those who study the female experience.

STUDIES OF DIFFERENCE

Feminist critics who are interested in determining the differences in male and female writing work from the assumption that gender determines everything, including value systems and language. Not all feminist critics agree, for they recognize that historically the concept of female difference has resulted in an assumption of female inferiority, leading them to argue that difference should no longer be an issue. Nevertheless, studies like those of Belenky and Gilligan have led critics to look for distinctive elements in texts by men and women. They compare and contrast what men and women write and how they write it. They examine not only their subjects but also their voice, syntax, and diction. And although such matters remain largely unresolved, the concern with male and female writing characteristics has resulted in increased attention to gay and lesbian texts and eventually has been influential in the establishment of gay studies programs.

One way this approach has influenced current criticism is evident in an expanded concept of which genres are to be accepted as literature. If works by female writers are to be deemed worthy of study, then the forms they have traditionally turned to, such as journals and letters, have to be included in the canon. The correspondence between Abigail Adams and her husband, John, who was away from home because of the American Revolution, is an example of the sorts of texts that interest feminist critics. For one thing, the letters allow the voice of Abigail, a woman who had much to say, to be heard. She was not likely to write a political treatise or poems exhorting the troops to battle, but she did write to her husband, and through those letters her concerns are still articulated. They are also typical of the kind of writing women have always done. Do they constitute literature? A feminist critic would argue that they do.

The Adams correspondence is interesting because of the contrast of content as well as the style of the two writers. Abigail begins both of her letters included here with a plea for more communication from John. She complains that he writes infrequently and that his letters are too brief. In answer, he does not apologize but explains that the "critical state of things" necessitates the brevity of his writing. He i: in matters of importance that make it impossible for him to write at greater l course, he also alludes, without excuse or apparent irony, to a "multiplicity tions" that presumably take up his time. Abigail also opens by inquiring ab work—asking about the state of the revolution and even devoting a short paragraph to patriotic statement that is sure to please him—before she turns to news of their home, the town, and finally her own state of mind. She ends with an overt feminist statement, calling men tyrants and asking her husband to recognize the rights of women to have voice and representation in the new government. John, on the other hand, after explaining that he has been too busy to write much, turns quickly to recounting the progress of the revolt and its effect on the colonies. It is an impersonal account, with no reference to his direct involvement with it. When he does address more personal issues, in answer to her description of the state of their Boston home, he assumes a patriarchal tone and discourses on issues of morality. Finally, in a response to her requests for his attention to the rights of women, he turns lighthearted, referring to her *gaieté de coeur* and describing her as "saucy." He treats her comments playfully, declaring that because men are already masters in name only, they cannot even think to repeal the system in which they seem to hold control lest they become completely subjected to "the despotism of the petticoat." He gives her appeals no serious thought.

The style of the two letters also has contrasts. Abigail's is full of personal references, the use of the pronoun *I,* whereas John's makes little reference to himself. John speaks primarily in the third person, narrating at much greater distance than does his wife. Abigail also describes her sentiments, explicitly stating her feelings. She says, for instance, "I wish you would ever write me a letter half as long as I write you," "I am fearful of the small-pox," and "I feel very differently at the approach of spring from what I did a month ago." John, in contrast, makes little reference to his own feelings. He says that he pities the children of the Solicitor General, but instead of indulging the sentiment, he uses it to make stern comments about morality. Later he speaks of being charmed by Abigail's gaiety, the sign of innocent femininity, and at the end expresses amusement, even laughter, at her silliness that asks for equality. The final mood is implicit in the ironic treatment he gives her concerns. The two not only choose to discuss different topics but also approach them from quite different perspectives: the personal and the impersonal, the subjective and the objective, the explicit and the implicit.

STUDIES OF POWER

The sociological aspects of feminism broached so delicately by Virginia Woolf become overt and explicit with today's outspoken feminists who complain of the imbalance of power between the sexes. Assuming that the economic system is at the root of the inequitable relationship, they attack both the economic and the social exploitation of women. They charge that women are oppressed by a group that consciously works to hold them down through its ideology. Michèle Barrett, who writes from a

Marxist point of view, argues that the way households and families are organized is related to the division of labor in a society, the systems of education, and the roles men and women play in the culture. Building on Virginia Woolf's belief that the conditions under which men and women produce literature affect how they write and what they write about, she argues that gender stereotyping is tied to material conditions.

The feminist critics who are interested in examining and protesting power relationships of men and women in literature have expanded their focus to include a number of subgroups that have also been marginalized in society. They frequently look at writers from cultures as varied and different as the black (African-American and other people of color), Hispanic, Asian-American, native American, Jewish, and lesbian ones. Some members of the black group, the most outspoken of the minorities, describe critics as racists and misogynists, object to the amount of attention paid to black male writers (instead of black female ones), and even charge white feminist critics with being interested only in white, upper-middle-class women. Their efforts have not all been directed to protest, however. They have also produced some valuable scholarship by compiling bibliographies of ignored black writers and their works, studying black female folk artists, and publishing slave narratives. They have traced the growing power and authority of black females, whose history in this country began in slavery, and they have celebrated the family and community nurtured by those women. Like the Marxists, these critics have highly political purposes.

The common thread uniting these disparate groups is the belief that the social organization has denied equal treatment to all its segments and that literature is a means of revealing and resisting that social order. To them, art and life are fused entities, making it the duty of the critic to work against stereotyping in literature, media, and public awareness; to raise the consciousness of those who are oppressed; and to bring about radical change in the power balance between the oppressors and the oppressed.

Whereas feminist critics in general have sometimes been criticized for having too little to say about the quality of literary texts, those concerned with issues of power and economics have been especially chided for their lack of attention to questions of aesthetic value. More interested in the sociological aspects of texts than in making a close reading of them, these readers have an especially political intent. Many of the English feminist critics who work from a Marxist perspective would belong to this group.

Critics who take this approach would be interested in the letters of Abigail and John Adams, because they show contrasting views of labor and economics. Hers express concern for the state of their personal property. She comments that their house, left empty by a doctor who has now moved on, is like a new asset, because it was worthless to them while it was occupied. She has asked a friend to take stock of what is left, as part of the process of evaluating their holdings. The house has been left dirty, obviously an objectionable state, but one that is less distressing than its destruction would have been. She also mentions the fate of others whose homes have been used by the enemy, noting that in some cases the inhabitants have left rent for their use or for damage done to furniture. She even mentions the state of the president's "mansion-house." Abigail's is a practical inventory of households—her own, those of her neighbors, and those of their leaders.

John, too, makes observations about the economy, but they are less personal than those of his wife. Attracted to an analysis of the broader situation, he is more philosophical than she. Speaking of the defense of Virginia, he comments, "The gentry are very rich, and the common people very poor. This inequality of property gives an aristocratical turn to all their proceedings." He recognizes the value of a less hierarchical society, one in which the classes are less distinctly defined. When he mentions their personal holdings, he maintains his impersonal tone, referring to "a certain house in Queen Street" rather than naming it as their own. He assumes the same attitude he held toward the "aristocratical turn" of the Virginians and applies it to his own family, warning, "Whenever vanity and gayety, a love of pomp and dress, furniture, equipage, buildings, great company, expensive diversions, and elegant entertainments get the better of the principles and judgments of men or women, there is no knowing where they will stop, nor into what evils, natural, moral, or political, they will lead us." His call for less attention to material acquisition and his desire for a less hierarchical society foreshadow the ideas to be later espoused by the Marxists.

The division of labor between man and woman, husband and wife, is also clear in these letters. It is John's duty to be away directing the affairs of the colonies, but Abigail is expected to remain at home with the family. Such a situation is not surprising in the eighteenth century. More interesting is the nature of the work they are expected to do. Whereas John's may involve physical courage but probably has more to do with using his authority to plan operations and direct groups of people, Abigail's responsibility for maintaining the family is considerably more lowly. In answer to his inquiry as to whether she has yet made saltpeter, she replies that she will try to do so after she makes soap and remarks that making clothes for the family takes much of her time. In addition, she is concerned about planting and sowing, about finding and providing food for all.

Finally, despite the candor with which Abigail presents her case to John regarding her desire for the equality of women, the terms she uses and the spirit in which he receives them indicate the reality of their relationship. She charges men with being "naturally tyrannical," acknowledges that they hold "the harsh title of master," and implores him to "put it out of the power of the vicious and the lawless to use us with cruelty and indignity with impunity." Despite his comments elsewhere about the desirability of equality among people, he fails to take her seriously. As he says, "As to your extraordinary code of laws, I cannot but laugh."

Obviously Abigail and John Adams do not belong to any of the minority groups named here. They were white, Anglo-Saxon founders of the United States, members of what in retrospect is definitely deemed to have been the "inner circle." They lived in Boston, a cultural city, had access to education, and through John wielded power and made policy. What would the minority feminist critics make of their correspondence?

Although there would seem to be less here for the minority critics to address than there is for the other groups of feminists, the final paragraph in John's letter is significant where their interests are concerned. In it he mentions, in a lighthearted manner, a number of minority groups: apprentices, students, Indians, "negroes," and "another tribe," women. Later he refers to "Tories, land-jobbers, trimmers, bigots, Canadians, Indians, negroes, Hanoverians, Hessians, Russians, Irish Roman Catholics, Scotch renegadoes," too. Clearly his intent is to treat the matter with humor, but by linking Abigail's "foolish" request with the unruly conduct of what he considers to be groups under the control and domination of their betters, he reveals his own prejudices. He betrays his own sense of superiority, his acceptance of the right to oppress and repress, despite his protestations against aristocracy. It could be charged, and certainly would be by minority feminists, that such attitudes are at the root of the racial and ethnic divisions that have marked the entire course of American history.

Studies of the Female Experience

The interest of some feminists in probing the unique nature of the female personality and experience has led the critics and writers among them to try to identify a specifically female tradition of literature. Such explorations have been particularly interesting to French feminists, who have found in Jacques Lacan's extensions of Freudian theory a basis for resisting the idea of a stable "masculine" authority or truth. Rejecting the idea of a male norm, against which women are seen as secondary and derivative, they call for a recognition of women's abilities that goes beyond the traditional binary oppositions such as male/female, and the parallel oppositions of active/passive, intellectual/emotional. Searching for the essence of feminine style in literature, they examine female images in the works of female writers and the elements thought to be typical of *l'écriture feminine*—such as blanks, unfinished sentences, silences, and exclamations. Early female images and goddesses become important as symbols of the power of women to resist and overcome male oppression. Images of motherhood are significant too, for childbearing and rearing involve power and creation. Of course, this approach runs the risk of creating female chauvinists who argue for a special, superior gender. It also risks creating a ghetto in which women's writing stands separate from the male tradition and is thereby weakened.

One such critic who has been influenced by Lacan is Hélène Cixous, who in "The Laugh of the Medusa" (1976) explores the nature of the female unconscious and issues a call for women to put their bodies into their writing. Connecting female writing with Lacan's Imaginary Order, a prelinguistic phase characterized by oneness between the child and the mother, she sees women's writing as coming from a primeval space that is free of the elements of Lacan's Symbolic Order, such as the Law of the Father. In it the Voice of the Mother becomes the source of feminine power and writing. Cixous's visionary perspective, which calls upon women to invent their own language, possibly heads toward the terminal marginalization of women's writing, despite the passion with which it is put forth.

Whereas feminists have often reacted negatively (even angrily) to some of Freud's idea about women—for example, that women suffer from an inevitable penis envy that makes them see themselves as *hommes manqués,* since Lacan, some of these feminists have been able to accept the "phallus" as a symbolic concept, using it as it once was used in ancient fertility cults. From him they take the position that males and females alike lack the wholeness of sexuality of full presence, leaving both with a yearning that can never be filled.

Abigail Adams would not have been able to think of herself in such terms, but throughout her letters it is clear that she looks at life around her and at her own responsibilities in a way that John does not. She is the nurturing caretaker of the family, fulfilling the expected, stereotypical female role. She offers, for example, to copy and send the instructions for the "proportions of the various sorts of powder fit for cannon, small-arms, and pistols" if it would be useful to John.

However, Abigail is more than just a helpmate or facilitator. She is a thinking individual, one who reverses the rational/irrational binary. John engages in a serious conversation with her about "Dunmore," and it is clear that he values her intellectual grasp of the situation. Her accounts of the work she does to maintain the household—making clothes, soap, and perhaps saltpeter—are evidence of the reversal of the active/passive binary often invoked in regard to male/female. She is a hardworking, involved, industrious woman, without whose efforts and energies the family, and by extension the society, could not survive.

Rhetorically, as noted in the discussion of studies of power, Abigail is careful to write what is likely to be pleasing to John. She inquires about his work, reiterates the rightness of the cause for which he is fighting, speaks at length about personal matters, and reveals her own feelings. Her voice is not that of her husband, even when she agrees with his sentiments. It is a distinctly female voice full of concern for others that comes from a particularly personal perspective.

WRITING FEMINIST CRITICISM

For those readers who are interested in examining issues concerning women and literature but who do not have a defined agenda to follow or promote, making a feminist reading of a male author's text (which includes most of the canon) involves realizing from the outset that it is androcentric and resisting that point of view. It means not necessarily reading from a traditionally male perspective. How does that resistance take place? For a female reader, it involves consciously refusing to reverse her role (that is, take on a male one) in order to identify with a male protagonist or to share a male point of view of a narrative. Instead of assuming that the masculine point of view, system of values, or manner of thinking is the universal norm, she will recognize that there is an alternative perspective: a woman's. Without such realization the female reader finds herself in a double bind. She is expected to identify with the male perspective while being reminded that to be male is not feminine. For a male feminist reader, it means adopting a new and possibly surprising perspective, that of trying to experience the narrative through the lens of the opposite gender. Of course, making a feminist reading of a feminist text means using a different approach. Instead of resisting, the reader will try to connect, try to find commonality and community.

A feminist reader will also look out for new female writers as well as help revive interest in forgotten or ignored ones. A study by Nina Baym showed that as late as 1977 the American canon of major writers did not include a single female novelist, even though female novelists have been a significant force in the field since the mid-nineteenth century. An androcentric canon generates androcentric interpretation, which leads to canonization of androcentric texts and the exclusion of gynocentric ones. The feminist reader will try to reverse that process by asserting the quality of texts produced by particular female writers, finding and promoting undervalued writers from the past, questioning the values that underlie literary acceptance, and defining a female tradition of letters. She will also make alternative readings of traditional works.

Prewriting

If you have the opportunity to choose the text you will examine for your feminist critique, you may want to select something by a female writer, especially if the work has not already received a good bit of notice from feminist critics. Regardless of the selection you are working on, you will initially find it helpful to focus on the characters in the text. They are an easily accessible indication of the author's attitudes and ideology. Some of the questions you can ask include the following:

- What stereotypes of women do you find? Are they oversimplified, demeaning, untrue? For example, are all blondes understood to be dumb?
- Examine the roles women play in a work. Are they minor, supportive, powerless, obsequious ones? Or are they independent and influential ones?
- Is the narrator a character in the narrative? If so, how does the male or female point of view affect the reader's perceptions?
- How do the male characters talk about the female characters?
- How do the male characters treat the female characters?
- How do the female characters act toward the male characters?
- Who are the socially and politically powerful characters?
- What attitudes toward women are suggested by the answers to these questions?
- Do the answers to these questions indicate that the work lends itself more naturally to a study of differences between the male and female characters, a study of power imbalances between the sexes (or perhaps other groups), or a study of unique female experience?

Drafting and Revising

Once you have determined which of the three approaches you want to follow, or how they work together to form the text, you can begin drafting your analysis.

The Introduction

One interesting way to open your discussion is to point out why a feminist critique is particularly appropriate for the text you are analyzing. For example, many established works have acquired traditional readings that can be challenged from a new point of view. You can easily explain that you intend to show why the accepted understanding is not the only possibility. In the case of the letters exchanged by John and Abigail Adams, for example, such an explanation would point out that it is his writings that are ordinarily examined by historians, not hers. Because she presents a different perspective on some of the same incidents and experiences he observed, her writings also deserve attention. Other rationales for a feminist analysis may lie in the characters, the situation, the cultural context in which a text was produced, or the author. Whatever your reason for making a feminist reading, explaining why it is a fitting one will help your reader follow the analysis more easily.

An alternative beginning is to connect the characters or events of the situation with one that has actually occurred. Because many feminist critics see literature as a way to understand and reform society, making such a connection can be powerful.

The Body

Because feminist studies serve so many different interests, your discussion can take a wide variety of approaches. To simplify your decision making, you can try working within one of the three categories discussed earlier: studies of difference, studies of power, or studies of the female experience. Of course, these are overlapping areas of attention, but you will probably want to center your analysis in one of them.

If the issue of gender differences attracts your attention, you will almost certainly want to select a work by a female writer for your study since you will be looking for what makes a female text different from one written by a male. You can ask questions such as the following:

- Is the genre one that is traditionally associated with male or female writers?
- Is the subject one that is of particular interest to women, perhaps one that is of importance in women's lives?
- What one-word label would accurately capture the voice of the narrator? Why is it appropriate?
- Is the work sympathetic to female characters?
- Are the female characters and the situations in which they are placed presented with complexity and in detail?
- How does the language differ from what you would expect from a writer of the opposite gender?
- How does the way the female characters talk influence the reader's perception of them?
- What are the predominant images? Why (or why are they not) associated with women's lives?
- Does the implied audience of the work include or exclude women? In the case of a male writer, is the work addressed to a mixed audience, or does it sound more like one man telling a story to another man?
- How do the answers to these questions support a case for this work's having been written in a particularly masculine or feminine style?

If you are interested in the relationships of the characters or in how things get done in the world of the text, you will probably investigate the balance (or imbalance) of power depicted in it. The following questions can help you arrive at some conclusions. Some of them are similar to those you asked while you were prewriting.

- Who is primarily responsible for making decisions in the world depicted: men or women?
- Do the female characters play an overt part in decision making? Or do they work behind the scenes?
- Who holds positions of authority and influence?
- Who controls the finances?
- Do the female characters play traditional female roles? Or do they assume some unusual ones?
- Are there any instances in which women are unfairly treated or ill treated?
- What kind of accomplishments do the female characters achieve?
- Are they honored for their accomplishments?
- Do the male characters consult the female characters before taking action, or merely inform them of it?
- Does the story approve or disapprove, condemn or glorify, the power structure as revealed by your answers to these questions?
- How is the female reader co-opted into accepting or rejecting the images of women presented in the work?

You may be interested in examining how the unique female experience is captured in the work you are to analyze. If so, you will want to consider questions like the following:

- Does the text reject the idea of a male norm of thinking and behavior that is stable and unchanging? If so, where?
- Is the writer's style characterized by blanks, gaps, silences, circularity?
- Are images of the female body important in the text?
- Are there references to female diseases or bodily functions?
- Do motherhood or those attitudes and behaviors characteristic of motherhood figure significantly in the text?
- Can you find instances in which the traditional binaries of male/female, intellectual/emotional, objective/subjective, and active/passive are reversed?
- What new circumstances do the reversals suggest?
- Can you find instances in which wholeness rather than otherness is associated with the female characters?
- What generalizations about the uniqueness of the female experience can you make based on the answers to these questions?

The Conclusion

The end of your paper is an appropriate place to state the generalizations and conclusions drawn from your questions. It should pull all of your references to the text into a single statement about what is particularly female (or male) about the way the work was written, about the power relationships depicted in it, or about its presentation of the nature of the female experience.

GLOSSARY OF TERMS USEFUL IN FEMINIST CRITICISM

Androcentric A term used to describe attitudes, practices, or social organizations that are based on the assumption that men are the model of being.

Gynocriticism A movement that examines the distinctive characteristics of the female experience, in contrast to earlier methods that explained the female by using male models. As applied to literature, gynocriticism is concerned with developing new ways to study the writing of women. Elaine Showalter designates four such perspectives: biological, linguistic, psychoanalytic, and cultural.

Imaginary Order A term used by Jacques Lacan to refer to the psychic stage during which the infant begins to recognize its separateness from other objects and to develop a sense of self.

L'Écriture feminine A term used by French critics to designate women's writing that has as its source the wholeness of Lacan's Imaginary Order.

Misogyny The hatred of women.

Oedipal attachment Sigmund Freud's theory that around the age of five a boy perceives his father to be a rival for the love of his mother.

Patriarchy A social system that is headed and directed by a male.

Symbolic Order A term used by Jacques Lacan to refer to the psychic stage in which an individual learns language and it shapes his identity.

RECOMMENDED WEB SITES

http://www/uni-koeln.de/phil-fak/englisch/datenbank/e_index.htm

Gender Inn, a searchable database providing access to more than 6,000 records pertaining to feminist theory, feminist literary criticism, and gender studies focusing on English and American literature. It also provides bibliographies on some areas of women's and gender studies. It is available in both English and German.

http://www.cddc.vt.edu/feminism/enin.html

A feminist theory Web site that includes more political theory than literary theory.

http://www.york.ac.uk/services/library/subjects/women/bibliographies/research_methods.htm

An annotated bibliography.

http://www.feminist.org/research/chronicles/biblio.html

A bibliography of American feminist issues.

http://www.york.ac.uk/services/library/subjects/women/bibliographies/literary_criticism.htm

An annotated bibliography of feminist aesthetics in literary, performing, and visual arts in 1970–1990.

http://www.york.ac.uk.services/library/subjects/women/bibliographies/feminist_methods.htm
Feminism, science, logic of inquiry, and methodology, with emphasis on social sciences, teaching, and research bibliography.

http://www.igc.apc.org/women/feminist.html
Links to feminist resources and concerns.

http://www.igc.apc.org/women/bookstores/widenets.html
Feminist bookstores worldwide.

http://www.ecoethics.net/bib/1997/clca-015.htm
A bibliography on ecofeminism.

SUGGESTED READING

Barrett, Michele. *Women's Oppression Today: Problems in Marxist Feminist Analysis.* London: Verso Editions, 1980.

Braidotta, Rosi. *Nomadic Subjects.* New York: Columbia Univ. Press, 1994.

Butler, Judith. *Gender Trouble: Feminism and the Subversion of Identity.* New York: Routledge, 1999.

Chodorow, Nancy. *The Reproduction of Mothering: Psychoanalysis and the Sociology of Gender.* Berkeley and Los Angeles: Univ. of California Press, 1999.

Cixous, Hélène. The Laugh of the Medusa. *Signs* 1 (1976): 875–893.

de Beauvoir, Simone. *The Second Sex.* Trans. H. M. Parshley. New York: Knopf, 1993.

Fetterly, Judith. *The Resisting Reader: A Feminist Approach to American Fiction.* Bloomington: Indiana Univ. Press, 1978.

Friedan, Betty. *The Feminine Mystique.* New York: Norton, 1997.

Gates, Henry Louis, Jr., ed. *Reading Black, Reading Feminist: A Critical Anthology.* New York: Meridian, 1990.

Gilbert, Sandra M., and Susan Gubar. *Madwoman in the Attic: The Woman Writer and the Nineteenth-Century Literary Imagination.* 2d ed. New Haven, Conn.: Yale Univ. Press, 2000.

Green, Gayle, and Coppélia Kahn, eds. *Making a Difference: Feminist Literary Criticism.* New York: Routledge, 1991.

Greer, Germaine. *The Female Eunuch.* New York: Farrar, Straus and Giroux, 2001.

Gubar, Susan. *Critical Condition: Feminism at the Turn of the Century.* New York: Columbia Univ. Press, 2000.

Heilbrun, Carolyn. *Hamlet's Mother and Other Women.* New York: Columbia Univ. Press, 1990.

Jackson, Stevi, and Sue Scott, eds. *Feminism and Sexuality.* New York: Columbia Univ. Press, 1996.

Meese, Elizabeth. *Crossing the Double-Cross: The Practice of Feminist Criticism.* Chapel Hill: Univ. of North Carolina Press, 1986.

Millett, Kate. *Sexual Politics.* Urbana: Univ. of Illinois Press, 2000.

Sedgwick, Eve. *Epistemology of the Closet.* Berkeley and Los Angeles: Univ. of California Press, 1990.

Showalter, Elaine, ed. *The New Feminist Criticism: Essays on Women, Literature, and Theory.* New York: Pantheon, 1985.
Warner, Michael, ed. *Fear of a Queer Planet.* Minneapolis: Univ. of Minnesota Press, 1993.
Wollstonecraft, Mary. *A Vindication of the Rights of Woman.* New York: Whitston, 1982.
Woolf, Virginia. *A Room of One's Own.* Bath, England: Chivers Press, 1999.

MODEL STUDENT ANALYSIS

The Masculine Sex-Parasite in Edith Wharton's "The Other Two"

Connie Herndon

> As her own memoirs and those of others make clear, Wharton was emphatically not a feminist in the ordinary sense of the word. On the contrary, she seems often to have gone out of her way to present herself as an old-fashioned "man's woman" who felt nothing but contempt for New Womanly strivings.
>
> Sandra M. Gilbert and Susan Gubar

In a chapter entitled "Angel of Devastation: Edith Wharton on the Arts of the Enslaved," Sandra M. Gilbert and Susan Gubar explore the contradictions between Edith Wharton's personal stance toward feminism, indicated above, and the feminist nature of her fiction. They argue that "despite all th[e] evidence that Edith Wharton was neither in theory nor in practice a feminist, her major fictions, taken together, constitute perhaps the most searching—and searing—feminist analysis of the construction of 'femininity' produced by any novelist in this century" (128). Thus, Wharton may be considered a professed nonfeminist who wrote feminist texts. Before reading anything about Edith Wharton herself, I sensed this contradiction regarding feminism when I read her short story "The Other Two." The story left me with mixed feelings and curiosity about Wharton's intentions regarding the interpretation of the female character, Alice Waythorn. With guidance from Gilbert and Gubar, I have better understood my frustrations and arrived at an interpretation of Alice Waythorn as a sacrificial example of Wharton's refusal to "elaborat[e] full-scale fantasies about the liberation and gratification of female desire or about the unleashing of female power" (Gilbert and Grubar, 129). In other words, Alice Waythorn is a typical rendering of Wharton's scathing view of the social system that produced female "sex-parasites" and that, to Wharton, seemed largely beyond reform (Gilbert and Gubar, 129).

Barbara A. White says that "The Other Two," which was published in 1904 as one of a collection of short stories entitled *The Descent of Man and Other Stories,* "depicts a newly married person's disillusionment with an initially admired spouse" (57). Although this is certainly true, I have already indicated that the story is meant to involve the female reader in a type of disillusionment also. To explain this opinion, the specifics of the situation that provides the subject of the story need to be reviewed. The "disillusioned married person" to whom White refers is Mr. Waythorn, newly married to Alice Waythorn, who has been married twice before her marriage to him. Though Mr. Waythorn, in the beginning, does not think he will have a problem with his wife's past, he has wrongly "fancied that a woman can shed her past like a man" (Wharton, 99). When he discovers that she cannot, that "Alice was bound to hers both by the circumstances which forced her into continued relation with it, and by the traces it had left on her nature" (Wharton, 99), he is disillusioned with her, thinking of her as, among other things, "a shoe that too many feet had worn" (98). "The circumstances which forced her into continued relation with [her past]" are that she has a child by the first husband and that her second husband has business dealings with Mr. Waythorn's firm. Thus, Mr. and Mrs. Waythorn find themselves constantly thrown together with one or the other (and, at the end, both) of Alice's ex-husbands. Mr. Waythorn's attempts to deal with this situation within proper social confines, as well as with the growing disillusionment he has with his wife as a result of it, make up this story.

The aspect of "The Other Two" that at first led me down a "feminist" path in my interpretation is the stereotypically oppressive character of Mr. Waythorn. As a woman, I am offended by his possessiveness, especially in the following passage when, watching Alice, he thinks, "They were his, those white hands with their flirting motions, his the light haze of hair, the lips and eyes. . . ." (83, Wharton's ellipsis points). Having been disturbed by recent manifestations of his divorced wife's past, including the immediate presence of her two ex-husbands in his life, Mr. Waythorn finds relief only in the feeling of ownership toward his wife. He feels comforted only when he objectifies and imaginatively dismembers the parts of her body and calls them his own. As a woman, I am deeply offended by this behavior, which Wharton describes as his "yielding again to the joy of possessorship" (83). Wharton's illustration of such behavior is clearly critical and meant to provoke female readers.

And yet, as my sympathies move away from Mr. Waythorn, they don't find a resting place with Alice Waythorn either. Though she is the object of her husband's oppressive views toward women, Alice seems never to be touched by his prejudices and, therefore, does not seem victimized by them. Though Mr. Waythorn's character provokes my anger, Mrs. Waythorn's character does not provoke my sympathy nor my loyalty. Gilbert and Gubar discuss what some critics have called Wharton's "'limitation of heart'—her apparent lack of sympathy for her characters, her coldness." (131). To Gilbert and Gubar, this accusation from critics can be explained as a "misperception of the grim delight with which she forced herself, and her readers, to face the social facts that made her women (and their men) what they were" (131). Thus, Wharton's lack of sympathy for Alice Waythorn has a purpose and is indicative of her attitude toward her characters in general.

But more than a lack of sympathy for Alice is at work in my response to the story. Not only is there a lack of sympathy for her character, but there is also a feeling of disapproval and repulsion toward her. To understand why, the characters of both Mr. and Mrs. Waythorn must be more carefully considered. There are two issues to be discussed. One is the crossing of masculine and feminine stereotypes in the characters (Mr. Waythorn is more feminine and Alice Waythorn more masculine). Second, there is the presence of the "sex-parasite" in Alice.

Upon finding Mr. Haskett (Alice's first husband) in his house the first time, Mr. Waythorn handles and thinks of himself thusly: "In his own room he flung himself down with a groan. He hated the *womanish* sensibility which made him suffer so acutely from the grotesque chances of life" (88, emphasis added). In this and numerous other examples, Mr. Waythorn is portrayed as having stereotypically feminine qualities. He is constantly worried about appearances, as when he is caught on the train with Varick (Alice's second husband) and sees someone he knows. When he "had a sudden vision of the picture he and Varick must present to an initiated eye, he jumped up with a muttered excuse" (79). Also, he is worried about appearances when Varick must come to visit him at his office to do business. Waythorn demonstrates his "womanish" concerns over propriety when, "waiting in his private room, [he] wondered what the others thought of it. . . . Waythorn could fancy the clerks smiling behind Varick's back as he was ushered in" (85). And, elsewhere, at the very beginning of the story, Waythorn reflects that "Her [Alice's] composure was restful to him; it acted as ballast to his somewhat unstable sensibilities" (72). In another instance, Waythorn is described as "always refus[ing] to recognize unpleasant contingencies till he found himself confronted with them, and then he saw them followed by a spectral train of consequences" (95). Waythorn's tendencies toward "unstable sensibilities," his oversensitive regard toward keeping up appearances, and his habit of avoiding and then overdramatizing problems are all stereotypes of the foolish and numskull female that are so familiar to us. Wharton's inversion of them, placing them within the foolish and offensive male character is a clever way to undermine such stereotypes.

On the other hand, Alice Waythorn is nearly the opposite of her husband, having "perfectly balanced nerves" as perceived by him (Wharton, 72). Furthermore, he characterizes her as having "a way of surmounting obstacles without seeming to be aware of them" (75). When he is still worrying about the upcoming visit of Mr. Haskett to their home, he looks at Mrs. Waythorn and notes that "she had obeyed his injunction and forgotten" about it (77). Of course it is her emotional control and ability to adapt to changing situations that eventually comes to burden Waythorn: "The fact that Alice took her change of husbands like a change of weather reduced the situation to mediocrity. He could have forgiven her for blunders, for excesses; for resisting Haskett, for yielding to Varick; for anything but her acquiescence and *her tact*" (99, emphasis added). Thus, Alice Waythorn is given all the stereotypically "masculine" characteristics that have been traditionally associated with the "strong male." The question to be addressed now is how to regard Alice's masculine qualities.

In thinking about the masculine qualities described in Alice Waythorn, it is important to consider another aspect of her character, an aspect that Gilbert and Gubar attribute to what they call the "sex-parasite." Quoting from Olive Schreiner in *An Olive Schreiner Reader,* Gilbert and Gubar (63) define the sex-parasite as "the effete wife, concubine or prostitute, clad in fine raiment, the work of others' fingers; fed on luxurious viands, the result of others' toil; waited on and tended by the labour of others" (Gilbert and Gubar, 143). This clearly describes Alice Waythorn, who has gradually climbed the social ladder through her succession of husbands. Alice's movement up in the social structure is evident in Mr. Waythorn's shock at the social station that he observes in Alice's first husband, Mr. Haskett. Waythorn spends a good deal of time trying to imagine his wife in "a phase of existence so different from anything with which he had connected her" (Wharton, 89). Furthermore, though "Varick . . . was a gentleman" (89) and "[h]e and Varick had the same social habits, spoke the same language, understood the same allusions" (90), Varick is clearly not as "well off" as Waythorn is. This is seen in Waythorn's surprise when he learns of the nature of Mr. Varick's business with his firm: "Waythorn wondered vaguely since when Varick had been dealing in 'important things.' Hitherto he had dabbled only in the shallow pools of speculation, with which Waythorn's office did not usually concern itself" (19). Clearly, then, Alice Waythorn has been on the move up since her first divorce. Alice's long history as a "wife-prostitute" is further obvious in Waythorn's concession that it might be "better to own a third of a wife who knew how to make a man happy than a whole one who had lacked opportunity to acquire the art" (100). Alice Haskett, with all her training, is definitely a master of the "art" of making a man happy. And what she has gotten in return is an increasingly more prestigious and luxurious position in the social structure.

We cannot like Alice Waythorn, because she is a sex-parasite. And her masculine, independent ways ironically do not help us to like her. Wharton's presentation of the sex-parasite in Alice Waythorn is representative of the kind of woman she despised (Gilbert). And yet Wharton was fully aware of "the process by which women are socialized as prisoners of sex, and more specifically the horror (to the 'lady' herself and others) of the cultural techniques of feminization that created the female 'sex' parasite" (Gilbert and Gubar, 129). In other words, though she despised this type of woman, she fully understood her and might even have considered herself one, for becoming a sex-parasite was virtually inescapable in her given social structure. Alice, as sex-parasite, represents the contemporary unreformed woman of Wharton's time. While feminists around Wharton were looking for ways to escape such a destiny, "Wharton mostly saw signs that said NO EXIT" (Gilbert and Gubar, 129). I think Wharton's pessimistic views regarding the potential for reform are clear in "The Other Two." Alice's masculinity is, in some ways, a warning that reform will lead only to a different, yet equally disturbing role for women. In this case, the warning is that women may become more like men, who, after all, are the ones we as women least want to resemble. Mr. Waythorn, with all his feminine characteristics, is portrayed as being silly and, eventually, rather inconsequential. Certainly, this is what we, as women, are trying to move away from. And yet, at the end of the story, when Alice Waythorn clearly has the upper hand, we are not satisfied because she is too manlike—she is not the type of woman we want to be, even if that means we would have the greater measure of power.

Wharton's pessimistic views about the possibility of a better social situation for women often manifests itself in female characters who disillusion female readers acquainted with more conventional, more romantic, and optimistic feminist ideas. This is certainly the case in "The Other Two." And yet Wharton's nonfeminist feminism, in the end, is a potent form of social criticism. In her refusal to grant women "full-scale fantasies about the liberation and gratification of female desire or about the unleashing of female power," (Gilbert and Gubar, 129), Wharton exercises what we today call tough love. Unwilling to scratch only at the surface of the social dynamics that create us, she makes us look deeper and longer at the female beasts that we are. For, as is evident in Alice Waythorn, if women are to be the enlightened ministers of a more humane world, we must do more than become equal to men in the same social structures in which we live lives of oppression. Equality within corruption will not reform us. A new and better world will require new social structures and better human beings, both male and female in kind.

Works Cited

Gilbert, Sandra M., and Susan Gubar. *Sexchanges.* Vol. 2 of *No Man's Land: The Place of the Woman Writer in the Twentieth Century.* New Haven, Conn.: Yale Univ. Press, 1989.

Wharton, Edith. The Other Two. In *The Descent of Man and Other Stories* (New York: Charles Scribner's Sons, 1904), 71–105.

White, Barbara A. *Edith Wharton: A Study of the Short Fiction.* Twayne's Studies in Short Fiction 30. New York: Twayne Publishers, 1991.

7

Reader-Response Criticism

'Tis the good reader that makes the good book.
Ralph Waldo Emerson, American essayist, poet, philosopher

The name *reader-response* tells the story. This approach to literary criticism turns the spotlight on the reader, without whose attention and reactions the text would be inert and meaningless. In one sense, it would not exist at all. It would be like the proverbial tree that makes no sound when it falls because there is nobody there to hear it.

HISTORICAL BACKGROUND

Readers have always responded to what they read, of course, but with the advent of reader-response analysis, the worst fears of the formalists came true: the audience was expected to shake off its deference to the authority of the text (or published critic's or classroom teacher's explanation of the text) and become an active participant in the creation of meaning. The focus moved away from thinking of a work as a self-contained aesthetic object to considering the experience that transpires when the reader and the work come together. No longer could any reading be taken as unbiased and objective. The reader had moved to center stage.

The ancient Greek orators and rhetoricians, with their concern for how to move and persuade an audience, could be called the literary ancestors of today's reader-response theorists. Both Plato and Aristotle were aware of the power of words to stir or convince people, although they did not hold the same opinions about the impact of doing so. Whereas the former had serious misgivings about using literature to arouse people's emotions, the latter recognized in it the capacity to quiet and strengthen an audience, as, for example, a tragedy can effect a catharsis that cleanses people of debilitating feelings and attitudes. Aristotle also explored the many ways in which an argument can be made convincing to listeners, and he thereby influenced the concern of Longinus, Cicero, Quintilian, and rhetoricians to this day in making choices about organization and style that will cause what they have to say to appeal to a particular group of people.

The more recent lineage of the reader-response critics can be traced to the work of I. A. Richards in the 1920s and Louise Rosenblatt in the 1930s. Richards, recognizing the wide variety of interpretations that a group of readers is likely to have for a single work, asked his students at Cambridge to write responses to short poems so that he could analyze their approaches. At that point Richards backed away from becoming a fully developed reader-response theorist, however, because he went on to categorize the students' reactions according to their "accuracy." That is, he ranked them, depending on their closeness to or distance from what he deemed to be the correct interpretation. Rosenblatt, largely ignored by readers pursuing formalist principles of criticism at the time her first works were published, offered a "transactional" theory of reading. As she explained it, a given text is not always read in the same way. Instead, readings vary with the purpose, needs, and concerns of the reader, who adopts a "stance" toward a text, an attitude that determines what signals to respond to in a text so that certain results can be achieved. The two opposing stances are the "efferent" one, in which the reader concentrates on information to be extracted from the writing, and the "aesthetic," which involves senses, feelings, and intuitions about "what is being lived through during the reading event." A piece of literature comes into being when it receives an aesthetic reading, which is produced by a merging of reader and text. As Rosenblatt explained, "At the aesthetic end of the spectrum, . . . the reader's primary purpose is fulfilled *during* the reading event, as he fixes his attention on the actual experience he is living through. This permits the whole range of responses generated by the text to enter into the center of awareness, and out of these materials he selects and weaves what he sees as the literary work of art" (*The Reader, the Text, the Poem,* 27–28).

The early work of Richards and Rosenblatt received renewed attention with the appearance of Walker Gibson and Wayne Booth, who, around midcentury, raised questions about the roles readers play. Gibson, pointing out that a text asks a reader to become what he calls a "mock reader," reintroduced the reader who becomes a participant in the creative act by playing the role the writer has designed for her, and the issue of where and how meaning is created reemerged as a significant concern among literary theorists. Booth recognized that a writer controls a reader through rhetorical strategies but did not go so far as to give readers the principal responsibility for making meaning. By then, the question, simply put, had become, Does the interpretation of a text depend primarily on the reader, the text itself (which can manipulate the reader), or a combination of the two? Further questions ensued: What is a text? Is the reader the book holder? The reader conceptualized by the writer? An ideal reader?

Reader-response critics do not answer such questions with a single voice. In fact, their approaches cover such a wide variety of concerns that sometimes the term *reader-response* seems to refer to a chaotic jumble of theories that may or may not have anything to do with each other. They can, however, be said to agree on a few basic principles, the most important of which is that they are primarily interested in the effect that a work has on a reader and the strategies that produce that effect. Interpretation of meaning is assumed to be an act of reading, thereby making the ultimate authority not the writer or the text but the reader. A literary work becomes, then, an evolving creation, as it is possible for there to be many interpretations of the same text by different readers, or several interpretations by a single reader at different times. As Wolfgang Iser explained, "The significance of the work, then, does not lie in the meaning sealed within the text, but in the fact that that meaning brings out what had previously been sealed within us" (*The Act of Reading,* 157).

The result? When readers accept the assumption that there is no one true interpretation, they discover rich, complex, diverse possibilities. When they recognize that there is no right or wrong answer but instead a variety of readings that grow out of individual experiences and feelings, literature becomes alive for them. When their own lives intersect with the text, it takes on vitality. As Louise Rosenblatt explained, "The reader brings to the work personality traits, memories of past events, present needs and preoccupations, a particular mood of the moment, and a particular physical condition. These and many other elements in a never-to-be-duplicated combination determine his interfusion with the peculiar contradiction of the text" (*Literature,* 30). The effect is not limited to the understanding of a text, however. It extends to the understanding of the self as well. Because reader-response criticism calls for introspection and reflection on one's own values and beliefs, it can lead the reader to deeper personal knowledge and greater cultural awareness.

Not surprisingly, some critics object to the intense subjectivity of such an approach. If a poem can have as many meanings as it has readers, they ask, can there be any shared experience of it? Can there be an intellectual discussion of it? Others complain that digressions into self-analysis diminish textual analysis. It makes the reader's life the primary focus, rather than the literary work. Though such arguments may have some merit, there is little doubt that in the end a reader-response analysis powerfully engages readers to move analytically both inward and outward, finding meaning in the text, the self, and the world.

MAKING A READER'S RESPONSE

To understand the discussion that follows, you will need to read the short story "The Masque of the Red Death," by Edgar Allan Poe, which begins on page 252.

GETTING STARTED

For some people a reader-response approach is startlingly different from the approach they are accustomed to taking. Instead of memorizing historical information, recognizing literary forms and techniques, or learning a prescribed interpretation, you will be asked to look inside and around yourself for ways to make the work meaningful.

INTERACTING WITH THE TEXT

Although the focus is always on the reader, there are several ways of thinking about the relationship he has with the text. Rosenblatt describes two of them, then advocates letting them work together in an approach that she calls **transactional.** As she explains it, in "the actual reading event" it can be said that the reader interprets the text (the reader acts on the text). Or we can say, the text produces a response in the reader (the text acts on the reader). Each of these phrasings, because it implies a single line of action by one separate element on another separate element, distorts the actual reading process. The relationship between reader and text is not linear. It is a situation, an event at a particular time and place in which each element conditions the other.

In preparation for making a transactional analysis, one that shows how reader and text come together to create meaning, it will be helpful to consider how each of the two "linear" processes works: how the text controls the reader and how the reader makes the text.

The Power of the Text

When you examine how a text controls the reader's responses, you acknowledge that it is a powerful manipulator. As Henry James once commented, "In every novel the work is divided between the writer and the reader; but the writer makes the reader very much as he makes his characters" ("The Novels of George Eliot").

To examine a text looking for how it produces certain effects on a reader means looking at it in much the same way as the group of critics known as the **structuralists** do (see chapter 8). Both reader-response critics and the structuralists assume that because readers come to a work with a certain literary competence, or what Jonathan Culler calls a set of shared reading conventions, they recognize signals they are accustomed to finding there and use them to make the expected interpretation. They know how they are expected to respond, and they do. They use the familiar cues to make new interpretations. Looking at the text to see how it causes readers to react in certain ways, then, involves asking how the codes, signs, signals, and rules work together to produce meaning. It means examining the relationships among the parts in an effort to define the system, known as the **grammar,** that governs them. The able reader recognizes the grammar because of her own life experiences and her reading background.

If the meaning of a text is recognizable because "informed" readers know the accepted conventions that underlie it, a work cannot be subject to an infinite number of interpretations, making it less important for readers to record their personal responses than to make generalizations about how interpretation is governed by the system under which the text was written. Although critics who have a structuralist bent recognize that different interpretations will be produced by different readers, they focus on the regularities they find in readers' strategies. Such generalizations extend beyond the text in question too, for it is not autonomous; it exists in the context of other texts, with which it shares common elements and, hence, meanings.

It is important to realize that sometimes an author can use recognizable conventions to "fool" the reader. As Stanley Fish points out in *Surprised by Sin,* a text can use predictable responses, such as the expectations typically evoked by a particular genre, to cause readers to make interpretations that later prove to be wrong.

Consequently, readers must be sophisticated enough to make adjustments to their interpretations as needed.

If you are primarily interested in how the text controls your response, you will want to examine how it shows you what you are to be thinking and feeling as it unfolds. This may involve a consideration of the author's intention and how it was carried out. Certainly it will entail looking closely at each element of the work for what it implies about the reader's behavior.

In "The Masque of the Red Death," for example, the reader gradually moves from enjoyment of (and vicarious participation in) the lighthearted revelries of the courtiers to "unutterable horror" at the final "dominion" of the Red Death. The isolation of the setting, the images of silence and darkness, and the diction ("gaudy," "fantastic," "blood-tinted panes," "ghastly," "grotesque," "delirious fancies," "bizarre") imply a world in which madness is the norm and the supernatural rules. Indeed, every component of the story—plot structure; patterns of expectation and satisfaction or expectation and disappointment; characterization; revelations and reversals; contrasting elements; image; symbol; figurative language; tone—contributes to the mounting uneasiness and final terror experienced by the reader. Consider, for example, the description of the rooms, one small element of the tale. The progress through each of the seven (a magical number) disquiets the reader. They are "irregularly disposed," we are told, with a "sharp turn at every twenty or thirty yards." Their colors, repeated in the stained glass windows to produce a claustrophobic effect, move in a disturbing sequence from blue to purple, then green, orange, white, violet, and finally black that is accentuated by window panes of "scarlet—a deep blood color." It is a sequence that begins with suggested innocence (blue) and ends in mystery and death (black and blood color). Or consider the effect of the contrasting sounds in the story. We are told, for example, that "the wild music of the orchestra" and light laughter of the dancers are interrupted when the hour is "stricken" (a word that carries the suggestion of illness) by the ebony clock, which has a sound that is "clear and loud and deep and exceedingly musical, but of so peculiar a note and emphasis that . . . the giddiest grew pale." The sound of the clock is made even more ominous by its contrast with the jovial noises of the partygoers and its effect on them.

To examine how a text controls a reader's response, you will find it helpful to ask questions such as these:

- What did the author intend for you to feel while reading this work, and how did he or she make you feel it?
- What are you dependent on in this work to help you make sense of what you read, such as descriptive passages, the narrator's voice, and contrasting viewpoints of characters?
- Do the events fall into a pattern you have met before?
- Are there opposites in the text that surprise you? Inform you? Keep you from anticipating what is coming?
- How do your previous experiences with this genre set up your expectations for how this text will operate?

- What images and events in the story are you already conditioned to approve or disapprove?
- How does the point of view affect (or control) your understanding?
- What similarities do you recognize between this work and other works—for example, themes, setting, characters?
- How does the text call upon what you know of the world to produce your response to the work?
- Did it cause you to make interpretations that you had to revise later by making new and different ones?
- What events or experiences were you led to anticipate? What mysteries were you asked to solve? What judgments were you expected to make?

The Reader as Producer of the Text

When the focus is turned directly on the reader as the chief source of interpretation, all of your thoughts, experiences, fantasies, and beliefs play a part in creating meaning. You will bring to a text a multitude of qualities that are yours alone: expectations, prejudices, stock responses, values, personal experiences, gender, age, past readings, even the circumstances of the present reading. These forces, according to Norman Holland, make a given work serve "highly personal, even idiosyncratic ends."

According to Holland, who uses psychology to explain the process of reading, each child receives a "primary identity" from his mother. It is our understanding of the kind of person we are. Because an "identity theme," like a musical theme, can have variations while it remains central to our being, when we read, we play our identity theme by re-creating the text in our own image. We "use the literary work to symbolize and finally replicate ourselves." As we do so, we find the means to cope with fears and desires buried in our own psyches. Consequently, responses vary just as personalities do. No two people will work through a text in the same way or arrive at the same point of understanding. That is not to say that a text lacks its own themes and structure. Nevertheless, any interpretation of them is, in the end, subjective.

David Bleich bases his case for the importance of the reader on the denials of modern scientists (such as Thomas Kuhn) that an objective world of facts exists. Because what is observed is inevitably changed by the circumstances of the observation, there can be no knowledge except subjective knowledge. Bleich, applying such theories to literature, argues that a text does not exist outside its readers, who are the observers. Whatever is offered as an "objective" analysis actually has roots in a personal response, for instead of discovering meaning in a text, readers develop meaning for it. The process begins with the individual but is subsequently shaped communally through question, challenge, and amendment in a group setting. What becomes known as fact (what meaning is developed) depends, he says, on the needs of the community.

Stanley Fish, calling his approach "affective stylistics," argues that readers create a text as they read it—word by word and sentence by sentence. He is interested in how readers' responses develop as the words and sentences succeed each other one by one—that is, how the style affects the reader. In his later work he describes interpretation as the product of **interpretive communities,** groups of informed, linguistically competent readers who read and make meaning based on assumptions and strategies that they hold in common. He denies the existence of an individual, subjective response because, as he points out, we have all internalized interpretive strategies based on assumptions about literature that have come to us from our institutions and cultural groups. We may belong to more than one such community. As Fish explains the process, a reader does not make an individual response that is altered by negotiation with others' responses but instead makes a response that from its inception is the product of a wider community of readers who share certain assumptions about how a text is read. In these terms, readers do not interpret a text. They create it.

In the case of "The Masque of the Red Death," your response can be affected by a number of forces that lie completely outside the text. If you have already read a number of stories by Poe, you will probably begin this one expecting something out of the ordinary, probably something mysterious and scary. Anticipation based on experience will predispose you to accept a confrontation with the fantastic. Once you begin to read, you will notice that much is not told. Despite the seemingly detailed descriptions of the castle apartments, for instance, the reader is left to supply the exact images mentioned only as a "multitude of gaudy and fantastic appearances" created by the tripod "bearing a brazier of fire" and the visual outlines of the "glare and glitter and piquancy and phantasm" of the great fete. The way they take shape for you will depend on other fiction you have read, movies you have seen, or possibly places you have been. Your impression may be altered even by whether you are reading this story at home alone late at night or whether you are in the library browsing room at school on a sunny spring morning.

When so much importance is placed on individual responses or those of interpretive communities, it almost seems as if a text can mean anything a reader says it means. It is critical to remember, then, that "wrong" readings can exist even when the reader is using this reader-response model. Mistaking one word for another, or misunderstanding the definition of a word, for example, can lead a reader to make inferences that are clearly off the mark. Although a wide variety of interpretations of a single work are possible using this approach, some simply will not fit. To make sure your interpretation is on point, ask yourself how much of it includes various features of the text and how much of it deals with aspects that do not reflect the text.

The following questions can help you discover your role in creating the texts you read.

- What did you expect to feel while reading this work?
- What was unsettling in what you read?
- How did you adapt what made you uncomfortable so that it more clearly fit what you desired?
- With what or whom did you most closely identify in the work? What identification gave you the most pleasure? The most displeasure?
- Did the work fit your picture of the way life is?

- What adjustments did you have to make so that it did not challenge the world as you know it?
- What does the work fail to tell you about characters and/or events? What imaginary or personal material did you use to supply what was missing?
- What memories does this work recall for you?
- Can you be sure you have not simply misread a passage—for example, by making a vocabulary mistake?
- If you reread this work using a different strategy, how would it become a different work?

The Reader and the Text as Coproducers

In practice, most reader-response critics do not think singly about how a text affects the reader or how a reader creates the text. Instead, they tend to apply both perspectives interactively. They work from the assumption that it is in the meeting of the two shapers of meaning that literature is created. As Louise Rosenblatt argues, "'The poem' cannot be equated solely with either the text or the experience of a reader." Instead, it is the relationship that exists between them. The former serves as a pattern that controls what the reader can make of it. The latter is called upon to fill in gaps, to hypothesize, imagine, and in general be a coproducer of the text. The poem (or the story) is created by the transaction that goes on between the two creators. As a result, new readings of a given text are always possible, but a text cannot mean whatever a given reader chooses to think it means. Any reading must be true to the work and to the reader as well.

Another way of explaining the interaction of reader and text is offered by Wolfgang Iser, a German phenomenologist who argues that it is impossible to separate anything from the mind that knows it. That makes the reader and text cocreators of meaning. A literary work, Iser says, is an intended act of the consciousness of a writer, an artistic effort that is then reexperienced in the consciousness of a reader, who engages in an aesthetic endeavor. The text supplies the materials and determines the boundaries for the creative act of reading. It creates for itself an **implied reader** and uses certain structures to predispose the actual reader, who brings her own unique set of experiences to the act of reading the text, to respond as the implied one. (Both are competent to decode the text.) It engages "the reader's imagination in the task of working things out for himself." As readers give life to the material presented by the text, as they deal with its "indeterminacy," created by the missing material and information, they influence the effect of what has been written. If the work is successful, it supplies neither too much nor too little but simply guides readers through to self-discovery.

If Poe's story pulled you through the series of lurid chambers to the final acknowledgment of the presence of the Red Death, leaving you hardly breathing, eyes fixed intently on each line, then the story worked for you. You recognized that you were to be an imaginative reader who was able to disregard the limitations of a realistic setting and thereby responded to the swift pace and mounting intensity of the narrative. Perhaps you identified with the guests and shared their response to the entrance of the masked figure, which, the narrator explains, is marked by terror, horror, and disgust. On the other hand, if you were unwilling to succumb to such a surreal plot, finding it simply too unbelievable even to generate sweaty palms, it was not a success. Your job is to explain what the effect on the reader was and analyze how the text and the reader were responsible for it.

Taken one step further, the transaction may occur between the mind of the author and the mind of the reader. The group known as the Geneva critics, for example, try to enter the mental universe of a writer, experiencing his unique consciousness. Individual works of literature grow unimportant in this process, as the purpose is not to understand a single work but to reconstitute in criticism the world of the writer. The goal is to share the inner reality of the author by considering his entire output.

To use the transactional model, you can begin by asking yourself some of the following questions:

- What kind of reader is implied by this text? For example, does it address you as if you are intelligent and well-informed, or as if you are inexperienced and innocent?
- What aspects of the text invite you to respond as that implied reader?
- How do you as an actual reader differ from the one that is implied?
- What gaps and vague outlines did you find yourself filling in?
- How did your perceptions and responses change as the work unfolded? What caused them to change?
- What contradictions did you perceive in the text—for example, characters who represent differing viewpoints? How did you resolve them?
- What do you know of the author's intent?
- List the most vivid images you remember from the text. How have you reconstructed them from your own experiences?
- What experiences of your own have you used to visualize and understand those presented in the text?

Period Responses, The Receptionists

It should be noted that there is another, somewhat different, form of reader-response criticism that asks the critic to examine the public's response to authors and works in a particular era. Known as **reception theory,** it recognizes that readers in different historical periods are not likely to interpret or judge a given work in precisely the same way and that as literary fashions and interests change, the characteristics that find favor in one century may be disparaged in the next. The receptionists peruse newspaper articles, study magazine reviews, and read personal letters to find evidence of how the public once viewed written material. They try to determine the expectations that readers were likely to have at a given time, based on their understanding of genres, works, and language. They look for what Robert Jauss calls the **horizon of expectations** of the reading public—that is, what they valued and looked for in a work.

The focus of the receptionists is easily understood when considering works that have at some point in time been rejected by the reading public but at other times have been held in high esteem. For example, Kate Chopin's *The Awakening,* today a popular and frequently taught novel, was given a hostile reception by the critics of her day. Her depiction of Edna Pontellier, a woman who remained unapologetic for her sensuality, was called "trite and sordid," and the author as well as the novel were deemed to be unacceptable in polite society. The America of a century ago was not ready to admit such a frank portrayal of female desire and indulgence. Its horizon of expectations did not include stories of such behavior. Sometimes the process is reversed, and a work that is well received early on receives negative criticism later. Mark Twain's *Huckleberry Finn,* for instance, has had the curious history of being alternately revered and castigated as readers in different eras proclaimed it to be sensitive or insensitive to various social issues.

The receptionists, whose work leads to interesting inferences about readers, authors, and their works, cannot make a final evaluation of the worth of a poem or story, because they demonstrate how its appeal may change from one time to another. Instead, they engage the past in a dialogue with the present, helping readers view the work from contrasting historical and cultural perspectives.

WRITING A READER-RESPONSE ANALYSIS

PREWRITING

To find a starting point for exploring where your personal experience and the text converge, you will find it helpful to make a few personal observations before, during, and after reading the text. They will help you to discover interpretive points for discussion. It is easy to begin by asking questions like these before you even pick up the book.

- How do I feel about reading this piece? Am I eager to begin? Curious about what I will find? Reluctant because I haven't liked other works by the same author?
- What do I already know about this work or this author?
- What do I already know about the time, place, or characters it depicts?
- What does the title suggest to me?

Noting your responses in a journal or log during a first reading can help you make generalizations later. You may still be at the questioning stage when you do this, or your ideas may have reached an advanced degree of development. Regardless of how far along you are in your thinking, here are some suggestions for you to think about during the initial reading.

- Are there quotations from the work that you would like to copy and save?
- What questions would you like to ask the author?
- What objections would you raise to what you are reading?
- Where do you experience confusion, disagreement, approval, or any other attitude or feeling?

- Compose a descriptive paragraph, poem, or short narrative about an experience the text brings to mind.

You can also make short responses after the first reading. They may be appropriate for a journal entry, or you may write them as separate texts. You can

- Describe how you feel about the work as soon as you finish it.
- Write a brief summary of the plot.
- Freewrite on a single line from a poem or on a sentence from a piece of prose.
- Identify a line or an image that immediately caught your attention, or one that you remember clearly. Why do you find it to be powerful?
- Think of someone or some experience that a character or situation in this work brings to mind.
- List the things you like about the work. Why do you like them?
- List those aspects of it that bother you. Why do they bother you?
- Identify any passages you do not understand.
- Choose what you would tell someone about this work if you could make only one comment.
- Consider how you might have acted had you been one of the characters.
- What else would you like to know about the characters or events?
- What values, beliefs, or assumptions of your own does this work affirm? Which of your values, beliefs, or assumptions does it challenge?
- Compose a letter (not to be sent) to the author or to one of the characters.
- Speculate on who should play the various parts in a filmed version of the work.

Drafting and Revising

The Introduction

Because you are making a reader-response analysis, it is appropriate to involve your audience in the introduction to your essay. In other words, you can try to provoke a strong response from your own reader. One way of doing so is to begin by recounting an incident from the work that elicits a particularly powerful reaction or quote a passage that holds strong emotion for most readers. For example, Edgar Allan Poe's description of the mysterious stranger who suddenly appears at the ball in "The Masque of the Red Death" ("The figure was tall and gaunt, and shrouded from head to foot in the habiliments of the grave") is not likely to provoke an inattentive yawn from anyone who reads it. It can send shivers down the spine of even the most passive reader. An essay that begins by quoting such a line will catch a reader's attention, and it can also effectively lead into a more detailed examination of how the reader and text are responsible for making the literary work.

The Body

The core of your paper will explain how the text controls the understanding and sympathies of the reader, will identify the personal material you have put into the text, and will describe how the two interact to create the text. In other words, it will show how you acquired information about the text and what responses that information created.

Part of your discussion, then, will center on the guidelines embodied in the text. It will note stereotypes, point of view, connotations, patterns, metaphors, foreshadowing, and images that guide your responses. It will question the accuracy of the information that is given and the reliability of the various characters. It will remark on those instances in which only partial information is provided and where the reader knows more than the characters. Even points at which the reader is misled will be significant.

You may want to describe your general impression of the work or how your initial impression of it changed to your final judgment. You may even want to point out what you have found that was recognizable from your own experiences, both personal and literary. All the incidents and characters that produced either validation of or challenge to your sense of the world (noticeable because of your own comfort or discomfort on meeting them) will be noted. It may be helpful to profile the character with whom you most closely identified or the incident that gave you the most pleasure or pain. If you found yourself remembering a personal experience that made the text more credible or moving, you will want to include it here. If you supplied material by imagining events that did not actually take place, you should mention those fantasies or speculations that helped to explain a character's motivation or enhance a bit of action. If you made adjustments in how you initially saw the text so that it was more in keeping with your usual way of seeing things, you will have a direct means of discovering your part in making this text. Even the expectations you had before reading it may be significant in explaining how you created it.

Finally, you will have to explain what resulted when the text and the reader came together. You will be looking for how the text invites responses by predisposing the reader to read in certain ways, and you will examine how the images provided by the text are modified by the reader's personal experience. Although certain norms or values are proffered by the text, it is the reader who decides whether or to what degree they should be accepted or rejected. The critic's job is to raise meaningful questions and to look for meaningful answers. In the process, a new reading of the text may emerge, and the reader may be changed as well.

The Conclusion

The body of your analysis will have presented numerous observations backed up by even more citations from the text. The conclusion, then, is the place to pull all the disparate pieces of information together into generalizations about the text. It need not be lengthy, but it should state the major effects the work has had on a reader and the causes that produced those effects. Finally, the conclusion should include an evaluation of how effectively the text elicited the desired responses, how deeply the reader became involved in constructing the text, and how the work was enriched by the mutual participation of text and reader. In other words, how well did the process work?

GLOSSARY OF TERMS USEFUL IN READER-RESPONSE CRITICISM

Geneva critics Readers who examine recurring themes and motifs that reveal a writer's essential being. They try to chart the writer's spiritual journey.

Grammar The system of rules that directs literary interpretation.

Horizon of expectations The linguistic and aesthetic expectations of a reader.

Implied reader Wolfgang Iser's term for a reader with the skills and qualities required by a text for it to have the intended effect.

Interpretive communities Stanley Fish's term for groups of competent, even sophisticated readers who make meaning based on assumptions and strategies they hold in common.

Narratology The study of narratives that seeks to show how one story's meaning emerges from its general structure, as opposed to its individual theme.

Phenomenology A modern branch of philosophy that asserts the perceiver's central role in determining meaning.

Reception theory A historical approach to a work that involves examining the changing responses to it on the part of the general reading public over a period of time.

Semiotics A science of signs that studies how meaning occurs and how structures allow it to operate.

Structuralists Critics who analyze literature following principles of linguistic theory. They seek to uncover the rules and codes by which a work is written and read and thereby to reveal the grammar of literature.

Transactional analysis An approach advocated by Louise Rosenblatt in which the critic considers how the reader interprets the text as well as how the text produces a response in her.

RECOMMENDED WEB SITES

Researchers interested in reader-response criticism should do a search for "human computer interaction," because it is the theory most usually associated with web writing. You will also find the following Web sites to be helpful.

http://www.cnr.edu/home/bmcmanus/readercrit.html
A student's definition with good links to other sites.

http://www.hu.mtu.edu/reader/
Reader Online, an online journal devoted to reader-response criticism.

http://divinity.lib.vanderbilt.edu/div/2504/reader.htm
A bibliography.

http://www.mdk12.org/practices/good_instruction/projectbetter/elangarts/ela-28-30.html
A study of reader-response criticism in K–12 classrooms.

http://www.brocku.ca/english/courses/4F70/rr.html
A survey of different reader-response approaches.

Suggested Reading

Bleich, David. *Subjective Criticism.* Baltimore: Johns Hopkins Univ. Press, 1978.
Booth, Wayne. *Rhetoric of Fiction.* 2d ed. Chicago: Univ. of Chicago Press, 1983.
Culler, Jonathan. *Structuralist Poetics: Structuralism, Linguistics, and the Study of Literature.* Ithaca, N.Y.: Cornell Univ. Press, 1975.
Fish, Stanley. *Is There a Text in This Class?* Cambridge: Harvard Univ. Press, 1980.
———. *Surprised by Sin: The Reader in "Paradise Lost."* 2d ed. Cambridge: Harvard Univ. Press, 1998.
Freund, Elizabeth. *The Return of the Reader: Reader-Response Criticism.* New York: Methuen, 1987.
Gibson, Walker. "Authors, Speakers, Readers, and Mock Readers." *College English* 5 (1950): 265–269.
Holland, Norman. *Five Readers Reading.* New Haven, Conn.: Yale Univ. Press, 1975.
———. Hamlet—My Greatest Creation. *Journal of the American Academy of Psychoanalysis* 3 (1975): 419–427.
Iser, Wolfgang. *The Act of Reading: A Theory of Aesthetic Response.* Baltimore: Johns Hopkins Univ. Press, 1978.
Jauss, Hans Robert. *Toward an Aesthetic of Reception.* Trans. T. Bahti. Minneapolis: Univ. of Minnesota Press, 1982.
Mailloux, Steven. *Interpretive Conventions: The Reader in the Study of American Fiction.* Ithaca, N.Y.: Cornell Univ. Press, 1984.
Rosenblatt, Louise. Writing and Reading: The Transactional Theory. *Reader* 20 (fall 1988): 7–31.
———. *The Reader, the Text, the Poem: The Transactional Theory of the Literary Work.* Carbondale: Southern Illinois Univ. Press, 1994.
———. *Literature as Exploration.* 5th ed. New York: Modern Language Association of America, 1995.
Scholes, Robert. *Structuralism in Literature: An Introduction.* New Haven, Conn.: Yale Univ. Press, 1974.
Tompkins, Jane. *Reader-Response Criticism: From Formalism to Post-Structuralism.* Baltimore: Johns Hopkins Univ. Press, 1980.

Model Student Analysis

Eudora Welty's Portrayal of the American Nightmare: A Reader-Response Analysis of "Death of a Traveling Salesman"

Larry Singleton

Eudora Welty's introductory paragraph of "Death of a Traveling Salesman" ends with the narrator giving the reader an intriguing description of the protagonist, R. J. Bowman: "He was feverish, and he was not quite sure of his way." Unlike Bowman, who is in a state of perplexity, readers of fiction at the beginning of the twenty-first century feel more empowered and willing to interact and trust their impressions about the fiction they read. As students, we are expected to respond to literature texts rather than to wait in a state of bewilderment until our revered professors impart an interpretation found "within" the text. Specifically, reader-response approaches have great utility in opening up texts for students. One example is approaching Eudora Welty's "Death of a Traveling Salesman" from five reader-response perspectives: "textual," "social," "cultural," "experiential," and "psychological" (Beach, *A Teacher's Introduction,* 7–8). In doing so, the transaction of reader and text produces quite different and involved interpretations from those one would encounter in more traditional approaches such as New Criticism. The interaction of the aforementioned five elements enriches and expands the text instead of searching for only some specific "meaning" within the text.

Before utilizing these five reader-response perspectives, a brief plot summary may prove helpful. "Death of a Traveling Salesman" is centered around the plight of R. J. Bowman, a single and lonely traveling salesman who has sold shoes throughout Mississippi for the last fourteen years. Bowman falls ill; however, before recovering fully, he decides to continue his journey toward Beulah, Mississippi. This becomes both a physical and a spiritual journey when Bowman is "lost" on a back-country trail and his car ends up in a ravine. As part of his spiritual journey, Bowman discovers a cabin and finds a woman inhabiting it whom he believes to be fifty years old and who reminds him of the one significant woman in his life: his grandmother. Notably, Welty does not name this character. Later Bowman meets Sonny, the woman's husband, whom Bowman first misidentifies as her son. Sonny's attire, specifically his wide black hat similar to Bowman's, evokes connections with the Bowman family past. Sonny uses his mule to pull Bowman's car out of the ravine; and upon his return, Sonny offers Bowman some of his bootleg whiskey, and the supposedly middle-aged matron of the house prepares a meal, creating an atmosphere of communion for Bowman.

Later, appropriately in the light, Bowman discovers the matron of the house to be Sonny's young and pregnant wife. Consequently, he cannot deal with this "fruitful marriage" and flees into the night to his awaiting car. The short story ends with Bowman's crumpling onto the road while "hearing" his heart making exploding noises to protest his actions.

Although this plot summary is useful in giving the reader an overview of the short story, a closer examination of the "implied reader," one textual approach, also proves useful. The author certainly envisions a fairly well-read individual, for the title of this short story is very close to Arthur Miller's famous play *Death of a Salesman,* and this association is reinforced by the similar names of the two protagonists: Loman and Bowman. Additionally, both characters are "ill" (delusional) and have bought into the materialistic "American dream." Although Willy Loman has not found happiness in pursuit of such a vision of being successful rather than living a life of adventure in Alaska, he commits suicide by means of a car accident in order to provide his son, Biff, with the insurance money he needs to pursue his dream of owning a ranch. At least, Loman does exhibit compassion toward his son. In contrast, Bowman leaves Sonny and his wife all the money in his billfold before he leaves, a great display by Bowman but an insult to Sonny and his belief that helping someone in need is a matter of honor, not one of monetary compensation. Thus, Loman is more "alive" in commiting suicide than Bowman is when fleeing Sonny's shotgun house.

However, Welty provides the "implied reader" with notable patterns, images, and connotations that guide the reader's interpretation. The reader obviously cannot miss Welty's paradoxical pattern of "feverish" life and cold death: the sun is "keeping its strength," yet the time setting is winter. There is the "feverish" Bowman and thoughts of his "dead grandmother." This brings up another recurring image in the short story, that of Bowman as a child lying in his grandmother's bed: Bowman wishing "he could fall into the big feather bed," his visualizing a cloud in the sky as being "like the bolster on his grandmother's bed," and his car being "rocked . . . like a grotesque child in a dark cradle." Of course, the words *grotesque* and *dark,* juxtaposed with *child* and *cradle,* connote a paradox of young, energetic life with "dark" death. The paradoxical pattern also occurs in reference to the strange "grandmother" figure who sits in the dark with Bowman yet has images of light and life associated with her: her eyes possess a "curious dulled brightness," and she owns, in her dark abode, a "red-and-yellow pieced quilt that looked like a map or a picture, a little like his grandmother's girlhood painting of Rome burning." Then there are the connotations of the other two characters in the short story: Sonny, the bearer of fire, and Redmond, the possessor of fire.

This opposition within the text channels the reader's possible interpretations. The remainder of this essay will provide one such interpretation.

In addition to intratextual elements, there are notable intertextual connections worth noting. One cannot help but notice the impact of a physical setting of isolation on the protagonist, something commonly seen in many American writers but especially telling in southern writers such as William Faulkner, Robert Penn Warren, Flannery O'Connor, as well as Eudora Welty. The virtual "wilderness" in "Death of a Traveling Salesman" is a common setting in the works of these writers, one where protagonists are afforded a "communal opportunity" to come to terms with isolation from their past and ultimately with mankind.

There are other intertextual connections worthy of discussion. Upon first reading the description of the countryside ("desolate hill country") and of Bowman's car falling into a ravine, I could not help but think of Flannery O'Connor's short story "A Good Man Is Hard to Find." In this selection, the grandmother experiences a moment of grace and communion with humanity before being shot by the "Misfit." Even more so than Willy Loman, she finally "lives" at the moment of her death. This contrasts with the fleeing Bowman's behavior. O'Connor's grandmother comes to terms with her humanity and accepts the

"Misfit" as her own son before he shoots her. Unlike this dynamic character, Bowman has opportunity after opportunity to come to terms with his past and become a more feeling and "humane" individual rather than a robotic salesman delivering practiced lines; but he does not.

Speaking of the importance of grandmother characters in the fiction of southern women, I cannot overlook the parallels and differences in the roles of Welty's Phoenix Jackson character in "A Worn Path" and the Phoenix-like and grandmotherly-seeming wife in "Death of a Traveling Salesman." Both characters seem ageless and have a golden glow. In the latter's case, Welty repeatedly describes objects associated with Sonny's wife in terms of a Phoenix-consuming fire: a "yellow cowhide seat," the "yellow pine boards" of her house, her "red-and-yellow pieced quilt," as well as her glowing eyes and "shining" teeth. Connecting these two characters lends credence to Sonny's wife being unnamed, because she, unlike the Phoenix, is not a successful catalyst in the development of Bowman, who returns to his "old ways" at the end of the short story. In essence, one can view Bowman's attempted rebirth as abortive.

Other significant aspects of "Death of a Traveling Salesman" are the social and cultural implications of southern literature's emphasis on the importance of the past as an integral part of the present. Time is not a continuum but is overlapping. This has agrarian and regionalistic significance. In this text, Welty implies that Bowman is moving backward in time, back to the young life of his maternal grandmother and grandfather before the birth of his mother. In doing so, Bowman encounters ancestors who hold time-honored traditions of mythological proportions yet traditions in an agrarian society that give meaning and purpose to life (doing for others without expecting monetary reward, honoring rituals of starting a fire and preparing food). Conversely, Bowman's life is one of materialistic modernity, isolation, and lack of communion with others through time-honored rituals. He is a "lost" soul separated from his past as a southerner. In effect, he is a "robotic" and programmed shell of a a man, indicative of the plight of individuals living in the more technological, fast-paced, and capitalistic world of the twentieth century.

This interpretation has intertextual support in the form of Bowman's destination: Beulah, a land of peace in *Pilgrim's Progress.* However, Bowman does not come to terms with his past and does not experience peace at the end of his journey, since he suffers a relapse of his heart/soul condition at the end. This seems appropriate, given that textual connotations of Bowman's name suggest a bow, an incomplete circle.

However, I cannot pass judgment on Bowman. Experientially and psychologically, I see much of myself in his situation. Like Bowman, I am a single southerner who knows a little about his family heritage and occasionally travels the dusty backroads of a fading rural south. Most of what I know about family and the all-important past consists of memories, bits and pieces of narratives told to me by long-dead relatives; yet these long-ago events and people do come to mind at strangely odd times, often by association with other present-day events or objects and animals, such as antiquated tractors and horses pictured in newspaper or magazine articles. Many would dismiss such connections and say they don't have time for such "insignificant distractions" and "digressions." In my twenties, I was guilty of exhibiting this attitude. However, now that I am older, I no longer view such occurrences as "digressions."

In addition, I can understand Bowman's fixation with materialism as his "savior." As a young man in his mid-twenties, I did not spend a great deal of time with aging relatives who offered a wealth of information about family lore. Instead, I pursued working fifty to sixty hours a week doing public relations work for what I thought was excellent pay, my ticket to purchase a new VCR, new clothes, and a new car. After three years of self-imposed servitude to such a superficial view of life, and after the deaths of two close older relatives, I began to realize what sort of isolated pursuer of the American dream (the materialistic version) I had become. Like Loman and Bowman, I had forgotten the importance of family, the past, and the importance of substantive dreams.

Fortunately, I did receive the support of my quickly diminishing family to pursue the study of literature that has accentuated the importance of the past and facilitated my attempt to complete as much of my "circle" as I can. Without such support, my fate and Bowman's may have been rather similar. Thus, this selection has promoted a better understanding of individuals like Bowman and myself ten years ago: "feverish" and confused souls who are "not quite sure of [their] way."

Work Cited

Beach, Richard. *A Teacher's Introduction to Reader-Response Theory.* Urbana, Ill.: National Council of Teachers of English, 1993.

8

Deconstruction

Deconstruction's admirers see it as a way that begins to let us question the presuppositions of the language we think in. Its detractors condemn its subtle and convoluted readings as narcissistic self-reflexivity.

Shirley F. Staton

The term *deconstruction* sends many readers running for cover, partly because it is one of the most radical approaches to reading that has appeared on the scene, but also because its terminology presents difficulties of its own. Why, then, does anyone want to understand it or use it to read a poem or story? Perhaps the best answer is that it provides a way of playing with language and meaning that teases and delights. It is not a methodology or school or even a philosophy. Instead, it is, says its founder Jacques Derrida, a strategy, some "rules for reading, interpretation and writing."

HISTORICAL BACKGROUND

Deconstruction is the best-known (and most significant) form of literary criticism known as **poststructuralism,** and in fact many people use the terms interchangeably. To understand the revolution that poststructuralism has created in literary criticism, it is necessary to look at some of its predecessors, both structuralism—the movement that it both incorporates and undermines—and those that structuralism itself challenged.

The revolutionary nature of deconstruction can be summarized by saying that in general it challenges the way Western civilization has conceived of the world since Plato. More specifically, it overturns the principles that have provided basic beliefs about truth and meaning since the eighteenth-century French philosopher, scientist, and mathematician René Descartes (1596–1650) applied the rational, inductive methods of science to philosophy. Refusing to accept the truth of anything without grounds for believing it to be true, he began with the one thing he could know, that consciousness of his thinking proved his own existence. *"Cogito, ergo sum,"* he declared. "I think, therefore I am." From that one certainty all other knowledge could proceed. The Cartesian approach, which elevated the importance of reason over passion, superstition, and imagination as a means of finding truth in the natural world, has had an impact well beyond the eighteenth century. It has helped shape the thinking of humanists, artists, and philosophers into the twenty-first century, providing them with the conviction that they could make a better world. If meaning and truth could be found by thinking and acting rationally, humankind could solve social problems, cure illnesses, and create new technologies. In short, through the use of reason progress was possible, perhaps inevitable.

The confidence inspired by such a worldview came into question toward the end of the nineteenth century with a radical revisioning of "reality" that took place in a wide variety of disciplines. The long-held view of the world as a knowable, objective entity that could be discovered through direct experience of the senses encountered serious challenges in fields as diverse as physics, linguistics, anthropology, and psychology. In philosophy, for example, thinkers such as Friedrich Nietzsche (1844–1900) began to question the existence of objective truth. Nietzsche even announced the death of God. Believing that traditional values had lost their influence over people, he called for the creation of new values that could replace them. He foresaw a "superman" who was strong and independent, freed from all values except those he deemed to be valid. Using different terminology, spokespersons from other areas of study echoed his denial of an ultimate reality that is static, unified, and absolute, to be replaced by an understanding of the world as relativistic, dynamic, and open. In 1905, for example, Albert Einstein published a paper that would change scientists' understanding of time, space, and reality. His ideas about the velocity of light challenged the assumption that there is such a thing as time that all clocks measure. In other words, the concept of absolute time was replaced with time as relevant to motion. Such thinking represented a fundamental shift in the way we see ourselves and our world. Later it would lead to questions about the nature of human behavior, belief, and morality. "Is *everything* relative?" the twentieth century would ask.

The study of language was not immune from such probing. For two hundred years, language had been viewed as a transparent medium through which reality could be set down and shaped into an aesthetic form. Finding meaning, which was assumed to be present, required finding the words that corresponded to objects perceived. Literature was taken to be mimetic, reflecting and presenting truths about life and the human condition. Because texts depicted life in a powerful way, they were thought to have a life of their own that could be discovered and analyzed. Enter the critic, whose job was to reveal their value and meaning. For example, the formalists (the New Critics, as distinguished from the Russian formalists), who carried the nineteenth-century empirical worldview into the twentieth century, saw a poem as a self-sufficient object possessing unity and form, operating within its own rules to resolve ambiguities, ironies, and paradoxes (see chapter 3). They sought to determine not what the poem means but how it means. There was no doubt that with the application of intellectual analysis, an understanding of form would lead to meaning.

Although an occasional doubter complained about the cold, unemotional nature of the close readings of the formalists, there was no uncertainty about the presence of ultimate meaning.

The power of the formalists, and their nineteenth-century heritage, began to break down in literary criticism with the appearance of the **phenomenological critics,** who rejected the formalists' inability (or unwillingness) to question how readers know a literary work, as exemplified by their refusal to investigate the author's intentions. The phenomenologists, who believe that meaning resides not in physical objects but in human consciousness as the object is registered in it, emphasize the reader in making literature (see chapter 7). Instead of a single best reading of a text, they accept the possibility of many readings, because a text cannot exist separate from the individual mind that perceives it. It cannot be explained as something unto itself; instead, it can be explained as an effect on a reader, and that effect will be different for each reader because of the experiences each brings to the reading. In addition, readers are called upon to supply missing material, to fill in textual gaps. They will do so using their own experience with literature and life, thereby creating even more difference in interpretations. In other words, as in other fields, it is no longer a given in literature that truth is static, absolute, and unified. Now it is deemed to be relative, dynamic, and open.

From the early part of the twentieth century came another set of ideas that was to have a significant impact on how people understand the world. Called structuralism, it is, in its broadest sense, a science that seeks to understand how systems work. Those who practice it are not so much interested in the operations (or aesthetics or meaning) of a single entity as they are in trying to describe the underlying (and not necessarily visible) principles by which it exists. Assuming that individual characteristics that can be noted on the surface are rooted in some general organization, structuralists collect observable information about an item or practice in order to discover the laws that govern it. For example, a structuralist studying urban American architecture of the twentieth century will be interested in the characteristics of a single building only insofar as they provide data that help define the bigger category of architectural objects to which that building belongs. A structural anthropologist may examine the customs and rituals of a single group of people in some remote part of the world not simply to understand them in particular but to discover underlying similarities between their society and others. Because behaviors that on the surface appear to be vastly different from each other may beneath that surface have commonalities that link the human beings that practice them, observations of concrete local phenomena allow the researcher to support assumptions about human society that cross cultural boundaries. Claude Lévy-Strauss, for example, found the mythologies of various cultures often to be only different versions of the same narrative. Their basic similarities of structure, which he called mythemes, he judged to be reflective of human concerns that are not culturally bound. In short, structuralists are looking not for structures in a physical sense but for patterns that underlie human behavior, experience, and creation.

A critical question has to do with the source of the structures themselves. Traditionally it has been assumed that they resided in the physical world. Human beings found meaning in what they perceived outside themselves. However, the structuralists argue from a different direction. According to them, structure comes from the human mind as it works to make sense of its world. Any given experience, they say, is so full of information that it would be overwhelming if there were no way of ordering it. The mind's defense is to sort and classify, make rules of process—that is, create a structure. It is such conceptual systems that make it possible for individuals to distinguish one type of object from another or to differentiate among members of the same category. This fairly radical idea placed meaning in the mind of human beings, not in external, objective reality. It is a short step from there to the idea that language, not sense experience or modes of consciousness, shapes who we are, what we think, what we understand reality to be.

When the structuralist approach was applied to language, it caused a significant departure from the traditional methods of study practiced by nineteenth-century philologists, who had examined language **diachronically,** that is, by tracing how words evolved in meaning or sound over time. The philologists compared the changes they found with those that had occurred in other languages and looked for causes. Their work assumed that language was mimetic, not a system with its own governing rules but one that reflected the world. A word, to them, was a symbol that was equal to the object or concept it represented. In contrast, French linguist Ferdinand de Saussure, today generally regarded as the father of modern linguistics, began to use a **synchronic** approach, looking at a language at one particular time in search of the principles that govern its functions, principles of which its users might not even be consciously aware. His studies led him to reject the idea that language is simply a tool to be used to represent a preexistent reality. That is, he did not accept the idea that it is mimetic or transparent. Instead, he argued that language is a system that has its own rules of operations. He called those general rules ***langue*** and referred to the applications that members of a particular speech community make of them in their iterations as ***parole.*** In other words, *langue,* sometimes referred to as a grammar, is the system within which individual verbalizations have meaning, and *parole* refers to the individual verbalizations. The rules of *langue,* which the individual speaker absorbs as a member of a culture, are manifested in *parole.* In his efforts to identify and explain how all this works, Saussure swept away the nineteenth-century correspondence model between words and things and gave us language that is connected only conventionally and arbitrarily to the world outside it.

One of the concepts important to Saussure's explanation of the language system is that of **signs,** which he describes as composed of two parts: a written or sound construction, known as the **signifier,** and its meaning, called the **signified.** The spoken or written form of *hat,* for example, is a signifier. The concept that flashes into your mind when you hear or read it is the signified. With the introduction of these terms, and the theory underlying them, Saussure transformed the sense of what a word is. He made it no longer possible to speak of a word as a symbol that represents a thing outside it, as it had conventionally been known. Because a signifier does not refer to some object in the world but to a concept in the mind, it is language, not the world external to us, that mediates our reality. We see only what it allows us to see both outside and inside ourselves. It structures our experience. Consider, for example, how speakers of different languages tend to have differing views of the world. They see the world through different structures.

The connection between the signifier and signified has several important characteristics. First of all, it is not a natural relationship but an arbitrary one. The signifier *hat* has no inherent link with the physical object you wear on your head. It could just as easily have been called a rose or a bed. Then how do a signifier and a signified become tied together? The relationship comes about through convention, an agreement on the part of speakers that the two are associated. Finally, we know one sign from another not because of meanings they inherently carry but because of the differences among them. The signifier *bat* is distinguishable from *hat,* for example, because they have different initial letters. Language, then, is arbitrary, conventional, and based on difference.

The concept of difference has additional ramifications that become important in deconstruction theory. This concept appears most clearly as opposites, which structuralists and others refer to as **binary oppositions.** They are contrasting concepts such as male/female, right/left, day/night, each of which makes it possible for us to understand the other more fully. We are able to understand black because we understand white, noise because we know silence.

Although structuralism has taken varied forms in different countries, the most influential theorists have been the French followers of Saussure. His ideas, and theirs, have been adopted and adapted by many disciplines besides linguistics. After all, wherever there is social behavior, there is likely to be a sign system, not necessarily one involving words. Saussure, in fact, proposed the development of a science called **semiology** that would investigate meaning through signs observable in cultural phenomena. Because language is the primary signifying system, it would be the chief focus of study, and research into other systems would follow the model used in studying it. At the same time in this country Charles Sanders Pierce was developing semiotics, which applied structuralist principles to the study of sign systems and the way meaning is derived from them. The point is the same: to treat all forms of social behavior as signifying systems that are defined by the structure of their interrelationships. The process provides anthropologists, sociologists, psychologists, and others with a way to go beneath external facts in order to examine the nature of the human experience. It has proved to be valuable in studying phenomena as disparate as Barbie dolls and the mythologies of little-known cultures.

Deconstruction, a product of the late 1960s, took structuralist ideas about the nature of the sign, the importance of difference and binary oppositions, and the role of language in mediating experience and extended them, sometimes in ways that contradicted the theories of the structuralists. It both built on and broke with structuralism, making deconstruction one of several poststructuralist theories that find their commonality in the idea that although some structuralist principles can be used to form a new understanding of reality, their interpretations of texts are too static and unchanging. They produce readings that posit fixed meanings. In contrast, the poststructuralists view texts as fluid, dynamic entities that are given new life with repeated readings and through interactions with other texts, thereby providing an ongoing plurality of meanings. Where the structuralists had provided a broadly applicable new method of arriving at meaning through an analysis of underlying codes and rules, deconstruction declared meaning to be essentially undecidable. What a text means and how it means, they said, cannot be determined because it is not possible to systematically find the grammar of a text. Instead, one can find many meanings in a single text, all of them possible and all of them replaceable by others. Instead of looking for structure, then, deconstruction looks for those places where texts contradict, and thereby deconstruct, themselves. Instead of showing how the conventions of a text work, it shows how they falter. The result is that a literary work can no longer have one unifying meaning that an authority (critic or author) can enunciate. Instead, meaning is accepted to be the outgrowth of various signifying systems within the text that may even produce contradictory meanings.

In the 1970s, deconstruction became a major influence on literary criticism in large part because of the strong influence of its originator and namer, the philosopher Jacques Derrida, whose major precursors were Friedrich Nietzsche and Martin Heidegger, known for their probing of such key concepts as knowledge, truth, and identity. In the United States, deconstruction became closely associated with Yale University because some of its better-known advocates were on the faculty there. In fact, in people's minds deconstruction remains closely associated with (and is sometimes referred to as) the Yale school of criticism.

The impact of deconstruction has not been welcomed by all readers, some of whom object that it robs literature of its significance, trivializes texts as simple word-play, and presents itself in unintelligible jargon. Humanists see it as a wedge between literature and life, even as a practice that shuts out ordinary readers unwilling to engage in the complex theorizing that deconstruction requires. In response, its defenders point out that it gives us a way to read more critically and honestly than previous systems have allowed us to do. It also provides means of discovering premises and ideologies that lurk unacknowledged in the language we use.

PRACTICING DECONSTRUCTION

Working from the assumption that language is inherently ambiguous, not the clear, efficient communicator that we would like to think it is, deconstruction recognizes that any human utterance has a multitude of possibilities for meaning. The simplest statement may be heard in a wide variety of ways, giving it a tendency to undermine itself by refuting what it appears to be saying. It contradicts itself as it moves from one meaning to another. How does this happen?

In deconstructive terms, Saussure's sign, the combination of a signifier and a signified that refers to a mental concept, is not a stable, unchanging entity. Using his predecessor's theory that language is a system based on differences, Derrida goes a step further to point out that any given signifier may point to several different signifieds. For example, a statement as uncomplicated as "The cherries are in the bowl" says more than the six words denote. The signifier "cherries" will evoke in our consciousness, and that of our listener/reader, a host of associations—other fruit, a still life, desserts, trees in bloom, allergies, obviously more than cherries in a bowl. Each of the signifieds (other fruit, a still life, and so on) in turn becomes a signifier because it leads to other associations, other signifieds. In short, a signifier has no single signified, or mental concept, as the structuralists assumed but leads instead to a chain of other signifiers.

The seemingly simple explanation of sign = signifier + signified can be complicated in some other ways as well. A person can speak ironically, for instance, saying one thing but meaning another. For example, imagine that you say to someone who has just run a stop sign and hit your car while driving over the speed limit, "How could you have run into me? You say you were driving so carefully." Although you would seem to be sympathetic to the other driver, you are actually accusing him of being irresponsible behind the wheel. Tone of voice can be meaningful here too. It can, by exaggeration, indicate irony, that the opposite of what is said is what is meant. It may also indicate a specially intended meaning behind a statement. By changing the vocal emphasis to different words, you change the meaning. For example, try reading the second sentence aloud stressing the first use of the word *you:* "*You* say you were driving so carefully." What does the statement imply? It suggests that the person who caused the accident is being defensive but is alone in claiming innocence. Now emphasize the second *you* and see how the meaning shifts. "You say *you* were driving so carefully" implies that the other driver has accused you of some improper driving practice. And so precise meaning slips away, suggesting many meanings, not a single, fixed, clearly identifiable one as the structuralists' principles defined.

Saussure argued that language refers not to objective reality but to mental concepts. In deconstructive terms, it does not even refer to mental concepts but only to itself. It consists of the ongoing play of signifiers that never come to rest. Our thinking, then, is always in flux, always subject to changing signifiers that move from one to another. We may wish for stability, but we are caught in language, which refuses to stay fixed. Such play does produce illusory effects of meanings, but the seeming significations are the results of a **trace,** which consists of what remains from the play of signifiers. Because we recognize a word by its differences from other words, it continues to have traces of those that it is not. A word (which is present) signals what is absent. This ongoing play Derrida calls ***différance,*** a deliberately ambiguous coined term combining the French words for "to defer" and "to differ," suggesting that meaning is always postponed, leaving in its place only the differences between signifiers. (Interestingly, in spoken French *différance* cannot be distinguished from *différence,* making its meaning even more uncertain.) *Différance* asserts that knowledge comes from dissimilarity and absence, making it dynamic and contextual. When these ideas are applied to a text, the concept of *différance* makes it impossible to think about that work in isolation. The meaning of any given text will be derived from its interrelatedness with other texts, in an ongoing process that gives it a series of possible meanings and readings.

Many people are made uncomfortable by the absence of a stable meaning. When they realize the extended consequences of such a proposition, they are likely to be even more disquieted, for if meaning is derived from what is not there—absence—and it is in the end undecidable, then there is no such thing as objective truth. As Derrida explains it, there is no **transcendental signified,** no ultimate reality or end to all the references from one sign to another, no unifying element to all things. Human beings resist an existence that lacks the certainty of unchanging meaning, a fixed center, because, as Derrida points out, humankind, at least in the Western world, is **logocentric;** that is, human beings want to believe that there is a centering principle in which all belief and actions are grounded and that certain metaphysical ideas are to be favored over others. They want to believe that there is a presence behind language and text. Throughout history such a center has been given many names: truth, God, Platonic Form, or essence. The salient characteristic, regardless of the name, is that each is stable and ongoing. Each provides an absolute from which all knowledge proceeds.

Actually, this type of thinking goes back to Aristotle, who declared that something cannot have a property and not have it, leading to the dualistic thinking characteristic of Western civilization. Such reasoning is most apparent in the tendency of Western metaphysics to see the world in terms of pairs of opposed centers of meaning, or binary oppositions. As on other occasions, Derrida borrows the idea from the structuralists, then elaborates on it by noting that in every such pair one member is privileged, or favored, over the other. For example, in the binary oppositions of male/female, good/evil, or truth/lies, the first in each pair is traditionally held by society to be superior. The privileged member defines itself by what it is not, its less valued partner. Not only do such oppositions exist among abstractions, but they also underlie all human acts. The ideology of a situation or a text can be determined by locating the binary oppositions in it and noting which are the privileged members.

Poststructuralists test binary oppositions to determine if they are indeed opposed, to challenge traditional assumptions and beliefs about what should be (and is) privileged, to question where they overlap and on what occasions they share their existence. The poststructuralists, including those who read from a deconstructive perspective, point out that oppositions are sometimes not so contrasting as they are thought to be. Perhaps something can be present and absent at the same time. Perhaps, they suggest, looking at the world as a series of opposed centers of meaning—such as right/wrong, good/evil, love/hate—oversimplifies its nature. Such thinking does not take into account the complexity of the way things are, leading to distortions of the truth. It requires that we suspend notice of contradictions in our effort to maintain the conventionally accepted arrangement of absolutes. Deconstruction resists such simplification by reversing the oppositions, thereby displacing meaning and offering another set of possibilities of meaning that arise from the new relations of difference.

One binary opposition of particular importance to Derrida is that of speech/writing. He objects to the practice of making speech the privileged member, a convention he calls **phonocentrism,** because it implies that the presence of a speaker makes communication more direct and accurate. Written words, which are merely copies of speech, are traditionally deemed to be inferior because they are less directly connected to the source. Speech is evidence of the presence of the speaker, but writing, which serves when the speaker is not there, points to absence. The binary emerging from this situation is presence/absence, with the former, declared through speaking, the privileged term. This is an essentially logocentric position because it puts the human being in the center, announcing her presence through language. It asserts presence (being) through speaking.

If there is no transcendental signified, no objective truth, then such binaries are not fixed and static. They are fluid, open to change. They can, says Derrida, be reversed. Any center can be decentered, thereby providing a new set of values and beliefs. At the very least, such a reversal makes it possible to see any given situation from a new perspective. A bigger assertion is that, by reversing the oppositions—displacing accepted meaning and reinscribing new values—one is able to get outside logocentric thought. Not only does Derrida reverse the speech/writing binary to see the terms in a new way, but he actually argues that writing must come before speech. That is, he reasons that speech is a form of writing. The two share certain features, as they are both signifying systems. When we interpret oral signs, we must do so by recognizing a pure form of the signifier, one that can be repeated (and recognized) again and again despite differences of pronunciation. But being capable of repetition is a characteristic of writing, whereas speech vanishes into the air. Because the repeatable signifier gives speech a characteristic of writing, Derrida says it is a special kind of writing.

Complicating the situation is that binary oppositions may overlap each other. They are not necessarily discrete entities. There are too many contradictions and associations involved with language to be able to separate them entirely. At the same time that they reinforce presence, they also remind us of what is missing, thereby complementing each other. Derrida refers to the unstable relationship of binary oppositions as **supplementation,** suggesting that each of the two terms adds something to the other and takes the place of the other. In his hands, for example, writing not only adds something to speech but also substitutes for it, though the substitution is never exact. It is never precisely what it completes. Supplementation exists in all aspects of human life and behavior.

The various ideas traditionally subscribed to by Western civilization are based on the assumption that conscious, integrated selves are at the center of human activity. Derrida calls that belief the **metaphysics of presence.** These ideas include our logocentrism (ties to words), phonocentrism (ties to words produced as sounds), and our acceptance of a transcendental signified (ultimate source of all knowledge). In short, they are beliefs about language and being that have been influential since Plato, but Derrida challenges them as flawed and erroneous because meaning is, in the end, undecidable. He defines the metaphysics of presence as "a set of themes whose character was the sign of a whole set of long-standing constraints" and adds, "These constraints were practiced at the price of contradictions, of denials, of dogmatic degrees. I proposed to analyze the non-closed and fissured system of these constraints under the name of logocentrism in the form that it takes in Western philosophy." By deconstructing these constraints, he is trying to open new ways of thinking and knowing. In terms of texts, he is giving readers a new way to read.

MAKING A DECONSTRUCTIVE ANALYSIS

To understand the discussion that follows, you will need to read "Stopping by Woods on a Snowy Evening," a poem by Robert Frost, found on page 256.

Whereas a traditional critical reading attempts to establish a meaning for a text, a deconstructive reading involves asking questions in an effort to show that what the text claims to be saying and what it is really saying are different. It tries to undermine the work's implied claim of having coherence, unity, and meaning and to show that it does not represent the truth of its subject. In fact, no final statement about its meaning can be made, for each reading is provisional, just one in a series of interpretations that decenter each other in ongoing play. In the absence of a transcendental signified, a text cannot be said to be tied to some center that existed before and outside it, and meaning can have no place to conclude, nothing in which to be subsumed.

A number of people have tried to summarize the process of deconstructing a text. Derrida himself explains it by saying that "the reading must always aim at a certain relationship, unperceived by the writer, between what he commands and what he does not command of the patterns of the language that he uses." As Sharon Crowley describes the process, it tries to "tease larger systemic motifs out of gaps, aberrations, or inconsistencies in a given text." It tries to find blind spots that a writer has absorbed from cultural systems. She adds that "deconstruction amounts to reading texts in order to rewrite them," as Derrida tries "to reread Western history to give voice to that which has been systematically silenced." (Paul de Man has perhaps had the most to say about "blind spots." In *Blindness and Insight,* he goes so far as to assert that critics achieve insight through their "peculiar blindness." He finds that they say something besides what they meant.)

Barbara Johnson's frequently quoted definition of deconstruction says that it occurs by "the careful teasing out of warring forces of signification within the text itself." Jonathan Culler says that "to deconstruct a discourse is to show how it undermines the philosophy it asserts, or the hierarchical oppositions on which it relies." A more detailed comment comes from J. Hillis Miller:

> Deconstruction as a mode of interpretation works by a careful and circumspect entering of each textual labyrinth. . . . The deconstructive critic seeks to find, by this process of retracing, the element in the system studied which is alogical, the thread in the text in question which will unravel it all, or the loose stone which will pull down the whole building. The deconstruction, rather, annihilates the ground on

which the building stands by showing that the text has already annihilated the ground, knowingly or unknowingly. Deconstruction is not a dismantling of the structure of a text but a demonstration that it has already dismantled itself.

The process is actually in some ways similar to the one used in formalism. That is, the reader engages in a close reading, a very close reading of the text, noting the presence and operation of all its elements. However, the end is radically different in the two approaches. Where formalism seeks to demonstrate that a work has essential unity despite the paradoxes and irony that create its inner tension, that it expresses a realizable truth, deconstruction seeks to show that a text has no organic unity or basis for presenting meanings, only a series of conflicting significations.

One way to begin is to follow Derrida's own process, which he calls "double reading." That is, you first go through a text in a traditional manner, pointing out where it seems to have determinate meanings. The first step in deconstructing Frost's "Stopping by Woods on a Snowy Evening," for example, might be to make a commentary on the narrator's desire for peace, the highly controlled form, or the cumulative effect of the images of night, winter, and sleep. On second reading, however, you would look for alternative meanings and use them to negate any specific one. Discovery of contradictory or incompatible meanings results in the deconstruction of a text. They undermine the grounds on which it is based, and meaning becomes indeterminate. The text is not unitary and unified in the manner that logocentrism promises. Recognizing that a text has multiple interpretations, the reader expects to interpret it over and over again. No single reading is irrevocable; it can always be displaced by a subsequent one. Thus interpretation becomes a creative act as important as the text undergoing interpretation. The pleasure lies in the discovery of new ways of seeing the work. Of course, because the reader must express those discoveries in logocentric language, the interpretation will deconstruct itself as well.

How do you find alternative meanings, especially if you are accustomed to assuming that there is an inherent meaning to be found, that it will be recognizable to other readers, and that the picture it gives of the world will be consonant with the way it really is? How do you find contradictory or incompatible meanings if you are used to finding *the* meaning of a text or passage?

You can begin by locating the binary oppositions in the text, identifying the member that is privileged and the one that is not. In "Stopping by Woods," for example, a number of hierarchical oppositions are quickly noted: silence/sound, nature/civilization, isolation/community, dark/light, stillness/activity, unconscious/conscious, and, by implication, death/life and dreams/reality. Looking at them carefully will give you a way of entering the poem deconstructively. For example, try to answer the following questions about them, and then compare your answers with the commentary that follows each one.

What values and ideas do the hierarchies reflect? Your answers to the question will define some of the preconceptions that influence the way the text is conventionally read.

If you accept the first of each of the paired terms to be the privileged one, you will read the poem as a statement about the value of experiencing peace, oneness with nature, acceptance of self. There is beauty in the moment, a sense of connection with primeval forces.

What do you find when you reverse the binary oppositions? What fresh perspectives on the poem emerge? Because the hierarchy is arbitrary and illusory, it can be turned upside down to provide a new view of the values and beliefs that underlie it. The new, unconventional relationships may radically change your perception of the terms or of the text.

The interesting aspect of the oppositions in this poem is that the terms that are privileged throughout most of it are reversed at the end when the traveler chooses to continue his journey. For the first three stanzas, silence is favored over sound, nature over civilization, isolation over community, and so on. When, however, the persona rejects the loveliness of the dark, deep woods and chooses to honor promises that lie outside them, he acknowledges that he lives in a world that expects him to renounce self-indulgent dreams and carry out his obligations. He is part of a society that honors community, activity, consciousness, and reality.

Although in this case the poet himself has provided a reversal, the reader still must ask what has been changed by it. What else is affected? What would be different, for example, if the traveler opted for nature, darkness, and dreams? What if the forces that attracted him so powerfully throughout most of the experience remained the privileged ones? What would be different if isolation were deemed to be more attractive than community? What if it were preferable to be alone, outside the company of friends and family? Then the woods would belong to nobody, or at least the narrator would not acknowledge their claim, and there would be no self-consciousness about being observed. Conformity to social norms and pressures (signaled by the horse) would cease to exist. The world would be marked by an absence of stress and the presence of peace. The narrator would be liberated from drudgery, labor, the burdens of responsibility that are implied by the penultimate line. Structure and regimentation would disappear, and in their place would be spontaneity and natural reactions. And perhaps most important, one would feel a sense of unity with nature. To be alone is for the moment appealing, posing as a provisional center of meaning.

Do you find any contradictions in the privileged members? That is, do the terms silence, isolation, stillness, *and* unconscious *seem consonant? Or are they incompatible?*

The privileged terms initially seem to fit easily into a single scene, but on closer analysis some inconsistencies emerge. There are contradictions in the poem that go unacknowledged. For example, the traveler enjoys the pleasures of isolation but ultimately opts for community. He savors the beauty of nature but chooses civilization. When he continues his journey, isolation and nature are decentered by community and civilization. In the end, contradictory hierarchies (isolation/community and community/isolation, nature/civilization and civilization/nature) are privileged by the protagonist even though they are incompatible. The opposed conditions cannot exist together, though that is never overtly acknowledged in the poem. Their incongruity underscores the fragmented, conflicted nature of the traveler himself. It also asserts the lack of fixed, unchanging meaning in poems or in life itself.

What else do the terms make you think of? What other hierarchies do they lead to? Such associations will suggest alternative readings, new terms that can decenter the ones currently controlling the interpretation.

Earlier it was noted that stillness, silence, isolation, and the rest seem by extension to suggest the unconscious and death. By establishing unconscious/conscious and death/life as major oppositions, the old reading about promises and duties is decentered and replaced with an interpretation having to do with renunciation of vitality and presence, a quite different set of concerns. In this way the chain of signifiers rolls over and over, moving from one provisional meaning to another.

How do the binary terms supplement each other? How does each help the reader to understand its opposing term? How do they reinforce both presence and absence?

At the end of Frost's poem, when the narrator exchanges the peace of aloneness (isolation) for reengagement with the world, then nature and civilization, and countryside and village, are not opposites, but experiences in the being of the narrator that decenter and supplement each other. He is attracted by the solace of the winter scene in the woods, but he chooses the world of obligations and work. He is not, of course, a unified being but a fragmented one who speaks from the unconscious and returns at the end to the conscious world. He exists in dream and reality.

Another deconstructive approach is to take what has heretofore seemed marginal and make it central. Elements customarily considered to be of minor interest can become the focus of interest, with binary oppositions and possible reversals of their own. The comment that ordinarily receives little attention is brought to the center to see what new understandings surface, or a minor character may be scrutinized as critical to what happens in the plot. For example, in "Stopping by Woods" a close look at the horse is revealing. Seemingly of slight importance to what happens in the poem or what it may mean, the horse turns out to be surprisingly significant. Described in this poem as "little" ("My little horse must think it queer / To stop without a farmhouse near"), he turns out to play a large role. He "gives his harness bells a shake," thereby reminding the narrator of responsibility, duty, and social judgments. He interrupts the silence with sound, supplanting the peacefulness of the moment with a call to activity and conformity, replacing absence with presence. The horse becomes, in a sense, the voice of the conscious and civilized world, which in itself is a commentary on that world. Nevertheless, the traveler exchanges his dreams for reality. The horse's bells, sounds that are not even language, displace isolation as a center of meaning and thereby change the direction of the poem. The animal's impact would easily go unnoticed, except that the deconstructionist moves him to center stage.

Any "hidden" contradictions and discrepancies between what the text seems to say and what it actually says are important. Such incongruities are often found in what is not said, in gaps of information, silences, questions, or sometimes figures of speech. The author's intent is of no help in this process because what the author thinks was said may not be the case at all. In fact, by identifying those places where a slip of language occurs, that is, where something is said that was not meant to be said, you have found a point at which a text begins to deconstruct itself. By discovering a pattern of such inconsistencies and trying to account for it, a different interpretation becomes possible. The reader of this poem wonders, for instance, about the distance between the terms used to describe the woods. They are said to be "lovely, dark, and deep." The first descriptive word connotes aesthetic pleasure, the next two a sense of threat or mystery. The solace that the narrator imputes to the woods is threatened. It is, finally, not there, or at least is there only momentarily. The woods have no permanent, stable, consistent self.

Looking at a binary opposition—such as presence/absence, for example, reversed by Derrida so that absence is favored—often helps a reader to deconstruct a text. In "Stopping by Woods," it is significant that the narrator's words come unspoken from the inner self. They appear to exist only in thought. Phonocentric views would give them a privileged position because they are closest to the man. They represent him, stand in for him, displace him. The inner words ultimately appear in writing, however, displacing speech (which in this case is unvoiced), which displaced unspoken thought, which initially displaced the man. The presence of being is far removed. The words of the persona are supplements (additions to and substitutions for) him. Further, the bells of the horse metaphorically make the horse a spokesperson for the community, thereby displacing its center. Sound has replaced speech. Animal has replaced people. Absence is thereby privileged over presence.

In sum, the narrator of "Stopping by Woods" is seen to be a logocentric being who looks for a center where there is none. Finding only momentary meaning, he moves on to seek a center in work and community. He yearns for peace but displaces it with obligations, because although unity is desirable, it is absent, only fleetingly available in the moment in the woods.

Finally, the deconstructive reader will place all structures in question, because an ultimate meaning is always deferred, and ambiguity remains. The purpose is to decenter each new center, to cast doubt on previous theories, never coming to rest on any one meaning but generating an infinite number of possible interpretations. The meaning of the protagonist's experience in "Stopping by Woods," for example, cannot in the long run be determined. The repetition of the last line resists interpretation or provides multiple readings, because its metaphoric ramifications remain ambiguous, unclear, full of possibilities, none of them final.

On subsequent readings, new levels of meaning will emerge with the inversion of other binary oppositions. Some will appear only after others have been explored. You may find yourself moving back and forth between different interpretations or successively displacing one with another. In either case, the unending play of *différance* prevents you from arriving at any decidable meaning, or any set of multiple meanings, for anything you say or write. Instead, there is an unending process, with every new reading holding the possibility of a new interpretation. Acceptance of shifting meanings challenges the previously held views of the reader, offering her freedom from the constraints of traditional assumptions and ideologies so that new ways of seeing are made possible.

WRITING A DECONSTRUCTIVE ANALYSIS

It should be noted at the outset that important voices have expressed concern about the appropriateness of viewing deconstruction as a critical approach. Not surprisingly, some critics resist what they see as the negativism found in its philosophical attack on the existence of meaning in literature (and life). Others object less to its destructive effects than to what they see as its tendency to trivialize literature and the act of reading, thereby threatening the privileged place they hold in academia. They accuse it of diminishing our capacity to appreciate and interpret literature. And almost everyone complains of its obscure and confusing terminology. David Hirsch's *The Deconstruction of Literature,* John Ellis's *Against Deconstruction,* and David Lehman's *Signs of the Times: Deconstruction and the Fall of Paul de Man,* for example, all question the validity of this approach.

Another kind of objection comes from Jane Tompkins, who argues against the practice of applying deconstructive principles to texts because it means using methods that are basically positivist and empirical and thereby contradictory to deconstruction. She writes,

> The point I want to make here is that you can't apply post-structuralism to literary texts. Why not? Because to talk about applying post-structuralism to literary texts assumes the following things: (1) that we have freestanding subjects, (2) that we have freestanding objects of investigation, (3) that there are freestanding methods, and (4) that what results when we apply reader to method and method to text is a freestanding interpretation. This series of assumptions revokes everything that Derrida is getting at in *"Différance,"* and that is implicit in Saussure's theory of language. . . . As we read literary texts, then, "we" are not applying a "method"; we are acting as an extension of the interpretive code, of those systems of difference that constitute us and the objects of our perception simultaneously.

Nevertheless, deconstructive readings can enrich one's experience with a text by providing an ongoing journey through it, each revealing a new way of thinking about it. Such studies proceed in different ways, but here are some suggestions to help you read from this perspective and write about your observations.

PREWRITING

A reading log can be particularly helpful with the deconstructive approach. As you go through a text for the first time, you can make notes as a formalist would, taking an interest in how meaning grows out of its various stylistic elements. You will identify tensions (in the form of paradox and irony) and be aware of how they are resolved. You will take note of how images, figurative language, and symbols come together to make a unified whole (see chapter 3). During the second reading, you can set aside your willingness to accept that there is an identifiable, stable meaning produced by the diction, imagery, symbols, and the rest and begin to probe unresolved, unexplained, or unmentioned matters. In your reading log you should record the undeveloped concerns that would, if they were explored, interrupt the assumed unity and meaning of the text.

The prewriting stage is also a good time to play with the binary oppositions that you find, first identifying those that initially seem most significant, then inferring the ideology that they present. The next step, as noted above in "Making a Deconstructive Analysis," is to reverse them, look for contradictions in them, and determine how they supplement each other. It is likely that this process will help you to find, in the terms of J. Hillis Miller, "the thread in the text in question which will unravel it all, or the loose stone which will pull down the whole building."

Another prewriting activity involves examining the figurative language of the text. By making a list of metaphors, for example, you have information that may reveal slippages of the language. Because figures of speech do not mean what they say, there is room for them to misstate what the author intended for them to say. You may find it helpful to put them on paper and, in writing, to play with their possibilities.

Much of the prewriting suggested here involves listing and note making. These strategies will aid analysis, but they will be helpful in the drafting stage only insofar as they provide ideas and information. Consequently, the more material you can generate at this point, the better off you will be when you begin to write.

DRAFTING AND REVISING

The Introduction

Given that deconstructive readings seek to displace previous ones, and sometimes to decenter standard, generally accepted interpretations, one way to open the discussion is to reiterate the conventional reading of a text. In other words, the introduction may simply be a restatement of the usual perception of what a work means or of how it operates, because by explaining how a story is usually read or how a character is normally perceived to be, you have a basis for deconstructing those views. Once you have established what is usually deemed to be so, you are set to state why it is not the only possible reading. Your argument for multiple readings will be the central focus of the body of the discussion that follows, but it is helpful to introduce that idea early on.

The Body

Your purpose in the body of your deconstructive analysis will be to demonstrate the limited perspective of the conventional reading. You may want to show how the ideology that the text tries to support is not supportable, an approach that is popular with Marxist and feminist deconstructive critics. In this case, as you study a particular text, you will also be deconstructing the larger contexts in which it exists. You will be suggesting, or overtly stating, that the order supported by it is also open to question, perhaps itself fraught with inconsistencies and illusory stability.

On the other hand, you may be more interested in presenting a series of possible readings, one decentering the other in an ongoing process. This approach will take the discussion a step further by showing how meaning is not simply an either-or situation but an unending series of possibilities, leaving meaning ultimately beyond deciding. In either case, you will want to demonstrate how and where the text falls apart because of its own inconsistencies, misstatements, or contradictions.

The thinking you did during the prewriting stage will be valuable here, but remember that all assertions will need to be supported with quotations and examples drawn from the text. The following questions can help you generate the basis of your discussion. If you developed your prewriting stage thoroughly, you will have already covered some of them.

- What is the primary binary opposition in the text?
- What associated binary oppositions do you find?
- Which terms in the oppositions are privileged?
- What elements in the work support the privileged terms?
- What statement of values or belief emerges from the privileged terms?
- What elements in the text contradict the hierarchies as presented?
- Where is the statement of values or belief contradicted by characters, events, or statements in the text?
- Are the privileged terms inconsistent? Do they present conflicting meanings?
- What associations do you have with the terms that complicate their opposition? That is, what associations keep you from accepting that the terms are all good or all bad?
- What new possibilities of understanding emerge when you reverse the binary oppositions?
- How does the reversal of oppositions tear down the intended statement of meaning?
- What contradictions of language, image, or event do you notice?
- Are there any significant omissions of information?
- Can you identify any irreconcilable views offered as coherent systems?
- What is left unnoticed or unexplained?
- How would a focus on different binary oppositions lead to a different interpretation?
- Where are the figures of speech so ambiguous that they suggest several (and perhaps contradictory) meanings?
- What usually overlooked minor figures or events can be examined as major ones?
- How does the focus of meaning shift when you make marginal figures central?
- What new vision of the situation presented by the text emerges for you?
- What new complications do you see that the conventional reading would have "smoothed over"?
- Why can you not make a definitive statement about the meaning of the text?

The Conclusion

If you have begun by rehearsing the conventional reading of the text under analysis, an effective way to end your essay is by making a comparison of that understanding and your deconstructive analysis, pointing out why the earlier one is not definitive. If you prefer, you may reiterate the several different ways in which the text can be read, thereby making the point that meaning is always provisional, always ready to give way to other meaning.

Glossary of Terms Useful in Understanding Deconstruction

Binary oppositions Dichotomies that are actually evaluative hierarchies. They underlie human acts and practices.

Diachronic A term used to describe an approach to the study of language that traces how and why words have evolved in meaning or sound over time.

Différance The term Derrida uses to indicate that meaning is based on differences, is always postponed, and is ultimately undecidable.

Langue The structure of a language that is used by all members of a particular language community.

Logocentrism The belief in an absolute or foundation that grounds the linguistic system and fixes the meaning of a spoken or written utterance.

Metaphysics of presence Beliefs including binary oppositions, logocentrism, and phonocentrism that have been the basis of Western philosophy since Plato.

Modernism A term used in a limited sense to designate the distinctive concepts and forms of literature and art since World War I (1914–1918) and used in a more general sense since the Enlightenment of the eighteenth century to designate concepts and forms characterized by a belief in science and the use of reason to solve the problems of humankind.

Parole A specific use of *langue*.

Phenomenology The philosophical perspective that assumes that a thinking subject and the object of which it is aware are inseparable. The Geneva critics, who read a text as the consciousness of an author put into words, are often described as practicing phenomenological criticism.

Phonocentrism The belief that speech is privileged over writing.

Poststructuralism Theories (including deconstruction, new historicism, and neo-Freudian theory) that are based on Ferdinand de Saussure's linguistic concepts but at the same time undermine them.

Sign The combination of a signifier and a signified.

Signified The concept of meaning indicated by a signifier.

Signifier A conventional sound utterance or written mark.

Semiology A science proposed by Saussure that would investigate meaning through signs observable in cultural phenomena.

Structuralism A science that seeks to understand how systems work. Those who practice it try to describe the underlying (and not necessarily visible) principles by which systems exist.

Supplement The unstable relationship between two binary oppositions that keeps them from being totally separate entities.

Synchronic A term used to describe an approach to the study of language that searches for the principles that govern its functions by examining a language at one particular point in time.

Trace The illusory effect of meaning that is left in a signifier by other signifiers, that is, what it is not.

Transcendental signified A fixed, ultimate center of meaning.

RECOMMENDED WEB SITES

http://educ.queensu.ca/~qbell/update/tint/postmodernism/post.html

Addresses issues of interest to teachers who want to integrate postmodern themes into their teaching. Called the Teacher's Guide to Postmodernism, it provides understandable explanations of complex concepts.

http://www.classics.cam.ac.uk/Faculty/structuralism.html

A brief overview of structuralism, with applications to classical literature. It includes an annotated bibliography of works of major figures of the movement.

http://www.aber.ac.uk/media/Documents/S4B/semiotic.html

Survey of major criticism of semiotics, entitled Semiotics for Beginners.

http://www.130.179.92.25/Arnason_DE/Derrida.html

An introduction to the basic concepts of Derrida. It also provides definitions of terms commonly used in discussions of deconstruction.

SUGGESTED READING

Abrams, M. H. The Deconstructive Angel. *Critical Inquiry* 3 (1977): 425–438.

Crowley, Sharon. *A Teacher's Introduction to Deconstruction.* Urbana, Ill.: National Council of Teachers of English, 1989.

Culler, Jonathan. *On Deconstruction: Theory and Criticism after Structuralism.* Ithaca, N.Y.: Cornell Univ. Press, 1982.

Derrida, Jacques. Living On: Border Lines. In *Deconstruction and Criticism.* Harold Bloom, Paul De Man, Jacques Derrida, Geoffrey H. Hartman, and J. Hillis Miller. New York: Continuum, 1980.

———. *Of Grammatology.* Trans. Gayatri Sival. Baltimore: Johns Hopkins Univ. Press, 1998.

Johnson, Barbara. *The Critical Difference: Essays in the Contemporary Rhetoric of Reading.* Baltimore: Johns Hopkins Univ. Press, 1980.

Miller, J. Hillis. Tradition and Difference. *Diacritics* 2.4 (1972): 6–13.

Scholes, Robert. Deconstruction and Criticism. *Critical Inquiry* 14 (1988): 278–295.

Tompkins, Jane. A Short Course in Post-Structuralism. In *Conversations,* ed. Charles Moran and Elizabeth Penfield, pp. 19–37. Urbana, Ill.: National Council of Teachers of English, 1990.

Model Student Analysis

Who Wants a Doughnut without a Hole? Deconstructive Criticism and the Failure of Meaning in Bobbie Ann Mason's "Shiloh"

Matt Dube

Many American short stories in the realist mode pursue the same narrative goal. In these stories, the narrator sets out to discover how his life is being ruined and to understand why. Bobbie Ann Mason's "Shiloh" (1982) is written in the realist mode and can be read as just this sort of domestic mystery. Leroy Moffitt has returned to living at home after years of driving a truck to discover his marriage is in trouble. He attempts to discover why his marriage is falling apart and then begin to repair it. Leroy discovers that his marital troubles began when his child, Randy, died from sudden infant death syndrome. This revelation, represented by the longest flashback in the story, falls somewhere beyond the halfway mark, where meaning in realistic stories is often disclosed. From there, Leroy and his wife, Norma Jean, go for a weekend to the Civil War battleground at Shiloh, and Leroy fights to save his marriage.

The deconstructive interpretive approach is informed by the same search for a central structuring incident, like the death of Randy in "Shiloh." The deconstructive critic is interested in locating the center of the story to understand how the story structures its own meaning. Traditionally, the deconstructive critic then moves to a study of the margins of the story, to prove that there is not a single central site for meaning. However, there is a separate tradition in deconstructive criticism, one inaugurated by Jacques Derrida in his essay-lecture "Structure, Sign, and Play in the Discourse of the Natural Sciences" (1970). In the essay, Derrida proposes a model whereby he is able to neutralize the center itself. He notes that the incest taboo, represented by Claude Lévy-Strauss as the universal center of all societies, regardless of local differences, is itself a site for mutually destructive contradictions. By invalidating the meaning center of the cultural systems, Derrida opens the cultures, and the study of them by social scientists, to the possibility of locating contingent meaning anywhere at all. "Shiloh" is engaged in a similar deconstructive critique of how the realist mode of American fiction creates meaning.

The flashback to the death of Randy, Leroy and Norma Jean's baby, is the single longest sustained flashback in the story, following as it does on the heels of Leroy's encounter with Stevie, his pot dealer. The flashback itself fills a lengthy paragraph, or rather doesn't fill it, for the memory of Randy is crowded out by the memory of the film that Norma Jean and Leroy were watching when Randy died, *Dr. Strangelove*. The flashback is motivated by and follows up a hint dropped earlier in the story, that Leroy and Norma Jean "had a child who died as an infant, years ago." That same passage continues to say this made the couple "feel awkward around one another," and more ominous still, "Leroy has read that for most people losing a child destroys a marriage." These concrete, factual comments have a certain authentic quality (despite, or perhaps because of, Leroy's admission that he can't place whether he read this somewhere or simply heard it on *Donahue*) that contrasts sharply with Leroy's feeling that he and his wife "are waking up out of a dream together." Mason suggests that it was the awkwardness over the death of their child that led Leroy to begin his life as a trucker. Now that an injury has forced him to abandon that career, he realizes that Randy's death has changed his relationship with Norma Jean, breaking it into periods before and after the tragedy. Since Randy died and Leroy began driving a big rig, he and his wife had talked little, but now that he is at home full-time, they are talking again. The struggle of the story, and of Leroy in his marriage, is to recuperate from the event of Randy's death, to exorcize Randy's spirit from the relationship the child haunts.

As much as the introductory sections of the story work to re-create the chronology of Leroy and Norma Jean's marriage and to posit Randy's death as the incident that caused the rupture that must be repaired, the flashback itself works to undo this comfortable sense of narrative meaning. In fact, when Randy is reintroduced into the story, it is through a chain of association, with Stevie, Leroy's dealer and the son of a prominent local doctor. Leroy says that Randy "would be about Stevie's age now," a statement that suggests an even closer similarity: that Randy would likely be just as delinquent, as ungrateful, and as brusque as Stevie, just as unlikely to help save Leroy's failing marriage. When Randy actually dies, Leroy and Norma Jean are watching *Dr. Strangelove* at the drive-in (one half of a double feature, of which they are unable to see the prophetically titled second half, *Lover, Come Back,* which in part is the narrative of "Shiloh"). Dead, Randy moves quickly from being a baby to being "a large doll" offered as "a present" and then "a sack of flour." Leroy himself can barely remember Randy, though it is easy for him to remember scenes from *Dr. Strangelove.* Randy is pronounced the victim of sudden infant death syndrome, a diagnosis reworded at the end of the flashback paragraph to become "crib death." This shift in diction mirrors a similar shift taking place with what has happened to Randy. First, a nurse says "It just happens sometimes," but later Leroy learns that "crib death is caused by a virus." Randy is completely written over, by his father's memories of the movie president, played by Peter Sellers, in the War Room; by Stevie, who could have been his classmate or even Randy himself; and by the doctor's shifting diagnosis. Finally, he is written over by the wording of the text itself: in both flashback and present day scenes, Randy is more often referred to as "the baby" than by his given name.

The story makes another move to displace Randy further from the central location he might hold in Leroy's catalog of failure and loss, and this final erasure is effected by substitution. Randy comes to be replaced by Shiloh, the Civil War battleground. Clearly, Mason means to riff on another way of reading "civil war," standing in for the conflict between Leroy and Norma Jean. But in the story, Shiloh itself takes on a significant and different meaning. Leroy's promise to build Norma Jean a house is synchronically displaced by the promise Norma Jean's mother, Mabel, made to return to Shiloh. The two frustrated desires merge in a shift that signals the beginning of the end of the story and identifies the trip as the solution to the larger problem of domestic grief. Mabel gives the trip further resonance by referring to it as a second honeymoon, recognizing in it an obvious attempt to fix a failed marriage. Norma Jean is shocked by her mother's choice of words, but she shouldn't be, because it comes from the same vocabulary her husband uses, that of daytime TV talk shows like *Donahue*.

Leroy and Norma Jean's trip is not a successful one. As the story ends, Norma Jean has announced that she is leaving Leroy. He watches her walk away from him across the site of the battle where "General Grant . . . shoved the Southerners back to Corinth, where Mabel and Jet Beasley were married years later." Leroy's story circles back geographically, but its narrative line is finally straightforward and unbroken. Mason writes, "Leroy knows he is leaving out a lot," but in a story that is motivated by synchronic displacement, as this one is, attempts to reconnect the signifier and signified necessarily foreground absence.

Bobbie Ann Mason is most often read, and rightly so, as part of an American realist movement that was the dominant mode for American short fiction in the 1980s. In this, she fits neatly beside writers like Raymond Carver and the literary "brat pack" of Jay McInerney, Brett Easton Ellis, and Tama Janowitz. However, the realist mode does not necessarily preclude a deconstructive reading of the story, as I think I have shown here. Realist fiction is in fact closely tied to cultural anthropology: both try to re-create a recognizable culture through the deployment of artifacts and rituals. As Derrida showed in "Structure, Sign, and Play in the Discourse of the Natural Sciences," such a system is particularly open to deconstructive techniques. The way Mason deconstructs the extended flashback, which could previously be read as a likely source for meaning in the story, does not mean that her story lacks all meaning or any appeal to the reader. Rather, it changes the stakes of what that story signifies and how we might respond to it.

The successful deconstruction of the central site of meaning, which here is the death of Norma Jean and Leroy's child, does not toss the story into the realm of unrecoverable metafiction, nor does it lessen the realism of the story. What it does, in fact, is to deepen the pathos of our response to Leroy's situation. There is nothing to lead us to believe that "reality" as represented in fiction must have meaning; in fact, such meanings often make the stories differ from the reader's own life experiences. In "Shiloh," Mason has used a deconstructive critique to neutralize the form of the realist story that imposes the kind of narrative meaning we rarely find in our lives. In the place of any central meaning, Mason instead offers the reader many possible alternate sites of meaning, all contingent on the pop culture in which her characters live. We can choose the contingent meaning of *Dr. Strangelove* or Wonder Woman, of Civil War history or *Donahue*. Mason has set the realist short story free from its need to structure all the events of its narrative into a univalent scheme for meaning. For the deconstructive critic, this is a liberation to be celebrated. For Leroy Moffitt, the loss of central meaning doesn't change the fact that his wife has walked away; it simply means that he will never know the reason why.

9

CULTURAL STUDIES: NEW HISTORICISM

The essential matter of history is not what happened but what people thought or said about it.

FREDERIC W. MAITLAND, English writer on law

As we noted with feminist and other critical approaches, the more recent the appearance of a particular perspective, the more difficult it is to define. The field of cultural studies is a prime example of the problem. Emerging in the 1960s, it has yet to settle into an accepted and agreed-upon set of principles and practices. In it you will recognize many theories that you have already met, ideas drawn from Marxism, feminism, popular culture, racial and ethnic studies, and more. It is not a single, standardized approach to literature (or anything else) but a field that binds its adherents together through some common interests and purposes, although they are addressed in widely divergent ways.

At present, three types of cultural studies that are getting particular notice are new historicism, postcolonialism, and American multiculturalism. Although each has its own distinct focus, they are all concerned with social and cultural forces that create a community or that threaten it. Those who look at texts from these points of view are eager to make more voices recognized by a broader circle of readers. In the long run, their approaches to reading can change the way readers conceive of a culture. Because cultural studies is still finding its way, this discussion will identify only a few commonalities that are shared by its different subgroups.

AN OVERVIEW OF CULTURAL STUDIES

Part of the difficulty in defining *cultural studies,* or even ***culture*** for that matter, is that the terms are so inclusive. If *culture* refers to the sum of the beliefs, institutions, arts, and behaviors of a particular people or time, cultural studies can be said to address an almost unthinkably broad body of knowledge: language, customs, legal system, literature, and more. Sometimes such a study is even interested in the culture of those who have responded to it. As it usually proceeds, however, a cultural study will address a particular topic, such as "Hispanic Women Writers of Texas," using the cultural context to arrive at generalizations about it. The intent is to connect historical, social, and economic knowledge surrounding the topic, one that may not seem to be very literary at all. Because any context is virtually unending, the critic never knows enough. As a result, interpretations made from a cultural studies perspective tend to be open-ended and continue to evolve as they are affected by new information. Nevertheless, a few generalizations can be made.

Groups engaged in cultural studies for the most part share the assumption that within any society is a dominant group that determines what is acceptable and unacceptable for the larger body. It defines the culture's tastes and values—in short, its ideology. Cultural critics are interested in those groups of people who do not belong to the dominant parties and who challenge the hegemony of the powerful. In the world of literature, they are the people Antonio Gramsci calls **subaltern** writers. However, wherever there is dominance, to some degree there is also defiance that makes it impossible for the powerful to prevent change indefinitely. Recognizing that **subjects** (people) are socially constructed, cultural critics work to change **power** structures where they are unequal, making the subjugated and marginalized more visible and influential makers of the culture. As James Berlin puts it, "The subject is the point of intersection of various discourses—discourses about class, race, gender, ethnicity, age, religion and the like—and it is influenced by those discourses." Consequently, it is necessary to "examine signifying practices in the formation of subjectivities within concrete material, social, and political conditions." Such a focus makes the field a highly politicized one, dedicated, as it is, to examining cultural forces in both literature and life with the intent of changing the way power is conceived.

The challenge presented to the power structure by groups such as African-Americans and gays and women has led to challenges in other arenas as well. In literature it has created a rejection of the concept of the "masterpiece." All the artifacts of a time or a people are of interest to the cultural critic, each to be treated with equal importance. There are no hierarchies of importance, no divisions between "fine art" and "popular art," between "high culture" and "low culture." Art itself is but one of many manifestations of a culture, one expression of it. Such an assumption makes cultural studies inevitably interdisciplinary. No single approach can provide the kind of analysis that broad social concerns demand. Literary criticism, in these terms, is a limited creature that needs the help of anthropology, sociology, psychology, linguistics, and more.

When literature is no longer given special reverence but is regarded as one of many areas of interest, its connections with the everyday world of work are inevitably involved, and at this point the influence of Marxism becomes particularly evident. It is reflected, for example, in the interest that cultural studies researchers have in how a work was produced. They question how a book achieved publication, who bought it, and how it was marketed.

In sum, cultural studies takes a broad view of human communities. Its practitioners challenge the status quo by trying to displace the powerful (whether "the powerful" be a literary canon or discriminatory institutions) and promote the voices (and thus the power) of those seldom heard. They do so by using knowledge and methods adopted from nonliterary fields to serve their belief that they can effect cultural change. For them, literature is a particularly productive means by which a culture can call attention to itself and assert its significance and worth.

With the increased self-awareness that has burgeoned since the 1960s among groups of people bound by common ties of race, ethnicity, history, and gender, a thorough discussion of cultural studies would become a book of its own. Even a consideration of how it affects literary criticism in general is beyond the scope of this presentation. Consequently, only three types of cultural studies will be looked at here: new historicism, postcolonialism, and American multiculturalism. They are not the only ones that could have been selected, but they are three that have received significant attention of late. The ways in which their adherents read and analyze texts can be applied to the literatures of other cultural groups.

ASSUMPTIONS, PRINCIPLES, AND GOALS OF NEW HISTORICISM

New historicism, which readers began to apply to texts in the late 1970s and early 1980s, attracted enough attention to challenge the prominent position then held by the deconstructionists. However, given that it is a radically new way of examining the human past, new historicism is difficult to pin down, partly because it is still changing and developing, and partly because it draws on widely diverse fields that seem to have little in common except their interest in the study of cultures. Sometimes it seems to be grounded in sociology, sometimes in psychology or economics, but the scope of investigation by the new historicists is never limited to any single field of study, because they see all parts of a given culture as shaping and being shaped by each other in such complex ways that any one approach is incapable of providing a complete picture of what has happened or, more important, what it means. Because new historicism is significantly different from traditional historical study, perhaps the best way to present its basic assumptions and principles is to begin by comparing it with its more familiar predecessor.

Traditional Historicism

At the simplest level, historians have traditionally been concerned with finding out what really happened at a given time and place. They worked to establish the factual accuracy of the stories that make up the record of the human past so that they could establish with as much certainty as possible that the account they rendered was a valid delineation of what had happened. To do so meant maintaining an objective stance, a position of distance from the scene of action that would allow them to see and state the truth about people and events. If they were successful in doing so, they would, by extension, manage to capture the sense of an entire age. They could find the essence of a period, the worldview that would unlock the meaning of its literature, art, politics, social behavior, and the rest. In looking at the broad sweep of history, they viewed the narratives they told as being linked to each other in a causal sequence that, it was assumed, would carry the world forward in a positive, progressive manner.

NEW HISTORICISM

The new historicists, most of them literary scholars, have challenged and resisted the assumptions and goals of traditional historicism. They deny, for example, that anyone can ever know exactly what happened at a given time and place. All that can be perceived is what has been handed down in artifacts and stories, making history a narration, not a pure, unadulterated set of precise observations. Thus, all history is subjectively known and set down, colored by the cultural context of the recorder, usually the person of power, leaving the stories of those who are powerless untold. Traditionally history has been recorded by the winners. The losers, or those who lack political or social power, have their stories to tell as well, and although they may not have published their stories in official documents or textbooks, they have circulated them as separate **discourses,** ways of seeing and talking about the world. The new historicist would want to hear all the stories, recognize all the voices.

Imagine, for example, trying to understand what took place at the Battle of Gettysburg and why it happened. No single explanation can account for the complexities and contradictions buried in it. A simple report of causes and effects behind the series of events would not explain what really happened. No reading of the battle in light of the spirit of the age would include all those who were involved: officers and volunteers, rural and urban troops, wives and children, blacks and whites. And, at the end of the battle, who could say that something positive had taken place? The new historicists do not claim to have the "truth" about a text or historical event but assert that the truth, if such a thing could even exist, would be narratologically and culturally contingent. History and literature, it seems, are more complicated than earlier readers had assumed.

Complicating the matter further is that not only are history's stories subjectively recorded, but they are also subjectively read and interpreted. Historians work from texts that have already been written (or told), recasting them in light of their own particular concerns, and regardless of their commitment to produce objective readings, they can never manage to do so because they cannot transcend their own values, experiences, and knowledge. Inevitably caught up in their own social and cultural contexts, they cannot escape the viewpoints provided by the ideas and institutions of their own day. Like the literary analyst, the historian who reads a "text" is involved in interpretation, reinforcing the subjectivity of any account of history.

Because it is impossible to maintain pure objectivity in the examination of history, historians are obligated to acknowledge the biases that are likely to color their interpretations. The more unaware they are of their tendencies to "read" history in particular ways, the more biased their accounts are likely to be. They are, therefore, ethically bound to admit their political and philosophical tendencies. The act of announcing one's own leanings is known as **self-positioning.**

As a result of the less than objective recording and readings of the past, history becomes a text, not simply a series of empirically verifiable events. Consequently, its study calls for a more interesting (and more valid) question than "What really happened?" In its place, the new historicist is drawn to ask, "What do the interpretations tell us about the interpreters?" or "How does what happened point to social conflicts?" or "How do the historical facts fit into ideologies of the day?" As Hayden White points out, what yesterday's historian would have seen as an event that actually occurred in the past, today's historian sees as a "text" to be interpreted, just as a poem or novel is interpreted by a critic.

The new historicists also challenge the existence of what is referred to as "the spirit of an age." Recognizing that any culture is made up of many disparate and conflicting strands, they deny that there is ever a single, unified worldview operating at a given period. To claim to have found the one perspective that would explain the beliefs, behaviors, and products of a time and place is an oversimplification. In place of a controlling narrative, the new historicists recognize many narratives produced by institutions and social strata that may hold contrasting bodies of belief and practice or differing modes of behavior. As they would put it, at any given period many discourses, or ways of seeing and thinking about the world, operate simultaneously. They clash and overlap and repeat, shaping and being shaped by each other. The political discourse of the court of Henry VIII in sixteenth-century England was not the discourse of the church of the time. To claim understanding of that rich period by considering only what the court was talking about and how it saw current events (and the court itself had many different discourses operating) or by examining only how the church viewed them would provide a severely limited sense of what was happening and what it meant. There was not, and there never is, say new historicists, a single history or a single worldview. Instead, many discourses come together in a complex cultural interaction. In fact, some new historicists charge that the very notion of a standardized culture is a false one that has been imposed by powerful institutions and classes as a way of maintaining their own interests.

Because new historicists are aware that no single discourse can explain the complexities of any event or artifact, they search out sources that have been overlooked in the past because of the emphasis on finding an overall explanation of a period's practices and products. Their investigations have led to an interest in the narratives of marginalized people and to some criticism for the importance given to nonmainstream materials. The quest is important, however, because it is through the stories people tell about themselves that they come to know who they are. To hear only the narratives of the dominant group would meaning ignoring others that have helped shape people, providing only a partial understanding of what and how ideologies are operating and interacting to form personal and group identities. Consider, for example, the sketchy picture Americans had of antebellum life before the slave narratives began to appear in the 1960s. Obviously a large part of what was known about pre–Civil War America was missing without those stories. The new historicists would question what the absence (silencing) of the slaves' discourse indicated about antebellum culture as well as the culture of the century that followed it. They might ask, for example, why the works of Frederick Douglass, well known in his own day, were out of print (and circulation) for decades following the Civil War. They would be interested in how the suppression fit the ideologies of the power structure.

The presence and use of power (and the lack thereof) is implicit in the search for previously silenced voices. Power is generated by shared discourses and wielded by those groups and institutions that are participants. They establish norms and define what is deemed acceptable. Discourses that differ from the norm and digress from what is acceptable are likely to be suppressed, or at least to go unrecognized, for they threaten the values generally espoused by a culture and the dominance of the powerful. Stephen Greenblatt points out that we define ourselves in relation to what we are not, making it necessary to demonize and objectify what we are not as "others." Designated as disruptive, foreign, and perhaps mad, the "others" are evidence of the rightness of our own power. Nevertheless, they are there, despite being ignored, scorned, or disapproved—that is, silenced—and without an awareness of them, one cannot understand the power structure itself.

Even the most powerful discourse is not permanent. Power moves through all social levels, by way of marriage, commerce, and intellectual exchange. While it reinforces its base in some cases, it inevitably stimulates opposition in others. As a result, culture is dynamic, with unstable, changing concepts of what is good and bad, acceptable and unacceptable. It is by hearing the repressed discourses as well as the dominant ones that the historian is able to discover complex relationships among ideologies that eventually provide an interpretation of what the stories of the past mean. At the very least, unearthing lost discourses and giving them value works against making an oversimplification of history by the acceptance of a master narrative, and it provides a more complete understanding of any text.

Finally, the new historicists deny that history has goals. In their reading of it, events do not necessarily march forward connected by cause and effect or constituting progress. After all, the concept of progress is likely to vary from one society to another, the characteristics attributed to it usually being those that belong to the society defining it. There is also the problem that cultures wax and wane. Powerful, affluent peoples do not stay at their peak forever. Even the Roman Empire eventually fell to the invaders known as barbarians.

NEW LITERARY HISTORICISM

Not surprisingly, such radical departures from the traditional ways of looking at history change the way we read literature. In fact, it should be noted that most of the new historicists are literary scholars. Under their aegis, the concept that a text imitates life—that it reflects its historical context—has either disappeared or seen serious changes. Gone are those approaches that used history, even history of the text, as background to literature and saw the work as a replication of people and behavior of that period (see chapter 2). In their place is the assumption that examination of an author's life to determine her intent and study of a historical period to find the spirit of the age reflected in the text are no longer directly relevant to literary scholarship because history is not expected to validate a text by providing facts that will prove its truth. Indeed, history cannot do so. Because it has been subjectively rendered, the facts are not and have never been known with certainty.

With such revised assumptions, the questions for readers are not "Were the characters based on real people?" or "Do the events recounted in the text re-create experiences from the author's life?" or "Does the text capture the spirit of the times accurately?" but "How does the text reveal and comment on the disparate discourses of the culture it depicts?" With that new question, history moves out from behind a literary work, and the various discourses of an era, one of them being literature, become coparticipants in a complex interaction that is the subject of study. Just as the historian contextualizes historical texts in the many discourses of a culture, so the critic interprets literary texts by viewing them as part of the same interchange. A work of literature is no longer read as an autonomous entity.

The several discourses will not all be representative of "high art" or even what has been known as "art" at all. In fact, according to the new historicists, all texts are social documents, and as such they both reflect and affect the world that produces them. Reading any single one renders an incomplete picture; understanding multiple documents requires piecing them together to produce an interpretation. Using such an approach means removing literature from its pedestal and accepting it as one discourse among many—some of them, such as scientific tracts, legal papers, and popular songs, seemingly distant from the sublimity traditionally attributed to literary works. Like other cultural artifacts, literature creates and is created by others. It demonstrates discourses as they conflict, overlap, and complement each other, and it conflicts with, overlaps, and complements other discourses. Literary interpretation involves acknowledging all the social concerns that surround a text, the customs, institutions, and social practices it depicts as well as those that are part of the life of the author. The job of the good reader is to negotiate the various forces claiming his attention and to find meaning in their interactions.

The good reader's job is complicated by the fact that the culture affects critics as well as texts. Just as a literary work exists in the midst of other discourses, so a critic cannot escape those of her own times. She is influenced by cultural norms and values, both public and private, so that instead of finding (and perhaps explaining) the "true" meaning of a work, she inevitably arrives at a unique interpretation, her own.

In sum, reading literature from a new historicist perspective involves accepting a new understanding of what a text is. Instead of assuming that it is a static, reflective artifact of a definable culture, this approach treats literature as a participant in a dynamic, changeable culture. The potential for change becomes important, because it means that literature has a role to play in the reformation of the society. With its help, power bases can be restructured and the marginalized recognized. Working from this position, the critic accepts the interrelatedness of all human activities, making it necessary to examine how all discourses, those contemporary with a text and those of readers that came later, affect the interpretation of literature. And once it has been acknowledged that what is deemed acceptable is not the same in all eras, it becomes necessary for the reader to admit the prejudices that have been generated by his own culture. The value of a new historicist reading is that it provides a more complete understanding of a text than could be discovered under the older system.

A brief word needs to be said about the related British movement known as **cultural materialism.** Like new historicism, it calls for a renewed awareness of the interrelatedness of human society and a deeper understanding of our own habits and beliefs, but it is more overtly political in its beliefs and goals. Organized in the mid-1960s, originally as an outgrowth of Marxist criticism, cultural materialism argues that the dominant class dictates what forms of art are to be considered superior at the expense of the culture of the working class, which, misunderstood and undervalued, is deemed to be inferior (see chapter 5). The cultural materialists work to erase any distinction between "high" and "low" forms of art, for, they argue, all texts can be analyzed to reveal how they shape a people's experience. All are carriers of ideologies that have the power to reinforce or transform those they touch. The dominant class defines what is acceptable with the goal of strengthening its own position of superiority and power, but the art of the excluded also has the power to reinforce those for whom it speaks and even to affect the entire culture, including the persons and institutions of power. It may be helpful to note that whereas new historicism tends to look at the operations of power from the top down and to concentrate on the pervasive nature of dominant power structures, thereby emphasizing the ways that the powerful produce (and appropriate) subversion in their own interest, cultural materialism looks at how power works from the bottom up and is more interested in the positive potential of subversion for producing real alternatives to dominant institutions of power and modes of knowing. Because literature is a means of effecting change, the job of the critic is to reveal the social purposes that may lie unrealized in a text, so that repressive ideologies of the powerful can be revealed and resisted.

HISTORICAL BACKGROUND

From the outset, the new literary historicism challenged several movements that preceded it. In particular it disputed the principles of traditional historicism and the New Criticism (formalism), both of which had dominated critical practice for several decades in the past.

Just as historians had customarily viewed the past as a series of movements and events that reflected a period's particular way of seeing the world, or as isolated achievements of individuals, literary historians had tended to see literature as an expression of the spirit of a particular time and place or as a series of masterpieces produced by a limited number of creative talents (see chapter 2). By positioning texts against a background of social and political information of the times in which they were produced, or in the context of biography, readers had a way of understanding another way of life, another culture. As the formalists pointed out, sometimes such a perspective was more historical than literary.

The New Critics went so far as to ignore the historical context of literary works, arguing that they belong to no particular era but instead are universal and timeless (see chapter 3). The formalists believed that it was not necessary to know the biography of the author or the cultural environment in which a work was produced, because it held its own aesthetic rules of being within itself. In a sense it existed like Keats's Grecian urn, outside of or above time. To consider a poem only in terms of itself, without reference as to why it came to be, who was influenced by it, what its purpose was, or how it changed the world meant not asking questions that many readers believe to be fundamental to understanding it. Those who objected began to challenge such a stance, raising issues about how a reader can understand literature without knowing where it came from and how it was received. At about the time that the New Critics were under attack from various postmodern theorists, the new historicists joined the skirmish by raising questions that further challenged their premises as well as those of traditional historical literary study.

An early shot was fired by literary scholar Stephen Greenblatt, who is regarded by many as the founder of new historicism. At least he provided the name by which the movement is known in this country by using the term in 1982 in an introduction to a special issue of the journal *Genre.* Well-schooled in the principles of New Criticism, Greenblatt resisted the narrowness of its view and began to publish articles and essays in which he probed the nature of literature and its relationship to the larger culture. His thinking attracted the interest of others, such as Louis Montrose, Jonathan Dollimore, and Catherine Gallagher, who were to become early new historicists. Together they questioned the objectivity of historians, the meaning of texts, the nature of literature, and the role of the critic. Several influences led them to do so.

The nineteenth-century philosopher Nietzsche had opened the discussion much earlier by asserting that people shape facts to suit their desires. He wrote, "Ultimately, man finds in things nothing but what he himself has imported into them." Nietzsche rejected the possibility of absolute truths or objective knowledge and in their place found that what is accepted as truth is that which corresponds to what has already been described as truth by those in power: political authorities, rulers, intellectuals, or simply the prevailing ideologies of the day. The new literary historicists have been more directly influenced by the French thinker Michel Foucault (1926–1984), who challenged many of the accepted concepts about history, culture, and society; by the ideas of Marxist scholars, who recognize the interconnected nature of society; and by the methodology of cultural anthropologists.

According to Foucault, history is neither linear nor teleological. That is, it cannot be explained as a series of causes and effects, and it is not necessarily going purposefully forward toward some known end. It is not a continuum in which truths about human nature and society remain constant. Instead, in Foucault's concept of history, what is accepted to be true changes. Each period establishes its own set of values or actions that people are expected to discuss, protect, and defend. Each develops its own standards of permissible behavior, its criteria for judging what is good or bad, and its system of rules for controlling what is to be said and for disseminating what is accepted as knowledge. Control may take the form of exclusion or prohibition, because what is considered normal or rational silences what is not, whether that be objects, rituals, or specific subjects.

Foucault was particularly interested in discourse, the language of a particular time and place that controls and preserves social relations. It can be thought of as ideology in action. He examined discursive practices in an effort to find the **episteme,** the rules and constraints outside which individuals cannot think or speak without running the risk of being excluded or silenced. The episteme designates which statements can be uttered, who or what institutions have the authority to name things and make judgments about them, how they are allowed to speak, the forms their expression can take, and what can be talked about. Persons and institutions representing "the norm," of which even they may be unconscious, have the power to determine that which is judged to be knowledge and truth, to dictate which subjects are valued and which are not.

Because human society is always more complicated than a single view can indicate, Foucault searched for who has not been allowed to speak and what topics have not been valued. To do so, he borrowed techniques and terminology from archaeology. He dug down past "final" readings of history to find what had been suppressed, ignored, or silenced, which may be just as important to understanding a culture as what has been accepted as knowledge. He examined subjects such as madness, prisons, and sexuality, which he felt had been discourse taboos for centuries. As he put it, they were subject to "rules of exclusion." For example, madness, which Foucault saw as a changing, historically conditioned notion, became a threat to society once reason was considered to be supreme, and thereby it had to be banned from society.

In these terms, literature becomes one of many interactive discourses, and studying it requires putting them together, the accepted with the excluded ones, even when they are contradictory. It is part of the record of human experience that was formed by the cultural conditions at a particular time and place. By reading literature in this way, one not only arrives at a more accurate picture of the past but also discovers knowledge that was lost in traditional historical and literary accounts because it belonged to those who were shut out from participating in the discussion, even when it was about subjects that were of significance to them.

Lately the work of Mikhail Bakhtin has provided new historicists with another way of thinking about the silenced and excluded. His concept of **carnival** features a culture behind the mainstream one, a marginalized one that subverts sanctioned hierarchies by turning the privileged symbols upside down or by putting them into common experience. When it does so, it mocks authority and resists mandatory social behavior. And throughout the process, carnival remains officially sanctioned. Interestingly, resistance is always a part of subjection. Dominance creates opposition that makes social change inevitable. The principle is evident in literature too, where the meanings of texts are never permanently subscribed to but modified by successive challenges from readers and critics. Continuously evolving interpretation makes it impossible to view a text as an organically unified entity.

Another key influence on new historicism has been Marxism, particularly its view of power, which recognizes that the dominant class tries to control the thinking of the people through many means, one of which is literature (see chapter 5). Following both the Marxists and Foucault, the new historicists acknowledge that the accepted practices of a culture keep the powerless in their place and serve the interests of the ruling classes by maintaining social divisions. However, texts can also be a means of overturning the status quo, and, according to new literary historicists—and more especially their British cousins the cultural materialists—critics have a role to play in revealing the political subtexts that lie beneath the conventional ones.

Marxism is also evident in the assumption that a text can be understood only in its cultural context. All actions in a society are connected to all other actions, and together they form the culture. From that position the literary new historicists reason that because a work is connected to the world that produced it, any understanding that does not include an awareness of the concerns of both the culture in general and the author in particular is incomplete. That is, knowledge of the material and historical circumstances of the production of a text is fundamental to comprehending it.

An additional influence on the practices of the new historicists comes from cultural anthropology. In particular, the methodology Clifford Geertz called **thick description** has proved to be helpful. Thick description involves the collection and interpretation of cultural details, close examination of social behavior that serves as the means for finding the codes by which people govern their choices and actions. Even small actions that seem to have no particular significance in themselves can, along with other actions, suggest how a given people see their world. In Geertz's methodology everything is important. Nothing is to be overlooked, because it is through the interconnections of details that meaning is revealed. The observer, however, can never be fully objective, for we are all biased by our own cultural forces. As Foucault points out, because historians too are subject to their epistemes, they must confront their own biases.

The growing interest in the literatures of people who have previously been ignored by the mainstream tradition is a step toward adapting Geertz's techniques to the study of literature. By collecting the many strands of concurrent storytelling available in any given era, critics and scholars can construct a richer, more complete account of that literary period. Recognition of the interactions of various traditions helps explain both the traditionally anthologized texts and those known only to members of the group that produced them, and it helps to keep them alive as well.

In sum, influenced by Foucault, Marxism, and cultural anthropology, the new literary historicists no longer see history as factual background but as one of many concurrent narrative discourses that can be (and will be) read and reread in light of the worldview of succeeding cultures. Analysis of a literary text involves listening to all the discourses while recognizing the inherently biased perspective of the listener. The process might be thought of as ongoing conversations among authors and readers of various eras in which no participant has a complete or objective understanding of the whole.

READING AS A NEW HISTORICIST

To understand the discussion that follows, you will need to read "The Sky Is Gray," by Ernest J. Gaines, which begins on page 257.

A new historicist analysis can pursue several different (but not unconnected) lines of inquiry. It can ask questions about the author's life and times, the life and times in which a work is set, the various discourses represented in it, the writer's intentions and the work's initial reception, and the various ways in which the work has been received since its initial appearance. The overlap of concerns in these queries will produce an interwoven analysis in which one topic complements and overlaps with the others.

THE WORLD OF THE AUTHOR AND THE TEXT

A look at the life of Ernest Gaines, for example, reveals a number of significant social forces that resulted in his 1963 writing of "The Sky Is Gray," a story about a young black boy growing up in the segregated South of the 1940s. The era in which Gaines wrote it was a turbulent one that wrestled with changing concepts of racial relationships, civil rights, and poverty—all of which are important aspects of "The Sky Is Gray." The era it recalls, however, was a very different one, one that Gaines himself knew from personal experience, family stories, African-American culture, and southern tradition. Although he had been living in California for fifteen years when he wrote it, had graduated from San Francisco State College, and held a creative writing fellowship at Stanford University, those earlier times remained viable in memory several decades later.

In some ways, in 1963 the issues of race, rights, and poverty were more powerful than they had been in Gaines's childhood. At the time he was writing the story, it had been six years since troops had been sent to Little Rock to ensure desegregation of the high school. Thurgood Marshall, who almost a decade earlier had won the *Brown* v. *Board of Education* case that led to the desegregation of public schools, was soon to become the first black justice appointed to the U.S. Supreme Court. Lyndon Johnson's War on Poverty would begin the next year. His Great Society, enacted by legislation introduced in 1965, would provide programs such as Medicare and Medicaid, and the Civil Rights Act of 1968, stressing open housing, was on the horizon. Newspapers, magazines, and television news routinely reported changes in the social system that had been in place since the Civil War. In short, the limited access to opportunity and the inequitable division of power taken for granted in "The Sky Is Gray" were being questioned during the time of its writing. Indeed, the denial of African-Americans' rights to schools and universities (education), the voting booth (political power), and lunch counters (social intercourse) was under siege.

In the story, however, James and his family lack all such rights. They are powerless. They do not even live close to centers of power where they might catch the notice of those who could change the dynamics of their situation. In fact, at the time of the story legal and social measures are firmly secured to keep blacks in their place. Through practice of segregation, maintained by those who have power, James and his family will remain powerless because of poverty, ignorance, and separation from the mainstream. For example, James and his mother sit in the bus behind the sign that says "Colored." When the dentist goes to lunch, they are locked out of his waiting room. To find food and shelter from the cold, they must go "back of town," passing by whites-only cafes but not looking in. By law and by social practice, the two of them have no choice but to endure. In such a context, the story becomes a quietly compelling political document testifying to social wrongs that cried out for attention and change.

Gaines was able to re-create that earlier time because he carried in his memory a strong sense of the place, its land, its people, and its culture. Like most of his work, the story is set in rural Louisiana, among the poor, black, bilingual populace of his native Point Coupée Parish. James lives in such a family. On his trip to see the dentist, for example, there is so little money that he must choose between buying something to eat and riding home on the bus, and racial discrimination dominates every choice he and his mother make in Bayonne, the small, bleak town that seems urban by comparison with the plot of land where they share their small house with Ty, Auntie, Val, Louis, and Walker.

Having listened as a child to the stories of the old people, Gaines understood the assumptions of his culture about family, attitudes, behavior, and values. From his early childhood experiences at River Lake Plantation, he had developed a sense of what it means to love the land but not own it, to live in the quarters in the shadow of the plantation house, to attend school and church in the same building and then in another town. As Gaines describes his identity, he says:

> I see myself as a writer, and I happen to have been born here [Louisiana]. I was born black. I was born on a plantation. I've lived in that interracial, or ethnic, mixture of the Cajun, and the big house owned by the Creoles—not Cajuns, but Creoles—and the blacks. I was associated very early with the Baptist church; I was christened as a Baptist. But I went to Catholic school, a little school in New Roads, my last three years in Louisiana. I had to go through their kind of discipline. I had to go to mass. I didn't go to confession or anything like that. I didn't take the Holy Sacrament. I had to go through all these kinds of things. My aunt who raised me and who was crippled spoke Creole. Some of the old ladies on the plantation and some of the old men spoke Creole. (*Porch Talk,* 80)

Gaines's young adulthood presented him with a broader context, one that included other races and ethnic groups and different relations between social classes. It introduced him to books and cities, a new world of experiences that would allow him to understand more clearly the nature of his own culture and the circumstances that had forged it. His respect for the strength of the people of the quarter, combined with knowledge of that bigger world where the social dictates and rules of decorum were different, allowed Gaines to depict the limitations imposed on his characters without dishonoring their dignity. As a result, "The Sky Is Gray" can illuminate the experience of people who up until its appearance had been mostly ignored, certainly underrepresented, and sometimes misrepresented in literature. In so doing, it develops several important themes that recur throughout Ernest Gaines's fiction.

The most evident one perhaps is the search for manhood, a manhood characterized by dignity that cannot be impugned by circumstances. The story ends with the words of James's mother, who in telling him to turn his collar down as it should be, explains, "You not a bum. . . . You a man." Long before that comment, however, her own behavior serves as a model of endurance and sacrifice. She goes hungry so that James can eat. "We don't take no handout," she tells Helena, the white lady who insists that she come into her kitchen and eat. She turns to leave the house rather than accept more salt meat than she has paid for. From such fierce determination and from such courage, James learns what is expected of him as a man. It is more than simple survival, which Mama also teaches him through the unpleasant duty of killing the redbird. It is survival with dignity in a harsh world that will systematically deny him his manhood.

Some themes deal with the old people who are connected to the land at the very time that change is approaching. There are tensions between the young, who are no longer willing to accept the burden the land imposes on them or the societal limitations they have inherited, and the old, who have endured them both. The scene in the dentist's office is a case in point. The radical young man who insists that everything, including the color of the grass and God himself, should be questioned offends the preacher and others who see his ranting as an attack on the institutions and beliefs that have allowed them to live with honor. The young man impugns their traditions and makes rifts in their solidarity by introducing a new way of looking at their lives, a new social code. Change will not be easy within the black community, even change that brings with it desirable rights and opportunities. It may even mean losing treasured aspects of the culture. For example, with increased literacy, what will happen to the rich oral tradition that formed Ernest Gaines himself? Will there continue to be a Monsieur Bayonne to pray over a tooth that aches? Will there be resources, some of them even superstitious ones, to fall back on when everything else fails? What is lost when solutions are standardized, when one size fits all?

And finally, there is the question of identity. Who is James to think he is? How does the black man define himself? In another Gaines story, "A Long Day in November," the character Munford says, "by looking at us he [the white man] knows what he is not." In a culture that has traditionally required that a person belong to one race or another, is the black man to do the same? In "The Sky Is Gray," James seems to recognize that although he honors his cultural background, being a man transcends racial designation. It requires acting responsibly and with integrity, traits not given to one race or the other. Gaines explains the situation when speaking of himself:

> I know who I am. I know that I was born in Pointe Coupée Parish. I know that I grew up on a plantation. I know about the old people around me who sacrificed everything for me to educate me. I know that I have written books. I know that my books have been translated into many languages. I know all these things about myself. I know that I care for my family. I know that I care for my friends. I know that I don't give a damn for my enemies. I know that I don't judge all whites as my enemies; I don't judge them as my friends, either. I know I have white friends. I don't say that all blacks are my friends, because I don't have too many black friends here. . . . I say I must go on and do my work, I must earn my living, I must do my teaching yet communicate with my friends, be with my friends, and all this sort of thing. (*Porch Talk,* 54)

DISCOURSES IN THE TEXT

Many voices are heard in "The Sky Is Gray," some of them new to readers of the 1960s. Before its appearance, few narratives based on the experiences of African-

Americans had joined the mainstream. Gaines himself notes that black writers had no influence on him as he learned his craft, simply because he could not check books out of the library when he was a child in Louisiana; and later in Vallejo, California, where he moved when he was fifteen, few books by black writers were available. Even in college in the early 1950s he was asked to read only passages from *Native Son,* and *Invisible Man* was newly published. In short, during his development as a writer, books by black writers were not there to show him the way. Consequently, Gaines's depiction of black families and experiences represented for the reading public a glimpse into what was virtually a new world for them, one characterized by pressures, practices, and traditions they had not met in literature before.

In addition to introducing the discourse of rural, poor, southern, black America, Gaines provided a depiction of another little-known culture, one composed of people of creole and Cajun lineage. Kate Chopin, who had drawn characters and settings from the communities of French and Spanish descendants in Louisiana, had been largely forgotten by the time Gaines began writing. Though her stories and certainly *The Awakening* would later find popularity with readers, in the early 1960s "The Sky Is Gray" depicted a world little known to most people who lived outside it. The discourses in it had been little heard or noticed.

Most audible are the African-American discourses. On the level of authenticity of expression, they resonate with rhythms and idioms that differ from those of urban, white America. Gaines acknowledges that he absorbed them as a child, listening to the stories people told sitting on the ditch bank or gathered around the fireplace at night. He says, "I came from a place where people sat around and chewed sugarcane and roasted sweet potatoes and peanuts in the ashes and sat on ditch banks and told tales and sat on porches and went into the swamps and went into the fields—that's what I came from" (*Porch Talk,* 37). That was not urban. Those situations were not the ones James Baldwin was writing about. They were voices not heard before in American literature.

As Marcia Gaudet and Carl Wooton point out in *Porch Talk,* Gaines's ability to catch the sound of these people talking was enhanced by his technical training and literary background: "Though he bases his narrative on the folk story-telling tradition, he is quite obviously not a folk storyteller. He is an artist who recognizes the value of the language and customs of his culture, and who consciously manipulates that material through techniques and in forms that occupy the mainstream of western literary tradition." Consequently, Gaines has been able to give readers not just black discourse but varieties of black discourse, not a one-dimensional perspective but conflicting and overlapping ones that deepen the authenticity of the portrayal. Even in "The Sky Is Gray" there are characters who represent differing discourses within the black community. Most obvious among them are the preacher and the revolutionary young man (who is probably more typical of the 1960s than the 1940s) in the dentist's office who finally come to blows over their differences. Not only do they represent contrasting views, but they also reflect the diversity that results from education. Whereas some of the characters are probably illiterate, others study and question. More subtly, there is difference in the innocence of Ty's childhood view of events, the piety of Monsieur Bayonne, and the tight-lipped stoicism of James's mother. They face the world with different expectations and different defenses, though all of them are closely bound together in rural black culture. It is not monolithic. It is not a single body of stereotypical characteristics.

Discourses besides those reflecting the black, creole, and Cajun cultures are also evident in "The Sky Is Gray." Gaines recognizes a number of significant influences on his writing that came from beyond the black community. He mentions the radio shows of the 1950s "where you can only hear things and they tell you what's going on"; jazz saxophonist Lester Young, who, instead of playing on the note, "plays around the note, or under the note, or above the note"; white writers (Twain, Fitzgerald, Hemingway, Turgenev); and the jumbled California culture (made up of blacks, Latinos, Filipinos, Japanese, Chinese, and whites) as all having played a part in the world he writes about and from. In his fiction there is no single discourse but a welter of complementary and conflicting and overlapping ones, just as there are in society itself.

Intentions and Reception

"The Sky Is Gray" could never be described as overtly supporting or undermining particular ideologies. It was not conceived as an explicitly political document. Nevertheless, in its poignant depiction of James (a boy old beyond his years), Mama (determined that he grow up to live with dignity), and Helena and Alnest (whose concern for suffering includes a sensitivity to the feelings of the sufferers), it challenges the power structure of the segregated society it depicts. It recognizes the complexity of human interaction, both intraracial and interracial, while it holds up the exchange between the older white couple and James and Mama as a model of what is possible even in a society built on wildly unequal divisions of power. In this way it can be said to undermine the discourses of the time and place in which it is set, but also to reflect clearly those in which it was produced. And although the legal strictures and mores of its setting have radically changed in the decades since its initial publication, it still manages to touch the emotions and the sense of ethics of contemporary readers, reminding them of what was and what must never be again.

Although Gaines does not talk about his work in political terms and generally asserts that he does not write for any particular audience, he has on occasion admitted that he would like to think that he writes for the black youth and the white youth of the South. Never interested in publishing just for money, just to sell books, he has stated that his purpose is to produce good writing, and if that touches young people who will make a better world than their predecessors experienced, he will be pleased.

Despite disclaimers about making money, economics has influenced publication of Gaines's fiction. His first novel, *Catherine Carmier,* went little noticed, making the stories he subsequently submitted unattractive to publishers. To get them into print, he had to produce a second novel before the stories were brought out. "The Sky Is Gray," which appeared in the collection *Bloodline,* had been earlier published in *Negro Digest.* At that time there seemed to be little recognition—except on the part of Dorothea Oppenheimer, who became Gaines's agent and close friend—of the artistry, authenticity, and power of the story. Today it is difficult to realize that perceptive editors did not recognize the relationship the story would go on to have with audiences over time. Now frequently anthologized and taught in schools and colleges, it stands as a historical document of what once was, continues to offer political challenge to unbalanced power structures, and poses, through the interactions of James, Mama, Helena, and Alnest, a model of interracial accord. It does not suggest that all the problems of the poor, the rural, or the races have been solved. It cannot be read from the perspective that progress is inevitable, but it clearly shows that there have been changes in the social system of the American South.

WRITING A NEW HISTORICIST LITERARY ANALYSIS

Throughout your analysis, and as you begin to shape it into a written report, you will hold certain assumptions about the text. You will assume that it has been marked by the time and place in which it was produced and that it reflects the time and place in which it is set. You will also presume that the text serves some purpose, even if the author and perhaps the reader are not consciously aware of what that intention is. In addition, you will accept that the reading you are making will be different from those of other readers, leading to multiple interpretations that are affected by changing cultural movements and evolving understandings of the time and place of production.

Prewriting

In the case of a new historicist analysis, prewriting may not be an accurate name for what you are likely to be doing. Because your attention will be on all the cultural forces surrounding (and infusing) the text with meaning, you will need to be well informed on a number of issues that lie outside it. Consequently, instead of pre*writing,* you may be pre*reading.* To acquire a comprehensive understanding of the cultural environment, you will probably need to do some library work, looking for information in the following areas:

- *The author.* Reading a biography can provide insight into the writer's concerns about personal experiences as well as about society in general. Such interests will affect the presentation of the people and times depicted in the text, whether or not the setting is the same as the one in which the author is working.
- *The cultural moment.* Not only will newspapers and magazines of the era report the issues of the day, but less explicitly they will also indicate the people's tastes. That is, they will provide information about the rules governing what was deemed to be acceptable and desirable at that time. Both the issues and tastes of the day are forces, albeit nonliterary ones, that impinge on what the text means. The tastes of the day, which you may find to be the more revealing, can be found sometimes in the public figures of the day who symbolize the codes of behavior approved by others. Sometimes they lurk in seemingly insignificant details, such as dress, family customs, advertising, or home decoration. Such research becomes

especially meaningful when the social codes and forces at work in a culture appear to be in conflict with each other.

- *The text.* Listening for all the voices, present and past as well as one's own, enriches and deepens possibilities for meaning. Although one narrative may be dominant, there is not a single one in any text. The world that the text presents is an interaction of different and dynamic discourses that shape and are shaped by each other.

DRAFTING AND REVISING

The Introduction

One way of opening your new historicist analysis is to present a general sketch of the era in which the text is set. An overall look at the time and place of the narrative can ground the discussion that follows. The guiding word here is *general.* The body of the essay will present specific information about politics, behaviors, figures, and institutions, so the introduction should do little more than present a panoramic view of the environment. You may want to think of it as an aerial photograph that shows the layout of the countryside. In the course of the discussion, you will provide close-up shots of that overview.

If you prefer to be more probing than such an introduction permits, an alternative opening is to move directly into your discussion about what the work contributes to your understanding of human experience in the particular time and place in which it is set. This approach involves making some generalizations about the text's interpretation of the culture it represents, which your ensuing discussion will go on to support. For example, you may want to comment on whether (and how) it supports or challenges the dominant discourses of its own era and those of later ones, or you may choose to explain how the text reveals the complexity of the period.

The Body

One way of organizing the body of your discussion comes directly from the prereading process described above. That is, you can address the three topics suggested by its categories of investigation: the world of the author, personal and public; the historical-cultural environment of the text, both the one it depicts and the one in which it was produced; and the internal world of the text itself, the discourses that generate the narrative. In the case of all three you should be attentive to the power structure that is in place, questioning inequalities and pointing out social forces that build community and those that destroy it.

Information about the author's life can shed light on the forces and issues that helped create the text. People and events that were significant to the writer, whether they were positive or negative experiences, can point directly to intent and purpose. Philosophical and political grounding can explain explicit and implicit social commentary. A writer's letters, interviews, and journals can provide comments that illuminate intended audiences and effects. To isolate such helpful information, you can ask some of the following questions.

- What were the formative experiences in the writer's life?
- Who were the significant people in the writer's life?
- What texts affected the writer's thinking?
- What religious-spiritual issues were important to the writer?
- What was the general political stance of the writer?
- What social class did the writer's family occupy?
- What social class did the writer as an adult aspire to belong to?
- How much social power did the writer's family have?
- From how many different social classes and types of work did the writer draw friends?
- From which social classes and types of work did the writer draw friends?
- What social issues were important to the writer?
- What public roles did the writer assume?
- What one-word label would describe the voice of the writer in this text?

Looking beyond the author to the culture in which he lived means examining events and texts that may seem to lie at some distance from the one under scrutiny. You will want to include social actions, relationships, and documents, all situations that involve exchanges of power. You will look for significance not only in major incidents but in minor details as well. Helpful information can be found by asking several kinds of questions. The first kind has to do with historical events of the period, such as the following:

- What were the major events of the period?
- What resistance was there to them and what was its source?
- What were the major controversies of the period?
- What or who represented the power bases in the controversy? Which group was dominant? Which ones were not?
- Who were the major figures of the period?
- What was the source of their power and influence?
- Who or what opposed (or at least resented) their power and influence?

Another avenue of inquiry regarding the work and the world outside of it deals with written texts of the period. It asks questions such as these:

- How do the purposes of this text agree with, repeat, or conflict with other literary texts of the same era?
- How is the style of this text similar to or different from other literary texts of the era?
- How does this text fit (or not fit) into the nonliterary texts of the same period?
- How has this text influenced and been influenced by other texts?

A third group of questions dealing with the work of literature and the world beyond it examines the interactions of the two, including the connections between the text and the world it depicts, the one in which it was published, and those of subsequent periods. You can ask questions like these.

- What would have attracted readers to this work at the time it was published? In later periods?
- What was its public and critical reception at the time of publication?
- What has changed about the way it has been read since its publication?
- What models of behavior does this work support?
- What do the answers to the preceding four questions tell you about the various cultures represented?
- How have values changed since the work was published?
- How have values changed since the period in which it is set?
- Has the text changed its culture or any other culture? If so, how?

In addition to examining the life and thought of the author and the cultural ambience of the work's times, you will need also to look intently at the text itself as a response to both of the other two areas of interest. To determine what commentary it offers regarding that larger world outside itself, you can ask the following questions.

- What various discourses do you meet in the text?
- Which ones are powerful?
- Which represent the experience of people who have traditionally been overlooked, marginalized, or misrepresented?
- What conflicts do you discern in the text between the discourse of the powerful and that of the powerless?
- How do they influence and shape each other by agreeing, complementing, or contradicting each other?
- How does this text support one or the other? What ideology does that support suggest?
- What are the social rules observed in the text?
- Is the text critical of them? Or does it treat them as models of behavior?
- How does this text support or challenge the values, beliefs, and/or practices of the culture it depicts?
- What does the ideological stance imply about the culture it depicts, that of the author's times, and that of subsequent periods?
- How does this text suggest that history does not necessarily proceed in an orderly, positive direction?

The Conclusion

If you have followed the suggestions offered here for drafting your essay, you may not have yet mentioned your own stance regarding the text. If that is the case, the conclusion provides an opportunity for you to make a disclaimer as to the certainty of your analysis. Because all readers are inevitably influenced by the times in which they live, nobody approaches a text from a completely unbiased perspective. In an effort to give as true an account of a text as is possible, the responsible new historicist critic will state her attitudes and the cultural principles that have led to the analysis. Such a declaration will not alter the slant of the critical comments, but it will give the reader a better chance of understanding their source and significance.

GLOSSARY OF TERMS USEFUL IN NEW HISTORICIST CRITICISM

Carnival A social practice that mocks authority and reverses hierarchies.
Cultural materialism The British counterpart of new literary historicism, significantly influenced by Marxist principles.
Culture The sum of the social patterns, traits, and products of a particular time or group of people.
Discourse Ways of thinking and talking about the world. Discourses promote specific kinds of power relations.
Episteme The system that defines the conditions for how a particular age views its world. It underlies the interaction of discourses of the period.
Power The ability or official capacity to exercise control. According to Foucault, the very terms used to describe something reflect power relations.
Self-positioning The announcement of one's own political and philosophical leanings.
Subalterns People of inferior status. Subaltern writers seek to make their marginalized cultures known and valued for their past and present.
Subject Because of their assumption that language shapes subjectivity, postmodernists sometimes use the term that designates a position in a sentence in place of the word *person.*
Thick description A term used by anthropologist Clifford Geertz to designate the collection of seemingly insignificant details that will reveal a culture.

RECOMMENDED WEB SITES

http://www.sou.edu/ENGLISH/Hedges/Sodashop/RCenter/Theory/Explaind/nhistexp.htm
A concise explanation of where new historicism came from and why it is practiced.

http://www.sou.edu/ENGLISH/IDTC/People/foucl t2.HTM
Limited information about Michel Foucault, but a wealth of links to more information on him.

http://www.cumber.edu/engl230/engl230/newhist.htm
Definitions, critical assumptions, and strategies of new historicism. The site has a limited amount of information.

http://www.as.wvu.edu/~lbrady/383newhist.html
Cites key assumptions, themes, and questions about new historicism. It is brief but helpful.

http://www.as.ua.edu/ant/Faculty/murphy/cultmat.htm

Extensive exploration of cultural materialism. It covers basic premises, leading figures, methodologies, and other topics.

SUGGESTED READING

Brannigan, John. *New Historicism and Cultural Materialism.* New York: St. Martin's Press, 1998.

Cox, Jeffrey N., and Larry J. Reynolds, eds. *New Historical Literary Study: Essays on Reproducing Texts, Representing History.* Princeton, N.J.: Princeton Univ. Press, 1993.

During, Simon. New Historicism. *Text and Performance Quarterly* 11 (July 1991): 171–189.

Foucault, Michel. *The Foucault Reader,* ed. Paul Rabinow. New York: Pantheon, 1984.

Gallagher, Catherine, and Stephen Greenblatt. *Practicing New Historicism.* Chicago: University of Chicago Press, 2000.

Gaudet, Marcia, and Carl Wooton. *Porch Talk with Ernest Gaines: Conversations on the Writer's Craft.* Baton Rouge: Louisiana State Univ. Press, 1990.

Greenblatt, Stephen. The Power of Forms and the Forms of Power. *Genre* 15 (1982): 1–4.

Michaels, Walter Benn. *The Gold Standard and the Logic of Naturalism.* Berkeley and Los Angeles: Univ. of California Press, 1987.

Thomas, Brook. The Historical Necessity for—and Difficulties with—New Historical Analysis in Introductory Literature Courses. *College English* 49 (September 1987): 509–522.

Veeser, H. Aram, ed. *The New Historicism.* New York: Routledge, 1989. (Note esp. Catherine Gallagher, "Marxism and the New Historicism," and Stephen Greenblatt, "Towards a Poetics of Culture.")

MODEL STUDENT ANALYSIS

Clothes as Power in Elizabethan England: A New Historicist Criticism of John Donne's "To His Mistress Going to Bed"

Brandy A. Harvey

John Donne's Elegy 19, "To His Mistress Going to Bed," provides each reader the possibility of a unique interpretation. The poem's narrator pleads with his mistress to remove her clothes, but his plea is expressed through symbols associated with war, religious allusions, and references to sexuality and sexual activity. With so many levels and, therefore, opportunities for interpretation, this plea for revelation is not clearly stated. What is most obvious in Elegy 19 is the narrator's struggle for desired power over his mistress in a day when the most powerful person in England, and among the most powerful people in the world, was Queen Elizabeth I, a woman.

The first four lines of the poem, with talk of the "foe" and the "fight," bring to mind a warlike situation. It is here that Donne introduces the idea of powerlessness and power:

Come, Madam, come, all rest my powers defy,
Until I labor, I in labor lie.

The poor narrator cannot even muster the power to sleep. Naturally, he turns to a woman to occupy his time, but he also turns to her as a source of the power he lacks. He asks her to come to him without putting up a fight, for he is weary and would fail to overcome her resistance:

The foe oft times, having the foe in sight,
Is tired with standing though he never fight.

The narrator is essentially saying to his "Madam" that she controls all and that he lies before her powerless.

In line 5 the narrator feels confident enough, powerful enough, to begin demanding the removal of her garments. Perhaps his lover has given him reason to feel this confidence, or perhaps he regains his sense of masculinity, his sense of power. The girdle, the breastplate, and the busk are all named, called upon for removal. Because these undergarments were worn by both men and women in the sixteenth century, various interpretations of the poem are possible. For example, is the lover really a woman, or could it be a man? The lover is more than likely a woman. While the poem offers the opportunity for discussion of homosexuality, Donne seems to be making a statement about the use of clothing as a source for power. Queen Elizabeth I, as well as other women of the sixteenth century, utilized clothing to aid in obtaining and maintaining power and status. The girdle, the breastplate, the bodice, and the busk all served to constrict and to conform, altering the appearance of the wearer, male and female. The purpose of these garments was to flatten the chest and elongate the body, forming a stiff, powerful, masculine figure. The narrator envies his mistress's power-asserting devices:

Off with that happy busk, which I envie,
That still can be, and still can stand so nigh.

Not only is he envious of the busk as a phallic symbol that remains "still" (stiff) indefinitely, but he also resents the fact that, wearing the same undergarments as men, his mistress has the ability to appear as powerful as any man.

As he imagines the removal of the masculine undergarments, he becomes more confident, more demanding, more powerful through her emasculation. She becomes womanly and is consequently associated with powerlessness, vulnerability. As her power is stripped away, literally, the narrator is empowered by his own masculinity in contrast to her femininity. There is a noted crescendo in words and tone. The narrator is finally confident that he is seeing the true woman instead of some character pretending to possess power. Because it is unclear whether or not the lover obeys his demands of removal, it is also unclear whether she merely pretends to wield power behind her masculine garments or whether she actually asserts this power. What is clear is that as the narrator imagines, or witnesses, the removal of his mistress's undergarments, he becomes more comfortable in exercising control over the situation.

His newfound power carries over into colonizing confidence as he explores and discovers her womanhood. She, the exotic, represents America, the New World, or these colonies represent her.

O my *America!* my *Newfoundland!*
My kingdom's safest, when with one man man'd.
My myne of precious stones: My Emperie,
How am I blest in thus discovering thee!

Given that man has the power to discover the colonies, he must have the power to explore and subjugate her as well. References to colonization are common in sixteenth-century works—Sir Philip Sidney's *Astrophel and Stella,* William Shakespeare's *Romeo and Juliet,* and the like—and are often associated with love and sexuality. It is fitting that as the narrator becomes more confident and more powerful in his mind, he should desire true freedom, the true freedom associated with being naked and the true freedom associated with America. By this point in Elegy 19 the narrator has regained all sense of power and will soon feel confident enough to request the presence of his mistress in bed.

The implications of power in the costume of the day overshadow all references to war and religion as the narrator's desire to explore and to "know" his mistress can be realized only after the removal of her power-wielding attire. Donne clearly relates the undergarments common to both men and women of the sixteenth century to the possession of power. The narrator's plea for revelation states much more than the sexual desires of the man. Donne reveals discomfort with the power asserted by women who, like Queen Elizabeth, are empowered by their undergarments.

10

More Cultural Studies: Postcolonialism and Multiculturalism

It is from those who have suffered the sentence of history—subjugation, domination, diaspora, displacement—that we learn our most enduring lessons for living and thinking.
Homi Bhabha, "The Postcolonial and the Postmodern"

We have already seen how new historicism uses knowledge and information from many fields, some of which have not traditionally been associated with literary studies. Critics working from a postcolonial or American multicultural perspective share that interest in going beyond the study of literature as literature, and they too have been influenced by anthropology, sociology, Marxism, feminism, popular culture studies, and other nonliterary disciplines that examine distinct groups of people in an attempt to explain how a culture is created, maintained, and weakened. In addition, they often use the methodologies of other disciplines, finding in the approaches of psychoanalysis or deconstruction the means of examining texts as part of a larger body of study, that of the culture itself.

POSTCOLONIALISM

To understand postcolonialism and its connection to literature requires looking first at its predecessor, colonialism, and its successor, neocolonialism. It hardly needs to be pointed out by now that because postcolonialism is a relatively new field of study, there is not total agreement about its principles and purposes. In this case, even its spelling (*post-colonialism* versus *postcolonialism*) is disputed. What follows, therefore, are generalizations that may not apply to everyone involved with postcolonial theory and the criticism of postcolonial literature.

HISTORICAL BACKGROUND

Interest in postcolonialism dates back to the 1950s when Alfred Sauvy coined the term *Third World* to refer to developing nations, such as those in Africa or South America. They differ from what has come to be known as the First World countries—those in most of Europe and the United States—which are characterized by industrialization, democracy, relative affluence, and similar cultural assumptions and beliefs. (The literature of postcolonial nations is still referred to by some, particularly Marxists, as being from the Third World.) The white populations of countries once belonging to the British Empire (Australia, Canada, New Zealand) and those of the former Soviet Union come somewhere between the developed and developing nations, and at the bottom of this hierarchy are the native populations who, although in some cases they compose the majority, are ruled by their white conquerors. Postcolonialism is interested in all but the First World, though because its members have historically been the oppressors, it too is involved in the discussion.

Colonialism is, simply, the subjection of one population to another. It is most clearly seen in physical conquest, but in its more subtle forms it involves political, economic, and cultural domination. The British rule in India, for example, involved not only the use of force to subdue the latter but also the imposition of British institutions and tastes. When people are colonized, their traditions and practices are supplanted by imitations of those of the colonizer. Parts of the indigenous one as elemental as food, clothing, and recreation tend to disappear, because they are either hidden or replaced, thereby removing that culture from history. **Postcolonialism** is concerned with what exists and happens after the end of colonial rule. The formal termination of colonial rule does not wipe out its legacy, and the culture that is left is a mixture of the colonized one and that of the colonizer, often marked by contrasts and antagonisms, resentment and blended practice. The two are no longer recognizable as separate cultures but exist as a mixed one.

It seems that the *post-* part of *postcolonialism* may be an overstatement of the way things really are, for today a new kind of colonialism is taking place. Weaker powers are no longer as likely to be taken by military conquest, but they are no less economically and culturally dominated. Major international corporations, drawn by the availability of cheap labor and cooperative local governments, practice what is known as **neocolonialism,** which has much the same effect as traditional imperialism. Under its aegis, the customs and traditional "ways" of the subjugated peoples are weakened, changed, and sometimes destroyed.

Although the term *postcolonial* was not in use until the late 1980s, Edward Said's *Orientalism,* an important influence, came out in 1978, and other theoretical texts date back to the 1960s. In his analysis, Said called attention to the pejorative stereotypes that the British, other Europeans, and Americans create of the peoples unlike themselves, thereby making it easier to justify military or economic conquest. Their view of the "other" world, "orientalism," is inevitably colored by their own cultural, political, and religious background, leading them to depict those unlike themselves as inferior and objectionable—for example, as lazy, deceitful, and irrational. The self, by contrast, is defined as good, upright, and moral. The Eastern nations are given all the negative characteristics the West does not want to see in itself. For example, the first reports of the Oklahoma City bombing attributed the deed to Middle Eastern terrorists, because it was impossible to think that an American would have done such a thing. In his early text, Said called upon the literary establishment to raise questions about colonization, imperialism, and constructions of the "other." Over the ensuing decades, postcolonial theory has probed those issues by examination of such subjects as language, feminism, oppression, cultural identity, and education. The intent is to feature what happens when one culture is dominated by another.

Knowing exactly which works fall into the category of postcolonial literature was a simpler matter before the 1980s, when it was called Commonwealth literature. The problem with that label was its grounding in British culture. It seemed to indicate that the literatures of native cultures still belonged to Britain. The term *postcolonial* has replaced it, although there is not total agreement as to what literatures it includes. Some readers assume that it refers to texts produced after the colonized countries became independent, but others take it to mean the texts produced from the time of colonization to the present.

Another complication is that in the English-speaking world, the term generally refers to the literature of cultures colonized by the British Empire, such as Australia, New Zealand, and Africa, all of which were dominated by white Europeans who imposed their own cultural traditions at the expense of those of the native population. Such a position ignores the literature of white settlers in colonized lands. Some readers argue that white writers in Canada or Australia should not be included because they still practice British traditions, share the same language, and belong to the same race. They were not oppressed. They did not have to hide their traditions. Others argue, on the other hand, that although the settlers were the colonizers, they (or their descendants) do not and did not belong to Britain in the same way that native-born citizens do. Their home is in the colonized country. Consequently, the literature of white settlers shares the **double consciousness (double vision)** of native peoples. That is, it views the world through the contrasting perspectives of both the colonizer and the colonized. It reflects the sense of belonging to neither, of being culturally displaced, a quality Homi Bhabha refers to as **unhomeliness.** The broadest view of postcolonial literature is that it is the literature written in English by people in formerly colonized countries, some of it authored by the colonizers and their descendants, but more of it by those they colonized.

The subject matter of postcolonial literature is marked by its concern for the ambiguity or loss of identity. Written by culturally displaced people, it investigates the clash of cultures in which one deems itself to be the superior one and imposes its own practices on the less powerful one. Its writers examine their histories, question how they should respond to the changes they see around them, and wonder what their society will become. They recognize in themselves the old culture and the new, elements of the native one and the imposed one. The result is writing that is critical of the conquerors and promotional about its own ideologies, which are particularly powerful because they are put there by writers and absorbed by readers without their necessarily realizing it.

Postcolonial criticism, which arose in the early 1990s, looks at the works of postcolonial writers but is not limited to them. Because its practitioners are interested in how the colonized came to accept the values of the more powerful culture and to resist them too, it looks at canonical texts as well as postcolonial ones. Attitudes toward the "other" are evident in works that may not, on the surface, seem to deal with colonialism at all. Helen Tiffin argues in "Post-colonial Literatures and Counter-discourse" that since a precolonial past cannot be regained, and contemporary identity cannot be free of that past, the real job of postcolonial criticism is "to investigate the means by which Europe imposed and maintained . . . colonial domination of so much of the rest of the world." She suggests that the way to do so is to use "canonical counter-discourse," a process in which one examines "a character or characters, or the basic assumptions of a British canonical text, and unveils [colonialist] assumptions, subverting the text for post-colonial purposes." By extension, the whole colonialist discourse in which it participates is revealed.

In another look at *Jane Eyre,* for example, Andrew Bennett and Nicholas Royle discover a strong racial theme in the novel. By bringing Bertha Mason, Rochester's creole wife (from the West Indies) to the center of the narrative, they make the allusions and images that refer to slavery and the slave trade, heretofore mostly ignored, important keys to prevailing social attitudes. Whereas traditional criticism has in large part overlooked Bertha, who lives as a madwoman locked in the attic, and left the assumptions about her unexamined, Bennett and Royle uncover the ideology implicit in the unquestioned acceptance of her invisibility, imprisonment, and displacement from her homeland. Before their analysis, she was seen as a threat because of her madness. They make it possible to view her, instead, as a sufferer who has been driven mad. The roles of villain and victim are reversed, providing through this new perspective on a much-read novel additional insight into colonialist and anticolonialist thinking.

BASIC ASSUMPTIONS

The lack of total agreement about what postcolonialism is or whom it involves makes it difficult to set down its basic principles and purposes. Further complicating the situation is that different cultures have responded to colonization in different ways, making it impossible to subscribe to any single way of approaching postcolonial studies. With those reservations in mind, the following assumptions and generalizations are generally accepted as important to postcolonial theory.

- Colonizers not only physically conquer territories but also practice **cultural colonization** by replacing the practices and beliefs of the native culture with their own values, governance, laws, and belief. The consequence is loss or modification of much of the precolonial culture.

- When their own culture is forbidden or devalued, natives come to see themselves as inferior to the conquerors. They abandon (or hide) their own cultural practices to adopt (imitate) those of the assumedly "superior" one.
- Colonial subjects practice **mimicry**—imitation of dress, language, behavior, even gestures—instead of resistance. Homi Bhabha points out that the mimicry is never exact, however. It "is at once resemblance and menace." The colonizer both wants and fears that the colonized will be like him because the imitation honors and, at the same time, undermines the "authoritative discourse" of colonialism.
- European colonizers believed that their ideals and experiences were universal. As a concept, **universalism** is evident in the characters and themes in European (and later American) literature.
- The European colonizers assumed the superiority of their own culture and the inferiority of the conquered ones. They thought of themselves as civilized, even advanced, and of the colonists as backward, even savage. Using their own culture as the standard for what any culture should be, a practice known as **Eurocentrism,** the powerful justified the imposition of their own culture on those they deemed to be of lesser status, the **subalterns.**
- The practice of **othering,** viewing as inferior beings those who are different from oneself, divides people and justifies hierarchies. Sometimes the dominant culture views the "other" as evil, in which case it is known as the **demonic other.**
- On other occasions, the "other" is deemed to have a natural beauty, to be the **exotic other.**
- Colonizers also become the colonized. In this two-way process, the Europeans too were affected by their contact with other cultures.
- The effects of past colonialism are still evident today, and a new form of colonialism is currently effected by international corporations operating in developing nations.
- The interaction of cultures creates blended ones, mixtures of the native and colonial, a process called **hybridity** or **syncretism.** Characterized by tensions and change, this process is dynamic, interactive, creative. As Bhabha explains in an interview with Gary Olson and Lynn Worsham, "For me, hybridization is a discursive, enunciatory, cultural, subjective process having to do with the struggle around authority, authorization, deauthorization, and the revision of authority. It's a social process. It's not about persons of diverse cultural tastes and fashions."

READING AS A POSTCOLONIALIST

To understand the discussion that follows, you should read the excerpt included here from Jill Ker Conway's autobiography, The Road from Coorain, *which begins on page 277.*

A postcolonial analysis begins with the assumption that examining the relationship between a text and its context will illuminate not only the given work but also the culture that produced and consumed it. In the end you may not agree with everything you find in either of them, but you will emerge with a deeper understanding of how and why a text is meaningful. In turn, the process gives greater validity to your judgments about a body of literature and the community associated with it. The postcolonial reader will generally be alert and sensitive to the presence of the following elements that recur in the literature.

Presentation of Colonialism

The central question of this kind of criticism addresses the stance of the text toward the mixed colonial culture that it depicts or that produced it. What attitudes does it reflect regarding the colonizers and the colonized? A wide range of viewpoints is possible here, for the historical development of a culture, the relationships of its cultural groups, and the daily stresses of mixing people of different backgrounds make for a complex situation. The understanding of such matters will likely be expressed in fairly subtle ways, and there may be no single unconflicted attitude, because questions of how the conquered and the conqueror can live comfortably with each other, even after years of trying, are not easily answered.

Colonialism is certainly one of the principal themes of Jill Ker Conway's autobiographical remembrance of growing up in Australia. In *The Road from Coorain* she not only identifies the colonialist mentalities she met (and was led to share) but also traces the means by which they were inculcated and maintained. She tells the story of her awakening to the fact that she has unconsciously absorbed colonial attitudes from her family and other families living similar kinds of lives in the outback. Her recognition of the elitism and estrangement from native life on that continent takes her by surprise as she moves from Coorain, the remote sheep farm in the bush, to Sydney after the death of her father, later to graduate school in America, and finally to her appointment as the first female president of Smith College. The awareness of the duality of her cultural roots is accompanied by the corresponding surprise of finding that being female set her apart in a similar way. Just as she was subtly informed at home and school and in society that Australia was inferior to Great Britain, so she was also confronted with implicit, and sometimes explicit, assumptions that she was less capable than the males in her world. Ironically, it was because she was female that she was allowed to pursue higher education, for, unlike her brothers, she was not expected to return to Coorain and run the sheep farm.

Treatment of Characters

It is in the portrayals of colonizers and the colonized that the larger picture becomes evident. The reader can begin by asking whether the depictions are positive or negative. Whose deeds are celebrated and whose reproved? The assumptions about characters, both spoken and unspoken, will indicate whether the work supports or resists the ideology and practices of colonialism.

Conway's depictions of the characters she knew as a girl are not simple ones. Some of the colorful personalities she met came to the sheep farm to work; others were landowning farmers like her parents. She remembers them with fondness, but she also recognizes that from the beginning the class distinctions were clear, and they became more firmly drawn after her move to Sydney. It was the families with close English connections who stood high in the hierarchy; it was those with the most English behavior who were most admired. At Abbotsleigh, for example, the school in which Conway was enrolled after her brief exposure to public education, the headmistress, Miss Everett, represented the "European cultural ideal," and the girls were expected to emulate her straight back, British accent, and athletic carriage. Looking back, Conway recognizes that something was lost by what she refers to as her "colonization." She speculates that had she remained in a public school, she might "have been obliged to come to terms with the Australian class system." She adds, "It would have been invaluable knowledge, and my vision of Australia would have been the better for it. It was to take me another fifteen years to see the world from my own Australian perspective, rather than from the British definition taught to my kind of colonial." Though her criticism is not bitter, and her depictions of Miss Everett and others at Abbotsleigh are affectionately drawn, her awareness of the limitations imposed by the colonial mentality is clear.

Validity of the Narrative

It is important to establish whether the events are exaggerated or not. Is political and cultural domination presented explicitly or allegorically? Is the whole story being told? Are some elements contrary to what actually happened? Are the rationalizations believable? Knowing something about the author, her background, opinions, and purposes can sometimes be helpful in this regard.

Because *The Road from Coorain* is autobiographical, and the writer has validity in the eyes of the reader, the narrative is straightforward and rings true. She does not indulge in exaggeration or even satire, except for an occasional comic look at human foibles.

Expressions of Nativism (Nationalism)

Out of a desire to resurrect the precolonial culture, some postcolonial writers consciously use elements of native culture and expunge elements of the imposed one. It is one way to rediscover native identity and declare its worth. Several problems lie in this approach, however. When writers publish works written in their own language, for instance, they are likely to meet a limited reading audience because too few people are likely to be proficient at comprehending it. Some people argue also that the attempt is inherently flawed because all cultures change, and even without the intervention of an outside oppressor, what once was, even if one could find it out, would no longer be. And, finally, postcolonial cultures are hybrid ones, and any attempt to go back to a "pure" culture is unrealistic.

Conway, writing as a native-born Australian but not as a member of the indigenous population, makes no attempt to disavow her British heritage. Instead, she writes from the postcolonial perspective of a hybrid culture that combines both the native one and the dominating one. Sometimes the contrasts make for illogical or amusing situations. For example, the requirement at Abbotsleigh that the girls wear uniforms designed for an English climate leaves them in summer in "starched green linen dresses with cream collars, the same [green flannel] blazer, beige socks, a cream panama hat, and the same brown gloves." She continues, "Woe betide the student caught shedding the blazer or the gloves in public, even when the thermometer was over 100 degrees. . . . No one paused to think that gloves and blazers had a function in damp English springs which they lacked entirely in our blazing summers." Such irrational practices left the girls, as Conway says, "only partially at home in our environment." She is referring to the sense of unhomeliness, of being caught between two cultures and not entirely at home in either of them. Another way of describing her situation is to say that she is experiencing double consciousness, for she has an awareness of being part of both the colonized and the colonizing cultures and thus being the recipient of all the conflicts and contrasts that exist between them.

Recurring Subjects and Themes

Some postcolonial texts look to the past, rehearsing the pains of othering and the humiliations of mimicry. They retell the stories of the initial colonization and trace changes in the native culture. Others record the sense of double consciousness and unhomeliness experienced by those who belong to both and to neither. Still other texts look to the future, reaching for a definition of the new hybrid identity (both personal and communal) and an ideology that will serve its needs. In all cases postcolonial texts reveal the complexity of cultural identity in a colonized world.

As already noted, *The Road from Coorain* is the story of Conway's double consciousness and unhomeliness as it evolves into a personal identity. It also points to the practice of mimicry as one of the chief ways by which the colonizer's presence was maintained. Nowhere is that more evident than at Abbotsleigh, where Eurocentrism reigned. The school made it clear by social rules, curriculum, and the example of its leaders that England was the standard by which all people and practices were to be measured. In the formality of the dinner table—where the girls, wearing green velvet dresses, were seated in descending order of age and class—in the absence of references to Australian art and literature in their classes, and in virtually all practices at Abbotsleigh, it was British culture that was imitated and admired. For example, Conway notes that, in the study of literature, she and her classmates "might have been in Sussex," because their reading consisted of Shakespeare and Shelley, not of the writers of their own country. Australia, then, was defined by default, by what it was not. The girls were left to conclude that because its countryside did not look like the Cotswolds and the Lake Country, it must be ugly; and because its paintings were not mentioned, there must not be any. History pointed out that people of any importance lived somewhere else. The teachers dutifully corrected the girls' speech so that it would conform to standard British pronunciation unmarred by Australian patterns. In short, "The best standards were derived from Great Britain, and should be emulated unquestioningly." And just in case the message was not clear, geography lessons featured maps with the holdings of the British Empire colored bright red. Obviously, the closest an Australian could come to being judged superior was by mimicry, by being British, even if only partly so.

Context

Every work has a context, and studying context lies at the heart of postcolonial literary study. Whereas interpreters of culture sometimes derive insights about it by reading its literature, a postcolonialist critic will look to almost every aspect of a culture to illuminate a text. Significant elements may be social or material; they may be drawn from the culture that produced the text or the culture of its interpreters. For the reader interested in deepening his understanding of a work, the process means examining the interaction of the two, which can be a time-consuming business if for no other reason than it is difficult to know when you have done enough. The complex relationship between text and context, which are both products and creators of each other, is called **negotiation.**

The context of Conway's story and the context of its telling are not the same. That is, it is told from the distance of another country, personal independence, and intellectual growth. She has written it from the perspective of one who has moved far enough away from a place and a personal history to achieve insight that is not often found while immersed in it. It is interesting to speculate, for example, whether Conway would have been moved to write about growing up entrenched in colonialist mentality if she had not left it behind. Then, too, the changing social attitudes of the 1960s and later must have been an influence on her, as they have been on others, to question the traditional ways of evaluating what is good and what should be, a process that is important to her story. The times and her changing place have allowed her to see her past with greater clarity, and her remembrances shed light on the times, past and present.

Minor Characters

As in the analysis of *Jane Eyre* mentioned earlier, previously unnoticed assumptions can sometimes be detected by paying attention to the characters that do not hold center stage. By noting their treatment and the language used to describe them, attitudes about colonizers and colonized peoples that have gone unnoticed, especially in canonical works, may become evident.

Conway's classmates at the public school she briefly attended are never mentioned by name, and perhaps they were never even known as individuals. In the full scope of the autobiography they play bit parts. Nevertheless, her brief encounter with them speaks volumes about the class structure of postwar Australia. For example, the superior attitude that she naturally assumed toward them, on the basis of the stereotypes and judgments given to her by her family and their friends, is symptomatic of the elitism common to their class. The jeering schoolmates are well aware of the social gulf between them, and they reflect an authentic Australian culture that is scorned by those who have assumed the colonizers' consciousness of class.

Political Statement and Innuendo

The question here is whether and how a work promotes resistance to colonialism. Does it make ideological statements or support a particular course of political, economic, or social action? Does it take up the case for or against a particular group of people? Or does it attempt to present the complexity of the situation without taking a stand toward it?

When Jill Ker Conway promotes resistance to colonialism, she does so quietly. Her book is not driven by a desire to rally crowds to march in the streets for a particular cause. Instead, it is a thoughtful recollection of how she came to recognize her own girlhood acceptance of a limited point of view that created in her, as an Australian, a sense of always being less than someone else. It was a sense of self that was derived both from her colonialist background and from growing up female. Although she names no black villains or conspirators, there is no mistaking her criticism of institutionalized social practices designed to ensure an inferior status for certain groups. It is clear that she regrets the negative sense of self imposed on both children and adults by the comparison of Australia with the revered Great Britain. Her escape from such smallness of vision came with her move to the United States for graduate study and her subsequent marriage to a Canadian. Her cultural identity has continued to grow, making in one sense for greater complexity of definition, but in another for deeper understanding of what it means to reject the colonial mentality as one works out an individual identity. In the end, her own liberation from colonialist boundaries and definitions and her assumption of an identity that has been enriched by numerous cultures makes her a model of what citizens of a shrinking world are likely to become. In that way her autobiography makes a quiet but powerful ideological statement.

Similarities

Homi Bhabha notes the possibilities for studying world literature not in terms of national traditions but in terms of postcolonial themes that cut across national boundaries. The reader would look, for example, at whether native populations from different countries have commonalities as a result of their experience of having been colonized. The study could take a number of different forms, depending on which groups the reader chose to study.

Conway could easily be the subject of such study, as she is not the only writer to address the issues named here. Undoubtedly, interesting comparisons could be made between her remembrances and those of others who grew up as natives in a homeland not entirely their own. Did they experience the same sense of double consciousness? Did they have the same knowledge of hybridity? Were they, too, expected to practice mimicry? For example, what correspondences and differences are to be found between *The Road from Coorain* and V. S. Naipaul's novel *A Bend in the River,* the story of a young Indian man who moves to an isolated African town and finds himself dangerously caught up in the clash of an old regime and the new one.

GLOSSARY OF TERMS USEFUL IN POSTCOLONIAL STUDIES

Colonialism The subjection of one culture by another. It may involve military conquest but extends to the imposition of the dominant power's values and customs on those of the conquered peoples.

Cultural colonization The imposition of the beliefs and social practices of the dominant power on the subjugated one, resulting in loss or change of the native culture.

Demonic other The view that those who are different from oneself are not only backward but also savage, even evil.

Double vision/double consciousness A sense of being part of both the colonized and the colonizing cultures, with all the conflicts and contrasts that involves. It is characteristic of indigenous peoples and later settlers.

Eurocentrism The assumption that European ideals and experiences are the standard by which all other cultures are to be measured and judged inferior.

Exotic other The view that those who are different from oneself possess an inherent dignity and beauty, perhaps because of their more undeveloped, natural state of being.

Hybridity/syncretism The quality of cultures that have characteristics of both the colonizers and the colonized. Marked by conflicts and tensions, they are continually changing and evolving.

Mimicry Imitation of the dress, manners, and language of the dominant culture by the oppressed one.

Negotiation The relationship between a text and its context, both the one that produced it and those that consume it. The assumption is that each affects the other in significant ways.

Neocolonialism Domination of a developing nation by international corporations attracted by cheap labor and manipulable political and legal systems.

Othering The assumption that those who are different from oneself are inferior beings.

Postcolonialism The study of a culture after the physical and/or political withdrawal of an oppressive power.

Postcolonial literary criticism Analysis that looks to uncover the colonialist or anticolonialist ideologies in a text.

Postcolonial literature The writings produced by members of the indigenous culture or by settlers (and their descendants) who have ties to both the invading culture and the oppressed one. (Agreement about the inclusion of the latter is not universal.) In English-speaking nations the term usually refers to the literature of former colonies of the British Empire.

Subalterns People of inferior status. Subaltern writers seek to make their marginalized cultures known and valued for their past and present.

Unhomeliness The sense of being culturally displaced, of being caught between two cultures and not "at home" in either of them. It is felt by those who lack a clearly defined cultural identity.

Universalism The belief that a great work of literature deals with certain themes and characters that are common in European literature. It is Eurocentric in nature.

AMERICAN MULTICULTURALISM

Since the 1960s, American society has undergone radical changes in how it conceives of social structures. School desegregation, new laws barring discrimination, and the demise of old ones that promoted it have opened the door to opportunity for people who had traditionally been shut out. Within such marginalized groups, the renaissance of valued traditions that differ from those of the dominant group has served to enhance self-esteem and reassert distinct identities. In turn, the richness of cultures that had heretofore been ignored or reviled has come to the attention not only of those who belong to them but of a wider public as well. The arts, crafts, rituals, and religion of American Indians, Hispanics, African-Americans, and other historically overlooked groups are now generating increasing interest in the many strands that make up American society, making people less confined by a single way of seeing their lives. Of all such groups, African-American culture, burdened with problems from the moment of its introduction to the New World, has probably received more attention than any of the others. For that reason, it will be discussed here as a model of how cultural studies of other marginalized groups can be made.

AFRICAN-AMERICAN LITERATURE

Although literature produced by African-Americans dates from their earliest presence in North America, notice by the mainstream was a long time coming to those writers who explored their own traditions and forms. Jupiter Hammon and Phyllis Wheatley, the first black man and woman to be published in what was to become this country, both practiced the literary traditions of white culture. Beginning in 1760, Hammon, the slave of Joseph Lloyd of Queens Village, Long Island, published poems and prose works that reflected his resignation to a life of obedience to his earthly master and to God. Wheatley, purchased as a young girl in 1761 by John Wheatley of Boston, was taught to read and write and quickly began to compose poems. Eventually she became the best-known American poet in England. Writing in the neoclassical style of Alexander Pope, she composed verses that reflected her privileged status, not a slave mentality. She never speaks with regret for the loss of her freedom. The theme of freedom was dominant, however, in the writing of other African-Americans during the slave period (1619–1865) and the period dedicated to readjustment and progress (1866–1917).

It was decades before black writers would again attract major attention from mainstream American culture. Not until the Harlem Renaissance of the 1920s would their work be celebrated by those outside their own circle. In that postwar decade, it shared the popularity that black music and dance found with whites, partly because it represented a departure from traditional forms. The culture that most of America had almost forgotten now seemed new and exciting, though attention waned again when the depression and World War II demanded its energies, returning in the 1940s with the appearance of social protest novels such as Richard Wright's *Black Boy.* By midcentury there was also interest in the black folk tradition, which was in danger of being lost. J. Mason Brewer, for example, collected and called on others to document a long and varied group of verbal artifacts, including religious tales; slave tales; "professor" stories; rich-soil tales (of Louisiana) and poor-land tales (of Alabama); the court story cycle of tales of the Arkansas Negro; humorous Mexican-Negro anecdotes; stories of Uncle Mose, the carefree Negro, the clever Negro, and the Mississippi delta; narratives of Georgia race prejudice; and ghost stories (*Black Expressions* 21). In the 1960s, black writers again claimed notice, but this time with a difference. Writing more consciously out of the African-American experience, they no longer asked for white approval of their works but wrote intentionally for black audiences. They no longer tried to conceal faults that might earn white criticism but instead turned to condemning the shortcomings of the dominant culture. Pity and mourning were replaced by an assertion of worth. The success of black writers over the past three decades has been astounding, with far too many prize-winning poets, essayists, playwrights, and fiction writers to name here.

Although the literature of black culture had been part of American history from the eighteenth century on, sometimes appearing in print, sometimes being passed on as an oral tradition, critics who understood the work were not. Anthologies of black literature were compiled in the 1920s, such as James Weldon Johnson's *The Book of American Negro Poetry* (1922), followed by Alain Locke's *The New Negro* (1925) and *Caroling Dusk,* brought out by Countee Cullen (1927). A second explosion of collections followed the appearance of Rosey Pool's *Beyond the Blues* in 1962. The readers were there, but where were the critics?

Clearly it was time for critical approaches that incorporated an understanding of the purposes of black artists and the forms and styles in which they worked. The standards held up as exemplary in the poetry and fiction of white writers were not always suitable for what African-American writers produced. Sometimes they did not fit. Needed were readers who could understand the forms and styles of black artists and interpret their works in ways that were valid, finding their uniqueness as well as discovering similarities and differences with the literatures of other cultures. Such interpretations would be based not on white standards but on what came to be known as the black aesthetic.

For African-American artists a black aesthetic would ease their struggle to find an identity in a world that was not theirs. It would encourage them to honor their own experience, not remake it in the image of white culture. By asserting a racial identity that was separate from and not dependent on white attitudes, principles, and practices, it would renounce the assumption that because the white experience is the model to follow, its rules and standards of judgment must be adopted. For the world at large, it would counter what Carolyn Gerald called the black community's "zero image," caused sometimes by the absence of visibility and sometimes by negative portraits that appeared in white films, literature, and art. In its most assertive form a black aesthetic would be a protest against white critics, editors, and publishers and their power to control what is written and published. More pragmatically, it would be the basis of a system of evaluating African-American art in terms of the special character of the black experience.

The problem lay in defining what that special character is. To arrive at a consensus about such a complex topic required thinking and talking about the function of black writers, examining their literary techniques, establishing the qualifications of black critics, and devising critical terminology. Although such discussions are still in progress, it is possible to specify some of the major points of interest. Like the aesthetic of all artists, the black aesthetic is concerned with the materials its artists work with, the purpose of their work, and how they go about doing it.

For black artists the material is black history, which is unlike that of any other group in America. Their unique past includes Africa, the Middle Passage, slavery, emancipation, northward migration, racism, and the civil rights, Black Power, and Black Arts movements, and it lacks some of the history that other Americans have enjoyed, such as the vision of this country as a land of rights, freedom, and opportunity. The result is a dual identity, one that both partakes of America and doesn't, one that shares the American experience but is denied it. Even today, the sense of belonging and being separate provides material not duplicated in any other American group. As Addison Gayle describes it in *The Black Aesthetic,* "One ever feels his twoness—an American, a Negro; two souls, two thoughts, two unreconciled strivings; two warring ideals in one dark body, whose dogged strength alone keeps it from being torn asunder" (xxii). Henry Louis Gates finds its traces in literature in what he calls "double-voicedness." In fact, he identifies that quality as the source of the uniqueness of black literature, for no other can lay claim to having its roots in both black and white cultures *(The Signifying Monkey).* (Some readers take his assertion to be overstated, because the work of white artists has certainly been influenced by black culture.)

The purpose of black art, like that of all art, varies with the artist. Nevertheless, African-American artists have a strong imperative to reclaim their culture by defining what is of value to them. Such a reclamation takes place by remembering history, defining identity, gaining recognition, and celebrating blackness. It requires that African-American literature announce itself as itself, not as a copy of other art. By so doing, it legitimizes the community it comes from and to some degree can be seen as revolutionary.

Black artists generally go about their work in the same way their white counterparts do. However, African-American writers are also noted for drawing on folk traditions that express their beliefs, values, and social mores. Their written narratives and poetry often come from an oral tradition that features folktales, common expressions, exaggeration, a notable lack of self-consciousness, and a closeness to nature. The influence of the folk tradition is found not only in literature, however; it is present in African-American music, such as the blues and work songs, as well.

Black artists are not limited to folk materials and techniques, though. Other traditions have also influenced how they do their work. Writing for *The Negro Digest* in 1968, Ron Karenga, for example, cites three characteristics of African art that can be found in the work of African-Americans. Both, he says, are functional, collective, and committing or committed. The function of African-American art, according to Karenga, is to make revolution. Its collective nature is evident in its presentation of real life and real people, and it is committed to permanent revolution.

READING AS A MULTICULTURALIST

To understand the discussion that follows, you will need to read an excerpt from The Eatonville Anthology, *a remembrance by Zora Neale Hurston, which begins on page 287.*

To approach a text from a multicultural perspective, a reader must look for more than material, purpose, and method. In the case of African-American writers, he needs to anticipate specific characteristics that distinguish their work. Don Lee states that such qualities can be most clearly recognized in music, because it is the black art form least affected by European-American culture ("Toward a Definition: Black Poetry of the Sixties," 235). Actually, these qualities are found in all aspects of black life—in the ways black people eat, speak, dance, dress, and walk. Such attributes are apparent, too, in written and spoken texts. When dealing with fiction, three topics to think about are narrative forms, diction, and style.

Narrative Forms

Many of the stories written by African-American authors are derived from the folk tradition, as was mentioned earlier. Although they have been adapted to serve modern audiences, they retain many of the elements of those earlier oral performances. Some of the most recognizable narrative forms include the following:

- *Folk tales.* Usually comic stories told to entertain and to pass time.
- *Tall tales.* Narratives that include exaggerated, unbelievable events and people.
- *Fables.* Animal stories, many with African roots, that make a moral point. They typically feature the hare, tortoise, fox, or spider.
- *Trickster stories.* Tales of John (or Jack), an unruly, disruptive character who manipulates people to make fools of them, then tries to clear himself by his wit when he is caught in a misdeed. His creative, inventive nature makes him seem bigger than life. One of the oldest mythical characters, the Trickster appears in folktales of many cultures. In African-American stories he often outwits the slave owner or, later, the policeman or landlord.
- *Why stories.* Narratives that humorously account for the origins of almost everything from creation to the ways of women.
- *Preacher tales.* Entertaining stories told from the pulpit and stories told about preachers.

- *Blues.* Earthy, honest commentaries on life's difficulties, some of them spiritual, some material, that offer no apology or defense but never admit defeat or ask for pity.
- *Satire.* The ridiculing of folly or stupidity. It is often humorous.
- *The dirty dozens.* Jeers directed at that which is held to be uplifting, holy, and decent. Although they are generated by loss of respect for a world that claims to honor such abstractions but crushes black people, they are often criticized for being obscene and disgusting.
- *Jokes.* Satirical anecdotes told at the expense of others, frequently white people, or to ridicule unfair social practices and stereotypes.

It is not surprising to find several of these narrative approaches in *The Eatonville Anthology,* by Zora Neale Hurston. She was well prepared to draw on African-American literary traditions to describe the vibrant characters of her childhood. She was, first of all, a natural storyteller who, among members of the Harlem Renaissance and even beyond that group, gained a reputation as a witty and skillful performer of oral narratives. In early childhood she was steeped in black culture, for until her mother's death when Hurston was eleven, she lived in Eatonville, Florida, an all-black town where she knew no white people. In addition, after migrating to New York City, she enrolled at Columbia University, where she studied anthropology under the renowned Franz Boas, generating in her a lifelong interest in Negro folk traditions.

The vignettes of *The Eatonville Anthology* are clearly cast in the oral tradition but are so skillfully managed in written form that the reader is not initially aware of the sophistication of the storyteller. On the one hand, the narrator is a wise and witty observer, recording people and their behavior in a standard dialect. On the other, she tells the stories by taking on the voices of the various characters: the pleading woman, Daisy the town vamp, even Mr. Dog and Miss Nancy Coon. She manages to re-create an oral narrative in a written text, maintaining throughout the dual roles of observer and participant. The simplicity and directness with which she does so obscures the difficulty of the task.

Most of the remembrances here are comic stories that make the reader laugh at human foibles. Old Man Anderson, for example, is so careful to protect his wagon from the train that he destroys it himself. And he never sees the train. And he never will. Even the troublemakers are drawn with a smile. Coon Taylor's forays into Joe Clarke's melon patch and sugarcane field are not depicted as "real stealing." Even those who are troubled affirm their situations. Mrs. Laura Crooms, much put upon by the vamp Daisy, talks a great deal about "leaving things in the hands of God." Then she fells Daisy with an ax handle and leaves her in a muddy ditch. The eighth entry, about Sewell, a man who lives by himself, is little more than a joke, or two jokes in four sentences about the same man.

Some of the stories approach the tall tale tradition. In "Village Fiction," men vie for the distinction of being the biggest liar, the evidence being unbelievable assertions about who they are and what they have seen. The final story picks up elements of the fable, using animals as characters. In the end, however, instead of making a moral point, it becomes a why story, for it explains how the dog's tongue got its crease down the middle. There is no preacher tale as such, but the final verse of the song found in "Double-Shuffle" takes a stab at that figure:

Would not marry uh preacher
Tell yuh de reason why
Every time he comes tuh town
He makes de chicken fly.

The blues are usually sung, but their commentary on life's difficulties is verbal. Mrs. Tony Roberts, the pleading woman in the opening selection, certainly moans the blues: "Lawd a mussy, Mis' Pierson, you ain't gonna gimme dat lil' eye-full uh greens fuh me an' mah chillen, is you? Don't be so graspin'; Gawd won't bless yuh. Gimme uh han'full mo'. Lawd, some folks is got everything, an' theys jes' as gripin' an stingy!" Although it is probably going too far to call Mrs. Roberts a Trickster figure, she is clearly a scam artist, but one who is not immune to being tricked herself. In the end, Mr. Clarke, the butcher, charges the slab of salt pork to her husband's account.

Each of the stories is built around a gentle satire that recognizes the foolishness of human beings. The characters may be flawed individuals, and the narrator enjoys exploiting their shortcomings, but they are not mean, unlikable individuals. They have their troubles, and they cause some of them too, but, like other comic characters, they manage to survive their difficulties and go on with their lives.

Diction

The language used by African-American writers varies all the way from strong dialect to standard American English. It appears in no single form. Nevertheless, some characteristics commonly appear. They include the following:

- Terse, pointed expressions that say much using few words. They sometimes take the form of proverbs or aphorisms.
- Informal language, sometimes labeled obscene, profane, or vulgar. It is the dialect of the street—alive and authentic.
- Language games that provide the user with ways of coping and surviving. They include jiving, sounding (delivering a direct insult), playing the dozens (sexually insulting a parent, usually the mother), and rapping.
- Signifying (or "signifyin'," as Henry Louis Gates uses the term to indicate its pronunciation), a particularly clever, playful way of giving an opinion about another person. Indirect and ironic, it is used to insult or ridicule another person or to pay someone a compliment. Gates uses the Signifying Monkey, the master Trickster of African-American folktales, as the embodiment of this process. For example, a person may pay a backhanded compliment to a friend, or one black writer may signify on another by making a parody of her literary structures.

Because of the several roles that the storyteller assumes in these vignettes, the language of *The Eatonville Anthology* is highly varied. The narrator speaks in standard forms, but Hurston is not averse to using informal expressions from time to time, as in the description of the double-shuffle. "Everybody happy, shining eyes, gleaming teeth. Feet dragged 'shhlap, shhlap! to beat out the time. No orchestra needed. Round and round! Back again, parse-me-la! shlap! shlap! Strut! Strut! Seaboard! Shlap! Shlap! Tiddy bumm! Mr. Clarke in the lead with Mrs. Moseley." Hurston is not reluctant to give her characters intense dialects either. In addition to the dialogue of Mrs. Tony Roberts, there is the conversation Daisy carries on with the men in front of the store–post office on Saturday night. As she says, "Who? Me? Ah don't keer whut Laura Crooms think. If she ain't a heavy hip-ted Mama enough to keep him, she don't need to come crying to me."

Though the language is informal, it does not approach anything that could be described as vulgar or obscene. Partly because of the age in which it was published, and probably because the author was female, some of the language games that are likely to be found in contemporary black writing are not present. The dialogue is, nevertheless, alive and real. It is believable language that Hurston took from the conversations she heard and knew.

In a few instances expressions seem compressed and pointed, meaning more than they actually say. When Mrs. McDuffy, for example is asked why she won't quit shouting in church even though her husband takes it as a personal affront and beats her for it, she simply replies that she can't "squinch the sperrit." No more need be said.

Many of the linguistic devices mentioned here, and more that are not, are covered by the term *signifying* (or signifyin'). Although signifying in the hands of a particularly clever user can be extraordinarily subtle, its appearance in *The Eatonville Anthology* is fairly apparent and understandable. In the description of Becky Moore, for example, the narrator seems to excuse her for any fault in the absence of a father for her children. We are told: "She has never stopped any of the fathers of her children from proposing, so if she has no father for her children it's not her fault. The men round about are entirely to blame." And Becky is thereby criticized. The other mothers are equally chided by the comment that they will not allow their children to play with hers because they think her condition is catching. The irony implicit in such statements provides a sense of play and fun for both the speaker and the audience.

Style

The narrative forms, characters, and typical language just described cause certain stylistic characteristics to recur with some regularity in the works of African-American writers. The following are likely to be encountered.

- *Exaggeration.* Found particularly in those stories that fall into the tall tale tradition.
- *Irony.* The indirection of signifying is created by saying one thing and meaning another, resulting in an ironic statement.
- *Rhymes.* Skillful repetition of vowels and consonants that makes a text lend itself to oral presentation.
- *Parody.* An effort to mock the work of another through repetition and variation.

- *Satire.* The ridicule of folly or stupidity. It is often humorous. The term can refer to an entire work but can also appear as a stylistic device that occurs now and then in a piece of writing. (See "Narrative Forms," above.)
- *Sardonic comedy.* The practice of making fun of adversity, as in jokes.
- *Superstitions.* Nonrational explanations of unusual occurrences.
- *Indirection.* Making a point without explicitly stating it. The technique allows the speaker to be subversive.

Such stylistic devices are easily noted in Hurston's work. Some have already been mentioned. The use of exaggeration, for example, abounds, giving the reader memorable portraits of the village liars—even of Tippy, the village dog, which has cheerfully survived dozens of attempts to get rid of him. Although *The Eatonville Anthology* is a prose work, the language is highly musical, breaking into rhyme only in the song recorded in "The Double-Shuffle" and in the concluding comment: "Stepped on a tin, mah story ends." Nevertheless, the recurrence of sound and the rhythm of the syntax enhance the stories and the characters that are in them. For example, listen to the courting dialogue of Mr. Dog and Mr. Rabbit as they seek to win Miss Coon's affection in the final selection. "'Miss Coon,' he says, 'Ma'am, also Ma'am which would you rather be—a lark flyin' or a dove a settin'?'" And in his turn, Mr. Rabbit is equally eloquent. "'Oh, Miss Nancy,' he says, 'Ma'am, also Ma'am, if you'd see me settin' straddle of a mud-cat leadin' a minnow, what would you think? Ma'am, also Ma'am?'" Aside from the images used in the proposals, a subtle music—typical of all of the pieces of the anthology—is created by the repeated short *a* sounds in *Nancy, Ma'am, straddle,* and *cat;* the initial *m* in *Miss, Ma'am, mud,* and *minnow;* and the *s* of *settin'* and *straddle;* and by rhythmic passages such as "a lark flyin'" or "a dove a settin'."

It is difficult to separate Hurston's use of irony, satire, and sardonic comedy into distinctive devices, because they work together throughout the *Anthology* to present a picture of a life that is not easy but is to be celebrated. It is a portrait of a village filled with the good and the bad, the strong and the weak, the troublemakers and those who would make things right. The storytelling is at once simple and complex, as the presentation is direct and uncluttered. However, the ironic statements and satirical viewpoint deepen what seems on the surface to be a series of naive portraits of village life. The underlying implication throughout is that life can be hard as well as good. In "Turpentine Love," for example, we are told that Jim Merchant fell in love with his wife when a dose of turpentine was accidentally spilled in her eye and she thereupon quit having fits. They have kept each other in good humor throughout a long marriage, even though she has had all her teeth pulled out. This brief portrait of a marriage contains a combination of the grotesque, the comic, and the beautiful. The narrator's implicit comment is that people's lives can be irrational, difficult, and wonderful, but that view is never directly stated; it is only implied through irony and satire that make *The Eatonville Anthology* as a whole a dark, if not sardonic, comedy.

Narrative has been a central means of black expression, probably because of the influence of the oral folk tradition, and thus the poetry of African-Americans shares many of its characteristics, particularly stylistic ones. Nevertheless, it has some of its own characteristics that distinguish it as a separate genre, though they are hard to pin down because they continue to evolve and develop. Undoubtedly, further analysis of that body of work will yield new understandings of it, but some generalizations are available for critical use.

Don Lee, examining the writing of black poets, found seven common characteristics in their poems:

1. polyrhythms, uneven, short, and explosive lines
2. intensity; depth, yet simplicity; spirituality, yet flexibility
3. irony; humor; signifying
4. sarcasm—a new comedy
5. direction; positive movement; teaching nation-building
6. subject matter—concrete; reflects a collective and personal life-style
7. music: the unique use of vowels and consonants with the developed rap demands that the poetry be real, and read out loud (Addison, *The Black Aesthetic,* 240)

Carolyn Rodgers has also attempted to establish poetic categories, naming ten major ones with twenty-three subdivisions. The chief categories she calls "signifying, teachin/rappin, coversoff, spaced, bein, love, shoutin, jazz, du-wah, and pyramid." Some of the subdivisions include "rundown, hipto, digup, and coatpull" (see Addison, *The Black Aesthetic,* 214.) Although her terminology would seem to stress content, all of the forms call upon the poet to be innovative and performative.

WRITING A CULTURAL STUDIES ANALYSIS

Because of the diversity of cultural studies, outlining a single approach to writing such criticism is not possible. The variety of questions that can be asked is likely to lead the writer in so many different directions that a single set of guidelines is not likely to be helpful here. However, some of the suggestions for composing introductions, organizing discussions, and making closing statements offered in the earlier chapters can be adapted and applied to postcolonial analyses and African-American criticism. Because the principles of writing do not change with the topics, you may find it profitable to look back at the preceding discussions about writing analyses to see what is applicable here as well.

RECOMMENDED WEB SITES

http://educ.queensu.ca/~qbell/update/tint/postmodernism/post.html

A discussion of several postmodern issues. Called the Teacher's Guide to Postmodernism, it covers slave narratives, stereotypes of native peoples in literature, and Ebonics.

http://landow.stg.brown.edu/post/misc/postov.html

Provides links to postcolonial authors, theory, bibliography, politics, history, and other topics.

http://www.stg.brown.edu/projects/hypertext/landow/post/poldiscourse/theorists.html
Discussions of eighteen postcolonial theorists, including Homi Bhabha, Salman Rushdie, and Edward Said.

SUGGESTED READING

Ashcroft, Bill, Gareth Griffiths, and Helen Tiffin. *The Empire Writes Back: Theory and Practice in Post-colonial Literatures.* New York: Routledge, 1989.

———, eds. *The Post-colonial Studies Reader.* New York: Routledge, 1995.

Awkward, Michael. *Inspiriting Influences: Tradition, Revision, and Afro-American Literature.* New York: Columbia Univ. Press, 1989.

Baker, Houston. *Blues, Ideology, and Afro-American Literature: A Vernacular Theory.* Chicago: Univ. of Chicago Press, 1984.

Bennett, Andrew, and Nicholas Royle. *Introduction to Literature, Criticism, and Theory.* London: Prentice Hall Europe, 1999.

Bhabha, Homi K. *The Location of Culture.* New York: Routledge, 1994.

Gates, Henry Louis. *The Signifying Monkey: A Theory of African-American Literary Criticism.* New York: Oxford Univ. Press, 1988.

Gayle, Addison, Jr., ed. *Black Expression: Essays by and about Black Americans in the Creative Arts.* New York: Weybright and Talley, 1969.

———. *The Black Aesthetic.* Garden City, N.Y.: Doubleday, 1971.

Loomba, Ania. *Colonialism/Postcolonialism.* London: Routledge, 1998.

Mitchell, Angelyn, ed. *Within the Circle: An Anthology of African American Literary Criticism from the Harlem Renaissance to the Present.* Durham, N.C.: Duke Univ. Press, 1994.

Morrison, Toni. *Playing in the Dark: Whiteness and the Literary Imagination.* New York: Vintage Books, 1993.

Olson, Gary A., and Lynn Worsham, eds. *Race, Rhetoric, and the Postcolonial.* Albany: State Univ. of New York Press, 1999.

Said, Edward. *Orientalism.* New York: Pantheon, 1978.

———. *Culture and Imperialism.* New York: Vintage Books, 1994.

Tiffin, Helen. Post-colonial Literatures and Counter-discourse. *Kunapipi* 9.3 (1987): 17–34.

Williams, Patrick, and Laura Chrisman, eds. *Colonial Discourse and Post-colonial Theory: A Reader.* New York: Columbia Univ. Press, 1994.

Young, Robert. *Colonial Desire: Hybridity in Theory, Culture, and Race.* London: Routledge, 1995.

MODEL STUDENT ANALYSES

Representations of Cultural Others in Angela Carter's "The Tiger's Bride"

Dennis Humphrey

Angela Carter's attempts to unmask Western culture's phallocentric view of the woman as "other" in her works have most often been examined from the perspective of feminism with some discussion of her postmodern or poststructural methods for stripping away the cultural facade of Western civilization's assignment of gender roles. In her examinations of "otherness" between women and men, Carter often makes use of themes and images that highlight otherness in a different context in order to establish a basis for comparison. In her short story "The Tiger's Bride," for example, Carter's most straightforward depiction of otherness draws upon the theme of "Beauty and the Beast." The "Beauty and the Beast" dichotomy between humanity and bestiality and its associated warnings against the deception of appearances provide a background for her portrayal of a Beauty who must reject the supposedly civilized society of her father, in which she exists as a commodity, and embrace the supposedly barbaric society of the Beast, in which she is free to discover her own true nature. Within the scope of the human/beast dichotomy, however, Carter intensifies the contrast between the two sides by associating the human father with Western civilization and by associating the Beast with the West's traditional other, the East or the Orient. Such depictions of the Oriental as cultural other are of particular interest to postcolonial critics because these depictions rely upon various stereotypes that cast the East as being not only different from but also inferior to the West. An examination of Carter's use of such stereotypes in "The Tiger's Bride" will reveal them as part of an orchestrated effort to show how the existence of cultural stereotypes serves to imprison some individuals and to exclude others.

Carter names the tiger, an animal indigenous only to Asia, as her Beast in the story's title rather than any of the more typical European representations of the beast such as the boar, the bear, or the wolf. Considered out of context, her choice of animal might be taken as an attempt to distinguish her story from traditional forms of the tale by giving her Beast a new look. However, Carter's numerous other references to the Orient reveal the tiger as part of a strategy that seeks to capitalize on Western stereotypes about the alien and inferior nature of other cultures. To Carter's Beauty, who hails from Russia in the North, "the treacherous South" of Italy with its decadent sophistication and gambling represents an evil other in itself (Carter 154–155). Into this alien setting comes the even more alien Beast. After her father loses Beauty to the Beast in a game of cards, at which the Beast has "the Devil's knack," Beauty recalls a story about "a tiger-man" from "Sumatra, in the Indies," with which her nurse "scared" her as a child (156, 158). When Beauty is taken back to the Beast's palazzo, she glimpses "suites of vaulted chambers opening one out of another like systems of Chinese boxes" (159). The Beast himself "wears a garment of Ottoman design," and fills his chamber with incense of a "thick, rich, wild scent," which "ascends in cursive blue from the smoke hole of a precious Chinese pot" (160). The mystical and exotic nature of these details surrounding the Beast serve to make him even more alien, and taken together, they show a sustained effort to establish a distinctly oriental atmosphere around him.

Another instance in which Carter evokes Western prejudice against other cultures occurs just after Beauty's father loses her to the Beast at cards. Beauty's father quotes a line from Shakespeare's *Othello:* "'Like the base Indian,'" [her father] said; he loved rhetoric. "'One whose hand, / Like the base Indian, threw a pearl away / Richer than all his tribe . . .' I have lost my pearl, my pearl beyond price." (Carter 157)

Proceeding directly from the content of the quoted passage, Carter's main purpose seems to be to point out that Beauty is being treated as a commodity by her father. In accordance with the passive role assigned to her by Western culture, Beauty is described in terms of a valuable possession that has been lost. Still, Carter chooses an example that also points out Western society's assumption of superiority over non-Western cultures. The image of the "base Indian" is one of an ignorant savage. Of course, the only thing of which the "base Indian" in the quoted passage can be called ignorant is the West's system of assigning monetary value, and the passage in both the story and the play shows how both Beauty and Desdemona are undervalued within the already degrading system in which they are considered as commodity or property. In addition, the reference to *Othello* is important because it invites a comparison of the many similarities between the Beast and the character Othello.

Othello, a non-European, is repeatedly compared to animals, such as "an old black ram" and "a Barbary horse" (*Othello* 1.1.88, 1.1.11–12). He is also described in such derogatory terms as "devil," "lascivious," and "barbarian" (1.1.91, 1.1.126, and 1.3.356). It is true that all of these derogatory descriptions of Othello are made by Iago, who hates him. However, the rhetoric needed to make such racial slurs against Othello seems to have been readily available for Iago's use, and the context clearly is not lost upon those to whom he describes Othello in such terms. Iago's derogatory language concerning Othello shows a cultural propensity to consider non-Europeans inferior. Othello is not an animal, but his status as a non-Westerner causes him to be seen as though he were.

In "The Tiger's Bride," the Beast *is* an animal. In a departure from the typical "Beauty and the Beast" tale, in which the Beast's animal appearance is only an illusion caused by some evil curse, this Beast is actually a tiger masquerading as a man. It would seem that this should make him alien enough to humans, but by linking the Beast to the Orient, Carter creates a tie to a real sense of the alien in the Western point of view. A big cat in a man's clothes is like a child's fairy tale, a giant-size Puss in Boots. It is pure fantasy. A tiger in oriental garb and surrounded by oriental imagery evokes a real and familiar sense of the alien and the exotic that is experienced by Westerners whenever they encounter anything oriental. Furthermore, the threatening nature of the Beast seems tied to his oriental nature as well. In contrast to the tiger Beast, who Beauty fears will "gobble" her up, Beauty's memory of an alleged bear-man who lived outside her village in Russia depicts the bear-man as "a good shepherd" (Carter 158–159). It is interesting that Beauty should be familiar from childhood with a story of a benign beast-man outside her village and yet assume that the oriental tiger Beast means to harm her.

The accumulation of oriental details around the Beast leads to an unsettling implication that the threatening and bestial nature of the Beast translates to a threatening and bestial nature in the oriental culture that he seems to represent. However, Carter's object throughout the story is to reveal the deception in appearances, especially those appearances that are created by Western ideologies that disenfranchise or marginalize certain individuals and groups, such as women and the people of other cultures. By portraying Western stereotypes concerning other cultures, she is in fact setting those stereotypes up for criticism. In the final scene of the story, as the Beast is licking away the "skins" of the identity assigned to Beauty by Western cultural traditions, Carter is revealing that all of the trappings of Western civilization are in fact illusion and that beneath that illusion lies Beauty's true nature (169). Within that true nature lies the "peaceable kingdom" in which she and the Beast can coexist (168). Postcolonial critics often condemn Western literature's tendency to try to universalize the human condition, but the main objections to such universals are that they assume the Western idea of human nature to be true in all cultures. The common ground that Carter finds for her Beauty and Beast lies beneath the level of all culture, in a sort of Edenic ideal where Beauty and the Beast may relate to one another without the interference of culturally assigned notions of good and evil. Such dreams of prelapsarian bliss are, of course, patently romantic, and as such they are as much a part of Western ideology as the stereotypes that Carter condemns. Still, the story's general strategy of revealing and critiquing the negative aspects of Western cultural ideologies and stereotypes remains effective, if not completely free from assumptions of its own.

One may ask how any fiction writer could criticize a situation without portraying it. Angela Carter's criticism of Western stereotypes is made possible because her use of those stereotypes draws them out into the open and shows them for what they really are, illusions that perpetuate the phallocentric and Eurocentric status quo in Western society. If her idea of a pure "peaceable kingdom" beneath the level of all culture seems to smack of Western romantic ideals, then perhaps it shows the depths to which cultural ideals define even the attempts to criticize them. According to Gödel's theorem, no mathematical system can completely define itself, but a larger system that contains it may. In the absence of a larger system, some uncertainty must remain. If Gödel's theorem may be extended to cultural studies, perhaps no complete reckoning of a culture may be made from within the context of that same culture. Still, whatever the statisticians might say, culture consists of more than a matter of mathematics. If Angela Carter's condemnation of Western stereotypes falls prey to its own criticism, perhaps it only makes its point that much more effectively by serving as both critique and case in point.

A Synopsis of Angela Carter's "The Tiger's Bride"

Angela Carter's short story "The Tiger's Bride" is a retelling of the classic fairy tale "Beauty and the Beast." In "The Tiger's Bride," Beauty's father loses her to the Beast in a game of cards. The Beast, whose true identity is concealed by his clothing and by the mask of a beautifully painted human face, must speak through the interpretation of his valet because "he has such a growling impediment in his speech." The Beast takes Beauty back to his palazzo, where she fears the Beast means to "gobble" her up. She discovers that the Beast's only request is to see her in the nude, after which she will be returned unharmed to her father along with all of the money her father had lost playing cards and "also a number of fine presents." She refuses. After she refuses several requests to appear nude before the Beast, the Beast offers to appear nude before her. She accepts. In a twist on the traditional "Beauty and the Beast" tale, in which the Beast is a human who has been cursed with a beastlike appearance, Beauty discovers that underneath his clothing and mask, the Beast is actually a real tiger. When she sees the tiger's true form, she removes her own clothing and appears nude before the Beast. The Beast offers to return her to her father the next day, along with all of the money and gifts in his original offer. Back in her room in the Beast's palazzo, Beauty looks into a mirror held by the clockwork lady's maid she had been given by the Beast. She sees the image of her father counting out the money and gifts from the Beast, and she realizes that she is nothing more to her father than another valuable possession. In another twist on the "Beauty and the Beast" tale, Beauty elects to join the Beast in his world, rather than helping the Beast to become human. She returns naked to the Beast, who licks off the layers of her skin to reveal a beautiful coat of fur.

Works Cited

Carter, Angela. "The Tiger's Bride." In *Burning Your Boats: The Collected Short Stories,* 154–169. New York: Penguin Books, 1995.

Shakespeare, William. *The Tragedy of Othello, the Moor of Venice* [1622]. In *The Riverside Shakespeare,* pp. 1203–1240. Boston: Houghton Mifflin, 1974.

Writing and Staging the White Man's Blues:
An Analysis of James Baldwin's *Blues for Mr. Charlie*

Lana Henry

The blues are about being alone and lonely, cast out and down-and-out, separated from home, mate, God, and the material comforts of life. As an African-American folk expression, the blues naturally reflect facets of that group's experience. How ironic, then, that a black man should write a "blues" piece for the white man, "Mister Charlie." Isn't it the black man who has been cast out and denied so much? Isn't he the one who has been abused and misused and who, therefore, has a reason to sing the blues? James Baldwin realized, however, as he made clear in his aptly titled introduction, "Notes for Blues," that separateness, isolation, and deprivation are also part of the white man's experience and, indeed, of all those living by the code of ignorance and hatred that accepts racial crime as inevitable and is, therefore, a crime in itself. This separation, according to Baldwin, is the separation of the individual from the knowledge and understanding of his own motivations and needs, as well as a separation of the earthly Christian church from its founder's teachings. The isolation is an isolation from the truth of every human being's potential worth—including one's own—and of the commonalities between races, which are greater than their differences. The deprivation is that of a community deprived of its totality, deprived of a mature self-awareness that recognizes all its members and their roots, deprived of the tolerance that forgives human imperfection, and deprived of the strength and honor that allow self-examination with clear eyes. It is the loneliness, the sadness, the desperation created by these conditions that are the notes for *Blues for Mister Charlie.*

Deeply moved by the vicious and racially motivated murder of fourteen-year-old Emmet Till in Mississippi in 1963, Baldwin based his play loosely on the event. His protagonist, Richard Henry, is a troubled young man returning to his southern hometown after an unsuccessful attempt to "make it" in the North. Embittered by this failure and his forced return to the racist world he had sought to flee, Richard recklessly breaks all the rules designed to keep blacks "in their place." For the ultimate of these transgressions—flirting with a white woman—he is murdered by Lyle Britten, the woman's husband. Though circumstantial evidence and motive point directly to Britten, the town is outraged that he is even arrested. He is, of course, acquitted of the crime but (like Till's murderers) boasts about his deed after the trial. Baldwin, however, does not allow his play to rest on stereotypes but rather seeks insight into the complex human realities on both sides of the color line. Ultimately, the play is guardedly optimistic about the ability of blacks and whites to work cooperatively to resolve the ignorance and bias that separate them.

It is clear that Baldwin is well acquainted with the blues—its motifs, its structure, its themes and motivations—for this knowledge is reflected in the arrangement and tension of his set, in the rhythm and progression of his scene shifts, in his characters' histories of struggle, and in his ability to transform their cliched parrotings into lean, honed-down nuggets that speak volumes for those histories, just as the formulaic lyrics of the blues do.

With its graphic illustration of a segregated community, the set reflects the tensions and contradictions of racial dichotomy as well as the separations and isolation that drive much of the blues. The most powerful and fundamental division is that of color. On one side of the town's main street is Blacktown; across the street and staring it down with ominous and incendiary opposition is Whitetown. All other divisions stem from and work in the service of this institutionalized color line. In his stage directions, Baldwin insists that the cross atop the black church and the flag atop the "blinding white" (81)* courthouse remain visible throughout the production. These are the visible symbols of a destructive distortion of the principle of "separation of church and state." In Mister Charlie's world, the state or law stands solidly on the side of Whitetown, offering no protection to the people of Blacktown, who turn instead to the church for comfort, strength, and guidance. This opposition also illustrates the division between secular law and divine law, one that will be underscored by the interchangeability of the pulpit and the witness stand.

In a clever application of visual doubling, Baldwin allows the pulpit and the witness stand to occupy the same space on stage. With this single, simple move, Baldwin juxtaposes "the true Word" of love, justice, and forgiveness taught by Christian scripture with the sworn-to-be-true words of legal testimony and thus calls into question the very nature and value of "truth" itself. The knowledge that Meridian's pulpit will be transformed into the seat where the official lie is sanctioned heightens the poignancy of the preacher's earnest prayer offered over his murdered son's body: "Now, when the children come, my Lord, and ask which road to follow, my tongue stammers and my heart fails. I will not abandon the land—this strange land, which is my home. But can I ask the children forever to sustain the cruelty inflicted on them by those who have been their masters, and who are now, in very truth, their kinfolk . . . ?" (77).

Further, Meridian's doubts reflect what the set has already indicated—that even the church itself is divided. It is divided into the "turn the other cheek" (101) brand of Christianity inherited by Meridian—"I've been a Christian all my life, like my Mama and Daddy before me and like their Mama and Daddy before them" (38)—and an acknowledgment that it is the condition of oppression itself that draws the black man to Christianity's promise of redemption: "I've had to think—would I have been such a Christian if I hadn't been born black?" (38). It is divided into those insisting upon rising above one's enemies (Meridian, Juanita) and those driven by a more impatient, self-esteeming, aggressive impulse attracted to revenge (Richard, Lorenzo). It is divided by the enticement of the North on the one hand and, on the other, the pride and loyalty to home and family that resist running from Mister Charlie. Like the character in the classic blues song recorded by Robert Johnson and many others after him, Meridian and his followers are standing at a crossroads evaluating the choices that will determine their future.

Meanwhile, Whitetown appears to be moving toward a crossroads of its own, albeit at the pace of a funeral dirge and in the syncopated rhythm of a disjointed community. Whitetown is rife with the conflicts that blues songs are written about, namely, sex and betrayal, financial hard times, and the hungers of a man without an emotional home. Lyle Britten was

---

* All page numbers refer to the 1964 Dial Press edition of the play.

Willa Mae Walker's "back door man," sexually obsessed with her but socially forbidden to acknowledge it. Lyle's history and hot temper have his wife worried about the possibility of his tomcatting around on those nights when she lies awake waiting for him in vain. The Brittens are struggling financially too, "barely holding *on*" (8), as Jo puts it, and after a lifetime of such struggle, Lyle is proud to be a survivor and determined not to lose any gains (including his status as a white man) that will make his son's "long journey" (115) easier. By having Lyle echo Meridian's identification with familial affinities, Baldwin emphasizes the men's common experience of being entrenched in and dedicated to a tradition—like that of racism—not of their own making:

> I've been doing hard work since I was a puppy. Like my Mama and Daddy before me, God rest their souls, and their Mama and Daddy before them. They wore theirselves out on the land—the land never gave them nothing. Nothing but an empty belly and some skinny kids. I'm the only one growed up to be a man. That's because I take after my Daddy . . . hard as any rock. And stubborn! . . . That little one ain't going to have nothing to worry about. (58)

Added to the sexual and financial doubts rumbling in the Britten household is the ominous specter of Lyle's arrest. The mere idea that a white man should be made to answer for the suspicion that he has killed a black man is a sure sign that social change is brewing, a prospect that has Whitetown worried and indignant. Lyle's exasperated musing speaks volumes for Mister Charlie's old order: "I don't know what's come over the folks in this town! . . . Raising so much fuss about a nigger—a northern nigger at that" (13). Whitetown is also disturbed by its own rambling, undomesticated bluesman, Parnell James. Parnell's torn loyalties ("I don't like it here. But I love it here"), his broader vision gained from travels and a superior education, and his duty as a public spokesperson render him a choral character who speaks from both sides of his mouth in an attempt to speak for both Whitetown and Blacktown (15). As a white man who has loved and befriended black people, Parnell detests racism but attempts to explain white people's motivations to his old friend Meridian:

> I know what we have done—and do. But you must have mercy on us. We have no other hope. . . .
>
> Please try to understand that it is not so easy to leap over fences, to give things up—all right, to surrender privilege! But if you were among the privileged you would know what I mean. It's not a matter of trying to hold *on;* the things, the privilege—are part of you, are *who* you are. It's in the *gut.* (40)

Torn between two worlds, Parnell is a man, like the blues rambler, without a comfortable place to hang his hat. He is like the "yellow nigger" described by George: "Boy, ain't they the worst kind? Their own folks don't want them, don't nobody want them, and you *can't* do nothing with them—you might be able to scare a black nigger, but you can't do nothing with a yellow nigger" (49–50). Though Parnell is the most socially progressive white man in the play, even he finds himself unprepared to make the right choice at the cross-roads if it means permanent and complete ostracism from what passes as his own tribe.

The apparent hopelessness of mending all the divisions in this bifurcated community is represented by both a physical and a metaphorical gulf, a seemingly bottomless, impenetrable gulf of darkness, ignorance, hatred, and blind custom. It is the gulf into which Lyle dumps Richard's body with no more regard than if he were garbage. It is the explosively poisonous gulf of the community's festering guilt. It is the gulf that fuels Mister Charlie's desperate clinging to an illusion of superiority, driving Lyle first to murder, then to denial, and finally, to an attempt to justify his crime with that ancient defensive refrain, "I'm a white man" (120). Lyle's defense is offered without any doubt as to its validity. To him, it is a self-explanatory universal as immutable as sunrise and sunset. Basic precepts, affinities, and prejudices such as this and bottom-line descriptions of the conditions of our lives, stated simply without frills or details, make blues music the universal language that it is. This stripped-down language is shared by the poor, the uneducated, and the marginalized of all races. Though it may accrue aesthetic appeal when coupled with humor, innuendo, rhyme, and other types of wordplay in the blues, thus earning the status of folk poetry, it is also the language of Mister Charlie's hate and ignorance.

Appropriately enough, Baldwin chooses to showcase the language of Mister Charlie's blues in a familiar blues setting—the kitchen. The metaphorical kitchen used as sexual innuendo in blues music becomes a literal one in Baldwin's play. Here, Whitetown gathers in a place of primal comfort, a place imbued with mother love, warmth, intimacy, and the satisfaction of hunger on many levels when the storm of Richard's murder threatens their world. It is here, among friends, where Mister Charlie feels most comfortable spouting his racist rhetoric. Thankfully, Baldwin is attuned enough to human nature to recognize behind that rhetoric a pain akin to the one that makes the bluesman howl. It is a pain born of loss, fear, inadequacy, truth, and guilt for one's sins. So Mister Charlie sings his old worn-out blues to comfort himself:

> What's happened to this town? It was peaceful here, we all got along, we didn't have no trouble.
>
> They had their ways, we had ours, and everything went along the way God intended.
>
> How come the colored people to hate us so much, all of a sudden? We *give* them everything they've got!
>
> They're a simple people—warm-hearted and good-natured. But they are very easily led, and now they are harkening to the counsel of these degenerate Communist race-mixers. And they don't know what terrible harm they can bring on themselves. Niggers can't learn like white folks, they ain't got the same interests.
>
> They got one interest. And it's just below the belly button. If you was to be raped by an orang-outang out of the jungle or a stallion, couldn't do you no worse than a nigger.

> You wouldn't be no more good for nobody. . . . That's why we men have got to be so vigilant.
>
> Well, goddammit, white men come before niggers! They *got* to! (48–54)

The guests in Jo's kitchen seemingly comfort themselves into oblivion, for they do not even recognize the horror of the fact that while Blacktown is burying one of its sons, they raise their glasses to his murderer, hailing him as the "jolly, good fellow" in a celebration of life.

Baldwin's experimentation with the structure of his play also reflects an understanding of the blues. In the shifts from present to past, from Whitetown to Blacktown and vice versa, I feel the rhythmic flow of the call-and-response pattern that is one of the backbones of African-American music, including the blues. This pattern, derived from and reflecting the African-American tradition of collective experience and expression, is established with the play's opening lines. Lyle's sadistic invocation over Richard's body—"And may every nigger like this nigger end like this nigger—face down in the weeds!" (2)—is answered across town with the inflammatory exhortations Meridian must use in his nonviolence training of the demonstrators: "You have to say it like you mean it—the way they really say it: nigger, nigger, nigger!" (2). The second shift from Whitetown to Blacktown continues this pattern of a thematic call and response. To Lyle's assertions in Whitetown that "they'll never convict me," Lorenzo "responds" from Blacktown, "And when they bring him to trial, I'm going to be right there every day—right across the street in that courthouse—where they been dealing death out to us for all these years" (16).

Later in act 1, Baldwin uses flashback to create temporal call-and-response dialogues that augment the tension created by the spatial scene-shifting. In one flashback, Richard dismays his grandmother with his confession of carrying a gun everywhere he goes. Later, in an attempt to compromise with his family and their teachings, Richard voluntarily hands his gun over to his father. Meridian's responses to this call from the past reveal how that memory must haunt him: "Maybe I was wrong not to let the people arm" (37), and "Must I be the man who watches while his people are beaten, chained, starved, clubbed, butchered?" (39).

Perhaps the most poignant use of the call-and-response pattern occurs in the trial scene when Blacktown responds, unseen and unheard by the court, to the old familiar parody of justice transpiring in that "blinding [and blinded] white" bastion of Mister Charlie's world. Effectively denied a voice on the jury by Jim Crow and intimidation, their witnesses harassed and subjected to character defamation, Blacktown largely recedes from the action of the courtroom. Their presence is communicated instead with an antiphonal and antithetical choral voice. Anticipating Jo Britten's reliance on the old standby defense of attempted rape, Blacktown eggs her on contemptuously, "Come on, bitch. We *know* what you going to say. Get it over with" (84). They are equally scornful of Papa D. for his continued congeniality with their enemy. In response to Whitetown's praise of him, Blacktown taunts Papa D., saying, "You can't be walking around here without no handkerchief! You might catch cold—after all *these* years!" (87). To the state's insinuating inquiries into Juanita's character, Blacktown snaps, "Why don't you come right out and ask her if she's a virgin, man? Save you time" (96). When Meridian is pushed to righteous ire, Blacktown champions his retort as they would a fine sermon, chanting, "Speak my man! Amen! Amen! Amen! Amen!" (104).

The play ends, as it began, at a crossroads. Whitetown is still firmly entrenched on its side of the road with the law defending its right to be there, and Lyle is acquitted and confident enough to admit his crime in public to the victim's father. But Whitetown has not escaped untouched or unmoved, for Parnell, shamed by his cowardice on the witness stand and recognizing that he now stands on the opposite side of the gulf from his tribe, is determined to try again. He has stood at the crossroads long enough to get a good look down both roads and knows that he must at least try to walk in the same direction as the students marching toward liberation. Juanita's noncommittal acceptance of his decision lets him know that it will not be an easy journey. Blacktown has been moved, as well. Meridian, that great symbol of the middle road, has also stood at the crossroads, pondering his choices long and hard. In the end, he is left with both the Bible—his parents' legacy, and a gun—his son's legacy, rather than a choice between the two. Armed with both, Meridian seems poised to attempt a transformation of that old crossroads, but his exit from the stage prevents drawing conclusions. Whatever his next move, Meridian's journey won't be easy either, but then, it never was. Despite this, and in keeping with the matter-of-fact tone that characterizes much of the blues, neither man surrenders to defeat or defense, offers apology, or solicits sympathy. It is sad that these two prime public voices and old friends are left standing alone, each to chart his own path, but facing the world alone is what the blues are all about.

Literary Selections

Chapter 2

WILLIAM FAULKNER

Barn Burning

The store in which the Justice of the Peace's court was sitting smelled of cheese. The boy, crouched on his nail keg at the back of the crowded room, knew he smelled cheese, and more: from where he sat he could see the ranked shelves close-packed with the solid, squat, dynamic shapes of tin cans whose labels his stomach read, not from the lettering which meant nothing to his mind but from the scarlet devils and the silver curve of fish—this, the cheese which he knew he smelled and the hermetic meat which his intestines believed he smelled coming in intermittent gusts momentary and brief between the other constant one, the smell and sense just a little of fear because mostly of despair and grief, the old fierce pull of blood. He could not see the table where the Justice sat and before which his father and his father's enemy (*our enemy* he thought in that despair; *ourn! mine and hisn both! He's my father!*) stood, but he could hear them, the two of them that is, because his father had said no word yet:

"But what proof have you, Mr. Harris?"

"I told you. The hog got into my corn. I caught it up and sent it back to him. He had no fence that would hold it. I told him so, warned him. The next time I put the hog in my pen. When he came to get it I gave him enough wire to patch up his pen. The next time I put the hog up and kept it. I rode down to his house and saw the wire I gave him still rolled on to the spool in his yard. I told him he could have the hog when he paid me a dollar pound fee. That evening a nigger came with the dollar and got the hog. He was a strange nigger. He said, 'He say to tell you wood and hay kin burn.' I said, 'What?' 'That whut he say to tell you,' the nigger said. 'Wood and hay kin burn.' That night my barn burned. I got the stock out but I lost the barn."

"Where is the nigger? Have you got him?"

"He was a strange nigger, I tell you. I don't know what became of him."

"But that's not proof. Don't you see that's not proof?"

"Get that boy up here. He knows." For a moment the boy thought too that the man meant his older brother until Harris said, "Not him. The little one. The boy," and, crouching, small for his age, small and wiry like his father, in patched and faded jeans even too small for him, with straight, uncombed, brown hair and eyes gray and wild as storm scud, he saw the men between himself and the table part and become a lane of grim faces, at the end of which he saw the Justice, a shabby, collarless, graying man in spectacles, beckoning him. He felt no floor under his bare feet; he seemed to walk beneath the palpable weight of the grim turning faces. His father, stiff in his black Sunday coat donned not for the trial but for the moving, did not even look at him. *He aims for me to lie,* he thought, again with that frantic grief and despair. *And I will have to do hit.*

"What's your name, boy?" the Justice said.

"Colonel Sartoris Snopes," the boy whispered.

"Hey?" the Justice said. "Talk louder. Colonel Sartoris? I reckon anybody named for Colonel Sartoris in this country can't help but tell the truth, can they?" The boy said nothing. *Enemy! Enemy!* he thought; for a moment he could not even see, could not see that the Justice's face was kindly nor discern that his voice was troubled when he spoke to the man named Harris: "Do you want me to question this boy?" But he could hear, and during those subsequent long seconds while there was absolutely no sound in the crowded little room save that of quiet and intent breathing it was as if he had swung outward at the end of a grape vine, over a ravine, and at the top of the swing had been caught in a prolonged instant of mesmerized gravity, weightless in time.

"No!" Harris said violently, explosively. "Damnation! Send him out of here!" Now time, the fluid world, rushed beneath him again, the voices coming to him again through the smell of cheese and sealed meat, the fear and despair and the old grief of blood:

"This case is closed. I can't find against you, Snopes, but I can give you advice. Leave this country and don't come back to it."

His father spoke for the first time, his voice cold and harsh, level, without emphasis: "I aim to. I don't figure to stay in a country among people who . . ." he said something unprintable and vile, addressed to no one.

"That'll do," the Justice said. "Take your wagon and get out of this country before dark. Case dismissed."

His father turned, and he followed the stiff black coat, the wiry figure walking a little stiffly from where a Confederate provost's man's musket ball had taken him in the heel on a stolen horse thirty years ago, followed the two backs now, since his older brother had appeared from somewhere in the crowd, no taller than the father but thicker, chewing tobacco steadily, between the two lines of grim-faced men and out of the store and across the worn gallery and down the sagging steps and among the dogs and half-grown boys in the mild May dust, where as he passed a voice hissed:

"Barn burner!"

Again he could not see, whirling; there was a face in a red haze, moonlike, bigger than the full moon, the owner of it half again his size, he leaping in the red haze toward the face, feeling no blow, feeling no shock when his head struck the earth, scrabbling up and leaping again, feeling no blow this time either and tasting no blood, scrabbling up to see the other boy in full flight and himself already leaping into pursuit as his father's hand jerked him back, the harsh, cold voice speaking above him: "Go get in the wagon."

It stood in a grove of locusts and mulberries across the road. His two hulking sisters in their Sunday dresses and his mother and her sister in calico and sunbonnets were already in it, sitting on and among the sorry residue of the dozen and more movings which even the boy could remember—the battered stove, the broken beds and chairs, the clock inlaid with mother-of-pearl, which would not run, stopped at some fourteen minutes past two o'clock of a dead and forgotten day and time, which had been his mother's dowry. She was crying, though when she saw him she drew her sleeve across her face and began to descend from the wagon. "Get back," the father said.

"He's hurt. I got to get some water and wash his . . ."

"Get back in the wagon," his father said. He got in too, over the tail-gate. His father mounted to the seat where the older brother already sat and struck the gaunt mules two savage blows with the peeled willow, but without heat. It was not even sadistic; it was exactly that same quality which in later years would cause his descendants to over-run the engine before putting a motor car into motion, striking and reining back in the same movement. The wagon went on, the store with its quiet crowd of grimly watching men dropped behind; a curve in the road hid it. *Forever* he thought. *Maybe he's done satisfied now, now that he has* . . . stopping himself, not to say it aloud even to himself. His mother's hand touched his shoulder.

"Does hit hurt?" she said.

"Naw," he said. "Hit don't hurt. Lemme be."

"Can't you wipe some of the blood off before hit dries?"

"I'll wash to-night," he said. "Lemme be, I tell you."

The wagon went on. He did not know where they were going. None of them ever did or ever asked, because it was always somewhere, always a house of sorts waiting for them a day or two days or even three days away. Likely his father had already arranged to make a crop on another farm before he . . . Again he had to stop himself. He (the father) always did. There was something about his wolflike independence and even courage when the advantage was at least neutral which impressed strangers, as if they got from his latent ravening ferocity not so much a sense of dependability as a feeling that his ferocious conviction in the rightness of his own actions would be of advantage to all whose interest lay with his.

That night they camped, in a grove of oaks and beeches where a spring ran. The nights were still cool and they had a fire against it, of a rail lifted from a nearby fence and cut into lengths—a small fire, neat, niggard almost, a shrewd fire; such fires were his father's habit and custom always, even in freezing weather. Older, the boy might have remarked this and wondered why not a big one; why should not a man who had not only seen the waste and extravagance of war, but who had in his blood an inherent voracious prodigality with material not his own, have burned everything in sight? Then he might have gone a step farther and thought that that was the reason: that niggard blaze was the living fruit of nights passed during those four years in the woods hiding from all men, blue or gray, with his strings of horses (captured horses, he called them). And older still, he might have divined the true reason: that the element of fire spoke to some deep mainspring of his father's being, as the element of steel or of powder spoke to other men, as the one weapon for the preservation of integrity, else breath were not worth the breathing, and hence to be regarded with respect and used with discretion.

But he did not think this now and he had seen those same niggard blazes all his life. He merely ate his supper beside it and was already half asleep over his iron plate when his father called him, and once more he followed the stiff back, the stiff and ruthless limp, up the slope and on to the starlit road where, turning, he could see his father against the stars but without face or depth—a shape black, flat, and bloodless as though cut from tin in the iron folds of the frockcoat which had not been made for him, the voice harsh like tin and without heat like tin:

"You were fixing to tell them. You would have told him." He didn't answer. His father struck him with the flat of his hand on the side of the head, hard but without heat, exactly as he had struck the two mules at the store, exactly as he would strike either of them with any stick in order to kill a horse fly, his voice still without heat or anger: "You're getting to be a man. You got to learn. You got to learn to stick to your own blood or you ain't going to have any blood to stick to you. Do you think either of them, any man there this morning, would? Don't you know all they wanted was a chance to get at me because they knew I had them beat? Eh?" Later, twenty years later, he was to tell himself, "If I had said they wanted only truth, justice, he would have hit me again." But now he said nothing. He was not crying. He just stood there. "Answer me," his father said.

"Yes," he whispered. His father turned.

"Get on to bed. We'll be there tomorrow."

Tomorrow they were there. In the early afternoon the wagon stopped before a paintless two-room house identical almost with the dozen others it had stopped before even in the boy's ten years, and again, as on the other dozen occasions, his mother and aunt got down and began to unload the wagon, although his two sisters and his father and brother had not moved.

"Likely hit ain't fitten for hawgs," one of the sisters said.

"Nevertheless, fit it will and you'll hog it and like it," his father said. "Get out of them chairs and help your Ma unload."

The two sisters got down, big, bovine, in a flutter of cheap ribbons; one of them drew from the jumbled wagon bed a battered lantern, the other a worn broom. His father handed the reins to the older son and began to climb stiffly over the wheel. "When they get unloaded, take the team to the barn and feed them." Then he said, and at first the boy thought he was still speaking to his brother: "Come with me."

"Me?" he said.

"Yes," his father said. "You."

"Abner," his mother said. His father paused and looked back—the harsh level stare beneath the shaggy, graying, irascible brows.

"I reckon I'll have a word with the man that aims to begin tomorrow owning me body and soul for the next eight months."

They went back up the road. A week ago—or before last night, that is—he would have asked where they were going, but not now. His father had struck him before last night but never before had he paused afterward to explain why; it was as if the blow and the following calm, outrageous voice still rang, repercussed, divulging nothing to him save the terrible handicap of being young, the light weight of his few years, just heavy enough to prevent his soaring free of the world as it seemed to be ordered but not heavy enough to keep him footed solid in it, to resist it and try to change the course of its events.

Presently he could see the grove of oaks and cedars and the other flowering trees and shrubs where the house would be, though not the house yet. They walked beside a fence massed with honey-suckle and Cherokee roses and came to a gate swinging open between two brick pillars, and now, beyond a sweep of drive, he saw the house for the first time and at that instant he forgot his father and the terror and despair both, and even when he remembered his father again (who had not stopped) the terror and despair did not return. Because, for all the twelve movings, they had sojourned until now in a poor country, a land of small farms and fields and houses, and he had never seen a house like this before. *Hit's big as a courthouse* he thought quietly, with a surge of peace and joy whose reason he could not have thought into words, being too young for that: *They are safe from him. People whose lives are a part of this peace and dignity are beyond his touch, he no more to them than a buzzing wasp: capable of stinging for a little moment but that's all; the spell of this peace and dignity rendering even the barns and stable and cribs which belong to it impervious to the puny flames he might contrive* . . . this, the peace and joy, ebbing for an instant as he looked again at the stiff black back, the stiff and implacable limp of the figure which was not dwarfed by the house, for the reason that it had never looked big anywhere and which now, against the serene columned backdrop, had more than ever that impervious quality of something cut ruthlessly from tin, depthless, as though, sidewise to the sun, it would cast no shadow. Watching him, the boy remarked the absolutely undeviating course which his father held and saw the stiff foot come squarely down in a pile of fresh droppings where a horse had stood in the drive and which his father could have avoided by a simple change of stride. But it ebbed only for a moment, though he could not have thought this into words either, walking on in the spell of the house, which he could even want but without envy, without sorrow, certainly never with that ravening and jealous rage which unknown to him walked in the ironlike black coat before him: *Maybe he will feel it too. Maybe it will even change him now from what maybe he couldn't help but be.*

They crossed the portico. Now he could hear his father's stiff foot as it came down on the boards with clocklike finality, a sound out of all proportion to the displacement of the body it bore and which was not dwarfed either by the white door before it, as though it had attained to a sort of vicious and ravening minimum not to be dwarfed by anything—the flat, wide, black hat, the formal coat of broadcloth which had once been black but which had now that friction-glazed greenish cast of the bodies of old house flies, the lifted sleeve which was too large, the lifted hand like a curled claw. The door opened so promptly that the boy knew the Negro must have been watching them all the time, an old man with neat grizzled hair, in a linen jacket, who stood barring the door with his body, saying, "Wipe yo foots, white man, fo you come in here. Major ain't home nohow."

"Get out of my way, nigger," his father said, without heat too, flinging the door back and the Negro also and entering, his hat still on his head. And now the boy saw the prints of the stiff foot on the doorjamb and saw them appear on the pale rug behind the machinelike deliberation of the foot which seemed to bear (or transmit) twice the weight which the body compassed. The Negro was shouting "Miss Lula! Miss Lula!" somewhere behind them, then the boy, deluged as though by a warm wave by a suave turn of carpeted stair and a pendant glitter of chandeliers and a mute gleam of gold frames, heard the swift feet and saw her too, a lady—perhaps he had never seen her like before either—in a gray, smooth gown with lace at the throat and an apron tied at the waist and the sleeves turned back, wiping cake or biscuit dough from her hands with a towel as she came up the hall, looking not at his father at all but at the tracks on the blond rug with an expression of incredulous amazement.

"I tried," the Negro cried. "I tole him to . . ."

"Will you please go away?" she said in a shaking voice. "Major de Spain is not at home. Will you please go away?"

His father had not spoken again. He did not speak again. He did not even look at her. He just stood stiff in the center of the rug, in his hat, the shaggy iron-gray brows twitching slightly above the pebble-colored eyes as he appeared to examine the house with brief deliberation. Then with the same deliberation he turned; the boy watched him pivot on the good leg and saw the stiff foot drag round the arc of the turning, leaving a final long and fading smear. His father never looked at it, he never once looked down at the rug. The Negro held the door. It closed behind them, upon the hysteric and indistinguishable woman-wail. His father stopped at the top of the steps and scraped his boot clean on the edge of it. At the gate he stopped again. He stood for a moment, planted stiffly on the stiff foot, looking back at the house. "Pretty and white, ain't it?" he said. "That's sweat. Nigger sweat. Maybe it ain't white enough yet to suit him. Maybe he wants to mix some white sweat with it."

Two hours later the boy was chopping wood behind the house within which his mother and aunt and the two sisters (the mother and aunt, not the two girls, he knew that; even at this distance and muffled by walls the flat loud voices of the two girls emanated an incorrigible idle inertia) were setting up the stove to prepare a meal, when he heard the hooves and saw the linen-clad man on a fine sorrel mare, whom he recognized even before he saw the rolled rug in front of the Negro youth following on a fat bay carriage horse—a suffused, angry face vanishing, still at full gallop, beyond the corner of the house where his father and brother were sitting in the two tilted chairs; and a moment later, almost before he could have put the axe down, he heard the hooves again and watched the sorrel mare go back out of the yard, already galloping again. Then his father began to shout one of the sisters' names, who presently emerged backward from the kitchen door dragging the rolled rug along the ground by one end while the other sister walked behind it.

"If you ain't going to tote, go on and set up the wash pot," the first said.

"You, Sarty!" the second shouted. "Set up the wash pot!" His father appeared at the door, framed against that shabbiness, as he had been against that other bland perfection, impervious to either, the mother's anxious face at his shoulder.

"Go on," the father said. "Pick it up." The two sisters stooped, broad, lethargic; stooping, they presented an incredible expanse of pale cloth and a flutter of tawdry ribbons.

"If I thought enough of a rug to have to git hit all the way from France I wouldn't keep hit where folks coming in would have to tromp on hit," the first said. They raised the rug.

"Abner," the mother said. "Let me do it."

"You go back and git dinner," his father said. "I'll tend to this."

From the woodpile through the rest of the afternoon the boy watched them, the rug spread flat in the dust beside the bubbling wash-pot, the two sisters stooping over it with that profound and lethargic reluctance, while the father stood over them in turn, implacable and grim, driving them though never raising his voice again. He could smell the harsh homemade lye they were using; he saw his mother come to the door once and look toward them with an expression not anxious now but very like despair; he saw his father turn, and he fell to with the axe and saw from the corner of his eye his father raise from the ground a flattish fragment of field stone and examine it and return to the pot, and this time his mother actually spoke: "Abner. Abner. Please don't. Please, Abner."

Then he was done too. It was dusk; the whippoorwills had already begun. He could smell coffee from the room where they would presently eat the cold food remaining from the mid-afternoon meal, though when he entered the house he realized they were having coffee again probably because there was a fire on the hearth, before which the rug now lay spread over the backs of the two chairs. The tracks of his father's foot were gone. Where they had been were now long, water-cloudy scoriations resembling the sporadic course of a lilliputian mowing machine.

It still hung there while they ate the cold food and then went to bed, scattered without order or claim up and down the two rooms, his mother in one bed, where his father would later lie, the older brother in the other, himself, the aunt, and the two sisters on pallets on the floor. But his father was not in bed yet. The last thing the boy remembered was the depthless, harsh silhouette of the hat and coat bending over the rug and it seemed to him that he had not even closed his eyes when the silhouette was standing over him, the fire almost dead behind it, the stiff foot prodding him awake. "Catch up the mule," his father said.

When he returned with the mule his father was standing in the black door, the rolled rug over his shoulder. "Ain't you going to ride?" he said.

"No. Give me your foot."

He bent his knee into his father's hand, the wiry, surprising power flowed smoothly, rising, he rising with it, on to the mule's bare back (they had owned a saddle once; the boy could remember it though not when or where) and with the same effortlessness his father swung the rug up in front of him. Now in the starlight they retraced the afternoon's path, up the dusty road rife with honeysuckle, through the gate and up the black tunnel of the drive to the lightless house, where he sat on the mule and felt the rough warp of the rug drag across his thighs and vanish.

"Don't you want me to help?" he whispered. His father did not answer and now he heard again that stiff foot striking the hollow portico with that wooden and clock-like deliberation, that outrageous overstatement of the weight it carried. The rug, hunched, not flung (the boy could tell that even in the darkness) from his father's shoulder struck the angle of wall and floor with a sound unbelievably loud, thunderous, then the foot again, unhurried and enormous; a light came on in the house and the boy sat, tense, breathing steadily and quietly and just a little fast, though the foot itself did not increase its beat at all, descending the steps now; now the boy could see him.

"Don't you want to ride now?" he whispered. "We kin both ride now," the light within the house altering now, flaring up and sinking. *He's coming down the stairs now,* he thought. He had already ridden the mule up beside the horse block; presently his father was up behind him and he doubled the reins over and slashed the mule across the neck, but before the animal could begin to trot the hard, thin arm came round him, the hard, knotted hand jerking the mule back to a walk.

In the first red rays of the sun they were in the lot, putting plow gear on the mules. This time the sorrel mare was in the lot before he heard it at all, the rider collarless and even bareheaded, trembling, speaking in a shaking voice as the woman in the house had done, his father merely looking up once before stooping again to the hame he was buckling, so that the man on the mare spoke to his stooping back:

"You must realize you have ruined that rug. Wasn't there anybody here, any of your women . . ." he ceased, shaking, the boy watching him, the older brother leaning now in the stable door, chewing, blinking slowly and steadily at nothing apparently. "It cost a hundred dollars. But you never had a hundred dollars. You never will. So I'm going to charge you twenty bushels of corn against your crop. I'll add it in your contract and when you come to the commissary you can sign it. That won't keep Mrs. de Spain quiet but maybe it will teach you to wipe your feet off before you enter her house again."

Then he was gone. The boy looked at his father, who still had not spoken or even looked up again, who was now adjusting the logger-head in the hame.

"Pap," he said. His father looked at him—the inscrutable face, the shaggy brows beneath which the gray eyes glinted coldly. Suddenly the boy went toward him, fast, stopping as suddenly. "You done the best you could!" he cried. "If he wanted hit done different why didn't he wait and tell you how? He won't git no twenty bushels! He won't git none! We'll gether hit and hide hit! I kin watch . . ."

"Did you put the cutter back in that straight stock like I told you?"

"No, sir," he said.

"Then go do it."

That was Wednesday. During the rest of that week he worked steadily, at what was within his scope and some which was beyond it, with an industry that did not need to be driven nor even commanded twice; he had this from his mother, with the difference that some at least of what he did he liked to do, such as splitting wood with the half-size axe which his mother and aunt had earned, or saved money somehow, to present him with at Christmas. In company with the two older women (and on one afternoon, even one of the sisters), he built pens for the shoat and the cow which were a part of his father's contract with the landlord, and one afternoon, his father being absent, gone somewhere on one of the mules, he went to the field.

They were running a middle buster now, his brother holding the plow straight while he handled the reins, and walking beside the straining mule, the rich black soil shearing cool and damp against his bare ankles, he thought *Maybe this is the end of it. Maybe even that twenty bushels that seems hard to have to pay for just a rug will be a cheap price for him to stop forever and always from being what he used to be;* thinking, dreaming now, so that his brother had to speak sharply to him to mind the mule: *Maybe he even won't collect the twenty bushels. Maybe it will all add up and balance and vanish—corn, rug, fire; the terror and grief, the being pulled two ways like between two teams of horses—gone, done with for ever and ever.*

Then it was Saturday; he looked up from beneath the mule he was harnessing and saw his father in the black coat and hat. "Not that," his father said. "The wagon gear." And then, two hours later, sitting in the wagon bed behind his father and brother on the seat, the wagon accomplished a final curve, and he saw the weathered paintless store with its tattered tobacco- and patent-medicine posters and the tethered wagons and saddle animals below the gallery. He mounted the gnawed steps behind his father and brother, and there again was the lane of quiet, watching faces for the three of them to walk through. He saw the man in spectacles sitting at the plank table and he did not need to be told this was a Justice of the Peace; he sent one glare of fierce, exultant, partisan defiance at the man in collar and cravat now, whom he had seen but twice before in his life, and that on a galloping horse, who now wore on his face an expression not of rage but of amazed unbelief which the boy could not have known was at the incredible circumstance of being sued by one of his own tenants, and came and stood against his father and cried at the Justice: "He ain't done it! He ain't burnt . . ."

"Go back to the wagon," his father said.

"Burnt?" the Justice said. "Do I understand this rug was burned too?"

"Does anybody here claim it was?" his father said. "Go back to the wagon." But he did not, he merely retreated to the rear of the room, crowded as that other had been, but not to sit down this time, instead, to stand pressing among the motionless bodies, listening to the voices:

"And you claim twenty bushels of corn is too high for the damage you did to the rug?"

"He brought the rug to me and said he wanted the tracks washed out of it. I washed the tracks out and took the rug back to him."

"But you didn't carry the rug back to him in the same condition it was in before you made the tracks on it."

His father did not answer, and now for perhaps half a minute there was no sound at all save that of breathing, the faint, steady suspiration of complete and intent listening.

"You decline to answer that, Mr. Snopes?" Again his father did not answer: "I'm going to find against you, Mr. Snopes. I'm going to find that you were responsible for the injury to Major de Spain's rug and hold you liable for it. But twenty bushels of corn seems a little high for a man in your circumstances to have to pay. Major de Spain claims it cost a hundred dollars. October corn will be worth about fifty cents. I figure that if Major de Spain can stand a ninety-five dollar loss on something he paid cash for, you can stand a five-dollar loss you haven't earned yet. I hold you in damages to Major de Spain to the amount of ten bushels of corn over and above your contract with him, to be paid to him out of your crop at gathering time. Court adjourned."

It had taken no time hardly, the morning was but half begun. He thought they would return home and perhaps back to the field, since they were late, far behind all other farmers. But instead his father passed on behind the wagon, merely indicating with his hand for the older brother to follow with it, and crossed the road toward the blacksmith shop opposite, pressing on after his father, overtaking him, speaking, whispering up at the harsh, calm face beneath the weathered hat: "He won't git no ten bushels neither. He won't git one. We'll . . ." until his father glanced for an instant down at him, the face absolutely calm, the grizzled eyebrows tangled above the cold eyes, the voice almost pleasant, almost gentle:

"You think so? Well, we'll wait till October anyway."

The matter of the wagon—the setting of a spoke or two and the tightening of the tires—did not take long either, the business of the tires accomplished by driving the wagon into the spring branch behind the shop and letting it stand there, the mules nuzzling into the water from time to time, and the boy on the seat with the idle reins, looking up the slope and through the sooty tunnel of the shed where the slow hammer rang and where his father sat on an upended cypress bolt, easily, either talking or listening, still sitting there when the boy brought the dripping wagon up out of the branch and halted it before the door.

"Take them on to the shade and hitch," his father said. He did so and returned. His father and the smith and a third man squatting on his heels inside the door were talking, about crops and animals; the boy, squatting too in the ammoniac dust and hoof-parings and scales of rust, heard his father tell a long and unhurried story out of the time before the birth of the older brother even when he had been a professional horsetrader. And then his father came up beside him where he stood before a tattered last year's circus poster on the other side of the store, gazing rapt and quiet at the scarlet horses, the incredible poisings and convolutions of tulle and tights and the painted leers of comedians, and said, "It's time to eat."

But not at home. Squatting beside his brother against the front wall, he watched his father emerge from the store and produce from a paper sack a segment of cheese and divide it carefully and deliberately into three with his pocket knife and produce crackers from the same sack. They all three squatted on the gallery and ate, slowly, without talking; then in the store again, they drank from a tin dipper tepid water smelling of the cedar bucket and of living beech trees. And still they did not go home. It was a horse lot this time, a tall rail fence upon and along which men stood and sat and out of which one by one horses were led, to be walked and trotted and then cantered back and forth along the road while the slow swapping and buying went on and the sun began to slant westward, they—the three of them—watching and listening, the older brother with his muddy eyes and his steady, inevitable tobacco, the father commenting now and then on certain of the animals, to no one in particular.

It was after sundown when they reached home. They ate supper by lamplight, then, sitting on the doorstep, the boy watched the night fully accomplish, listening to the whippoorwills and the frogs, when he heard his mother's voice: "Abner! No! No! Oh, God. Oh, God. Abner!" and he rose, whirled, and saw the altered light through the door where a candle stub now burned in a bottle neck on the table and his father, still in the hat and coat, at once formal and burlesque as though dressed carefully for some shabby and ceremonial violence, emptying the reservoir of the lamp back into the five-gallon kerosene can from which it had been filled, while the mother tugged at his arm until he shifted the lamp to the other hand and flung her back, not savagely or viciously, just hard, into the wall, her hands flung out against the wall for balance, her mouth open and in her face the same quality of hopeless despair as had been in her voice. Then his father saw him standing in the door.

"Go to the barn and get that can of oil we were oiling the wagon with," he said. The boy did not move. Then he could speak.

"What . . ." he cried. "What are you . . ."

"Go get that oil," his father said. "Go."

Then he was moving, running, outside the house, toward the stable: this the old habit, the old blood which he had not been permitted to choose for himself, which had been bequeathed him willy nilly and which had run for so long (and who knew where, battening on what of outrage and savagery and lust) before it came to him. *I could keep on,* he thought. *I could run on and on and never look back, never need to see his face again. Only I can't. I can't,* the rusted can in his hand now, the liquid sploshing in it as he ran back to the house and into it, into the sound of his mother's weeping in the next room, and handed the can to his father.

"Ain't you going to even send a nigger?" he cried. "At least you sent a nigger before!"

This time his father didn't strike him. The hand came even faster than the blow had, the same hand which had set the can on the table with almost excruciating care flashing from the can toward him too quick for him to follow it, gripping him by the back of his shirt and on to tiptoe before he had seen it quit the can, the face stooping at him in breathless and frozen ferocity, the cold, dead voice speaking over him to the older brother who leaned against the table, chewing with that steady, curious, sidewise motion of cows:

"Empty the can into the big one and go on. I'll catch up with you."

"Better tie him up to the bedpost," the brother said.

"Do like I told you," the father said. Then the boy was moving, his bunched shirt and the hard, bony hand between his shoulder-blades, his toes just touching the floor, across the room and into the other one, past the sisters sitting with spread heavy thighs in the two chairs over the cold hearth, and to where his mother and aunt sat side by side on the bed, the aunt's arms about his mother's shoulders.

"Hold him," the father said. The aunt made a startled movement. "Not you," the father said. "Lennie. Take hold of him. I want to see you do it." His mother took him by the wrist. "You'll hold him better than that. If he gets loose don't you know what he is going to do? He will go up yonder." He jerked his head toward the road. "Maybe I'd better tie him."

"I'll hold him," his mother whispered.

"See you do then." Then his father was gone, the stiff foot heavy and measured upon the boards, ceasing at last.

Then he began to struggle. His mother caught him in both arms, he jerking and wrenching at them. He would be stronger in the end, he knew that. But he had no time to wait for it. "Lemme go!" he cried. "I don't want to have to hit you!"

"Let him go!" the aunt said. "If he don't go, before God, I am going up there myself!"

"Don't you see I can't?" his mother cried. "Sarty! Sarty! No! No! Help me, Lizzie!"

Then he was free. His aunt grasped at him but it was too late. He whirled, running, his mother stumbled forward on to her knees behind him, crying to the nearer sister: "Catch him, Net! Catch him!" But that was too late too, the sister (the sisters were twins, born at the same time, yet either of them now gave the impression of being, encompassing as much living meat and volume and weight as any other two of the family) not yet having begun to rise from the chair, her head, face, alone merely turned, presenting to him in the flying instant an astonishing expanse of young female features untroubled by any surprise even, wearing only an expression of bovine interest. Then he was out of the room, out of the house, in the mild dust of the starlit road and the heavy rifeness of honey-suckle, the pale ribbon unspooling with terrific slowness under his running feet, reaching the gate at last and turning in, running, his heart and lungs drumming, on up the drive toward the lighted house, the lighted door. He did not knock, he burst in, sobbing for breath, incapable for the moment of speech; he saw the astonished face of the Negro in the linen jacket without knowing when the Negro had appeared.

"De Spain!" he cried, panted. "Where's . . ." then he saw the white man too emerging from a white door down the hall. "Barn!" he cried. "Barn!"

"What?" the white man said. "Barn?"

"Yes!" the boy cried. "Barn!"

"Catch him!" the white man shouted.

But it was too late this time too. The Negro grasped his shirt, but the entire sleeve, rotten with washing, carried away, and he was out that door too and in the drive again, and had actually never ceased to run even while he was screaming into the white man's face.

Behind him the white man was shouting, "My horse! Fetch my horse!" and he thought for an instant of cutting across the park and climbing the fence into the road, but he did not know the park nor how high the vine-massed fence might be and he dared not risk it. So he ran on down the drive, blood and breath roaring; presently he was in the road again though he could not see it. He could not hear either: the galloping mare was almost upon him before he heard her, and even then he held his course, as if the very urgency of his wild grief and need must in a moment more find him wings, waiting until the ultimate instant to hurl himself aside and into the weed-choked roadside ditch as the horse thundered past and on, for an instant in furious silhouette against the stars, the tranquil early summer night sky which, even before the shape of the horse and rider vanished, stained abruptly and violently upward: a long, swirling roar incredible and soundless, blotting the stars, and he springing up and into the road again, running again, knowing it was too late yet still running even after he heard the shot and, an instant later, two shots, pausing now without knowing he had ceased to run, crying "Pap! Pap!", running again before he knew he had begun to run, stumbling, tripping over something and scrabbling up again without ceasing to run, looking backward over his shoulder at the glare as he got up, running on among the invisible trees, panting, sobbing, "Father! Father!"

At midnight he was sitting on the crest of a hill. He did not know it was midnight and he did not know how far he had come. But there was no glare behind him now and he sat now, his back toward what he had called home for four days anyhow, his face toward the dark woods which he would enter when breath was strong again, small, shaking steadily in the chill darkness, hugging himself into the remainder of his thin, rotten shirt, the grief and despair now no longer terror and fear but just grief and despair. *Father. My father,* he thought. "He was brave!" he cried suddenly, aloud but not loud, no more than a whisper: "He was! He was in the war! He was in Colonel Sartoris' cav'ry!" not knowing that his father had gone to that war a private in the fine old European sense, wearing no uniform, admitting the authority of and giving fidelity to no man or army or flag, going to war as Malbrouck himself did: for booty—it meant nothing and less than nothing to him if it were enemy booty or his own.

The slow constellations wheeled on. It would be dawn and then sun-up after a while and he would be hungry. But that would be tomorrow and now he was only cold, and walking would cure that. His breathing was easier now and he decided to get up and go on, and then he found that he had been asleep because he knew it was almost dawn, the night almost over. He could tell that from the whippoorwills. They were everywhere now among the dark trees below him, constant and inflectioned and ceaseless, so that, as the instant for giving over to the day birds drew nearer and nearer, there was no interval at all between them. He got up. He was a little stiff, but walking would cure that too as it would the cold, and soon there would be the sun. He went on down the hill, toward the dark woods within which the liquid silver voices of the birds called unceasing—the rapid and urgent beating of the urgent and quiring heart of the late spring night. He did not look back.

Chapter 3

JAMES JOYCE

Araby

North Richmond Street, being blind, was a quiet street except at the hour when the Christian Brothers' School set the boys free. An uninhabited house of two storeys stood at the blind end, detached from its neighbours in a square ground. The other houses of the street, conscious of decent lives within them, gazed at one another with brown imperturbable faces.

The former tenant of our house, a priest, had died in the back drawingroom. Air, musty from having been long enclosed, hung in all the rooms and the waste room behind the kitchen was littered with old useless papers. Among these I found a few papercovered books, the pages of which were curled and damp: *The Abbot* by Walter Scott, *The Devout Communicant* and *The Memoirs of Vidocq.* I liked the last best because its leaves were yellow. The wild garden behind the house contained a central apple tree and a few straggling bushes under one of which I found the late tenant's rusty bicycle pump. He had been a very charitable priest; in his will he had left all his money to institutions and the furniture of his house to his sister.

When the short days of winter came dusk fell before we had well eaten our dinners. When we met in the street the houses had grown sombre. The space of sky above us was the colour of everchanging violet and towards it the lamps of the street lifted their feeble lanterns. The cold air stung us and we played till our bodies glowed. Our shouts echoed in the silent street. The career of our play brought us through the dark muddy lanes behind the houses where we ran the gantlet of the rough tribes from the cottages, to the back doors of the dark dripping gardens where odours arose from the ashpits, to the dark odorous stables where a coachman smoothed and combed the horse or shook music from the buckled harness. When we returned to the street light from the kitchen windows had filled the areas. If my uncle was seen turning the corner we hid in the shadow until we had seen him safely housed. Or if Mangan's sister came out on the doorstep to call her brother in to his tea we watched her from our shadow peer up and down the street. We waited to see whether she would remain or go in and if she remained we left our shadow and walked up to Mangan's steps resignedly. She was waiting for us, her figure defined by the light from the half-opened door. Her brother always teased her before he obeyed and I stood by the railings looking at her. Her dress swung as she moved her body and the soft rope of her hair tossed from side to side.

Every morning I lay on the floor in the front parlour watching her door. The blind was pulled down to within an inch of the sash so that I could not be seen. When she came out on the doorstep my heart leaped. I ran to the hall, seized my books and followed her. I kept her brown figure always in my eye and when we came near the point at which our ways diverged I quickened my pace and passed her. This happened morning after morning. I had never spoken to her except for a few casual words and yet her name was like a summons to all my foolish blood.

Her image accompanied me even in places the most hostile to romance. On Saturday evenings when my aunt went marketing I had to go to carry some of the parcels. We walked through the flaring streets, jostled by drunken men and bargaining women, amid the curses of labourers, the shrill litanies of shop boys who stood on guard by the barrels of pigs' cheeks, the nasal chanting of street singers who sang a *come-all-you* about O'Donovan Rossa or a ballad about the troubles in our native land. These noises converged in a single sensation of life for me: I imagined that I bore my chalice safely through a throng of foes. Her name sprang to my lips at moments in strange prayers and praises which I myself did not understand. My eyes were often full of tears (I could not tell why) and at times a flood from my heart seemed to pour itself out into my bosom. I thought little of the future. I did not know whether I would ever speak to her or not or, if I spoke to her, how I could tell her of my confused adoration. But my body was like a harp and her words and gestures were like fingers running upon the wires.

One evening I went into the back drawingroom in which the priest had died. It was a dark rainy evening and there was no sound in the house. Through one of the broken panes I heard the rain impinge upon the earth, the fine incessant needles of water playing in the sodden beds. Some distant lamp or lighted window gleamed below me. I was thankful that I could see so little. All my senses seemed to desire to veil themselves and, feeling that I was about to slip from them, I pressed the palms of my hands together until they trembled, murmuring: *O love! O love!* many times.

At last she spoke to me. When she addressed the first words to me I was so confused that I did not know what to answer. She asked me was I going to *Araby*. I forget whether I answered yes or no. It would be a splendid bazaar, she said; she would love to go.

—And why can't you? I asked.

While she spoke she turned a silver bracelet round and round her wrist. She could not go, she said, because there would be a retreat that week in her convent. Her brother and two other boys were fighting for their caps and I was alone at the railings. She held one of the spikes, bowing her head towards me. The light from the lamp opposite our door caught the white curve of her neck, lit up the hair that rested there and, falling, lit up the hand upon the railing. It fell over one side of her dress and caught the white border of a petticoat, just visible as she stood at ease.

—It's well for you, she said.

—If I go, I said, I will bring you something.

What innumerable follies laid waste my waking and sleeping thoughts after that evening! I wished to annihilate the tedious intervening days. I chafed against the work of school. At night in my bedroom and by day in the classroom her image came between me and the page I strove to read. The syllables of the word *Araby* were called to me through the silence in which my soul luxuriated and cast an eastern enchantment over me. I asked for leave to go to the bazaar on Saturday night. My aunt was surprised and hoped it was not some freemason affair. I answered few questions in class. I watched my master's face pass from amiability to sternness; he hoped I was not beginning to idle. I could not call my wandering thoughts together. I had hardly any patience with the serious work of life which, now that it stood between me and my desire, seemed to me child's play, ugly monotonous child's play.

On Saturday morning I reminded my uncle that I wished to go to the bazaar in the evening. He was fussing at the hallstand, looking for the hatbrush, and answered me curtly:

—Yes, boy, I know.

As he was in the hall I could not go into the front parlour and lie at the window. I left the house in bad humour and walked slowly towards the school. The air was pitilessly raw and already my heart misgave me.

When I came home to dinner my uncle had not yet been home. Still it was early. I sat staring at the clock for some time and when its ticking began to irritate me I left the room. I mounted the staircase and gained the upper part of the house. The high cold empty gloomy rooms liberated me and I went from room to room singing. From the front window I saw my companions playing below in the street. Their cries reached me weakened and indistinct and, leaning my forehead against the cool glass, I looked over at the dark house where she lived. I may have stood there for an hour seeing nothing but the brownclad figure cast by my imagination, touched discreetly by the lamplight at the curved neck, at the hand upon the railings and at the border below the dress.

When I came downstairs again I found Mrs Mercer sitting at the fire. She was an old garrulous woman, a pawnbroker's widow who collected used stamps for some pious purpose. I had to endure the gossip of the teatable. The meal was prolonged beyond an hour and still my uncle did not come. Mrs Mercer stood up to go: she was sorry she couldn't wait any longer but it was after eight o'clock and she did not like to be out late as the night air was bad for her. When she had gone I began to walk up and down the room, clenching my fists. My aunt said:

—I'm afraid you may put off your bazaar for this night of Our Lord.

At nine o'clock I heard my uncle's latchkey in the halldoor. I heard him talking to himself and heard the hallstand rocking when it had received the weight of his overcoat. I could interpret these signs. When he was midway through his dinner I asked him to give me the money to go to the bazaar. He had forgotten.

—The people are in bed and after their first sleep now, he said.

I did not smile. My aunt said to him energetically:

—Can't you give him the money and let him go? You've kept him late enough as it is.

My uncle said he was very sorry he had forgotten. He said he believed in the old saying: *All work and no play makes Jack a dull boy.* He asked me where I was going and when I had told him a second time he asked me did I know *The Arab's Farewell to His Steed.* When I left the kitchen he was about to recite the opening lines of the piece to my aunt.

I held a florin tightly in my hand as I strode down Buckingham Street towards the station. The sight of the streets thronged with buyers and glaring with gas recalled to me the purpose of my journey. I took my seat in a third class carriage of a deserted train. After an intolerable delay the train moved out of the station slowly. It crept onward among ruinous houses and over the twinkling river. At Westland Row Station a crowd of people pressed at the carriage doors; but the porters moved them back, saying that it was a special train for the bazaar. I remained alone in the bare carriage. In a few minutes the train drew up beside an improvised wooden platform. I passed out on to the road and saw by the lighted dial of a clock that it was ten minutes to ten. In front of me was a large building which displayed the magical name.

I could not find any sixpenny entrance and, fearing that the bazaar would be closed, I passed in quickly through a turnstile, handing a shilling to a wearylooking man. I found myself in a big hall girdled at half its height by a gallery. Nearly all the stalls were closed and the greater part of the hall was in darkness. I recognised a silence like that which pervades a church after a service. I walked into the centre of the bazaar timidly. A few people were gathered about the stalls which were still open. Before a curtain over which the words *Café Chantant* were written in coloured lamps two men were counting money on a salver. I listened to the fall of the coins.

Remembering with difficulty why I had come I went over to one of the stalls and examined porcelain vases and flowered teasets. At the door of the stall a young lady was talking and laughing with two young gentlemen. I remarked their English accents and listened vaguely to their conversation.

—O, I never said such a thing!

—O, but you did!

—O, but I didn't!

—Didn't she say that?

—She did. I heard her.

—O, there's a . . . fib!

Observing me the young lady came over and asked me did I wish to buy anything. The tone of her voice was not encouraging: she seemed to have spoken to me out of a sense of duty. I looked humbly at the great jars that stood like eastern guards at either side of the dark entrance to her stall and murmured:

—No, thank you.

The young lady changed the position of one of the vases and went back to the two young men. They began to talk of the same subject. Once or twice the young lady glanced at me over her shoulder.

I lingered before her stall, though I knew my stay was useless, to make my interest in her wares seem the more real. Then I turned away slowly and walked down the middle of the bazaar. I allowed the two pennies to fall against the sixpence in my pocket. I heard a voice call from one end of the gallery that the light was out. The upper part of the hall was now completely dark.

Gazing up into the darkness I saw myself as a creature driven and derided by vanity: and my eyes burned with anguish and anger.

Chapter 4

NATHANIEL HAWTHORNE

YOUNG GOODMAN BROWN

From The Complete Novels and Selected Tales of Nathaniel Hawthorne, *ed. Norman Holmes Pierson (New York: Random House, Modern Library, 1937), pp. 1033–1042.*

Young Goodman Brown came forth at sunset into the street at Salem village; but put his head back, after crossing the threshold, to exchange a parting kiss with his young wife. And Faith, as the wife was aptly named, thrust her own pretty head into the street, letting the wind play with the pink ribbons of her cap while she called to Goodman Brown.

"Dearest heart," whispered she, softly and rather sadly, when her lips were close to his ear, "prithee put off your journey until sunrise and sleep in your own bed to-night. A lone woman is troubled with such dreams and such thoughts that she's afeard of herself sometimes. Pray tarry with me this night, dear husband, of all nights in the year."

"My love and my Faith," replied young Goodman Brown, "of all nights in the year, this one night must I tarry away from thee. My journey, as thou callest it, forth and back again, must needs be done 'twixt now and sunrise. What, my sweet, pretty wife, dost thou doubt me already, and we but three months married?"

"Then God bless you!" said Faith, with the pink ribbons; "and may you find all well when you come back."

"Amen!" cried Goodman Brown. "Say thy prayers, dear Faith, and go to bed at dusk, and no harm will come to thee."

So they parted; and the young man pursued his way until, being about to turn the corner by the meeting-house, he looked back and saw the head of Faith still peeping after him with a melancholy air, in spite of her pink ribbons.

"Poor little Faith!" thought he, for his heart smote him. "What a wretch am I to leave her on such an errand! She talks of dreams, too. Me-thought as she spoke there was trouble in her face, as if a dream had warned her what work is to be done tonight. But no, no; 't would kill her to think it. Well, she's a blessed angel on earth; and after this one night I'll cling to her skirts and follow her to heaven."

With this excellent resolve for the future, Goodman Brown felt himself justified in making more haste on his present evil purpose. He had taken a dreary road, darkened by all the gloomiest trees of the forest, which barely stood aside to let the narrow path creep through, and closed immediately behind. It was all as lonely as could be; and there is this peculiarity in such a solitude, that the traveller knows not who may be concealed by the innumerable trunks and the thick boughs overhead; so that with lonely footsteps he may yet be passing through an unseen multitude.

"There may be a devilish Indian behind every tree," said Goodman Brown to himself; and he glanced fearfully behind him as he added, "What if the devil himself should be at my very elbow!"

His head being turned back, he passed a crook of the road, and, looking forward again, beheld the figure of a man, in grave and decent attire, seated at the foot of an old tree. He arose at Goodman Brown's approach and walked onward side by side with him.

"You are late, Goodman Brown," said he. "The clock of the Old South was striking as I came through Boston, and that is full fifteen minutes agone."

"Faith kept me back a while," replied the young man, with a tremor in his voice, caused by the sudden appearance of his companion, though not wholly unexpected.

It was now deep dusk in the forest, and deepest in that part of it where these two were journeying. As nearly as could be discerned, the second traveller was about fifty years old, apparently in the same rank of life as Goodman Brown, and bearing a considerable resemblance to him, though perhaps more in expression than features. Still they might have been taken for father and son. And yet, though the elder person was as simply clad as the younger, and as simple in manner too, he had an indescribable air of one who knew the world, and who would not have felt abashed at the governor's dinner table or in King William's court, were it possible that his affairs should call him thither. But the only thing about him that could be fixed upon as remarkable was his staff, which bore the likeness of a great black snake, so curiously wrought that it might almost be seen to twist and wriggle itself like a living serpent. This, of course, must have been an ocular deception, assisted by the uncertain light.

"Come, Goodman Brown," cried his fellow-traveller, "this is a dull pace for the beginning of a journey. Take my staff, if you are so soon weary."

"Friend," said the other, exchanging his slow pace for a full stop, "having kept covenant by meeting thee here, it is my purpose now to return whence I came. I have scruples touching the matter thou wot'st of."

"Sayest thou so?" replied he of the serpent, smiling apart. "Let us walk on, nevertheless, reasoning as we go; and if I convince thee not thou shalt turn back. We are but a little way in the forest yet."

"Too far! too far!" exclaimed the goodman, unconsciously resuming his walk. "My father never went into the woods on such an errand, nor his father before him. We have been a race of honest men and good Christians since the days of the martyrs; and shall I be the first of the name of Brown that ever took this path and kept"—

"Such company, thou wouldst say," observed the elder person, interpreting his pause. "Well said, Goodman Brown! I have been as well acquainted with your family as with ever a one among the Puritans; and that's no trifle to say. I helped your grandfather, the constable, when he lashed the Quaker woman so smartly through the streets of Salem; and it was I that brought your father a pitch-pine knot, kindled at my own hearth, to set fire to an Indian village, in King Philip's war. They were my good friends, both; and many a pleasant walk have we had along this path, and returned merrily after midnight. I would fain be friends with you for their sake."

"If it be as thou sayest," replied Goodman Brown, "I marvel they never spoke of these matters; or, verily, I marvel not, seeing that the least rumor of the sort would have driven them from New England. We are a people of prayer, and good works to boot, and abide no such wickedness."

"Wickedness or not," said the traveller with the twisted staff, "I have a very general acquaintance here in New England. The deacons of many a church have drunk the communion wine with me; the selectmen of divers towns make me their chairman; and a majority of the Great and General Court are firm supporters of my interest. The governor and I, too—But these are state secrets."

"Can this be so?" cried Goodman Brown, with a stare of amazement at his undisturbed companion. "Howbeit, I have nothing to do with the governor and council; they have their own ways, and are no rule for a simple husbandman like me. But, were I to go on with thee, how should I meet the eye of that good old man, our minister, at Salem village? Oh, his voice would make me tremble both Sabbath day and lecture day."

Thus far the elder traveller had listened with due gravity; but now burst into a fit of irrepressible mirth, shaking himself so violently that his snake-like staff actually seemed to wriggle in sympathy.

"Ha! ha! ha!" shouted he again and again; then composing himself, "Well, go on, Goodman Brown, go on; but, prithee, don't kill me with laughing."

"Well, then, to end the matter at once," said Goodman Brown, considerably nettled, "there is my wife, Faith. It would break her dear little heart; and I'd rather break my own."

"Nay, if that be the case," answered the other, "e'en go thy ways, Goodman Brown. I would not for twenty old women like the one hobbling before us that Faith should come to any harm."

As he spoke he pointed his staff at a female figure on the path, in whom Goodman Brown recognized a very pious and exemplary dame, who had taught him his catechism in youth, and was still his moral and spiritual adviser, jointly with the minister and Deacon Gookin.

"A marvel, truly, that Goody Cloyse should be so far in the wilderness at nightfall," said he. "But with your leave, friend, I shall take a cut through the woods until we have left this Christian woman behind. Being a stranger to you, she might ask whom I was consorting with and whither I was going."

"Be it so," said his fellow-traveller. "Betake you to the woods, and let me keep the path."

Accordingly the young man turned aside, but took care to watch his companion, who advanced softly along the road until he had come within a staff's length of the old dame. She, meanwhile, was making the best of her way, with singular speed for so aged a woman, and mumbling some indistinct words—a prayer, doubtless—as she went. The traveller put forth his staff and touched her withered neck with what seemed the serpent's tail.

"The devil!" screamed the pious old lady.

"Then Goody Cloyse knows her old friend?" observed the traveller, confronting her and leaning on his writhing stick.

"Ah, forsooth, and is it your worship indeed?" cried the good dame. "Yea, truly is it, and in the very image of my old gossip, Goodman Brown, the grandfather of the silly fellow that now is. But—would your worship believe it?—my broomstick hath strangely disappeared, stolen, as I suspect, by that unhanged witch, Goody Cory, and that, too, when I was all anointed with the juice of smallage, and cinquefoil, and wolf's bane"—

"Mingled with fine wheat and the fat of a new-born babe," said the shape of old Goodman Brown.

"Ah, your worship knows the recipe," cried the old lady, cackling aloud. "So, as I was saying, being all ready for the meeting, and no horse to ride on, I made up my mind to foot it; for they tell me there is a nice young man to be taken into communion to-night. But now your good worship will lend me your arm, and we shall be there in a twinkling.

"That can hardly be," answered her friend. "I may not spare you my arm, Goody Cloyse; but here is my staff, if you will."

So saying, he threw it down at her feet, where, perhaps, it assumed life, being one of the rods which its owner had formerly lent to the Egyptian magi. Of this fact, however, Goodman Brown could not take cognizance. He had cast up his eyes in astonishment, and, looking down again, beheld neither Goody Cloyse nor the serpentine staff, but his fellow-traveller alone, who waited for him as calmly as if nothing had happened.

"That old woman taught me my catechism," said the young man; and there was a world of meaning in this simple comment.

They continued to walk onward, while the elder traveller exhorted his companion to make good speed and persevere in the path, discoursing so aptly that his arguments seemed rather to spring up in the bosom of his auditor than to be suggested by himself. As they went, he plucked a branch of maple to serve for a walking stick, and began to strip it of the twigs and little boughs, which were wet with evening dew. The moment his fingers touched them they became strangely withered and dried up as with a week's sunshine. Thus the pair proceeded, at a good free pace, until suddenly, in a gloomy hollow of the road, Goodman Brown sat himself down on the stump of a tree and refused to go any farther.

"Friend," said he, stubbornly, "my mind is made up. Not another step will I budge on this errand. What if a wretched old woman do choose to go to the devil when I thought she was going to heaven: is that any reason why I should quit my dear Faith and go after her?"

"You will think better of this by and by," said his acquaintance, composedly. "Sit here and rest yourself a while; and when you feel like moving again, there is my staff to help you along."

Without more words, he threw his companion the maple stick, and was as speedily out of sight as if he had vanished into the deepening gloom. The young man sat a few moments by the roadside, applauding himself greatly, and thinking with how clear a conscience he should meet the minister in his morning walk, nor shrink from the eye of good old Deacon Gookin. And what calm sleep would be his that very night, which was to have been spent so wickedly, but so purely and sweetly now, in the arms of Faith! Amidst these pleasant and praiseworthy meditations, Goodman Brown heard the tramp of horses along the road, and deemed it advisable to conceal himself within the verge of the forest, conscious of the guilty purpose that had brought him thither, though now so happily turned from it.

On came the hoof tramps and the voices of the riders, two grave old voices, conversing soberly as they drew near. These mingled sounds appeared to pass along the road, within a few yards of the young man's hiding-place; but, owing doubtless to the depth of the gloom at that particular spot, neither the travellers nor their steeds were visible. Though their figures brushed the small boughs by the wayside, it could not be seen that they intercepted, even for a moment, the faint gleam from the strip of bright sky athwart which they must have passed. Goodman Brown alternately crouched and stood on tiptoe, pulling aside the branches and thrusting forth his head as far as he durst without discerning so much as a shadow. It vexed him the more, because he could have sworn, were such a thing possible, that he recognized the voices of the minister and Deacon Gookin, jogging along quietly, as they were wont to do, when bound to some ordination or ecclesiastical council. While yet within hearing, one of the riders stopped to pluck a switch.

"Of the two, reverend sir," said the voice like the deacon's, "I had rather miss an ordination dinner than to-night's meeting. They tell me that some of our community are to be here from Falmouth and beyond, and others from Connecticut and Rhode Island, besides several of the Indian powwows, who, after their fashion, know almost as much deviltry as the best of us. Moreover, there is a goodly young woman to be taken into communion."

"Mighty well, Deacon Gookin!" replied the solemn old tones of the minister. "Spur up, or we shall be late. Nothing can be done, you know, until I get on the ground."

The hoofs clattered again; and the voices, talking so strangely in the empty air, passed on through the forest, where no church had ever been gathered or solitary Christian prayed. Whither, then, could these holy men be journeying so deep into the heathen wilderness? Young Goodman Brown caught hold of a tree for support, being ready to sink down on the ground, faint and overburdened with the heavy sickness of his heart. He looked up to the sky, doubting whether there really was a heaven above him. Yet there was the blue arch, and the stars brightening in it.

"With heaven above and Faith below, I will yet stand firm against the devil!" cried Goodman Brown.

While he still gazed upward into the deep arch of the firmament and had lifted his hands to pray, a cloud, though no wind was stirring, hurried across the zenith and hid the brightening stars. The blue sky was still visible, except directly overhead, where this black mass of cloud was sweeping swiftly northward. Aloft in the air, as if from the depths of the cloud, came a confused and doubtful sound of voices. Once the listener fancied that he could distinguish the accents of towns-people of his own, men and women, both pious and ungodly, many of whom he had met at the communion table, and had seen others rioting at the tavern. The next moment, so indistinct were the sounds, he doubted whether he had heard aught but the murmur of the old forest, whispering without a wind. Then came a stronger swell of those familiar tones, heard daily in the sunshine at Salem village, but never until now from a cloud of night. There was one voice of a young woman, uttering lamentations, yet with an uncertain sorrow, and entreating for some favor, which, perhaps, it would grieve her to obtain; and all the unseen multitude, both saints and sinners, seemed to encourage her onward.

"Faith!" shouted Goodman Brown, in a voice of agony and desperation; and the echoes of the forest mocked him, crying, "Faith! Faith!" as if bewildered wretches were seeking her all through the wilderness.

The cry of grief, rage, and terror was yet piercing the night, when the unhappy husband held his breath for a response. There was a scream, drowned immediately in a louder murmur of voices, fading into far-off laughter, as the dark cloud swept away, leaving the clear and silent sky above Goodman Brown. But something fluttered lightly down through the air and caught on the branch of a tree. The young man seized it, and beheld a pink ribbon.

"My Faith is gone!" cried he, after one stupefied moment. "There is no good on earth; and sin is but a name. Come, devil; for to thee is this world given."

And, maddened with despair, so that he laughed loud and long, did Goodman Brown grasp his staff and set forth again, at such a rate that he seemed to fly along the forest path rather than to walk or run. The road grew wilder and drearier and more faintly traced, and vanished at length, leaving him in the heart of the dark wilderness, still rushing onward with the instinct that guides mortal man to evil. The whole forest was peopled with frightful sounds—the creaking of the trees, the howling of wild beasts, and the yell of Indians; while sometimes the wind tolled like a distant church bell, and sometimes gave a broad roar around the traveller, as if all Nature were laughing him to scorn. But he was himself the chief horror of the scene, and shrank not from its other horrors.

"Ha! ha! ha!" roared Goodman Brown when the wind laughed at him. "Let us hear which will laugh loudest. Think not to frighten me with your deviltry. Come witch, come wizard, come Indian powwow, come devil himself, and here comes Goodman Brown. You may as well fear him as he fear you."

In truth, all through the haunted forest there could be nothing more frightful than the figure of Goodman Brown. On he flew among the black pines, brandishing his staff with frenzied gestures, now giving vent to an inspiration of horrid blasphemy, and now shouting forth such laughter as set all the echoes of the forest laughing like demons around him. The fiend in his own shape is less hideous than when he rages in the breast of man. Thus sped the demoniac on his course, until, quivering among the trees, he saw a red light before him, as when the felled trunks and branches of a clearing have been set on fire, and throw up their lurid blaze against the sky, at the hour of midnight. He paused, in a lull of the tempest that had driven him onward, and heard the swell of what seemed a hymn, rolling solemnly from a distance with the weight of many voices. He knew the tune; it was a familiar one in the choir of the village meeting-house. The verse died heavily away, and was lengthened by a chorus, not of human voices, but of all the sounds of the benighted wilderness pealing in awful harmony together. Goodman Brown cried out, and his cry was lost to his own ear by its unison with the cry of the desert.

In the interval of silence he stole forward until the light glared full upon his eyes. At one extremity of an open space, hemmed in by the dark wall of the forest, arose a rock, bearing some rude, natural resemblance either to an altar or a pulpit, and surrounded by four blazing pines, their tops aflame, their stems untouched, like candles at an evening meeting. The mass of foliage that had overgrown the summit of the rock was all on fire, blazing high into the night and fitfully illuminating the whole field. Each pendent twig and leafy festoon was in a blaze. As the red light arose and fell a numerous congregation alternately shone forth, then disappeared in shadow, and again grew, as it were, out of the darkness, peopling the heart of the solitary woods at once.

"A grave and dark-clad company," quoth Goodman Brown.

In truth they were such. Among them, quivering to and fro between gloom and splendor, appeared faces that would be seen next day at the council board of the province, and others which, Sabbath after Sabbath, looked devoutly heavenward, and benignantly over the crowded pews, from the holiest pulpits in the land. Some affirm that the lady of the governor was there. At least there were high dames well known to her, and wives of honored husbands, and widows, a great multitude, and ancient maidens, all of excellent repute, and fair young girls, who trembled lest their mothers should espy them. Either the sudden gleams of light flashing over the obscure field bedazzled Goodman Brown, or he recognized a score of the church members of Salem village famous for their especial sanctity. Good old Deacon Gookin had arrived, and waited at the skirts of that venerable saint, his revered pastor. But, irreverently consorting with these grave, reputable, and pious people, these elders of the church, these chaste dames and dewy virgins, there were men of dissolute lives and women of spotted fame, wretches given over to all mean and filthy vice, and suspected even of horrid crimes. It was strange to see that the good shrank not from the wicked, nor were the sinners abashed by the saints. Scattered also among their pale-faced enemies were the Indian priests, or powwows, who had often scared their native forest with more hideous incantations than any known to English witchcraft.

"But where is Faith?" thought Goodman Brown; and, as hope came into his heart, he trembled.

Another verse of the hymn arose, a slow and mournful strain, such as the pious love, but joined to words which expressed all that our nature can conceive of sin, and darkly hinted at far more. Unfathomable to mere mortals is the lore of fiends. Verse after verse was sung; and still the chorus of the desert swelled between like the deepest tone of a mighty organ; and with the final peal of that dreadful anthem there came a sound, as if the roaring wind, the rushing streams, the howling beasts, and every other voice of the unconcerted wilderness were mingling and according with the voice of guilty man in homage to the prince of all. The four blazing pines threw up a loftier flame, and obscurely discovered shapes and visages of horror on the smoke wreaths above the impious assembly. At the same moment the fire on the rock shot redly forth and formed a glowing arch above its base, where now appeared a figure. With reverence be it spoken, the figure bore no slight similitude, both in garb and manner, to some grave divine of the New England churches.

"Bring forth the converts!" cried a voice that echoed through the field and rolled into the forest.

At the word, Goodman Brown stepped forth from the shadow of the trees and approached the congregation, with whom he felt a loathful brotherhood by the sympathy of all that was wicked in his heart. He could have well-nigh sworn that the shape of his own dead father beckoned him to advance, looking downward from a smoke wreath, while a woman, with dim features of despair, threw out her hand to warn him back. Was it his mother? But he had no power to retreat one step, not to resist, even in thought, when the minister and good old Deacon Gookin seized his arms and led him to the blazing rock. Thither came also the slender form of a veiled female, led between Goody Cloyse, that pious teacher of the catechism, and Martha Carrier, who had received the devil's promise to be queen of hell. A rampant hag was she. And there stood the proselytes beneath the canopy of fire.

"Welcome, my children," said the dark figure, "to the communion of your race. Ye have found thus young your nature and your destiny. My children, look behind you!"

They turned; and flashing forth, as it were, in a sheet of flame, the fiend worshippers were seen; the smile of welcome gleamed darkly on every visage.

"There," resumed the sable form, "are all whom ye have reverenced from youth. Ye deemed them holier than yourselves, and shrank from your own sin, contrasting it with their lives of righteousness and prayerful aspirations heavenward. Yet here are they all in my worshipping assembly. This night it shall be granted you to know their secret deeds: how hoary-bearded elders of the church have whispered wanton words to the young maids of their households; how many a woman, eager for widows' weeds, has given her husband a drink at bedtime and let him sleep his last sleep in her bosom; how beardless youths have made haste to inherit their fathers' wealth; and how fair damsels—blush not, sweet ones—have dug little graves in the garden, and bidden me, the sole guest to an infant's funeral. By the sympathy of your human hearts for sin ye shall scent out all the places—whether in church, bedchamber, street, field, or forest—where crime has been committed, and shall exult to behold the whole earth one stain of guilt, one mighty blood spot. Far more than this. It shall be yours to penetrate, in every bosom, the deep mystery of sin, the fountain of all wicked arts, and which inexhaustibly supplies more evil impulses than human power—than my power at its utmost—can make manifest in deeds. And now, my children, look upon each other."

They did so; and, by the blaze of the hell-kindled torches, the wretched man beheld his Faith, and the wife her husband, trembling before that unhallowed altar.

"Lo, there ye stand, my children," said the figure, in a deep and solemn tone, almost sad with its despairing awfulness, as if his once angelic nature could yet mourn for our miserable race. "Depending upon one another's hearts, ye had still hoped that virtue were not all a dream. Now are ye undeceived. Evil is the nature of mankind. Evil must be your only happiness. Welcome again, my children, to the communion of your race."

"Welcome," repeated the fiend worshippers, in one cry of despair and triumph.

And there they stood, the only pair, as it seemed, who were yet hesitating on the verge of wickedness in this dark world. A basin was hollowed, naturally, in the rock. Did it contain water, reddened by the lurid light? or was it blood? or, perchance, a liquid flame? Herein did the shape of evil dip his hand and prepare to lay the mark of baptism upon their foreheads, that they might be partakers of the mystery of sin, more conscious of the secret guilt of others, both in deed and thought, than they could now be of their own. The husband cast one look at his pale wife, and Faith at him. What polluted wretches would the next glance show them to each other, shuddering alike at what they disclosed and what they saw!

"Faith! Faith!" cried the husband, "look up to heaven, and resist the wicked one."

Whether Faith obeyed he knew not. Hardly had he spoken when he found himself amid calm night and solitude, listening to a roar of the wind which died heavily away through the forest. He staggered against the rock, and felt it chill and damp; while a hanging twig, that had been all on fire, besprinkled his cheek with the coldest dew.

The next morning young Goodman Brown came slowly into the street of Salem village, staring around him like a bewildered man. The good old minister was taking a walk along the graveyard to get an appetite for breakfast and meditate his sermon, and bestowed a blessing, as he passed, on Goodman Brown. He shrank from the venerable saint as if to avoid an anathema. Old Deacon Gookin was at domestic worship, and the holy words of his prayer were heard through the open window. "What God doth the wizard pray to?" quoth Goodman Brown. Goody Cloyse, that excellent old Christian, stood in the early sunshine at her own lattice, catechizing a little girl who had brought her a pint of morning's milk. Goodman Brown snatched away the child as from the grasp of the fiend himself. Turning the corner by the meeting-house, he spied the head of Faith, with the pink ribbons, gazing anxiously forth, and bursting into such joy at sight of him that she skipped along the street and almost kissed her husband before the whole village. But Goodman Brown looked sternly and sadly into her face, and passed on without a greeting.

Had Goodman Brown fallen asleep in the forest and only dreamed a wild dream of a witch-meeting?

Be it so if you will; but, alas! it was a dream of evil omen for young Goodman Brown. A stern, a sad, a darkly meditative, a distrustful, if not a desperate man did he become from the night of that fearful dream. On the Sabbath day, when the congregation were singing a holy psalm, he could not listen because an anthem of sin rushed loudly upon his ear and drowned all the blessed strain. When the minister spoke from the pulpit with power and fervid eloquence, and, with his hand on the open Bible, of the sacred truths of our religion, and of saint-like lives and triumphant deaths, and of future bliss or misery unutterable, then did Goodman Brown turn pale, dreading lest the roof should thunder down upon the gray blasphemer and his hearers. Often, waking suddenly at midnight, he shrank from the bosom of Faith; and at morning or eventide, when the family knelt down at prayer, he scowled and muttered to himself, and gazed sternly at his wife, and turned away. And when he had lived long, and was borne to his grave a hoary corpse, followed by Faith, an aged woman, and children and grandchildren, a goodly procession, besides neighbors not a few, they carved no hopeful verse upon his tombstone, for his dying hour was gloom.

Chapter 5

GUY DE MAUPASSANT

THE DIAMOND NECKLACE

From Selected Tales of Guy de Maupassant, *ed. Faye Commins (New York: Random House, 1950), pp. 137–144.*

She was one of those pretty, charming young ladies, born, as if through an error of destiny, into a family of clerks. She had no dowry, no hopes, no means of becoming known, appreciated, loved, and married by a man either rich or distinguished; and she allowed herself to marry a petty clerk in the office of the Board of Education.

She was simple, not being able to adorn herself; but she was unhappy, as one out of her class; for women belong to no caste, no race; their grace, their beauty, and their charm serving them in the place of birth and family. Their inborn finesse, their instinctive elegance, their suppleness of wit are their only aristocracy, making some daughters of the people the equal of great ladies.

She suffered incessantly, feeling herself born for all delicacies and luxuries. She suffered from the poverty of her apartment, the shabby walls, the worn chairs, and the faded stuffs. All these things, which another woman of her station would not have noticed, tortured and angered her. The sight of the little Breton, who made this humble home, awoke in her sad regrets and desperate dreams. She thought of quiet antechambers, with their Oriental hangings, lighted by high, bronze torches, and of the two great footmen in short trousers who sleep in the large armchairs, made sleepy by the heavy air from the heating apparatus. She thought of large drawing-rooms, hung in old silks, of graceful pieces of furniture carrying bric-à-brac of inestimable value, and of the little perfumed coquettish apartments, made for five o'clock chats with most intimate friends, men known and sought after, whose attention all women envied and desired.

When she seated herself for dinner, before the round table where the tablecloth had been used three days, opposite her husband who uncovered the tureen with a delighted air, saying: "Oh! the good potpie! I know nothing better than that—" she would think of the elegant dinners, of the shining silver, of the tapestries peopling the walls with ancient personages and rare birds in the midst of fairy forests; she thought of the exquisite food served on marvelous dishes, of the whispered gallantries, listened to with the smile of the sphinx, while eating the rose-colored flesh of the trout or a chicken's wing.

She had neither frocks nor jewels, nothing. And she loved only those things. She felt that she was made for them. She had such a desire to please, to be sought after, to be clever, and courted.

She had a rich friend, a schoolmate at the convent, whom she did not like to visit, she suffered so much when she returned. And she wept for whole days from chagrin, from regret, from despair, and disappointment.

One evening her husband returned elated, bearing in his hand a large envelope.

"Here," said he, "here is something for you."

She quickly tore open the wrapper and drew out a printed card on which were inscribed these words:

> "The Minister of Public Instruction and Madame George Ramponneau ask the honor of Mr. and Mrs. Loisel's company Monday evening, January 18, at the Minister's residence."

Instead of being delighted, as her husband had hoped, she threw the invitation spitefully upon the table murmuring:

"What do you suppose I want with that?"

"But, my dearie, I thought it would make you happy. You never go out, and this is an occasion, and a fine one! I had a great deal of trouble to get it. Everybody wishes one, and it is very select; not many are given to employees. You will see the whole official world there."

She looked at him with an irritated eye and declared impatiently:

"What do you suppose I have to wear to such a thing as that?"

He had not thought of that; he stammered:

"Why, the dress you wear when we go to the theater. It seems very pretty to me—"

He was silent, stupefied, in dismay, at the sight of his wife weeping. Two great tears fell slowly from the corners of his eyes toward the corners of his mouth; he stammered:

"What is the matter? What is the matter?"

By a violent effort, she had controlled her vexation and responded in a calm voice, wiping her moist cheeks:

"Nothing. Only I have no dress and consequently I cannot go to this affair. Give your card to some colleague whose wife is better fitted out than I."

He was grieved, but answered:

"Let us see, Matilda. How much would a suitable costume cost, something that would serve for other occasions, something very simple?"

She reflected for some seconds, making estimates and thinking of a sum that she could ask for without bringing with it an immediate refusal and a frightened exclamation from the economical clerk.

Finally she said, in a hesitating voice:

"I cannot tell exactly, but it seems to me that four hundred francs ought to cover it."

He turned a little pale, for he had saved just this sum to buy a gun that he might be able to join some hunting parties the next summer, on the plains at Nanterre, with some friends who went to shoot larks up there on Sunday. Nevertheless, he answered:

"Very well. I will give you four hundred francs. But try to have a pretty dress."

The day of the ball approached and Mme. Loisel seemed sad, disturbed, anxious. Nevertheless, her dress was nearly ready. Her husband said to her one evening:

"What is the matter with you? You have acted strangely for two or three days."

And she responded: "I am vexed not to have a jewel, not one stone, nothing to adorn myself with. I shall have such a poverty-laden look. I would prefer not to go to this party."

He replied: "You can wear some natural flowers. At this season they look very *chic.* For ten francs you can have two or three magnificent roses."

She was not convinced. "No," she replied, "there is nothing more humiliating than to have a shabby air in the midst of rich women."

Then her husband cried out: "How stupid we are! Go and find your friend Mrs. Forestier and ask her to lend you her jewels. You are well enough acquainted with her to do this."

She uttered a cry of joy: "It is true!" she said. "I had not thought of that."

The next day she took herself to her friend's house and related her story of distress. Mrs. Forestier went to her closet with the glass doors, took out a large jewel-case, brought it, opened it, and said: "Choose, my dear."

She saw at first some bracelets, then a collar of pearls, then a Venetian cross of gold and jewels and of admirable workmanship. She tried the jewels before the glass, hesitated, but could neither decide to take them nor leave them. Then she asked:

"Have you nothing more?"

"Why, yes. Look for yourself. I do not know what will please you."

Suddenly she discovered, in a black satin box, a superb necklace of diamonds, and her heart beat fast with an immoderate desire. Her hands trembled as she took them up. She placed them about her throat against her dress, and remained in ecstasy before them. Then she asked, in a hesitating voice, full of anxiety:

"Could you lend me this? Only this?"

"Why, yes, certainly."

She fell upon the neck of her friend, embraced her with passion, then went away with her treasure.

The day of the ball arrived. Mme. Loisel was a great success. She was the prettiest of all, elegant, gracious, smiling, and full of joy. All the men noticed her, asked her name, and wanted to be presented. All the members of the Cabinet wished to waltz with her. The Minister of Education paid her some attention.

She danced with enthusiasm, with passion, intoxicated with pleasure, thinking of nothing, in the triumph of her beauty, in the glory of her success, in a kind of cloud of happiness that came of all this homage, and all this admiration, of all these awakened desires, and this victory so complete and sweet to the heart of woman.

She went home toward four o'clock in the morning. Her husband had been half asleep in one of the little salons since midnight, with three other gentlemen whose wives were enjoying themselves very much.

He threw around her shoulders the wraps they had carried for the coming home, modest garments of everyday wear, whose poverty clashed with the elegance of the ball costume. She felt this and wished to hurry away in order not to be noticed by the other women who were wrapping themselves in rich furs.

Loisel retained her: "Wait," said he. "You will catch cold out there. I am going to call a cab."

But she would not listen and descended the steps rapidly. When they were in the street, they found no carriage; and they began to seek one, hailing the coachmen whom they saw at a distance.

They walked along toward the Seine, hopeless and shivering. Finally they found on the dock one of those old, nocturnal *coupés* that one sees in Paris after nightfall, as if they were ashamed of their misery by day.

It took them as far as their door in Martyr Street, and they went wearily up to their apartment. It was all over for her. And on his part, he remembered that he would have to be at the office by ten o'clock.

She removed the wraps from her shoulders before the glass, for a final view of herself in her glory. Suddenly she uttered a cry. Her necklace was not around her neck.

Her husband, already half undressed, asked: "What is the matter?"

She turned toward him excitedly:

"I have—I have—I no longer have Mrs. Forestier's necklace."

He arose in dismay: "What! How is that? It is not possible."

And they looked in the folds of the dress, in the folds of the mantle, in the pockets, everywhere. They could not find it.

He asked: "You are sure you still had it when we left the house?"

"Yes, I felt it in the vestibule as we came out."

"But if you had lost it in the street, we should have heard it fall. It must be in the cab."

"Yes. It is probable. Did you take the number?"

"No. And you, did you notice what it was?"

"No."

They looked at each other utterly cast down. Finally, Loisel dressed himself again.

"I am going," said he, "over the track where we went on foot, to see if I can find it."

And he went. She remained in her evening gown, not having the strength to go to bed, stretched upon a chair, without ambition or thoughts.

Toward seven o'clock her husband returned. He had found nothing.

He went to the police and to the cab offices, and put an advertisement in the newspapers, offering a reward; he did everything that afforded them a suspicion of hope.

She waited all day in a state of bewilderment before this frightful disaster. Loisel returned at evening with his face harrowed and pale; he had discovered nothing.

"It will be necessary," said he, "to write to your friend that you have broken the clasp of the necklace and that you will have it repaired. That will give us time to turn around."

She wrote as he dictated.

At the end of a week, they had lost all hope. And Loisel, older by five years, declared:

"We must take measures to replace this jewel."

The next day they took the box which had inclosed it, to the jeweler whose name was on the inside. He consulted his books.

"It is not I, Madame," said he, "who sold this necklace; I only furnished the casket."

Then they went from jeweler to jeweler seeking a necklace like the other one, consulting their memories, and ill, both of them, with chagrin and anxiety.

In a shop of the Palais-Royal, they found a chaplet of diamonds which seemed to them exactly like the one they had lost. It was valued at forty thousand francs. They could get it for thirty-six thousand.

They begged the jeweler not to sell it for three days. And they made an arrangement by which they might return it for thirty-four thousand francs if they found the other one before the end of February.

Loisel possessed eighteen thousand francs which his father had left him. He borrowed the rest.

He borrowed it, asking for a thousand francs of one, five hundred of another, five louis of this one, and three louis of that one. He gave notes, made ruinous promises, took money of usurers and the whole race of lenders. He compromised his whole existence, in fact, risked his signature, without even knowing whether he could make it good or not, and, harassed by anxiety for the future, by the black misery which surrounded him, and by the prospect of all physical privations and moral torture, he went to get the new necklace, depositing on the merchant's counter thirty-six thousand francs.

When Mrs. Loisel took back the jewels to Mrs. Forestier, the latter said to her in a frigid tone:

"You should have returned them to me sooner, for I might have needed them."

She did open the jewel-box as her friend feared she would. If she should perceive the substitution, what would she think? What should she say? Would she take her for a robber?

Mrs. Loisel now knew the horrible life of necessity. She did her part, however, completely, heroically. It was necessary to pay this frightful debt. She would pay it. They sent away the maid; they changed their lodgings; they rented some rooms under a mansard roof.

She learned the heavy cares of a household, the odious work of a kitchen. She washed the dishes, using her rosy nails upon the greasy pots and the bottoms of the stewpans. She washed the soiled linen, the chemises and dishcloths, which she hung on the line to dry; she took down the refuse to the street each morning and brought up the water, stopping at each landing to breathe. And, clothed like a woman of the people, she went to the grocer's, the butcher's, and the fruiterer's, with her basket on her arm, shopping, haggling, defending to the last sou her miserable money.

Every month it was necessary to renew some notes, thus obtaining time, and to pay others.

The husband worked evenings, putting the books of some merchants in order, and nights he often did copying at five sous a page.

And this life lasted for ten years.

At the end of ten years, they had restored all, all, with interest of the usurer, and accumulated interest besides.

Mrs. Loisel seemed old now. She had become a strong, hard woman, the crude woman of the poor household. Her hair badly dressed, her skirts awry, her hands red, she spoke in a loud tone, and washed the floors, using large pails of water. But sometimes, when her husband was at the office, she would seat herself before the window and think of that evening party of former times, of that ball where she was so beautiful and so flattered.

How would it have been if she had not lost that necklace? Who knows? Who knows? How singular is life, and how full of changes! How small a thing will ruin or save one!

One Sunday, as she was taking a walk in the Champs-Elysées to rid herself of the cares of the week, she suddenly perceived a woman walking with a child. It was Mrs. Forestier, still young, still pretty, still attractive. Mrs. Loisel was affected. Should she speak to her? Yes, certainly. And now that she had paid, she would tell her all. Why not?

She approached her. "Good morning, Jeanne."

Her friend did not recognize her and was astonished to be so familiarly addressed by this common personage. She stammered:

"But, Madame—I do not know—You must be mistaken—"

"No, I am Matilda Loisel."

Her friend uttered a cry of astonishment: "Oh! my poor Matilda! How you have changed—"

"Yes, I have had some hard days since I saw you; and some miserable ones—and all because of you—"

"Because of me? How is that?"

"You recall the diamond necklace that you loaned me to wear to the Commissioner's ball?"

"Yes, very well."

"Well, I lost it."

"How is that, since you returned it to me?"

"I returned another to you exactly like it. And it has taken us ten years to pay for it. You can understand that it was not easy for us who have nothing. But it is finished and I am decently content."

Madame Forestier stopped short. She said:

"You say that you bought a diamond necklace to replace mine?"

"Yes. You did not perceive it then? They were just alike."

And she smiled with a proud and simple joy. Madame Forestier was touched and took both her hands as she replied:

"Oh! my poor Matilda! Mine were false. They were not worth over five hundred francs!"

Chapter 6

LETTERS OF ABIGAIL AND JOHN ADAMS

Abigail Adams

March 31, 1776

I wish you would ever write me a letter half as long as I write you, and tell me, if you may, where your fleet are gone; what sort of defense Virginia can make against our common enemy; whether it is so situated as to make an able defense. Are not the gentry lords, and the common people vassals? Are they not like the uncivilized vassals Britain represents us to be? I hope their riflemen, who have shown themselves very savage and even blood-thirsty, are not a specimen of the generality of the people. I am willing to allow the colony great merit for having produced a Washington; but they have been shamefully duped by a Dunmore.

I have sometimes been ready to think that the passion for liberty cannot be equally strong in the breasts of those who have been accustomed to deprive their fellow-creatures of theirs. Of this I am certain, that it is not founded upon that generous and Christian principle of doing to others as we would that others should do unto us.

Do not you want to see Boston? I am fearful of the small-pox, or I should have been in before this time. I got Mr. Crane to go to our house and see what state it was in. I find it has been occupied by one of the doctors of a regiment; very dirty, but no other damage has been done to it. The few things which were left in it are all gone. I look upon it as a new acquisition of property—a property which one month ago I did not value at a single shilling, and would with pleasure have seen it in flames.

The town in general is left in a better state than we expected; more owing to a precipitate flight than any regard to the inhabitants; though some individuals discovered a sense of honor and justice, and have left the rent of the houses in which they were, for the owners, and the furniture unhurt, or, if damaged, sufficient to make it good. Others have committed abominable ravages. The mansion-house of your President is safe, and the furniture unhurt; while the house and furniture of the Solicitor General have fallen a prey to their own merciless party. Surely the very fiends feel a reverential awe for virtue and patriotism, whilst they detest the parricide and traitor.

I feel very differently at the approach of spring from what I did a month ago. We knew not then whether we could plant or sow with safety, whether where we had tilled we could reap the fruits of our own industry, whether we could rest in our own cottages or whether we should be driven from the seacoast to seek shelter in the wilderness; but now we feel a temporary peace, and the poor fugitives are returning to their deserted habitations.

Though we felicitate ourselves, we sympathize with those who are trembling lest the lot of Boston should be theirs. But they cannot be in similar circumstances unless pusillanimity and cowardice should take possession of them. They have time and warning given them to see the evil and shun it.

I long to hear that you have declared an independency. And, by the way, in the new code of laws which I suppose it will be necessary for you to make, I desire you would remember the ladies and be more generous and favorable to them than your ancestors. Do not put such unlimited power into the hands of the husbands. Remember, all men would be tyrants if they could. If particular care and attention is not paid to the ladies, we are determined to foment a rebellion, and will not hold ourselves bound by any laws in which we have no voice or representation.

That your sex are naturally tyrannical is a truth so thoroughly established as to admit of no dispute; but such of you as wish to be happy willingly give up the harsh title of master for the more tender and endearing one of friend. Why, then, not put it out of the power of the vicious and the lawless to use us with cruelty and indignity with impunity? Men of sense in all ages abhor those customs which treat us only as the vassals of your sex; regard us then as beings placed by Providence under your protection, and in imitation of the Supreme Being make use of that power only for our happiness.

Abigail Adams

April 5, 1776

I want to hear much oftener from you than I do. March 8th was the last date of any that I have yet had. You inquire of me whether I am making saltpetre. I have not yet attempted it, but after soap-making believe I shall make the experiment. I find as much as I can do to manufacture clothing for my family, which would else be naked. I know of but one person in this part of the town who has made any. That is Mr. Tertius Bass, as he is called, who has got very near a hundred-weight which has been found to be very good. I have heard of some others in the other parishes. Mr. Reed, of Weymouth, has been applied to, to go to Andover to the mills which are now at work, and he has gone.

I have lately seen a small manuscript describing the proportions of the various sorts of powder fit for cannon, small-arms, and pistols. If it would be of any service your way I will get it transcribed and send it to you. Every one of your friends sends regards, and all the little ones. Adieu.

John Adams

April 14, 1776

You justly complain of my short letters, but the critical state of things and the multiplicity of avocations must plead my excuse. You ask where the fleet is? The inclosed papers will inform you. You ask what sort of defense Virginia can make? I believe they will make an able defense. Their militia and minute-men have been some time employed in training themselves, and they have nine battalions of regulars, as they call them, maintained among them, under good officers, at the Continental expense. They have set up a number of manufactories of firearms, which are busily employed. They are tolerably supplied with powder, and are successful and assiduous in making saltpetre. Their neighboring sister, or rather daughter colony of North Carolina, which is a warlike colony, and has several battalions at the Continental expense, as well as a pretty good militia, are ready to assist them, and they are in very good spirits and seem determined to make a brave resistance. The gentry are very rich, and the common people very poor. This inequality of property gives an aristocratical turn to all their proceedings, and occasions a strong aversion in their patricians to "Common Sense." But the spirit of these Barons is coming down, and it must submit. It is very true, as you observe, they have been duped by Dunmore. But this is a common case. All the colonies are duped, more or less, at one time and another. A more egregious bubble was never blown up than the story of Commissioners coming to treat with the Congress, yet it has gained credit like a charm, not only with, but against the clearest evidence. I never shall forget the delusion which seized our best and most sagacious friends, the dear inhabitants of Boston, the winter before last. Credulity and the want of foresight are imperfections in the human character, that no politician can sufficiently guard against.

You give me some pleasure by your account of a certain house in Queen Street. I had burned it long ago in imagination. It rises now to my view like a phoenix. What shall I say of the Solicitor General? I pity his pretty children. I pity his father and his sisters. I wish I could be clear that it is no moral evil to pity him and his lady. Upon repentance, they will certainly have a large share in the compassions of many. But let us take warning, and give it to our children. Whenever vanity and gayety, a love of pomp and dress, furniture, equipage, buildings, great company, expensive diversions, and elegant entertainments get the better of the principles and judgments of men or women, there is no knowing where they will stop, nor into what evils, natural, moral, or political, they will lead us.

Your description of your own *gaieté de coeur* charms me. Thanks be to God, you have just cause to rejoice, and may the bright prospect be obscured by no cloud. As to declarations of independency, be patient. Read our privateering laws and our commercial laws. What signifies a word?

As to your extraordinary code of laws, I cannot but laugh. We have been told that our struggle has loosened the bonds of government everywhere; that children and apprentices were disobedient; that schools and colleges were grown turbulent; that Indians slighted their guardians, and negroes grew insolent to their masters. But your letter was the first intimation that another tribe, more numerous and powerful than all the rest, were grown discontented. This is rather too coarse a compliment, but you are so saucy, I won't blot it out. Depend upon it, we know better than to repeal our masculine systems. Although they are in full force, you know they are little more than theory. We dare not exert our power in its full latitude. We are obliged to go fair and softly, and, in practice, you know we are the subjects. We have only the name of masters, and rather than give up this, which would completely subject us to the despotism of the petticoat, I hope General Washington and all our brave heroes would fight; I am sure every good politician would plot, as long as he would against despotism, empire, monarchy, aristocracy, oligarchy, or ochlocracy. A fine story, indeed! I begin to think the ministry as deep as they are wicked. After stirring up Tories, land-jobbers, trimmers, bigots, Canadians, Indians, negroes, Hanoverians, Hessians, Russians, Irish Roman Catholics, Scotch renegadoes, at last they have stimulated the ——— to demand new privileges and threaten to rebel.

Chapter 7

EDGAR ALLAN POE

The Masque of the Red Death

From The Gold Bug and Other Tales and Poems *(New York: Macmillan, 1945), pp. 164–171.*

The "Red Death" had long devastated the country. No pestilence had ever been so fatal, or so hideous. Blood was its Avatar and its seal—the redness and the horror of blood. There were sharp pains, and sudden dizziness, and then profuse bleeding at the pores, with dissolution. The scarlet stains upon the body and especially upon the face of the victim, were the pest ban which shut him out from the aid and from the sympathy of his fellow-men. And the whole seizure, progress and termination of the disease, were the incidents of half an hour.

But the Prince Prospero was happy and dauntless and sagacious. When his dominions were half depopulated, he summoned to his presence a thousand hale and light-hearted friends from among the knights and dames of his court, and with these retired to the deep seclusion of one of his castellated abbeys. This was an extensive and magnificent structure, the creation of the prince's own eccentric yet august taste. A strong and lofty wall girdled it in. This wall had gates of iron. The courtiers, having entered, brought furnaces and massy hammers and welded the bolts. They resolved to leave means neither of ingress or egress to the sudden impulses of despair or of frenzy from within. The abbey was amply provisioned. With such precautions the courtiers might bid defiance to contagion. The external world could take care of itself. In the meantime it was folly to grieve, or to think. The prince had provided all the appliances of pleasures. There were buffoons, there were improvisatori, there were ballet-dancers, there were musicians, there was Beauty, there was wine. All these and security were within. Without was the "Red Death."

It was toward the close of the fifth or sixth month of his seclusion, and while the pestilence raged most furiously abroad, that the Prince Prospero entertained his thousand friends at a masked ball of the most unusual magnificence.

It was a voluptuous scene, that masquerade. But first let me tell of the rooms in which it was held. There were seven—an imperial suite. In many palaces, however, such suites form a long and straight vista, while the folding doors slide back nearly to the walls on either hand, so that the view of the whole extent is scarcely impeded. Here the case was very different; as might have been expected from the duke's love of the *bizarre*. The apartments were so irregularly disposed that the vision embraced but little more than one at a time. There was a sharp turn at every twenty or thirty yards, and at each turn a novel effect. To the right and left, in the middle of each wall, a tall and narrow Gothic window looked out upon a closed corridor which pursued the windings of the suite. These windows were of stained glass whose color varied in accordance with the prevailing hue of the decorations of the chamber into which it opened. That at the eastern extremity was hung, for example, in blue—and vividly blue were its windows. The second chamber was purple in its ornaments and tapestries, and here the panes were purple. The third was green throughout, and so were the casements. The fourth was furnished and lighted with orange—the fifth with white—the sixth with violet. The seventh apartment was closely shrouded in black velvet tapestries that hung all over the ceiling and down the walls, falling in heavy folds upon a carpet of the same material and hue. But in this chamber only, the color of the windows failed to correspond with the decorations. The panes here were scarlet—a deep blood color. Now in no one of the seven apartments was there any lamp or candelabrum, amid the profusion of golden ornaments that lay scattered to and fro or depended from the roof. There was no light of any kind emanating from lamp or candle within the suite of chambers. But in the corridors that followed the suite, there stood, opposite to each window, a heavy tripod, bearing a brazier of fire that projected its rays through the tinted glass and so glaringly illumined the room. And thus were produced a multitude of gaudy and fantastic appearances. But in the western or black chamber the effect of the fire-light that streamed upon the dark hangings through the blood-tinted panes was ghastly in the extreme, and produced so wild a look upon the countenances of those who entered, that there were few of the company bold enough to set foot within its precincts at all.

It was in this apartment, also, that there stood against the western wall, a gigantic clock of ebony. Its pendulum swung to and fro with a dull, heavy, monotonous clang; and when the minute-hand made the circuit of the face, and the hour was to be stricken, there came from the brazen lungs of the clock a sound which was clear and loud and deep and exceedingly musical, but of so peculiar a note and emphasis that, at each lapse of an hour, the musicians of the orchestra were constrained to pause, momentarily, in their performance, to hearken to the sound; and thus the waltzers perforce ceased their evolutions; and there was a brief disconcert of the whole gay company; and, while the chimes of the clock yet rang, it was observed that the giddiest grew pale, and the more aged and sedate passed their hands over their brows as if in confused reverie or meditation. But when the echoes had fully ceased, a light laughter at once pervaded the assembly; the musicians looked at each other and smiled as if at their own nervousness and folly, and made whispering vows, each to the other, that the next chiming of the clock should produce in them no similar emotion; and then, after the lapse of sixty minutes (which embrace three thousand and six hundred seconds of the Time that flies), there came yet another chiming of the clock, and then were the same disconcert and tremulousness and meditation as before.

But, in spite of these things, it was a gay and magnificent revel. The tastes of the duke were peculiar. He had a fine eye for colors and effects. He disregarded the *decora* of mere fashion. His plans were bold and fiery, and his conceptions glowed with barbaric lustre. There are some who would have thought him mad. His followers felt that he was not. It was necessary to hear and see and touch him to be *sure* that he was not.

He had directed, in great part, the movable embellishments of the seven chambers, upon occasion of this great *fête;* and it was his own guiding taste which had given character to the masqueraders. Be sure they were grotesque. There were much glare and glitter and piquancy and phantasm—much of what has been since seen in "Hernani." There were arabesque figures with unsuited limbs and appointments. There were delirious fancies such as the madman fashions. There was much of the beautiful, much of the wanton, much of the *bizarre,* something of the terrible, and not a little of that which might have excited disgust. To and fro in the seven chambers there stalked, in fact, a multitude of dreams. And these—the dreams—writhed in and about, taking hue from the rooms, and causing the wild music of the orchestra to seem as the echo of their steps. And, anon, there strikes the ebony clock which stands in the hall of the velvet. And then, for a moment, all is still, and all is silent save the voice of the clock. The dreams are stiff-frozen as they stand. But the echoes of the chime die away—they have endured but an instant—and a light, half-subdued laughter floats after them as they depart. And now again the music swells, and the dreams live, and writhe to and fro more merrily than ever, taking hue from the many-tinted windows through which stream the rays from the tripods. But to the chamber which lies most westwardly of the seven, there are now none of the maskers who venture; for the night is waning away; and there flows a ruddier light through the blood-colored panes; and the blackness of the sable drapery appals; and to him whose foot falls upon the sable carpet, there comes from the near clock of ebony a muffled peal more solemnly emphatic than any which reaches *their* ears who indulge in the more remote gaieties of the other apartments.

But these other apartments were densely crowded, and in them beat feverishly the heart of life. And the revel went whirlingly on, until at length there commenced the sounding of mid-night upon the clock. And then the music ceased, as I have told; and the evolutions of the waltzers were quieted; and there was an uneasy cessation of all things as before. But now there were twelve strokes to be sounded by the bell of the clock; and thus it happened, perhaps, that more of thought crept, with more of time, into the meditations of the thoughtful among those who revelled. And thus, too, it happened, perhaps, that before the last echoes of the last chime had utterly sunk into silence, there were many individuals in the crowd who had found leisure to become aware of the presence of a masked figure which had arrested the attention of no single individual before. And the rumor of this new presence having spread itself whisperingly around, there arose at length from the whole company a buzz, or murmur, expressive of disapprobation and surprise—then, finally, of terror, of horror, and of disgust.

In an assembly of phantasms such as I have painted, it may well be supposed that no ordinary appearance could have excited such sensation. In truth the masquerade license of the night was nearly unlimited; but the figure in question had out-Heroded Herod, and gone beyond the bounds of even the prince's indefinite decorum. There are chords in the hearts of the most reckless which cannot be touched without emotion. Even with the utterly lost, to whom life and death are equally jests, there are matters of which no jest can be made. The whole company, indeed, seemed now deeply to feel that in the costume and bearing of the stranger neither wit nor propriety existed. The figure was tall and gaunt, and shrouded from head to foot in the habiliments of the grave. The mask which concealed the visage was made so nearly to resemble the countenance of a stiffened corpse that the closest scrutiny must have had difficulty in detecting the cheat. And yet all this might have been endured, if not approved, by the mad revellers around. But the mummer had gone so far as to assume the type of the Red Death. His vesture was dabbled in *blood*—and his broad brow, with all the features of the face, was besprinkled with the scarlet horror.

When the eyes of Prince Prospero fell upon this spectral image (which with a slow and solemn movement, as if more fully to sustain its *rôle,* stalked to and fro among the waltzers) he was seen to be convulsed, in the first moment with a strong shudder either of terror or distaste; but, in the next, his brow reddened with rage.

"Who dares?" he demanded hoarsely of the courtiers who stood near him—"who dares insult us with this blasphemous mockery? Seize him and unmask him—that we may know whom we have to hang at sunrise, from the battlements!"

It was in the eastern or blue chamber in which stood the Prince Prospero as he uttered these words. They rang throughout the seven rooms loudly and clearly—for the prince was a bold and robust man, and the music had become hushed at the waving of his hand.

It was in the blue room where stood the prince, with a group of pale courtiers by his side. At first, as he spoke, there was a slight rushing movement of this group in the direction of the intruder, who at the moment was also near at hand, and now, with deliberate and stately step, made closer approach to the speaker. But from a certain nameless awe with which the mad assumptions of the mummer had inspired the whole party, there were found none who put forth hand to seize him; so that, unimpeded, he passed within a yard of the prince's person; and, while the vast assembly, as if with one impulse, shrank from the centres of the rooms to the walls, he made his way uninterruptedly, but with the same solemn and measured step which had distinguished him from the first, through the blue chamber to the purple—through the purple to the green—through the green to the orange—through this again to the white—and even thence to the violet, ere a decided movement had been made to arrest him. It was then, however, that the Prince Prospero, maddening with rage and the shame of his own momentary cowardice, rushed hurriedly through the six chambers, while none followed him on account of a deadly terror that had seized upon all. He bore aloft a drawn dagger, and had approached, in rapid impetuosity, to within three or four feet of the retreating figure, when the latter, having attained the extremity of the velvet apartment, turned suddenly and confronted his pursuer. There was a sharp cry—and the dagger dropped gleaming upon the sable carpet, upon which, instantly afterwards, fell prostrate in death the Prince Prospero. Then, summoning the wild courage of despair, a throng of the revellers at once threw themselves into the black apartment, and, seizing the mummer, whose tall figure stood erect and motionless within the shadow of the ebony clock, gasped in unutterable horror at finding the grave-cerements and corpse-like mask which they handled with so violent a rudeness, untenanted by any tangible form.

And now was acknowledged the presence of the Red Death. He had come like a thief in the night. And one by one dropped the revellers in the blood-bedewed halls of their revel, and died each in the despairing posture of his fall. And the life of the ebony clock went out with that of the last of the gay. And the flames of the tripods expired. And Darkness and Decay and the Red Death held illimitable dominion over all.

Chapter 8

ROBERT FROST

Stopping by Woods on a Snowy Evening

Whose woods these are I think I know.
His house is in the village, though;
He will not see me stopping here
To watch his woods fill up with snow.

My little horse must think it queer
To stop without a farmhouse near
Between the woods and frozen lake
The darkest evening of the year.

He gives his harness bells a shake
To ask if there is some mistake.
The only other sound's the sweep
Of easy wind and downy flake.

The woods are lovely, dark, and deep,
But I have promises to keep,
And miles to go before I sleep,
And miles to go before I sleep.

Chapter 9

ERNEST J. GAINES

THE SKY IS GRAY

1

Go'n be coming in a few minutes. Coming round that bend down there full speed. And I'm go'n get out my handkerchief and wave it down, and we go'n get on it and go.

I keep on looking for it, but Mama don't look that way no more. She's looking down the road where we just come from. It's a long old road, and far's you can see you don't see nothing but gravel. You got dry weeds on both sides, and you got trees on both sides, and fences on both sides, too. And you got cows in the pastures and they standing close together. And when we was coming out here to catch the bus I seen the smoke coming out of the cows's noses.

I look at my mama and I know what she's thinking. I been with Mama so much, just me and her, I know what she's thinking all the time. Right now it's home—Auntie and them. She's thinking if they got enough wood—if she left enough there to keep them warm till we get back. She's thinking if it go'n rain and if any of them go'n have to go out in the rain. She's thinking 'bout the hog—if he go'n get out, and if Ty and Val be able to get him back in. She always worry like that when she leaves the house. She don't worry too much if she leave me there with the smaller ones, 'cause she know I'm go'n look after them and look after Auntie and everything else. I'm the oldest and she say I'm the man.

I look at my mama and I love my mama. She's wearing that black coat and that black hat and she's looking sad. I love my mama and I want put my arm round her and tell her. But I'm not supposed to do that. She say that's weakness and that's crybaby stuff, and she don't want no crybaby round her. She don't want you to be scared, either. 'Cause Ty's scared of ghosts and she's always whipping him. I'm scared of the dark, too, but I make 'tend I ain't. I make 'tend I ain't 'cause I'm the oldest, and I got to set a good sample for the rest. I can't ever be scared and I can't ever cry. And that's why I never said nothing 'bout my teeth. It's been hurting me and hurting me close to a month now, but I never said it. I didn't say it 'cause I didn't want act like a crybaby, and 'cause I know we didn't have enough money to go have it pulled. But, Lord, it been hurting me. And look like it wouldn't start till at night when you was trying to get yourself little sleep. Then soon 's you shut your eyes—ummm-ummm, Lord, look like it go right down to your heartstring.

"Hurting, hanh?" Ty'd say.

I'd shake my head, but I wouldn't open my mouth for nothing. You open your mouth and let that wind in, and it almost kill you.

I'd just lay there and listen to them snore. Ty there, right 'side me, and Auntie and Val over by the fireplace. Val younger than me and Ty, and he sleeps with Auntie. Mama sleeps round the other side with Louis and Walker.

I'd just lay there and listen to them, and listen to that wind out there, and listen to that fire in the fireplace. Sometimes it'd stop long enough to let me get little rest. Sometimes it just hurt, hurt, hurt. Lord, have mercy.

2

Auntie knowed it was hurting me. I didn't tell nobody but Ty, 'cause we buddies and he ain't go'n tell nobody. But some kind of way Auntie found out. When she asked me, I told her no, nothing was wrong. But she knowed it all the time. She told me to mash up a piece of aspirin and wrap it in some cotton and jugg it down in that hole. I did it, but it didn't do no good. It stopped for a little while, and started right back again. Auntie wanted to tell Mama, but I told her, "Uh-uh." 'Cause I knowed we didn't have any money, and it just was go'n make her mad again. So Auntie told Monsieur Bayonne, and Monsieur Bayonne came over to the house and told me to kneel down 'side him on the fireplace. He put his finger in his mouth and made the Sign of the Cross on my jaw. The tip of Monsieur Bayonne's finger is some hard, 'cause he's always playing on that guitar. If we sit outside at night we can always hear Monsieur Bayonne playing on his guitar. Sometimes we leave him out there playing on the guitar.

Monsieur Bayonne made the Sign of the Cross over and over on my jaw, but that didn't do no good. Even when he prayed and told me to pray some, too, that tooth still hurt me.

"How you feeling?" he say.

"Same," I say.

He kept on praying and making the Sign of the Cross and I kept on praying, too.

"Still hurting?" he say.

"Yes, sir."

Monsieur Bayonne mashed harder and harder on my jaw. He mashed so hard he almost pushed me over on Ty. But then he stopped.

"What kind of prayers you praying, boy?" he say.

"Baptist," I say.

"Well, I'll be—no wonder that tooth still killing him. I'm going one way and he pulling the other. Boy, don't you know any Catholic prayers?"

"I know 'Hail Mary,'" I say.

"Then you better start saying it."

"Yes, sir."

He started mashing on my jaw again, and I could hear him praying at the same time. And, sure enough, after while it stopped hurting me.

Me and Ty went outside where Monsieur Bayonne's two hounds was and we started playing with them. "Let's go hunting," Ty say. "All right," I say; and we went on back in the pasture. Soon the hounds got on a trail, and me and Ty followed them all 'cross the pasture and then back in the woods, too. And then they cornered this little old rabbit and killed him, and me and Ty made them get back, and we picked up the rabbit and started on back home. But my tooth had started hurting me again. It was hurting me plenty now, but I wouldn't tell Monsieur Bayonne. That night I didn't sleep a bit, and first thing in the morning Auntie told me to go back and let Monsieur Bayonne pray over me some more. Monsieur Bayonne was in his kitchen making coffee when I got there. Soon's he seen me he knowed what was wrong.

"All right, kneel down there 'side that stove," he say. "And this time make sure you pray Catholic. I don't know nothing 'bout that Baptist, and I don't want know nothing 'bout him."

3

Last night Mama say, "Tomorrow we going to town."

"It ain't hurting me no more," I say. "I can eat anything on it."

"Tomorrow we going to town," she say.

And after she finished eating, she got up and went to bed. She always go to bed early now. 'Fore Daddy went in the Army, she used to stay up late. All of us sitting out on the gallery or round the fire. But now, look like soon's she finish eating she go to bed.

This morning when I woke up, her and Auntie was standing 'fore the fireplace. She say: "Enough to get there and get back. Dollar and a half to have it pulled. Twenty-five for me to go, twenty-five for him. Twenty-five for me to come back, twenty-five for him. Fifty cents left. Guess I get little piece of salt meat with that."

"Sure can use it," Auntie say. "White beans and no salt meat ain't white beans."

"I do the best I can," Mama say.

They was quiet after that, and I made 'tend I was still sleep.

"James, hit the floor," Auntie say.

I still made 'tend I was asleep. I didn't want them to know I was listening.

"All right," Auntie say, shaking me by the shoulder. "Come on. Today's the day."

I pushed the cover down to get out, and Ty grabbed it and pulled it back.

"You, too, Ty," Auntie say.

"I ain't getting no teef pulled," Ty say.

"Don't mean it ain't time to get up," Auntie say. "Hit it, Ty."

Ty got up grumbling.

"James, you hurry up and get in your clothes and eat your food," Auntie say. "What time y'all coming back?" she say to Mama.

"That 'leven o'clock bus," Mama say. "Got to get back in that field this evening."

"Get a move on you, James," Auntie say.

I went in the kitchen and washed my face, then I ate my breakfast. I was having bread and syrup. The bread was warm and hard and tasted good. And I tried to make it last a long time.

Ty came back there grumbling and mad at me.

"Got to get up," he say. "I ain't having no teefes pulled. What I got to be getting up for?"

Ty poured some syrup in his pan and got a piece of bread. He didn't wash his hands, neither his face, and I could see that white stuff in his eyes.

"You the one getting your teef pulled," he say. "What I got to get up for. I bet if I was getting a teef pulled, you wouldn't be getting up. Shucks; syrup again. I'm getting tired of this old syrup. Syrup, syrup, syrup. I'm go'n take with the sugar diabetes. I want me some bacon sometime."

"Go out in the field and work and you can have your bacon," Auntie say. She stood in the middle door looking at Ty. "You better be glad you got syrup. Some people ain't got that—hard's time is."

"Shucks," Ty say. "How can I be strong."

"I don't know too much 'bout your strength," Auntie say; "but I know where you go'n be hot at, you keep that grumbling up. James, get a move on you; your mama waiting."

I ate my last piece of bread and went in the front room. Mama was standing 'fore the fireplace warming her hands. I put on my coat and my cap, and we left the house.

4

I look down there again, but it still ain't coming. I almost say, "It ain't coming yet," but I keep my mouth shut. 'Cause that's something else she don't like. She don't like for you to say something just for nothing. She can see it ain't coming, I can see it ain't coming, so why say it ain't coming. I don't say it, I turn and look at the river that's back of us. It's so cold the smoke's just raising up from the water. I see a bunch of pool-doos not too far out—just on the other side the lilies. I'm wondering if you can eat pool-doos. I ain't too sure, 'cause I ain't never ate none. But I done ate owls and blackbirds, and I done ate redbirds, too. I didn't want kill the redbirds, but she made me kill them. They had two of them back there. One in my trap, one in Ty's trap. Me and Ty was go'n play with them and let them go, but she made me kill them 'cause we needed the food.

"I can't," I say. "I can't."

"Here," she say. "Take it."

"I can't," I say. "I can't. I can't kill him, Mama, please."

"Here," she say. "Take this fork, James."

"Please, Mama, I can't kill him," I say.

I could tell she was go'n hit me. I jerked back, but I didn't jerk back soon enough.

"Take it," she say.

I took it and reached in for him, but he kept on hopping to the back.

"I can't, Mama," I say. The water just kept on running down my face. "I can't," I say.

"Get him out of there," she say.

I reached in for him and he kept on hopping to the back. Then I reached in farther, and he pecked me on the hand.

"I can't, Mama," I say.

She slapped me again.

I reached in again, but he kept on hopping out my way. Then he hopped to one side and I reached there. The fork got him on the leg and I heard his leg pop. I pulled my hand but 'cause I had hurt him.

"Give it here," she say, and jerked the fork out my hand.

She reached in and got the little bird right in the neck. I heard the fork go in his neck, and I heard it go in the ground. She brought him out and helt him right in front of me.

"That's one," she say. She shook him off and gived me the fork. "Get the other one."

"I can't, Mama," I say. "I'll do anything, but don't make me do that."

She went to the corner of the fence and broke the biggest switch over there she could find. I knelt 'side the trap, crying.

"Get him out of there," she say.

"I can't, Mama."

She started hitting me 'cross the back. I went down on the ground, crying.

"Get him," she say.

"Octavia?" Auntie say.

'Cause she had come out of the house and she was standing by the tree looking at us.

"Get him out of there," Mama say.

"Octavia," Auntie say, "explain to him. Explain to him. Just don't beat him. Explain to him."

But she hit me and hit me and hit me.

I'm still young—I ain't no more than eight; but I know now; I know why I had to do it. (They was so little, though. They was so little. I 'member how I picked the feathers off them and cleaned them and helt them over the fire. Then we all ate them. Ain't had but a little bitty piece each, but we all had a little bitty piece, and everybody just looked at me 'cause they was so proud.) Suppose she had to go away? That's why I had to do it. Suppose she had to go away like Daddy went away? Then who was go'n look after us? They had to be somebody left to carry on. I didn't know it then, but I know it now. Auntie and Monsieur Bayonne talked to me and made me see.

5

Time I see it I get out my handkerchief and start waving. It's still 'way down there, but I keep waving anyhow. Then it come up and stop and me and Mama get on. Mama tell me go sit in the back while she pay. I do like she say, and the people look at me. When I pass the little sign that say "White" and "Colored," I start looking for a seat.

I just see one of them back there, but I don't take it, 'cause I want my mama to sit down herself. She comes in the back and sit down, and I lean on the seat. They got seats in the front, but I know I can't sit there, 'cause I have to sit back of the sign. Anyhow, I don't want sit there if my mama go'n sit back here.

They got a lady sitting 'side my mama and she looks at me and smiles little bit. I smile back, but I don't open my mouth, 'cause the wind'll get in and make that tooth ache. The lady take out a pack of gum and reach me a slice, but I shake my head. The lady just can't understand why a little boy'll turn down gum, and she reach me a slice again. This time I point to my jaw. The lady understands and smiles little bit, and I smile little bit, but I don't open my mouth, though.

They got a girl sitting 'cross from me. She got on a red overcoat and her hair's plaited in one big plait. First, I make 'tend I don't see her over there, but then I start looking at her little bit. She make 'tend she don't see me, either, but I catch her looking that way. She got a cold, and every now and then she h'ist that little handkerchief to her nose. She ought to blow it, but she don't. Must think she's too much a lady or something.

Every time she h'ist that little handkerchief, the lady 'side her say something in her ear. She shakes her head and lays her hands in her lap again. Then I catch her kind of looking where I'm at. I smile at her little bit. But think she'll smile back? Uh-uh. She just turn up her little old nose and turn her head. Well, I show her both of us can turn us head. I turn mine too and look out at the river.

The river is gray. The sky is gray. They have pool-doos on the water. The water is wavy, and the pool-doos go up and down. The bus go round a turn, and you got plenty trees hiding the river. Then the bus go round another turn, and I can see the river again.

I look toward the front where all the white people sitting. Then I look at that little old gal again. I don't look right at her, 'cause I don't want all them people to know I love her. I just look at her little bit, like I'm looking out that window over there. But she knows I'm looking that way, and she kind of look at me, too. The lady sitting 'side her catch her this time, and she leans over and says something in her ear.

"I don't love him nothing," that little old gal says out loud.

Everybody back there hear her mouth, and all of them look at us and laugh.

"I don't love you, either," I say. "So you don't have to turn up your nose, Miss."

"You the one looking," she say.

"I wasn't looking at you," I say. "I was looking out that window, there."

"Out that window, my foot," she say. "I seen you. Everytime I turned round you was looking at me."

"You must of been looking yourself if you seen me all them times," I say.

"Shucks," she say, "I got me all kind of boyfriends."

"I got girlfriends, too," I say.

"Well, I just don't want you getting your hopes up," she say.

I don't say no more to that little old gal 'cause I don't want have to bust her in the mouth. I lean on the seat where Mama sitting, and I don't even look that way no more.

When we get to Bayonne, she jugg her little old tongue out at me. I make 'tend I'm go'n hit her, and she duck down 'side her mama. And all the people laugh at us again.

6

Me and Mama get off and start walking in town. Bayonne is a little bitty town. Baton Rouge is a hundred times bigger than Bayonne. I went to Baton Rouge once—me, Ty, Mama, and Daddy. But that was 'way back yonder, 'fore Daddy went in the Army. I wonder when we go'n see him again. I wonder when. Look like he ain't ever coming back home. . . . Even the pavement all cracked in Bayonne. Got grass shooting right out the sidewalk. Got weeds in the ditch, too; just like they got at home.

It's some cold in Bayonne. Look like it's colder than it is home. The wind blows in my face, and I feel that stuff running down my nose. I sniff. Mama says use that handkerchief. I blow my nose and put it back.

We pass a school and I see them white children playing in the yard. Big old red school, and them children just running and playing. Then we pass a café, and I see a bunch of people in there eating. I wish I was in there 'cause I'm cold. Mama tells me keep my eyes in front where they belong.

We pass stores that's got dummies, and we pass another café, and then we pass a shoe shop, and that bald-head man in there fixing on a shoe. I look at him and I butt into that white lady, and Mama jerks me in front and tells me stay there.

We come up to the courthouse, and I see the flag waving there. This flag ain't like the one we got at school. This one here ain't got but a handful of stars. One at school got a big pile of stars—one for every state. We pass it and we turn and there it is—the dentist office. Me and Mama go in, and they got people sitting everywhere you look. They even got a little boy in there younger than me.

Me and Mama sit on that bench, and a white lady come in there and ask me what my name is. Mama tells her and the white lady goes on back. Then I hear somebody hollering in there. Soon's that little boy hear him hollering, he starts hollering, too. His mama pats him and pats him, trying to make him hush up, but he ain't thinking 'bout his mama.

The man that was hollering in there comes out holding his jaw. He is a big old man and he's wearing overalls and a jumper.

"Got it, hanh?" another man asks him.

The man shakes his head—don't want open his mouth.

"Man, I thought they was killing you in there," the other man says. "Hollering like a pig under a gate."

The man don't say nothing. He just heads for the door, and the other man follows him.

"John Lee," the white lady says. "John Lee Williams."

The little boy juggs his head down in his mama's lap and holler more now. His mama tells him go with the nurse, but he ain't thinking 'bout his mama. His mama tells him again, but he don't even hear her. His mama picks him up and takes him in there, and even when the white lady shuts the door I can still hear little old John Lee.

"I often wonder why the Lord let a child like that suffer," a lady says to my mama. The lady's sitting right in front of us on another bench. She's got on a white dress and a black sweater. She must be a nurse or something herself, I reckon.

"Not us to question," a man says.

"Sometimes I don't know if we shouldn't," the lady says.

"I know definitely we shouldn't," the man says. The man looks like a preacher. He's big and fat and he's got on a black suit. He's got a gold chain, too.

"Why?" the lady says.

"Why anything?" the preacher says.

"Yes," the lady says. "Why anything?"

"Not us to question," the preacher says.

The lady looks at the preacher a little while and looks at Mama again.

"And look like it's the poor who suffers the most," she says. "I don't understand it."

"Best not to even try," the preacher says. "He works in mysterious ways—wonders to perform."

Right then little John Lee bust out hollering, and everybody turn they head to listen.

"He's not a good dentist," the lady says. "Dr. Robillard is much better. But more expensive. That's why most of the colored people come here. The white people go to Dr. Robillard. Y'all from Bayonne?"

"Down the river," my mama says. And that's all she go'n say, 'cause she don't talk much. But the lady keeps on looking at her, and so she says, "Near Morgan."

"I see," the lady says.

7

"That's the trouble with the black people in this country today," somebody else says. This one here's sitting on the same side me and Mama's sitting, and he is kind of sitting in front of that preacher. He looks like a teacher or somebody that goes to college. He's got on a suit, and he's got a book that he's been reading. "We don't question is exactly our problem," he says. "We should question and question and question—question everything."

The preacher just looks at him a long time. He done put a toothpick or something in his mouth, and he just keeps on turning it and turning it. You can see he don't like that boy with that book.

"Maybe you can explain what you mean," he says.

"I said what I meant," the boy says. "Question everything. Every stripe, every star, every word spoken. Everything."

"It 'pears to me that this young lady and I was talking 'bout God, young man," the preacher says.

"Question Him, too," the boy says.

"Wait," the preacher says. "Wait now."

"You heard me right," the boy says. "His existence as well as everything else. Everything."

The preacher just looks across the room at the boy. You can see he's getting madder and madder. But mad or no mad, the boy ain't thinking 'bout him. He looks at that preacher just's hard's the preacher looks at him.

"Is this what they coming to?" the preacher says. "Is this what we educating them for?"

"You're not educating me," the boy says. "I wash dishes at night so that I can go to school in the day. So even the words you spoke need questioning."

The preacher just looks at him and shakes his head.

"When I come in this room and seen you there with your book, I said to myself, 'There's an intelligent man.' How wrong a person can be."

"Show me one reason to believe in the existence of a God," the boys says.

"My heart tells me," the preacher says.

"'My heart tells me,'" the boys says. "'My heart tells me.' Sure, 'My heart tells me.' And as long as you listen to what your heart tells you, you will have only what the white man gives you and nothing more. Me, I don't listen to my heart. The purpose of the heart is to pump blood throughout the body, and nothing else."

"Who's your paw, boy?" the preacher says.

"Why?"

"Who is he?"

"He's dead."

"And your mon?"

"She's in Charity Hospital with pneumonia. Half killed herself, working for nothing."

"And 'cause he's dead and she's sick, you mad at the world?"

"I'm not mad at the world. I'm questioning the world. I'm questioning it with cold logic, sir. What do words like Freedom, Liberty, God, White, Colored mean? I want to know. That's why *you* are sending us to school, to read and to ask questions. And because we ask these questions, you call us mad. No sir, it is not us who are mad."

"You keep saying 'us'?"

"'Us.' Yes—us. I'm not alone."

The preacher just shakes his head. Then he looks at everybody in the room—everybody. Some of the people look down at the floor, keep from looking at him. I kind of look 'way myself, but soon's I know he done turn his head, I look that way again.

"I'm sorry for you," he says to the boy.

"Why?" the boy says. "Why not be sorry for yourself? Why are you so much better off than I am? Why aren't you sorry for these other people in here? Why not be sorry for the lady who had to drag her child into the dentist office? Why not be sorry for the lady sitting on that bench over there? Be sorry for them. Not for me. Some way or the other I'm going to make it."

"No, I'm sorry for you," the preacher says.

"Of course, of course," the boy says, nodding his head. "You're sorry for me because I rock that pillar you're leaning on."

"You can't ever rock the pillar I'm leaning on, young man. It's stronger than anything man can ever do."

"You believe in God because a man told you to believe in God," the boy says. "A white man told you to believe in God. And why? To keep you ignorant so he can keep his feet on your neck."

"So now we the ignorant?" the preacher says.

"Yes," the boy says. "Yes." And he opens his book again.

The preacher just looks at him sitting there. The boy done forgot all about him. Everybody else make 'tend they done forgot the squabble, too.

Then I see that preacher getting up real slow. Preacher's a great big old man and he got to brace himself to get up. He comes over where the boy is sitting. He just stands there a little while looking down at him, but the boy don't raise his head.

"Get up, boy," preacher says.

The boy looks up at him, then he shuts his book real slow and stands up. Preacher just hauls back and hit him in the face. The boy falls back 'gainst the wall, but he straightens himself up and looks right back at that preacher.

"You forgot the other cheek," he says.

The preacher hauls back and hit him again on the other side. But this time the boy braces himself and don't fall.

"That hasn't changed a thing," he says.

The preacher just looks at the boy. The preacher's breathing real hard like he just run up a big hill. The boy sits down and opens his book again.

"I feel sorry for you," the preacher says. "I never felt so sorry for a man before."

The boy makes 'tend he don't even hear that preacher. He keeps on reading his book. The preacher goes back and gets his hat off the chair.

"Excuse me," he says to us. "I'll come back some other time. Y'all, please excuse me."

And he looks at the boy and goes out the room. The boy h'ist his hand up to his mouth one time to wipe 'way some blood. All the rest of the time he keeps on reading. And nobody else in there say a word.

8

Little John Lee and his mama come out the dentist office, and the nurse calls somebody else in. Then little bit later they come out, and the nurse calls another name. But fast's she calls somebody in there, somebody else comes in the place where we sitting, and the room stays full.

The people coming in now, all of them wearing big coats. One of them says something 'bout sleeting, another one says he hope not. Another one says he think it ain't nothing but rain. 'Cause, he says, rain can get awful cold this time of year.

All round the room they talking. Some of them talking to people right by them, some of them talking to people clear 'cross the room, some of them talking to anybody'll listen. It's a little bitty room, no bigger than us kitchen, and I can see everybody in there. The little old room's full of smoke, 'cause you got two old men smoking pipes over by that side door. I think I feel my tooth thumping me some, and

I hold my breath and wait. I wait and wait, but it don't thump me no more. Thank God for that.

I feel like going to sleep, and I lean back 'gainst the wall. But I'm scared to go to sleep. Scared 'cause the nurse might call my name and I won't hear her. And Mama might go to sleep, too, and she'll be mad if neither one of us heard the nurse.

I look up at Mama. I love my mama. I love my mama. And when cotton come I'm go'n get her a new coat. And I ain't go'n get a black one, either. I think I'm go'n get her a red one.

"They got some books over there," I say. "Want read one of them?"

Mama looks at the books, but she don't answer me.

"You got yourself a little man there," the lady says.

Mama don't say nothing to the lady, but she must've smiled, 'cause I seen the lady smiling back. The lady looks at me a little while, like she's feeling sorry for me.

"You sure got that preacher out here in a hurry," she says to that boy.

The boy looks up at her and looks in his book again. When I grow up I want be just like him. I want clothes like that and I want keep a book with me, too.

"You really don't believe in God?" the lady says.

"No," he says.

"But why?" the lady says.

"Because the wind is pink," he says.

"What?" the lady says.

The boy don't answer her no more. He just reads in his book.

"Talking 'bout the wind is pink," that old lady says. She's sitting on the same bench with the boy and she's trying to look in his face. The boy makes 'tend the old lady ain't even there. He just keeps on reading. "Wind is pink," she says again. "Eh, Lord, what children go'n be saying next?"

The lady 'cross from us bust out laughing.

"That's a good one," she says. "The wind is pink. Yes sir, that's a good one."

"Don't you believe the wind is pink?" the boys says. He keeps his head down in the book.

"Course I believe it, honey," the lady says. "Course I do." She looks at us and winks her eye. "And what color is grass, honey?"

"Grass? Grass is black."

She bust out laughing again. The boy looks at her.

"Don't you believe grass is black?" he says.

The lady quits her laughing and looks at him. Everybody else looking at him, too. The place quiet, quiet.

"Grass is green, honey," the lady says. "It was green yesterday, it's green today, and it's go'n be green tomorrow."

"How do you know it's green?"

"I know because I know."

"You don't know it's green," the boy says. "You believe it's green because someone told you it was green. If someone had told you it was black you'd believe it was black."

"It's green," the lady says. "I know green when I see green."

"Prove it's green," the boy says.

"Sure, now," the lady says. "Don't tell me it's coming to that."

"It's coming to just that," the boy says. "Words mean nothing. One means no more than the other."

"That's what it all coming to?" that old lady says. That old lady got on a turban and she got on two sweaters. She got a green sweater under a black sweater. I can see the green sweater 'cause some of the buttons on the other sweater's missing.

"Yes ma'am," the boy says. "Words mean nothing. Action is the only thing. Doing. That's the only thing."

"Other words, you want the Lord to come down here and show Hisself to you?" she says.

"Exactly, ma'am," he says.

"You don't mean that, I'm sure?" she says.

"I do, ma'am," he says.

"Done, Jesus," the old lady says, shaking her head.

"I didn't go 'long with that preacher at first," the other lady says; "but now—I don't know. When a person say the grass is black, he's either a lunatic or something's wrong."

"Prove to me that it's green," the boy says.

"It's green because the people say it's green."

"Those same people say we're citizens of these United States," the boy says.

"I think I'm a citizen," the lady says.

"Citizens have certain rights," the boy says. "Name me one right that you have. One right, granted by the Constitution, that you can exercise in Bayonne."

The lady don't answer him. She just looks at him like she don't know what he's talking 'bout. I know I don't.

"Things changing," she says.

"Things are changing because some black men have begun to think with their brains and not their hearts," the boy says.

"You trying to say these people don't believe in God?"

"I'm sure some of them do. Maybe most of them do. But they don't believe that God is going to touch these white people's hearts and change things tomorrow. Things change through action. By no other way."

Everybody sit quiet and look at the boy. Nobody says a thing. Then the lady 'cross the room from me and Mama just shakes her head.

"Let's hope that not all your generation feel the same way you do," she says.

"Think what you please, it doesn't matter," the boy says. "But it will be men who listen to their heads and not their hearts who will see that your children have a better chance than you had."

"Let's hope they ain't all like you, though," the old lady says. "Done forgot the heart absolutely."

"Yes ma'am, I hope they aren't all like me," the boy says. "Unfortunately, I was born too late to believe in your God. Let's hope that the ones who come after will have your faith—if not in your God, then in something else, something definitely that they can lean on. I haven't anything. For me, the wind is pink, the grass is black."

9

The nurse comes in the room where we all sitting and waiting and says the doctor won't take no more patients till one o'clock this evening. My mama jumps up off the bench and goes up to the white lady.

"Nurse, I have to go back in the field this evening," she says.

"The doctor is treating his last patient now," the nurse says. "One o'clock this evening."

"Can I at least speak to the doctor?" my mama asks.

"I'm his nurse," the lady says.

"My little boy's sick," my mama says. "Right now his tooth almost killing him."

The nurse looks at me. She's trying to make up her mind if to let me come in. I look at her real pitiful. The tooth ain't hurting me at all, but Mama say it is, so I make 'tend for her sake.

"This evening," the nurse says, and goes on back in the office.

"Don't feel 'jected, honey," the lady says to Mama. "I been round them a long time—they take you when they want to. If you was white, that's something else; but we the wrong color."

Mama don't say nothing to the lady, and me and her go outside and stand 'gainst the wall. It's cold out there. I can feel that wind going through my coat. Some of the other people come out of the room and go up the street. Me and Mama stand there a little while and we start walking. I don't know where we going. When we come to the other street we just stand there.

"You don't have to make water, do you?" Mama says.

"No, ma'am," I say.

We go on up the street. Walking real slow. I can tell Mama don't know where she's going. When we come to a store we stand there and look at the dummies. I look at a little boy wearing a brown overcoat. He's got on brown shoes, too. I look at my old shoes and look at his'n again. You wait till summer, I say.

Me and Mama walk away. We come up to another store and we stop and look at them dummies, too. Then we go on again. We pass a café where the white people in there eating. Mama tells me keep my eyes in front where they belong, but I can't help from seeing them people eat. My stomach starts to growling 'cause I'm hungry. When I see people eating, I get hungry; when I see a coat, I get cold.

A man whistles at my mama when we go by a filling station. She makes 'tend she don't even see him. I look back and I feel like hitting him in the mouth. If I was bigger, I say; if I was bigger, you'd see.

We keep on going. I'm getting colder and colder, but I don't say nothing. I feel that stuff running down my nose and I sniff.

"That rag," Mama says.

I get it out and wipe my nose. I'm getting cold all over now—my face, my hands, my feet, everything. We pass another little café, but this'n for white people, too, and we can't go in there, either. So we just walk. I'm so cold now I'm 'bout ready to say it. If I knowed where we was going I wouldn't be so cold, but I don't know where we going. We go, we go, we go. We walk clean out of Bayonne. Then we cross the street and we come back. Same thing I seen when I got off the bus this morning. Same old trees, same old walk, same old weeds, same old cracked pave—same old everything.

I sniff again.

"That rag," Mama says.

I wipe my nose real fast and jugg that handkerchief back in my pocket 'fore my hand gets too cold. I raise my head and I can see David's hardware store. When we come up to it, we go in. I don't know why, but I'm glad.

It's warm in there. It's so warm in there you don't ever want to leave. I look for the heater, and I see it over by them barrels. Three white men standing round the heater talking in Creole. One of them comes over to see what my mama want.

"Got any axe handles?" she says.

Me, Mama and the white man start to the back, but Mama stops me when we come up to the heater. She and the white man go on. I hold my hands over the heater and look at them. They go all the way to the back, and I see the white man pointing to the axe handles 'gainst the wall. Mama takes one of them and shakes it like she's trying to figure how much it weighs. Then she rubs her hand over it from one end to the other end. She turns it over and looks at the other side, then she shakes it again, and shakes her head and puts it back. She gets another one and she does it just like she did the first one, then she shakes her head. Then she gets a brown one and do it that, too. But she don't like this one, either. Then she gets another one, but 'fore she shakes it or anything, she looks at me. Look like she's trying to say something to me, but I don't know what it is. All I know is I done got warm now and I'm feeling right smart better. Mama shakes this axe handle just like she did the others, and shakes her head and says something to the white man. The white man just looks at his pile of axe handles, and when Mama pass him to come to the front, the white man just scratch his head and follows her. She tells me come on and we go on out and start walking again.

We walk and walk, and no time at all I'm cold again. Look like I'm colder now 'cause I can still remember how good it was back there. My stomach growls and I suck it in to keep Mama from hearing it. She's walking right 'side me, and it growls so loud you can hear it a mile. But Mama don't say a word.

10

When we come up to the courthouse, I look at the clock. It's got quarter to twelve. Mean we got another hour and a quarter to be out here in the cold. We go and stand 'side a building. Something hits my cap and I look up at the sky. Sleet's falling.

I look at Mama standing there. I want stand close 'side her, but she don't like that. She say that's crybaby stuff. She say you got to stand for yourself, by yourself.

"Let's go back to that office," she says.

We cross the street. When we get to the dentist office I try to open the door, but I can't. I twist and twist, but I can't. Mama pushes me to the side and she twist the knob, but she can't open the door, either. She turns 'way from the door. I look at her, but I don't move and I don't say nothing. I done seen her like this before and I'm scared of her.

"You hungry?" she says. She says it like she's mad at me, like I'm the cause of everything.

"No, ma'am," I say.

"You want eat and walk back, or you rather don't eat and ride?"

"I ain't hungry," I say.

I ain't just hungry, but I'm cold, too. I'm so hungry and cold I want to cry. And look like I'm getting colder and colder. My feet done got numb. I try to work my toes, but I don't even feel them. Look like I'm go'n die. Look like I'm go'n stand right here and freeze to death. I think 'bout home. I think 'bout Val and Auntie and Ty and Louis and Walker. It's 'bout twelve o'clock and I know they eating dinner now. I can hear Ty making jokes. He done forgot 'bout getting up early this morning and right now he's probably making jokes. Always trying to make somebody laugh. I wish I was right there listening to him. Give anything in the world if I was home round the fire.

"Come on," Mama says.

We start walking again. My feet so numb I can't hardly feel them. We turn the corner and go on back up the street. The clock on the courthouse starts hitting for twelve.

The sleet's coming down plenty now. They hit the pave and bounce like rice. Oh, Lord; oh, Lord, I pray. Don't let me die, don't let me die, don't let me die, Lord.

11

Now I know where we going. We going back of town where the colored people eat. I don't care if I don't eat. I been hungry before. I can stand it. But I can't stand the cold.

I can see we go'n have a long walk. It's 'bout a mile down there. But I don't mind. I know when I get there I'm go'n warm myself. I think I can hold out. My hands numb in my pockets and my feet numb, too, but if I keep moving I can hold out. Just don't stop no more, that's all.

The sky's gray. The sleet keeps on falling. Falling like rain now—plenty, plenty. You can hear it hitting the pave. You can see it bouncing. Sometimes it bounces two times 'fore it settles.

We keep on going. We don't say nothing. We just keep on going, keep on going.

I wonder what Mama's thinking. I hope she ain't mad at me. When summer come I'm go'n pick plenty cotton and get her a coat. I'm go'n get her a red one.

I hope they'd make it summer all the time. I'd be glad if it was summer all the time—but it ain't. We got to have winter, too. Lord, I hate the winter. I guess everybody hate the winter.

I don't sniff this time. I get out my handkerchief and wipe my nose. My hands's so cold I can hardly hold the handkerchief.

I think we getting close, but we ain't there yet. I wonder where everybody is. Can't see a soul but us. Look like we the only two people moving round today. Must be too cold for the rest of the people to move round in.

I can hear my teeth. I hope they don't knock together too hard and make that bad one hurt. Lord, that's all I need, for that bad one to start off.

I hear a church bell somewhere. But today ain't Sunday. They must be ringing for a funeral or something.

I wonder what they doing at home. They must be eating. Monsieur Bayonne might be there with his guitar. One day Ty played with Monsieur Bayonne's guitar and broke one of the strings. Monsieur Bayonne was some mad with Ty. He say Ty wasn't go'n ever 'mount to nothing. Ty can go just like Monsieur Bayonne when he ain't there. Ty can make everybody laugh when he starts to mocking Monsieur Bayonne.

I used to like to be with Mama and Daddy. We used to be happy. But they took him in the Army. Now, nobody happy no more. . . . I be glad when Daddy comes home.

Monsieur Bayonne say it wasn't fair for them to take Daddy and give Mama nothing and give us nothing. Auntie say, "Shhh, Etienne. Don't let them hear you talk like that." Monsieur Bayonne say, "It's God truth. What they giving his children? They have to walk three and a half miles to school hot or cold. That's anything to give for a paw? She's got to work in the field rain or shine just to make ends meet. That's anything to give for a husband?" Auntie say, "Shhh, Etienne, shhh." "Yes, you right," Monsieur Bayonne say. "Best don't say it in front of them now. But one day they go'n find out. One day." "Yes, I suppose so," Auntie say. "Then what, Rose Mary?" Monsieur Bayonne say. "I don't know, Etienne," Auntie say. "All we can do is us job, and leave everything else in His hand . . ."

We getting closer, now. We getting closer. I can even see the railroad tracks.

We cross the tracks, and now I see the café. Just to get in there, I say. Just to get in there. Already I'm starting to feel little better.

12

We go in. Ahh, it's good. I look for the heater; there 'gainst the wall. One of them little brown ones. I just stand there and hold my hands over it. I can't open my hands too wide 'cause they almost froze.

Mama's standing right 'side me. She done unbuttoned her coat. Smoke rises out of the coat, and the coat smells like a wet dog.

I move to the side so Mama can have more room. She opens out her hands and rubs them together. I rub mine together, too, 'cause this keep them from hurting. If you let them warm too fast, they hurt you sure. But if you let them warm just little bit at a time, and you keep rubbing them, they be all right every time.

They got just two more people in the café. A lady back of the counter, and a man on this side the counter. They been watching us ever since we come in.

Mama gets out the handkerchief and count up the money. Both of us know how much money she's got there. Three dollars. No, she ain't got three dollars, 'cause she had to pay us way up here. She ain't got but two dollars and a half left. Dollar and a half to get my tooth pulled, and fifty cents for us to go back on, and fifty cents worth of salt meat.

She stirs the money round with her finger. Most of the money is change 'cause I can hear it rubbing together. She stirs it and stirs it. Then she looks at the door. It's still sleeting. I can hear it hitting 'gainst the wall like rice.

"I ain't hungry, Mama," I say.

"Got to pay them something for they heat," she says.

She takes a quarter out the handkerchief and ties the handkerchief up again. She looks over her shoulder at the people, but she still don't move. I hope she don't spend the money. I don't want her spending it on me. I'm hungry, I'm almost starving I'm so hungry, but I don't want her spending the money on me.

She flips the quarter over like she's thinking. She's must be thinking 'bout us walking back home. Lord, I sure don't want walk home. If I thought it'd do any good to say something, I'd say it. But Mama makes up her own mind 'bout things.

She turns 'way from the heater right fast, like she better hurry up and spend the quarter 'fore she change her mind. I watch her go toward the counter. The man and the lady look at her, too. She tells the lady something and the lady walks away. The man keeps on looking at her. Her back's turned to the man, and she don't even know he's standing there.

The lady puts some cakes and a glass of milk on the counter. Then she pours up a cup of coffee and sets it 'side the other stuff. Mama pays her for the things and comes on back where I'm standing. She tells me sit down at the table 'gainst the wall.

The milk and the cakes's for me; the coffee's for Mama. I eat slow and I look at her. She's looking outside at the sleet. She's looking real sad. I say to myself, I'm go'n make all this up one day. You see, one day, I'm go'n make all this up. I want say it now; I want tell her how I feel right now; but Mama don't like for us to talk like that.

"I can't eat all this," I say.

They ain't got but just three little old cakes there. I'm so hungry right now, the Lord knows I can eat a hundred times three, but I want my mama to have one.

Mama don't even look my way. She knows I'm hungry, she knows I want it. I let it stay there a little while, then I get it and eat it. I eat just on my front teeth, though, 'cause if cake touch that back tooth I know what'll happen. Thank God it ain't hurt me at all today.

After I finish eating I see the man go to the juke box. He drops a nickel in it, then he just stand there a little while looking at the record. Mama tells me keep my eyes in front where they belong. I turn my head like she say, but then I hear the man coming toward us.

"Dance, pretty?" he says.

Mama gets up to dance with him. But 'fore you know it, she done grabbed the little man in the collar and done heaved him 'side the wall. He hit the wall so hard he stop the juke box from playing.

"Some pimp," the lady back of the counter says. "Some pimp."

The little man jumps up off the floor and starts toward my mama. 'Fore you know it, Mama done sprung open her knife and she's waiting for him.

"Come on," she says. "Come on. I'll gut you from your neighbo to your throat. Come on."

I go up to the little man to hit him, but Mama makes me come and stand 'side her. The little man looks at me and Mama and goes on back to the counter.

"Some pimp," the lady back of the counter says. "Some pimp." She starts laughing and pointing at the little man. Yes sir, you a pimp, all right. Yes sir-ree."

13

"Fasten that coat, let's go," Mama says.

"You don't have to leave," the lady says.

Mama don't answer the lady, and we right out in the cold gain. I'm warm right now—my hands, my ears, my feet—but know this ain't go'n last too long. It done sleet so much now you got ice everywhere you look.

We cross the railroad tracks, and soon's we do, I get cold. That wind goes through this little old coat like it ain't even there. I got on a shirt and a sweater under the coat, but that wind don't pay them no mind. I look up and I can see we got a long way to go. I wonder if we go'n make it 'fore I get too cold.

We cross over to walk on the sidewalk. They got just one sidewalk back here, and it's over there.

After we go just a little piece, I smell bread cooking. I look, then I see a baker shop. When we get closer, I can smell it more better. I shut my eyes and make 'tend I'm eating. But I keep them shut too long and I butt up 'gainst a telephone post. Mama grabs me and see if I'm hurt. I ain't bleeding or nothing and she turns me loose.

I can feel I'm getting colder and colder, and I look up to see how far we still got to go. Uptown is 'way up yonder. A half mile more, I reckon. I try to think of something. They say think and you won't get cold. I think of that poem, "Annabel Lee." I ain't been to school in so long—this bad weather—I reckon they done passed "Annabel Lee" by now. But passed it or not, I'm sure Miss Walker go'n make me recite it when I get there. That woman don't never forget nothing. I ain't never seen nobody like that in my life.

I'm still getting cold. "Annabel Lee" or no "Annabel Lee," I'm still getting cold. But I can see we getting closer. We getting there gradually.

Soon's we turn the corner, I see a little old white lady up in front of us. She's the only lady on the street. She's all in black and she's got a long black rag over her head.

"Stop," she says.

Me and Mama stop and look at her. She must be crazy to be out in all this bad weather. Ain't got but a few other people out there, and all of them's men.

"Y'all done ate?" she says.

"Just finish," Mama says.

"Y'all must be cold then?" she says.

"We headed for the dentist," Mama says. "We'll warm up when we get there."

"What dentist?" the old lady says. "Mr. Bassett?"

"Yes, ma'am," Mama says.

"Come on in," the old lady says. "I'll telephone him and tell him y'all coming."

Me and Mama follow the old lady in the store. It's a little bitty store, and it don't have much in there. The old lady takes off her head rag and folds it up.

"Helena?" somebody calls from the back.

"Yes, Alnest?" the old lady says.

"Did you see them?"

"They're here. Standing beside me."

"Good. Now you can stay inside."

The old lady looks at Mama. Mama's waiting to hear what she brought us in here for. I'm waiting for that, too.

"I saw y'all each time you went by," she says. "I came out to catch you, but you were gone."

"We went back of town," Mama says.

"Did you eat?"

"Yes, ma'am."

The old lady looks at Mama a long time, like she's thinking Mama might be just saying that. Mama looks right back at her. The old lady looks at me to see what I have to say. I don't say nothing. I sure ain't going 'gainst my mama.

"There's food in the kitchen," she says to Mama. "I've been keeping it warm."

Mama turns right around and starts for the door.

"Just a minute," the old lady says. Mama stops. "The boy'll have to work for it. It isn't free."

"We don't take no handout," Mama says.

"I'm not handing out anything," the old lady says. "I need my garbage moved to the front. Ernest has a bad cold and can't go out there."

"James'll move it for you," Mama says.

"Not unless you eat," the old lady says. "I'm old, but I have my pride, too, you know."

Mama can see she ain't go'n beat this old lady down, so she just shakes her head.

"All right," the old lady says. "Come into the kitchen."

She leads the way with that rag in her hand. The kitchen is a little bitty little old thing, too. The table and the stove just 'bout fill it up. They got a little room to the side. Somebody in there laying 'cross the bed—'cause I can see one of his feet. Must be the person she was talking to: Ernest or Alnest—something like that.

"Sit down," the old lady says to Mama. "Not you," she says to me. "You have to move the cans."

"Helena?" the man says in the other room.

"Yes, Alnest?" the old lady says.

"Are you going out there again?"

"I must show the boy where the garbage is, Alnest," the old lady says.

"Keep that shawl over your head," the old man says.

"You don't have to remind me, Alnest. Come, boy," the old lady says.

We go out in the yard. Little old back yard ain't no bigger than the store or the kitchen. But it can sleet here just like it can sleet in any big back yard. And 'fore you know it, I'm trembling.

"There," the old lady says, pointing to the cans. I pick up one of the cans and set it right back down. The can's so light, I'm go'n see what's inside of it.

"Here," the old lady says. "Leave that can alone."

I look back at her standing there in the door. She's got that black rag wrapped round her shoulders, and she's pointing one of her little old fingers at me.

"Pick it up and carry it to the front," she says. I go by her with the can, and she's looking at me all the time. I'm sure the can's empty. I'm sure she could've carried it herself—maybe both of them at the same time. "Set it on the sidewalk by the door and come back for the other one," she says.

I go and come back, and Mama looks at me when I pass her. I get the other can and take it to the front. It don't feel a bit heavier than that first one. I tell myself I ain't go'n be nobody's fool, and I'm go'n look inside this can to see just what I been hauling. First, I look up the street, then down the street. Nobody coming. Then I look over my shoulder toward the door. That little old lady done slipped up there quiet 's mouse, watching me again. Look like she knowed what I was go'n do.

"Ehh, Lord," she says. "Children, children. Come in here, boy, and go wash your hands."

I follow her in the kitchen. She points toward the bathroom, and I go in there and wash up. Little bitty old bathroom, but it's clean, clean. I don't use any of her towels; I wipe my hands on my pants legs.

When I come back in the kitchen, the old lady done dished up the food. Rice, gravy, meat—and she even got some lettuce and tomato in a saucer. She even got a glass of milk and a piece of cake there, too. It looks so good, I almost start eating 'fore I say my blessing.

"Helena?" the old man says.

"Yes, Alnest?"

"Are they eating?"

"Yes," she says.

"Good," he says. "Now you'll stay inside."

The old lady goes in there where he is and I can hear them talking. I look at Mama. She's eating slow like she's thinking. I wonder what's the matter now. I reckon she's thinking 'bout home.

The old lady comes back in the kitchen.

"I talked to Dr. Bassett's nurse," she says. "Dr. Bassett will take you as soon as you get there."

"Thank you, ma'am," Mama says.

"Perfectly all right," the old lady says. "Which one is it?"

Mama nods toward me. The old lady looks at me real sad. I look sad, too.

"You're not afraid, are you?" she says.

"No, ma'am," I say.

"That's a good boy," the old lady says. "Nothing to be afraid of. Dr. Bassett will not hurt you."

When me and Mama get through eating, we thank the old lady again.

"Helena, are they leaving?" the old man says.

"Yes, Alnest."

"Tell them I say good-bye."

"They can hear you, Alnest."

"Good-bye both mother and son," the old man says. "And may God be with you."

Me and Mama tell the old man good-bye, and we follow the old lady in the front room. Mama opens the door to go out, but she stops and comes back in the store.

"You sell salt meat?" she says.

"Yes."

"Give me two bits worth."

"That isn't very much salt meat," the old lady says.

"That's all I have," Mama says.

The old lady goes back of the counter and cuts a big piece off the chunk. Then she wraps it up and puts it in a paper bag.

"Two bits," she says.

"That looks like awful lot of meat for a quarter," Mama says.

"Two bits," the old lady says. "I've been selling salt meat behind this counter twenty-five years. I think I know what I'm doing."

"You got a scale there," Mama says.

"What?" the old lady says.

"Weigh it," Mama says.

"What?" the old lady says. "Are you telling me how to run my business?"

"Thanks very much for the food," Mama says.

"Just a minute," the old lady says.

"James," Mama says to me. I move toward the door.

"Just one minute, I said," the old lady says.

Me and Mama stop again and look at her. The old lady takes the meat out of the bag and unwraps it and cuts 'bout half of it off. Then she wraps it up again and juggs it back in the bag and gives the bag to Mama. Mama lays the quarter on the counter.

"Your kindness will never be forgotten," she says. "James," she says to me.

We go out, and the old lady comes to the door to look at us. After we go a little piece I look back, and she's still there watching us.

The sleet's coming down heavy, heavy now, and I turn up my coat collar to keep my neck warm. My mama tells me turn it right back down.

"You not a bum," she says. "You a man."

Chapter 10

JILL KER CONWAY

EXCERPT FROM *THE ROAD FROM COORAIN*

Because Christmas recalled our father's death, it was a difficult feast for us. Nevertheless, we had one of my mother's succulent roast turkeys and her ambrosial plum puddings before the boys left to spend the rest of the summer at Coorain. During January, we began to talk seriously about where I would attend school. My mother was daunted by the prospect of more private school fees as our debts grew and our assets dwindled. Did I think I would like the local state school? she asked me. We could see it each time we took a train—it was right beside the railway station, empty at present, surrounded by an acre of unkempt ground. I was startled. I had taken on my parents' values sufficiently to see this proposal as a distinct coming down in the world. Recognizing the worry in my mother's eyes, I said I would.

The first day of school in February was hot, 105 degrees. The school, a brick building with an iron roof, was like a furnace, and its inhabitants, teachers and students, wilted as the day wore on. I hated it from the moment I walked in the door. I was a snob, and I knew the accents of the teachers and most of the students were wrong by the exacting standards we'd had drummed into us at home. Worse still was the unruly behavior of everyone of every age. Boys pulled my hair when I refused to answer questions I took as rude or impudent; girls stuck out their tongues and used bad language. Teachers lost their tempers and caned pupils in front of the class. Few books were opened as the staff waged a losing battle to establish order. Recess and lunchtime were purgatorial. Crowds, or so it seemed to me, of jeering boys and a few girls gathered around to taunt me about my accent. "Stuck up, ain't you," they yelled, as I faced them in stubborn silence.

They were right. Now I was in a more diverse social universe than I had known at Coorain. I had no idea how to behave or what the rules were for managing social boundaries. I had been friends, one could say special friends, with Shorty, or with Ron Kelly, but that was in a simple world where we each knew our respective places. Here, I knew only that the old rules could not possibly apply. Everyone around me spoke broad Australian, a kind of speech my parents' discipline had ruthlessly eliminated. My interrogators could unquestionably be described by that word my mother used as a blanket condemnation of lower-class people, customs, and forms of behavior. They were "common." My encounter was a classic confrontation for the Australia of my generation. I, the carefully respectable copier of British manners, was being called to raucous and high-spirited account by the more vital and unquestionably authentic Australian popular culture. I was too uncertain to cope. I faced them in silence till the bell rang and we returned to the pandemonium of the unruly classroom.

After school, the same group assembled to escort me home to the accompaniment of catcalls and vivid commentaries on my parentage. I knew these city children could not outlast someone who was used to walking ten or twelve miles a day behind a herd of sheep, so our comic crocodile set out. I, stalking in front in frozen indignation, my attendant chorus gradually wilting as I led them along hot pavements and across streets where the heat had begun to melt the tarmac. After the last one had tired and dropped away, I made my way home where my mother was ostentatiously doing nothing in the front garden, on the watch for my arrival.

We had our afternoon tea in blissful silence. Finally she asked me how the day had gone. "It was all right," I said, determined not to complain. She studied my face thoughtfully. "You don't have to go back," she said. "I made a mistake. That's not the right school for you." Years later, I asked how she guessed what my day had been like. "I didn't have to ask," she said. "You were a child whose face was always alight with curiosity. When you came home that day, your face was closed. I knew you wouldn't learn anything there."

In fact, had I persevered I would have learned a great deal, though little of it from the harassed and overworked teachers in the ill-equipped classrooms. I'd have been obliged to come to terms with the Australian class system, and to see my family's world from the irreverent and often hilarious perspective of the Australian working class. It would have been invaluable knowledge, and my vision of Australia would have been the better for it. It was to take me another fifteen years to see the world from my own Australian perspective, rather than from the British definition taught to my kind of colonial. On the other hand, had I learned that earthy irreverence in my schooldays, it would have ruled out the appreciation of high culture in any form. My mother had no training for that appreciation, but she knew instinctively to seek it for her children. She did not reflect much about the underlying conflicts in Australian culture. She was simply determined that I would be brought up to abhor anything "common," and that, despite her financial worries, I would have the best education available in the Australia she knew.

The next day, my mother acted decisively. By some wizardry peculiarly hers, she persuaded the headmistress of Abbotsleigh, one of the most academically demanding of the private schools for girls in Sydney, to accept me as a pupil in the last year of the Junior School. Although there were long waiting lists for admission to the school, I was to begin at once, as a day girl, and become a boarder the next term.

Before being formally enrolled, I was taken for an interview with Miss Everett, the headmistress. To me she seemed like a benevolent being from another planet. She was over six feet tall, with the carriage and gait of a splendid athlete. Her dress was new to me. She wore a tweed suit of soft colors and battered elegance. She spoke in the plummy tones of a woman educated in England, and her intelligent face beamed with humor and curiosity. When she spoke, the habit of long years of teaching French made her articulate her words clearly and so forcefully that the unwary who stood too close were in danger of being sprayed like the audience too close to the footlights of a vaudeville show. "She looks strapping," she cheerfully commented to my mother, after talking to me for a few minutes alone. "She can begin tomorrow." Thereafter, no matter how I misbehaved, or what events brought me into her presence, I felt real benevolence radiating from Miss Everett.

The sight of her upright figure, forever striding across the school grounds, automatically caused her charges to straighten their backs. Those who slouched were often startled to have her appear suddenly behind them and seize their shoulders to correct their posture. Perhaps because she liked my stiff back we began a friendship that mattered greatly in my future. I never ceased to wonder at her, for Miss Everett was the first really free spirit I had ever met. She was impatient with bourgeois Australian culture, concerned about ideas, restless with the constraints of a Board of Trustees dominated by the low church evangelical Anglican archdiocese of Sydney, and she never bothered to conceal her feelings. She had been a highly successful amateur athlete, and had earned her first degree in French literature at the Sorbonne. After Paris, she had studied modern literature in Germany. To me and to many others, she was a true bearer of European cultural ideals in Australia. She loved learning for itself, and this made her a most unusual schoolteacher. The academic mentality in the Australia of my childhood focused on knowledge as a credential, a body of information one had to use as a mechanic would his tools. With her French training, she saw her academic task as one of conveying to her charges the kinds of disciplines which released the mind for creativity and speculation. This, to many of her peers, was a subversive goal. She was a successful headmistress because she was also an astute politician, bending before the winds of provincial prejudice whenever they blew strongly over issues of discipline and behavior. But it was characteristic of her that she made her mind up about flouting the waiting lists of daughters of old girls because she'd been struck during our ten minutes together by the range of my vocabulary. My mother and I had had a hard few years, she had remarked to get us started. "Yes," I said, "we have lived through a great natural catastrophe." She wanted eleven-year-olds who thought that way in her school and cheerfully ignored the admission rules.

Thereafter, I hurried quickly past the desert of the local state school to the railway station and rode the seven minutes south to Wahroonga, the suburb of my new school. On my path homeward, I only once saw my former attendant chorus ranging restlessly about the local state school grounds. Seeing me, they took flight like a flock of birds, alighting by the fence as I strode past. I was prepared for hostility, but they were remarkably genial. "We don't blame you for leaving this fucking school, Jill," the ringleader shouted cheerfully. "It's no bloody good." I was too young and insecure to wonder what a good school might have made of such high-spirited pupils, and I had as yet no sense of injustice that the difference between our chances for education were as night and day. At Abbotsleigh, even though I was immediately ushered into a classroom of thirty-six total strangers, it seemed as though I had already arrived in paradise. Many students were boarders from distant country areas who had also had to overcome their shyness and become social beings. At breaks between classes they understood my tongue-tied silence. I was placed at a desk next to one of the kindest and most helpful members of the class, and two girls were deputed to see to it that I was not lonely my first day. I could scarcely believe my good fortune. Better still, the teacher, Miss Webb, a woman in her late twenties, knew exactly when to put the class to work, and when to relax and allow high spirits to run relatively free. Our classroom was an orderly and harmonious place where the subjects were taught well and the students encouraged to learn. Even the strange ritual of the gymnasium was less puzzling. The teachers were used to bush children and took the time to explain what the exercises were for, or to tell me that I would soon learn the eye hand coordination I lacked.

Our curriculum was inherited from Great Britain, and consequently it was utterly untouched by progressive notions in education. We took English grammar, complete with parsing and analysis, we were drilled in spelling and punctuation, we read English poetry and were tested in scansion, we read English fiction, novels, and short stories and analyzed the style. Each year, we studied a Shakespeare play, committing much of it to memory, and performing scenes from it on April 23 in honor of Shakespeare's birthday.

We might have been in Sussex for all the attention we paid to Australian poetry and prose. It did not count. We, for our part, dutifully learned Shakespeare's imagery drawn from the English landscape and from English horticulture. We memorized Keats's "Ode to Autumn" or Shelley on the skylark without ever having seen the progression of seasons and the natural world they referred to. This gave us the impression that great poetry and fiction were written by and about people and places far distant from Australia. Palgrave's *Golden Treasury* or the Oxford collection of romantic poetry we read were so beautiful it didn't seem to matter, though to us poetry was more like incantation than related to the rhythms of our own speech. As for landscape, we learned by implication that ours was ugly, because it deviated totally from the landscape of the Cotswolds and the Lake Country, or the romantic hills and valleys of Constable.

After English (eight classes a week) came history (five times a week). We learned about Roman Britain and memorized a wonderful jumble of Angles, Saxons, Picts, and Boadicea. In geography (three times a week), we studied the great rivers of the world. They were the Ganges, the Indus, the Amazon, the Plate, the Rhine, the Danube, the Nile, the Congo, the St. Lawrence, and the Mississippi. When the question was raised, Australia was defined once again by default. Our vast continent had no great river system; its watercourses flowed inland to Lake Eyre, an anomaly which was quickly dismissed as a distraction from the business at hand. Once a week, we read scripture, sticking to the Old Testament and learning its geography as a distraction from its bloodthirsty tribal battles. Nothing in the instruction suggested that this sacred subject bore any relation to our daily lives, although because we read the Bible, we were supposed to be particularly well behaved during this class.

In mathematics, we studied arithmetic and simple geometry, five times a week. The textbooks were English, and the problems to be solved assumed another natural environment. It was possible to do them all as a form of drill without realizing that the mathematical imagination helped one explore and analyze the continuities and discontinuities of the order which lay within and beneath natural phenomena. We learned to treat language as magical, but not numbers and their relationships. Somehow we knew that mathematics was important, as a form of intellectual discipline. However, our problems to solve had to do with shopping and making change, pumping water from one receptacle to another at constant volumes, or measuring the areas of things. These did not encourage the visualizing of shapes and relationships, let alone hint at the wonders of physics.

Once a week we had choir lessons, lessons in painting and drawing, and in sewing. The sewing was of the nonutilitarian type, embroidery or crewel work. The art concerned lessons in perspective, conveyed with no historical context describing the development of Western ideas about the representation of objects. Choir was group instruction in singing and the reading of music. All these practical subjects assumed some previous background which I did not possess, so that I fiddled away the hour and a half appearing busy enough to escape rebuke, but never really undertaking any project. In choir, I soon learned that I could not carry a tune and that it was better to move my mouth soundlessly and look interested. My imagination might have been fired by reproductions of great painting and sculpture, but we did not look at them. Nor did our classes ever hint at the great body of Australian painting which already existed, or the vitality of the artistic efflorescence taking place in our own city even as we studied. As with our study of art, we were not taught what music *was*. It was enough that a lady knew how to carry a tune and to read music. Those who were talented mastered performance, but the rest of us were left to learn about music and dance as forms of expression on our own.

Although our curriculum ignored our presence in Australia, the school itself demonstrated how the Australian landscape could be enhanced by a discerning eye. Its ample grounds were a far cry from the barren setting of my local state school with its hot dusty building and gritty yard. It stood on twenty or so acres rising up a hillside toward one of the highest points of the gentle hills which made up the terrain between Sydney Harbor and the entrance to the Hawkesbury River, to the north of the Harbor. The school's residential buildings clustered along the main high way running north from Sydney, the Pacific Highway. Behind them, close to the main entrance, two groups of classroom buildings formed a quadrangle with a residence and the administration buildings. Patches of bush had been manicured a little to control steep grades down to two levels of playing fields. Paths led to more dispersed dormitories, and around them were plantings which created places for day students to sit outside at lunch, and for boarders to enjoy during the weekend. Rose gardens, jacarandas, jasmine, honeysuckle, mock-orange, peach, plum, and quince trees perfumed the air in spring, and the planting pulled out the contours of the land without interrupting the sense of the wildness of the pockets of bush skillfully left to separate different grades and functional areas. Tucked away at the northern end were banks of tennis courts and closer to the main buildings were basketball courts and a sunken court with a high cement wall at which budding tennis stars honed their backhand and leapt to smash their forehand drive.

In this setting thronged some three hundred pupils in the Junior School, and another eight hundred or so students in high school grades. Much about our way of life symbolized the colonial mentality. Its signs were visible in the maps on our classroom walls, extended depictions of the globe with much of Africa, all of the Indian subcontinent, parts of Southeast Asia, half of North America, colored the bright red of the British Empire. Our uniforms, copies of those of English schools, indicated that we were only partially at home in our environment. In winter, we wore pine green tunics, cream blouses, green flannel blazers, dark brown cotton stockings, green velour hats, and brown cotton gloves. In summer, we wore starched green linen dresses with cream collars, the same blazer, beige socks, a cream panama hat, and the same brown gloves. Woe betide the student caught shedding the blazer or the gloves in public, even when the thermometer was over 100 degrees. She was letting down the school, behaving unbecomingly, and betraying the code involved in being a lady. Ladies, we learned, did not consider comfort more important than propriety in dress or manners. Disciplinary action was taken instantly when it was learned that an Abbotsleigh student had not leapt to her feet in train or bus to offer her seat to an older person, male or female. Speaking loudly, sitting in public in any fashion except bolt upright with a ramrod-straight back, were likewise sorts of behavior which let down the school. When the more rebellious asked why this was so, the answer was clear and unequivocal. We were an elite. We were privileged girls and young women who had an obligation to represent the best standards of behavior to the world at large. The best standards were derived from Great Britain, and should be emulated unquestioningly. Those were the standards which had led to such a sizable part of the map of the globe being colored red, and we let them slip at our peril. No one paused to think that gloves and blazers had a function in damp English springs which they lacked entirely in our blazing summers.

Speech was another important aspect of deportment. One's voice must be well modulated and purged of all ubiquitous Australian diphthongs. Teachers were tireless in pointing them out and stopping the class until the offender got the word right. Drills of "how now brown cow" might have us all scarlet in the face with choked schoolgirl laughter, but they were serious matters for our instructors, ever on guard against the diphthongs that heralded cultural decline.

The disciplinary system also modeled the British heritage. We were an elite. Ergo we were born to be leaders. However, the precise nature of the leadership was by no means clear. For some of our mentors, excelling meant a fashionable marriage and leadership in philanthropy. For others, it meant intellectual achievement and the aspiration to a university education. Since the great majority of the parents supporting the school favored the first definition, the question of the social values which should inform leadership was carefully glossed over. Eminence in the school's hierarchy could come from being a lively and cheerful volunteer, a leader in athletics, or from intellectual achievement. The head girl was always carefully chosen to offend no particular camp aligned behind the competing definitions. She was always a good-natured all-rounder.

The discipline code and the manner of its administration might well have been designed to prepare us to be subalterns in the Indian army, or district officers in some remote jungle colony. The routine running of the school was managed by class captains and prefects selected by the headmistress. Prefects administered the rules of behavior and imposed penalties without there being any recourse to a higher authority. Cheating or letting down the side were far more serious offenses than failures of sensitivity. Theft was the ultimate sin. It being Australia, prowess at sports excused most breaches of the rules or failures of decorum. Bookishness and dislike for physical activity, on the other hand, aroused dark suspicions and warranted disciplinary action for the slightest infringement of the rules.

Hardiness was deemed more important than imagination. Indeed, an observer might have believed that the school's founders had been inspired by John Locke and Mistress Masham. Boarders rose at 6:30 a.m. to take cold showers even in midwinter. The aim was to encourage everyone to run at least a mile before breakfast, although slugabeds and poor planners could manage a frantic dash for breakfast without too frequent rebukes.

While this regimen might be seen as a precursor of later obsessions with health and fitness, our diet undid whatever benefits our routine of exercise conferred. We lived on starch, over-cooked meat, and endless eggs and bacon. Fruit appeared in one's diet only if parents intervened and arranged for special supplies to be made available outside meal hours. Slabs of bread and butter accompanied every meal, so that the slimmest figures thickened and susceptible complexions became blotchy.

What meals lacked in culinary style they made up for in formality. A mistress or a sixth-form boarder sat at the head of each long rectangular table. The rest of us, bathed and changed into a required green velvet dress for evenings, sat in descending order of age and class until the youngest and most recently arrived sat at the distant foot of the table. Food was served by the teacher or sixth former at the head of the table, and the rules of conduct decreed that one might not ask for more or less, and that one must endure in silence until someone farther up the table noticed that one needed salt, pepper, butter, tea, or whatever seasonings made our tasteless dishes palatable. Foibles in food were not tolerated. If a student refused to eat the main dish and the teacher in charge noticed, it would be served to her again at subsequent meals until it was deemed that a satisfactory amount had been consumed. The youngest were required to wait to be spoken to before starting a conversation, as though those seated higher up the table were royalty. People who made too much noise or displayed unseemly manners were sent from the room and left hungry until the next meal.

All these rules might have made for stilted behavior, but in fact, they barely subdued the roar of conversation in the boarders' dining room, and only modestly curtailed the animal spirits of the younger students intent at one and the same time on getting more than their share of food, and on whatever form of mischief might disconcert the figure of authority seated at the head of the table.

After I became a boarder in my second term, I looked forward to the two hours which followed dinner, hours when the whole boarding population gathered for carefully supervised preparation for the next day's classes. I could usually finish what was required in short order, and then I could relish the quiet. The day of classes and the afternoon of games seemed to my bush consciousness to be too full of voices. I liked to sit and read poetry, to race ahead in the history book and ponder the events described. I also liked occasionally to manage some feat of wickedness in total silence, such as to wriggle undetected from one end of the "prep" room to the other to deliver some innocuous note or message. Ron Kelly's training in hunting had given me the patience required to move silently, and the satisfaction of going about my own business rather than following orders appealed to me deeply.

Much of my time during the first year or so of my schooling at Abbotsleigh was taken up with the pleasure of defying adult authority and systematically flouting the rules. Lights out in the evening was merely a license to begin to roam about the school, to climb out the window and appear as a somewhat dusty apparition in someone else's dormitory. Restrictions on what one could bring back to school in the way of food were an invitation to figure out the multifarious opportunities for concealing forbidden chocolates, sponge cakes, fruit cakes, soft drinks, and other bulky items as one returned to school from weekly trips to the dentist or weekends of freedom at midterm. Locks on the door of the tuck-shop were no barrier to country children used to dismantling doors and reassembling them.

These escapades were natural reactions to regimentation. They were also my first opportunity to rebel without the danger of doing psychological damage to adults of whom I was prematurely the care giver. It was a delicious and heady feeling undimmed even when my mother was told of my misbehavior. She took it that I was keeping bad company, although this was hardly reflected in my academic performance. I knew that I was being perversely carefree and irresponsible for the first time in my life. I could not articulate a criticism of my mother yet, but I could see the pretenses behind many of the school's rules, and I enjoyed being hypercritical of the people who tried to make me sleep and wake to a schedule, always wear clean socks on Sundays, and never forget my gloves when leaving the school.

After one rebellious scrape led to my being gated over the Easter break, my mother called on Miss Everett and began to apologize for my bad conduct. Miss Everett, with an imperious wave of the hand, interrupted her in mid-sentence. "My dear Mrs. Ker, don't fuss. There's nothing to worry about. I've yet to see Jill's mind fully extended, and I look forward to the day when I do. When she's really interested, she'll forget about breaking rules." These comments, duly reported to my brothers, led to much teasing, and examinations of my head to detect signs of stretching, but they also gave me some freedom from my mother's pressure for perfect conduct, freedom which I badly needed.

I was not a popular student. No one could call me pretty. I had ballooned on the school's starchy diet, developed a poor complexion, and I looked the embodiment of adolescent ungainliness. Moreover, my pride prevented me from seizing opportunities to correct my lack of coordination. I could not bear to begin tennis lessons with the seven-year-old beginners, but could not pretend to play like my classmates, who had been coached for years. A month after arriving as a boarder, I purchased a magnifying glass, found a quiet spot in the sun, and burned the carefully inscribed name off my tennis racket. Once I was satisfied with the job, I turned the racket in at the school's lost property office and escaped further lessons by bewailing the loss of my racket. Basketball was different. Everyone was beginning that game more or less as I began. With diligence my height could be turned to advantage and I earned a place on a team. Thereafter, afternoons could be filled with basketball practice, and Saturday mornings with competition. I liked the excitement of the game, although I never learned to treat a game as a game, and not to care about losing.

I was as intellectually precocious as I was socially inept. I never understood the unspoken rule which required that one display false modesty and hang back when there was a task to be done, waiting to be asked to undertake it. I also took a long time to learn the social hierarchies of the place: whose parents were very rich, whose family had titled relatives in England, whose mother dressed in the height of fashion, which families owned the most stylish holiday retreats. My boarder friends were mainly the daughters of the real backcountry, people who were homesick for the bush and their families and accepted the school as a term which must be served uncomplainingly.

I liked getting out from under the pressure of my mother's company, but at the same time, I was burdened by the sense that she had taken on two jobs, a secretarial one by day and a nursing one at night, in order to pay my fees. As soon as she had delivered me to Abbotsleigh as a boarder, my mother moved back to my grandmother's house, settled Bob in a rented room down the road, and began to work in earnest. Once she had satisfied herself that she could earn enough to pay Barry's and my school fees and pay the rent for herself and my older brother, she began to concentrate her energies on the kind of investment which would be needed to make Coorain profitable again. She had no thought of selling it, but planned to revive it as a sheep-raising venture once it rained. She had a sure instinct for the economics of a small business, and long before others in our drought-stricken district began to think about restocking, she had realized that if she waited for the rain to fall before buying sheep, the price would be so high it would be years before she paid off the cost of the purchase. Once the drought had broken in areas two to three hundred miles from

Coorain, she began to look for suitable sale sheep to form the basis for rebuilding the Coorain flock. She planned to hire a drover to walk her purchases through the stock routes in country where the rains had come until the drought broke at Coorain. On the day she borrowed sixteen hundred pounds from her woolbroker and signed the papers to purchase twelve hundred Merino ewes, she arrived home to learn that there had been two and a half inches of rain at Coorain. The value of her purchase had doubled within a matter of hours and she was rightly jubilant. Two weeks later, there was another inch and a half of rain and by the time the new sheep were delivered by their drover to Coorain, it was producing luxuriant pasture. From that day on our finances were assured, thanks to her inspired gamble.

None of the new earnings were frittered away on improving our style of life. Instead, every penny went back into building up the property, replacing buried fences, repairing the stockyards, buying new equipment. My mother kept on at one of her jobs, found us an inexpensive house to rent in an unfashionable, lower-middle-class suburb to the west of the city, and gradually began to reunite the family.

The reunion at the end of my second term as a boarder at Abbotsleigh brought together a group of young people on the edge of major life changes. Bob, at nineteen, was a young man impatient to savor life, and in search of the adventure he had once expected to find in wartime. Barry, at seventeen, was intent on leaving the King's School before completing high school. He had by then been in boarding school for seven years, and he was convinced that he would learn more from work experience and evening study than during an eighth year of routine in the closed world of the school he no longer enjoyed. I, approaching thirteen years old, looked and felt an awkward adolescent. Our mother, now in her forty-ninth year, looked her years, but she had regained some of her old vitality. Release from stress, and the chance to recoup the family fortunes at Coorain, had restored some of her beautiful coloring and brought back a sparkle to her eyes.

Although many men friends, including our favorite, Angus Waugh, tried to persuade her to marry again, she rebuffed them all. She had loved our father deeply, and she clearly did not want to share the raising of their children with anyone else. She still found herself swept by waves of anger and grief at his loss. Strangers who sat opposite her in the train or the local bus would occasionally be startled by the gaze of hatred she turned on them. She would literally be possessed by rage that other men were alive while her husband was dead.

The intensity of her feelings did not bode well for anyone's peace of mind as we children moved at various paces toward adulthood. She was out of touch with the mood of the postwar world we were entering. She now found it hard to imagine vocations for her sons except the land and the life of a grazier. The boys, understandably, given our recent experiences, did not want to embark on that path. I, for my part, was teetering on the edge of a more mature awareness of the people in my world. I found my brothers entrancing, developed romantic crushes on their friends, and tagged along as often as possible on their diversions.

These were mainly concerned with music, music being the one sociable activity at home my mother approved of and encouraged. Bob began to study the trumpet, Barry the clarinet, while their circle of friends revolved around jazz concerts, listening to recordings of the great jazz musicians, and studying music theory. Our tiny rented house was often crammed with young men participating in or listening to the latest jazz session. When the small living room could not contain the noise of the excited improvisation, I would be dispatched to sit on the curb across the street to listen and report how it really sounded. Doubtless, had we lived in a stuffier neighborhood there would have been complaints about the noise. Our kindly neighbors approved of a widowed mother keeping her sons at home and away from the Australian obsession with pubs and gambling.

My mother's code of thrift, sobriety, and industry had served her well growing up in a simpler Australian society, but it had little appeal for her children, hungry for excitement and experience, and made aware of a more complex society by their urban schooling. Postwar Australia was a society transformed by the economic stimulus of the Second World War. In contrast to the cautious mentality inherited by the generation shaped by the Depression, we were agog with the excitement of prosperity, and the questions raised by Australia's wartime contact with American culture. We went to American movies, used American slang, and listened to American music.

The boys, reluctant to remain dependent on their widowed mother, seized the best jobs they could find, unaware that it was in their long-term interest to attend university and acquire professional training. In my mother's generation, higher education was a luxury available to a tiny elite. In ours, it would become a necessary doorway to opportunity. The choice of early employment meant that Bob and Barry did not find excitement and challenge in the fairly routine tasks which made up their jobs with woolbrokers. They sought excitement instead in music, and later in the world of fast cars and road racing. By reason of my gender, I was not marked out for a career connected with the land. Moreover, as our finances improved it was possible for my mother to dream that I would fulfill her ambition: attend university and become a doctor. So the stereotypes of gender worked in my favor. Unlike my brothers, I grew up knowing that my life would be lived in peacetime, and that it was an unspoken expectation that I would finish high school and attend the University of Sydney.

ZORA NEALE HURSTON

EXCERPT FROM *THE EATONVILLE ANTHOLOGY*

From I Love Myself When I Am Laughing . . . and Then Again When I Am Looking Mean and Impressive *by Zora Neale Hurston, edited by Alice Walker. New York: HarperCollins Publishers, 1979.*

1
The Pleading Woman

MRS. TONY ROBERTS is the pleading woman. She just loves to ask for things. Her husband gives her all he can rake and scrape, which is considerably more than most wives get for their housekeeping, but she goes from door to door begging for things.

She starts at the store. "Mist' Clarke," she sing-songs in a high keening voice, "gimme lil' piece uh meat tuh boil a pot uh greens wid. Lawd knows me an' mah chillen is so hongry! Hits uh SHAME! Tony don't fee-ee-eee-ed me!"

Mr. Clarke knows that she has money and that her larder is well stocked, for Tony Roberts is the best provider on his list. But her keening annoys him and he rises heavily. The pleader at his elbow shows all the joy of a starving man being seated at a feast.

"Thass right Mist' Clarke. De Lawd loveth de cheerful giver. Gimme jes' a lil' piece 'bout dis big (indicating the width of her hand) an' de Lawd'll bless yuh."

She follows this angel-on-earth to his meat tub and superintends the cutting, crying out in pain when he refuses to move the knife over just a teeny bit mo'.

Finally, meat in hand, she departs, remarking on the meanness of some people who give a piece of salt meat only two-fingers wide when they were plainly asked for a hand-wide piece. Clarke puts it down to Tony's account and resumes his reading.

With the slab of salt pork as a foundation, she visits various homes until she has collected all she wants for the day. At the Piersons, for instance: "Sister Pierson, plee-ee-ease gimme uh han'ful uh collard greens fuh me an' mah po' chillen! 'Deed, me an' mah chillen is so hongry. Tony doan' fee-ee-eed me!"

Mrs. Pierson picks a bunch of greens for her, but she springs away from them as if they were poison. "Lawd a mussy, Mis' Pierson, you ain't gonna gimme dat lil' eye-full uh greens fuh me an' mah chillen, is you? Don't be so graspin'; Gawd won't bless yuh. Gimme uh han'full mo'. Lawd, some folks is got everything, an' theys jes' as gripin' an stingy!"

Mrs. Pierson raises the ante, and the pleading woman moves on to the next place, and on and on. The next day, it commences all over.

2
Turpentine Love

JIM MERCHANT is always in good humor—even with his wife. He says he fell in love with her at first sight. That was some years ago. She has had all her teeth pulled out, but they still get along splendidly.

He says the first time he called on her he found out that she was subject to fits. This didn't cool his love, however. She had several in his presence.

One Sunday, while he was there, she had one, and her mother tried to give her a dose of turpentine to stop it. Accidentally, she spilled it in her eye and it cured her. She never had another fit, so they got married and have kept each other in good humor ever since.

3

BECKY MOORE has eleven children of assorted colors and sizes. She has never been married, but that is not her fault. She has never stopped any of the fathers of her children from proposing, so if she has no father for her children it's not her fault. The men round about are entirely to blame.

The other mothers of the town are afraid that it is catching. They won't let their children play with hers.

4
Tippy

SYKES JONES' FAMILY all shoot craps. The most interesting member of the family—also fond of bones, but of another kind—is Tippy, the Jones' dog.

He is so thin, that it amazes one that he lives at all. He sneaks into village kitchens if the housewives are careless about the doors and steals meats, even off the stoves. He also sucks eggs.

For these offenses he has been sentenced to death dozens of times, and the sentences executed upon him, only they didn't work. He has been fed bluestone, strychnine, nux vomica, even an entire Peruna bottle beaten up. It didn't fatten him, but it didn't kill him. So Eatonville has resigned itself to the plague of Tippy, reflecting that it has erred in certain matters and is being chastened.

In spite of all the attempts upon his life, Tippy is still willing to be friendly with anyone who will let him.

5
The Way of a Man with a Train

OLD MAN ANDERSON lived seven or eight miles out in the country from Eatonville. Over by Lake Apopka. He raised feed-corn and cassava and went to market with it two or three times a year. He bought all of his victuals wholesale so he wouldn't have to come to town for several months more.

He was different from citybred folks. He had never seen a train. Everybody laughed at him for even the smallest child in Eatonville had either been to Maitland or Orlando and watched a train go by. On Sunday afternoons all of the young people of the village would go over to Maitland, a mile away, to see Number 35 whizz southward on its way to Tampa and wave at the passengers. So we looked down on him a little. Even we children felt superior in the presence of a person so lacking in wordly knowledge.

The grown-ups kept telling him he ought to go see a train. He always said he didn't have time to wait so long. Only two trains a day passed through Maitland. But patronage and ridicule finally had its effect and Old Man Anderson drove in one morning early. Number 78 went north to Jacksonville at 10:20. He drove his light wagon over in the woods beside the railroad below Maitland, and sat down to wait. He began to fear that his horse would get frightened and run away with the wagon. So he took him out and led him deeper into the grove and tied him securely. Then he returned to his wagon and waited some more. Then he remembered that some of the train-wise villagers had said the engine belched fire and smoke. He had better move his wagon out of danger. It might catch fire. He climbed down from the seat and placed himself between the shafts to draw it away. Just then 78 came thundering over the trestle spouting smoke, and suddenly began blowing for Maitland. Old Man Anderson became so frightened he ran away with the wagon through the woods and tore it up worse than the horse ever could have done. He doesn't know yet what a train looks like, and says he doesn't care.

6
Coon Taylor

COON TAYLOR never did any real stealing. Of course, if he saw a chicken or a watermelon he'd take it. The people used to get mad but they never could catch him. He took so many melons from Joe Clarke that he set up in the melon patch one night with his shotgun loaded with rock salt. He was going to fix Coon. But he was tired. It is hard work being a mayor, postmaster, storekeeper and everything. He dropped asleep sitting on a stump in the middle of the patch. So he didn't see Coon when he came. Coon didn't see him either, that is, not at first. He knew the stump was there, however. He had opened many of Clarke's juicy Florida Favorite on it. He selected his fruit, walked over to the stump and burst the melon on it. That is, he thought it was the stump until it fell over with a yell. Then he knew it was no stump and departed hastily from those parts. He had cleared the fence when Clarke came to, as it were. So the charge of rock-salt was wasted on the desert air.

During the sugar-cane season, he found he couldn't resist Clarke's soft green cane, but Clarke did not go to sleep this time. So after he had cut six of eight stalks by the moonlight, Clarke rose up out of the cane strippings with his shotgun and made Coon sit right down and chew up the last one of them on the spot. And the next day he made Coon leave his town for three months.

7
Village Fiction

JOE LINDSAY is said by Lum Boger to be the largest manufacturer of prevarications in Eatonville; Brazzle (late owner of the world's leanest and meanest mule) contends that his business is the largest in the state and his wife holds that he is the biggest liar in the world.

Exhibit A—He claims that while he was in Orlando one day he saw a doctor cut open a woman, remove everything—liver, lights and heart included—clean each of them separately; the doctor then washed out the empty woman, dried her out neatly with a towel and replaced the organs so expertly that she was up and about her work in a couple of weeks.

8

SEWELL is a man who lives all to himself. He moves a great deal. So often, that 'Lige Moseley says his chickens are so used to moving that every time he comes out into his backyard the chickens lie down and cross their legs, ready to be tied up again.

He is baldheaded; but he says he doesn't mind that, because he wants as little as possible between him and God.

9

MRS. CLARKE is Joe Clarke's wife. She is a soft-looking, middle-aged woman, whose bust and stomach are always holding a get-together.

She waits on the store sometimes and cries every time he yells at her which he does every time she makes a mistake, which is quite often. She calls her husband

"Jody." They say he used to beat her in the store when he was a young man, but he is not so impatient now. He can wait until he goes home.

She shouts in Church every Sunday and shakes the hand of fellowship with everybody in the Church with her eyes closed, but somehow always misses her husband.

10

MRS. MCDUFFY goes to Church every Sunday and always shouts and tells her "determination." Her husband always sits in the back row and beats her soon as they get home. He says there's no sense in her shouting, as big a devil as she is. She just does it to slur him. Elijah Moseley asked her why she didn't stop shouting, seeing she always got a beating about it. She says she can't "squinch the sperrit." Then Elijah asked Mr. McDuffy to stop beating her, seeing that she was going to shout anyway. He answered that she just did it for spite and that his fist was just as hard as her head. He could last just as long as she. So the village let the matter rest.

11
Double-Shuffle

BACK IN THE GOOD OLD DAYS before the World War, things were very simple in Eatonville. People didn't fox-trot. When the town wanted to put on its Sunday clothes and wash behind the ears, it put on a "breakdown." The daring younger set would two-step and waltz, but the good church members and the elders stuck to the grand march. By rural canons dancing is wicked, but one is not held to have danced until the feet have been crossed. Feet don't get crossed when one grand marches.

At elaborate affairs the organ from the Methodist church was moved up to the hall and Lizzimore, the blind man presided. When informal gatherings were held, he merely played his guitar assisted by any volunteer with mouth organs or accordions.

Among white people the march is as mild as if it had been passed on by Volstead. But it still has a kick in Eatonville. Everybody happy, shining eyes, gleaming teeth. Feet dragged 'shhlap, shhlap! to beat out the time. No orchestra needed. Round and round! Back again, parse-me-la! shlap! shlap! Strut! Strut! Seaboard! Shlap! Shlap! Tiddy bumm! Mr. Clarke in the lead with Mrs. Moseley.

It's too much for some of the young folks. Double shuffling commences. Buck and wing. Lizzimore about to break his guitar. Accordion doing contortions. People fall back against the walls, and let the soloist have it, shouting as they clap the old, old double shuffle songs.

'Me an' mah honey got two mo' days
Two mo' days tuh do de buck'

Sweating bodies, laughing mouths, grotesque faces, feet drumming fiercely. Deacons clapping as hard as the rest.

"Great big nigger, black as tar
Trying tuh git tuh hebben on uh 'lectric car."

"Some love cabbage, some love kale
But I love a gal wid a short skirt tail."

Long tall angel—steppin' down,
Long white robe an' starry crown.

'Ah would not marry uh black gal (bumm bumm!)
Tell yuh de reason why
Every time she comb her hair
She make de goo-goo eye.

Would not marry a yaller gal (bumm bumm!)
Tell yuh de reason why
Her neck so long an' stringy
Ahm 'fraid she'd never die.

Would not marry uh preacher
Tell yuh de reason why
Every time he comes tuh town
He makes de chicken fly.

When the buck dance was over, the boys would give the floor to the girls and they would parse-me-la with a slye eye out of the corner to see if anybody was looking who might "have them up in church" on conference night. Then there would be more dancing. Then Mr. Clarke would call for everybody's best attention and announce that *'freshments was served! Every gent'man would please take his lady by the arm and scorch her right up to de table fur a treat!*

Then the men would stick their arms out with a flourish and ask their ladies: "You lak chicken? Well, then, take a wing." And the ladies would take the proffered "wings" and parade up to the long table and he served. Of course most of them had brought baskets in which were heaps of jointed and fried chicken, two or three kinds of pies, cakes, potato pone and chicken purlo. The hall would separate into happy groups about the baskets until time for more dancing.

But the boys and girls got scattered about during the war, and now they dance the fox-trot by a brand new piano. They do waltz and two-step still, but no one now considers it good form to lock his chin over his partner's shoulder and stick out behind. One night just for fun and to humor the old folks, they danced, that is, they grand marched, but everyone picked up their feet. *Bah!!*

12
The Head of the Nail

Daisy Taylor was the town vamp. Not that she was pretty. But sirens were all but non-existent in the town. Perhaps she was forced to it by circumstances. She was quite dark, with little bushy patches of hair squatting over her head. These were held down by shingle-nails often. No one knows whether she did this for artistic effect or for lack of hairpins, but there they were shining in the little patches of hair when she got all dressed for the afternoon and came up to Clarke's store to see if there was any mail for her.

It was seldom that anyone wrote to Daisy, but she knew that the men of the town would be assembled there by five o'clock, and some one could usually be induced to buy her some soda water or peanuts.

Daisy flirted with married men. There were only two single men in town. Lum Boger, who was engaged to the assistant school-teacher, and Hiram Lester, who had been off to school at Tuskegee and wouldn't look at a person like Daisy. In addition to other drawbacks, she was pigeon-toed and her petticoat was always showing so perhaps he was justified. There was nothing else to do except flirt with married men.

This went on for a long time. First one wife and then another complained of her, or drove her from the preserves by threat.

But the affair with Crooms was the most prolonged and serious. He was even known to have bought her a pair of shoes.

Mrs. Laura Crooms was a meek little woman who took all of her troubles crying, and talked a great deal of leaving things in the hands of God.

The affair came to a head one night in orange picking time. Crooms was over at Oneido picking oranges. Many fruit pickers move from one town to the other during the season.

The *town* was collected at the store-postoffice as is customary on Saturday nights. The *town* has had its bath and with its week's pay in pocket fares forth to be merry. The men tell stories and treat the ladies to soda-water, peanuts and peppermint candy.

Daisy was trying to get treats, but the porch was cold to her that night.

"Ah don't keer if you don't treat me. What's a dirty lil nickel?" She flung this at Walter Thomas. "The everloving Mister Crooms will gimme anything atall Ah wants."

"You better shet up yo' mouf talking 'bout Albert Crooms. Heah his wife comes right now."

Daisy went akimbo. "Who? Me! Ah don't keer whut Laura Crooms think. If she ain't a heavy hip-ted Mama enough to keep him, she don't need to come crying to me."

She stood making goo-goo eyes as Mrs. Crooms walked upon the porch. Daisy laughed loud, made several references to Albert Crooms, and when she saw the mail-bag come in from Maitland she said, "Ah better go in an' see if Ah ain't got a letter from Oneido."

The more Daisy played the game of getting Mrs. Crooms' goat, the better she liked it. She ran in and out of the store laughing until she could scarcely stand. Some of the people present began to talk to Mrs. Crooms—to egg her on to halt Daisy's boasting, but she was for leaving it all in the hands of God. Walter Thomas kept on after Mrs. Crooms until she stiffened and resolved to fight. Daisy was inside when she came to this resolve and never dreamed anything of the kind could happen. She had gotten hold of an envelope and came laughing and shouting, "Oh, Ah can't stand to see Oneido lose!"

There was a box of ax-handles on display on the porch, propped up against the door jamb. As Daisy stepped upon the porch, Mrs. Crooms leaned the heavy end of one of those handles heavily upon her head. She staggered from the porch to the ground and the timid Laura, fearful of a counter-attack, struck again and Daisy toppled into the town ditch. There was not enough water in there to do more than muss her up. Every time she tried to rise, down would come that ax-handle again. Laura was fighting a scared fight. With Daisy thoroughly licked, she retired to the store porch and left her fallen enemy in the ditch. But Elijah Moseley, who was some distance down the street when the trouble began arrived as the victor was withdrawing. He rushed up and picked Daisy out of the mud and began feeling her head.

"Is she hurt much?" Joe Clarke asked from the doorway.

"I don't know," Elijah answered, "I was just looking to see if Laura had been lucky enough to hit one of those nails on the head and drive it in."

Before a week was up, Daisy moved to Orlando. There in a wider sphere, perhaps, her talents as a vamp were appreciated.

13
Pants and Cal'line

SISTER CAL'LINE POTTS was a silent woman. Did all of her laughing down inside, but did the thing that kept the town in an uproar of laughter. It was the general opinion of the village that Cal'line would do anything she had a mind to. And she had a mind to do several things.

Mitchell Potts, her husband, had a weakness for women. No one ever believed that she was jealous. She did things to the women, surely. But most any townsman would have said that she did them because she liked the novel situation and the queer things she could bring out of it.

Once he took up with Delphine—called Mis' Pheeny by the town. She lived on the outskirts on the edge of the piney woods. The town winked and talked. People don't make secrets of such things in villages. Cal'line went about her business with her thin black lips pursed tight as ever, and her shiny black eyes unchanged.

"Dat devil of a Cal'line's got somethin' up her sleeve!" The town smiled in anticipation.

"Delphine is too big a cigar for her to smoke. She ain't crazy," said some as the weeks went on and nothing happened. Even Pheeny herself would give an extra flirt to her over-starched petticoats as she rustled into church past her of Sundays.

Mitch Potts said furthermore, that he was tired of Cal'line's foolishness. She had to stay where he put her. His African soup-bone (arm) was too strong to let a woman run over him. 'Nough was 'nough. And he did some fancy cussing, and he was the fanciest cusser in the county.

So the town waited and the longer it waited, the odds changed slowly from the wife to the husband.

One Saturday, Mitch knocked off work at two o'clock and went over to Maitland. He came back with a rectangular box under his arm and kept straight on out to the barn to put it away. He ducked around the corner of the house quickly, but even so, his wife glimpsed the package. Very much like a shoe-box. So!

He put on the kettle and took a bath. She stood in her bare feet at the ironing board and kept on ironing. He dressed. It was about five o'clock but still very light. He fiddled around outside. She kept on with her ironing. As soon as the sun got red, he sauntered out to the barn, got the parcel and walked away down the road, past the store and into the piney woods. As soon as he left the house, Cal'line slipped on her shoes without taking time to don stockings, put on one of her husband's old Stetsons, worn and floppy, slung the axe over her shoulder and followed in his wake. He was hailed cheerily as he passed the sitters on the store porch and answered smiling sheepishly and passed on. Two minutes later passed his wife, silently, unsmilingly, and set the porch to giggling and betting.

An hour passed perhaps. It was dark. Clarke had long ago lighted the swinging kerosene lamp inside.

14

ONCE 'WAY BACK YONDER before the stars fell all the animals used to talk just like people. In them days dogs and rabbits was the best of friends—even tho both of them was stuck on the same gal—which was Miss Nancy Coon. She had the sweetest smile and the prettiest striped and bushy tail to be found anywhere.

They both run their legs nigh off trying to win her for themselves—fetching nice ripe persimmons and such. But she never give one or the other no satisfaction.

Finally one night Mr. Dog popped the question right out. "Miss Coon," he says, "Ma'am, also Ma'am which would you ruther be—a lark flyin' or a dove a settin'?"

Course Miss Nancy she blushed and laughed a little and hid her face behind her bushy tail for a spell. Then she said sorter shy like, "I does love yo' sweet voice, brother dawg—but—I ain't jes' exactly set my mind yit."

Her and Mr. Dog set on a spell, when up comes hopping Mr. Rabbit wid his tail fresh washed and his whiskers shining. He got right down to business and asked Miss Coon to marry him, too.

"Oh, Miss Nancy," he says, "Ma'am, also Ma'am, if you'd see me settin' straddle of a mud-cat leadin' a minnow, what would you think? Ma'am also Ma'am?" Which is a out and out proposal as everybody knows.

"Youse awful nice, Brother Rabbit and a beautiful dancer, but you cannot sing like Brother Dog. Both you uns come back next week to gimme time for to decide."

They both left arm-in-arm. Finally Mr. Rabbit says to Mr. Dog. "Taint no use in me going back—she ain't gwinter have me. So I mought as well give up. She loves singing, and I ain't got nothing but a squeak."

"Oh, don't talk that a way," says Mr. Dog, tho' he is glad Mr. Rabbit can't sing none.

"Thass all right, Brer Dog. But if I had a sweet voice like you got, I'd have it worked on and make it sweeter."

"How! How! How!" Mr. Dog cried, jumping up and down.

"Lemme fix it for you, like I do for Sister Lark and Sister Mocking-bird."

"When? Where?" asked Mr. Dog, all excited. He was figuring that if he could sing just a little better Miss Coon would be bound to have him.

"Just you meet me t'morrer in de huckleberry patch," says the rabbit and off they both goes to bed.

The dog is there on time next day and after a while the rabbit comes loping up.

"Mawnin', Brer Dawg," he says kinder chippy like. "Ready to git yo' voice sweetened?"

"Sholy, sholy, Brer Rabbit. Let's we all hurry about it. I wants tuh serenade Miss Nancy from the piney woods tuh night."

"Well, den, open yo' mouf and poke out yo' tongue," says the rabbit.

No sooner did Mr. Dog poke out his tongue than Mr. Rabbit split it with a knife and ran for all he was worth to a hollow stump and hid hisself.

The dog has been mad at the rabbit ever since.

Anybody who don't believe it happened, just look at the dog's tongue and he can see for himself where the rabbit slit it right up the middle.

Stepped on a tin, mah story ends.

Information at a Glance

Purposes and Assumptions

Approach	Purpose(s)	Assumption(s)
Familiar	To understand literature in the context of an author's biography and/or historical period.	Literature reflects the life and world of its author.
Formalist	To value a literary work for its own intrinsic properties.	Literature is an utterance of abstract, absolute truths about reality.
Psychological	To determine meanings that are suggested but not overtly stated.	(1) Literature comes from the unconscious of a writer, expressing meanings that even he or she may not recognize. (2) A character's nature is revealed by more than external actions: slips of language, dreams, symbols.
Marxist	To reveal how those in control of the means of production manipulate the rest and thereby change the system.	Economics controls all aspects of a society. The material, not the spiritual, is all important.
Feminist	(1) To read with heightened awareness of the nature, social roles, and treatment of female characters. (2) To recognize ignored and undervalued female writers.	Because society is and has been basically patriarchal, the talents and products of women have been undervalued, leaving them without visible power.
Reader-response	To include the reader in constructing the meaning of a text.	Whatever a text means is at least partially the product of a reader's interaction with it.
Deconstructionist	To demonstrate the multiplicity of meanings in a given text.	Meaning is always provisional, not stable, united, or unchanging.

New historicist	To understand a text as a product and maker of complex and sometimes conflicting historical forces.	Because a text is the product of more than a single contributing source, it is not explainable simply as the reflection of a controlling idea of a given period.
Postcolonialist	To examine the literature of colonized peoples and that of the descendants of their colonizers, featuring what happens when one culture is dominated by another.	Physical conquest of a culture leads to loss or serious modification of it, resulting in uncertainty of identity for both the conquered and the colonizers, who live in a mixed culture often marked by contrasts and antagonisms, resentment, and blended practice.
Multiculturalist	To identify and analyze the literatures of racial and ethnic minorities in order to discover their unique characteristics and worldviews.	The literature of historically marginalized groups provides a rich source of works for analysis.

Strategies, Strengths, and Weaknesses

APPROACH	STRATEGY OR STRATEGIES	STRENGTH	WEAKNESS
Familiar	Read literature as a reflection of major events, figures, and ideas of a period.	Provides a framework for tracing growth and development of literary ideas and styles.	Subordinates literary concerns to nonliterary ones.
Formalist	Read closely to see how tensions in diction and style are resolved into a unified whole.	Shows how meaning is a product of form.	Looks for a single best interpretation.
Psychological	Pay close attention to unconscious motivations and meanings expressed indirectly through dreams, language, and symbols.	Reveals meanings that are not explicitly stated.	Can degenerate into nonliterary jargon or arrive at unjustified interpretations.
Marxist	Identify the powerful individuals or groups in the text and show how they create the superstructure that controls the proletariat.	Connects literature with life—that is, with everyday concerns about economics, class, and power.	Is essentially nonliterary—that is, does not take aesthetic matters into account.

Feminist	(1) Examine the roles and treatment of female characters. (2) Discover (or reintroduce) works by neglected female writers.	Gives attention to traditionally overlooked aspects of a text and to heretofore ignored writers.	Can become narrowly focused, leaving out other important aspects of a text.
Reader-response	Connect the life experiences and worldviews of the reader with the text.	Makes the reader an active coparticipant in creating a text, not simply a passive receiver of it.	Can produce idiosyncratic readings.
Deconstructionist	Identify those places where misstatements, gaps, and inconsistencies in a text undermine what it claims to be saying.	Opens up a text to an unending series of new interpretations.	Uses difficult, specialized vocabulary.
New historicist	Acknowledge all the social concerns that surround and infuse a text, particularly the power structures of the culture it depicts and that of the author's world.	Accepts any written text as worthy of serious analysis (not just those composed in traditional literary genres).	May neglect literary elements of a text for its political aspects.
Postcolonialist	Determine the stance of a text regarding colonialism, postcolonialism, and/or neocolonialism.	Generates understanding of cultures as well as texts.	Can be more concerned with social criticism than literary criticism.
Multiculturalist	Identify materials, purposes, and styles that are characteristic of a racial or ethnic minority.	Liberates the minority from dependence on mainstream standards of performance.	Divides cultural groups from one another.

INDEX